*The Biblical Seminar*
*83*

# Canaan and Israel
# in Antiquity

# CANAAN
# AND ISRAEL
# IN ANTIQUITY

## AN INTRODUCTION

# K.L. NOLL

SHEFFIELD ACADEMIC PRESS
*A Continuum imprint*
LONDON • NEW YORK

Published by Sheffield Academic Press Ltd
The Tower Building, 11 York Road, London SE1 7NX
370 Lexington Avenue, New York NY 10017-6550

www.SheffieldAcademicPress.com
www.continuumbooks.com

British Library Cataloguing-in-Publication Data

A catalogue record for this book is available from the British Library

Typeset by Sheffield Academic Press
Printed on acid-free paper in Great Britain by The Cromwell Press, Melksham, Wiltshire

ISBN   1-84127-318-X (hardback)
       1-84127-258-2 (paperback)

CONTENTS

LIST OF FIGURES

# ABBREVIATIONS

| | |
|---|---|
| *ANET* | James B. Pritchard (ed.), *Ancient Near Eastern Texts Relating to the Old Testament* (Princeton: Princeton University Press, 1950) |
| *BASOR* | *Bulletin of the American Schools of Oriental Research* |
| *BibInt* | *Biblical Interpretation: A Journal of Contemporary Approaches* |
| *CBQ* | *Catholic Biblical Quarterly* |
| *IEJ* | *Israel Exploration Journal* |
| *Int* | *Interpretation* |
| *JBL* | *Journal of Biblical Literature* |
| *JR* | *Journal of Religion* |
| *JSOT* | *Journal for the Study of the Old Testament* |
| JSOTSup | *Journal for the Study of the Old Testament*, Supplement Series |
| *SJOT* | *Scandinavian Journal of the Old Testament* |
| *ZAH* | *Zeitschrift für Althebraistik* |
| *ZAW* | *Zeitschrift für die alttestamentliche Wissenschaft* |

PREFACE

This book has been written for an intelligent reader who has not yet encountered academic study of the ancient world. If it is a successful introduction, that reader can move smoothly from this volume into deeper study, and will develop a profound respect for the ancient peoples of the Near East, whose lives have been recalled in these pages.

Two factors motivated me to write this volume. First was my growing dissatisfaction as a teacher with the standard English-language introductory handbooks. Some are too complex for an uninitiated reader. Others have become dated as our field of research has undergone radical changes. Another group promote religious convictions that render the textbook unsuitable for use in an academic setting.

A second motivation has been the rewarding interaction I have enjoyed with students at the Mont Alto campus of Penn State University. Frequently the enthusiasm of the student with a religious background turns to anxiety as she or he discovers my class lectures and discussions do not reinforce the doctrines of the faith. Nevertheless, a gratifying discovery awaits. Academic research does not undermine an intellectually healthy religious faith. History is not heresy! These chapters have been composed for the many students who have been willing to share their thoughts, concerns and disgust with me through after-class and e-mail conversations as they traveled along a path toward that discovery.

Since my purpose is to offer a first step, I have avoided complexities that would only confuse, simplified complexities that could not be avoided, and repeated some themes and details for emphasis. Apparatus has been restricted to an absolute minimum. Bibliography is restricted to English-language scholarship and only selected items, because I prefer not to overwhelm the beginner with a 'Suggested Additional Reading' list that is indigestible. I hope experts will overlook these inadequacies, teachers will supplement the text through creative class discussions, and students will benefit from the resulting clarity of presentation. Unless noted otherwise, translations from ancient documents are my own. I thank Philip R. Davies for his enthusiastic support of this project and the friendly staff at Sheffield Academic Press for their professionalism at every stage. Warm thanks go to my darling wife, Tina, who helped with copy-editing, maps and charts, and whose wit and wisdom have sustained me for more than 20 joyful years.

This book was completed many months before the terrorist attack against New York City and Washington D.C., September 11, 2001. As we were going to press, that horrible Tuesday morning reminded the world that religion can be a force of evil as well as good. I wrote this volume to honor the ancient dead. Now, I hope, it will honor recent dead, the victims of religious hatred. May this book do its small part to teach that history is never the possession of one people, that truth is never the property of only one tradition and that any god who demands violence against the innocent is a god unworthy of worship.

Chapter 1

## CANAAN AND ISRAEL: AN OVERVIEW

*Introduction*

This short chapter provides a general overview to prepare for later chapters, especially Chapters 4 to 10. It is recommended that the information presented here be reviewed regularly as later chapters are read.

*What's in a Name?*

The terms 'Canaan' and 'Israel' are difficult to define. Each word was employed by ancient writers in several ways.

'Canaan' was a geographic term designating the eastern shore of the Mediterranean Sea (very roughly modern Lebanon and Israel). However, ancient writers often used Canaan as an ethnic term, designating not the land but the people who lived in the land. As such, the Canaanites were never a genuinely cohesive ethnic group since a variety of cultures and competing world views could be included under this single label. For example, biblical writers speak of Canaanites as only one of many ethnic groups in Canaan, along with Amorites, Hittites, Hivites, Girgashites, Jebusites and Perizzites, to name just a few. This way of writing was imprecise, to say the least. Neither the Bible nor any other ancient source enables a modern archaeologist to distinguish clearly between such groups in the material remains of Palestine. Since the ancient Israelites lived in the land of Canaan, they were also 'Canaanites'. *Everyone* who lived in ancient Canaan was a Canaanite. Gradually, the term shifted in meaning, so that 'Canaanites' eventually became identical to 'Phoenicians', the people who lived on the coast of the lands now called Syria and Lebanon.

In ancient writings, 'Israel' is a much more complex and problematic term than 'Canaan'. Although 'Israel' is a very common label in the Bible, it is rare in other writings. For example, the word 'Israel' appears only once in ancient Egyptian texts. This is very strange, since the Egyptians were near neighbors to the Israelites throughout ancient times and knew all Canaan's inhabitants well. Apparently, from the Egyptian point of view, Israel was just one more Canaanite group. Other ancient neighbors of the Israelites also display very little or no interest in the word 'Israel'. Neo-Assyrian writings, which mention the Israelite kings on a regular basis, almost never call them 'Israelite' kings. Rather, they refer to them by the dynastic label *bit humri*, which meant 'the House of [King] Omri'. Several very close neighbors of Israel mention the name 'Israel', but these are the exceptions.

In the Bible, Israel is the alternate name for a man named Jacob, son of Isaac, grandson of Abraham (see Gen. 32.29). Also in the Bible, Israel is the name of an ethnic group, the Israelites. The Bible connects the man Israel to the people Israel by telling a story in which the man fathers 12 sons who in turn 'father' 12 tribes of people. The 12 tribes are, collectively, the people called 'Israel'. A story of this kind has a name; scholars who study world folklore call it an 'eponymic legend'. An eponym is a person, real or imagined, who has given his name to a later group of people. The legend is the story, real or imagined, that explains the eponym.

Modern anthropologists have discovered that eponymic legends are common in many traditional (non-modern) societies. Ethnic identity is defined by telling a story of kinship. Frequently, the story does not so much reflect a biological reality as it reflects a social or political reality. When groups of people enter into relationship with one another, begin to cooperate for agricultural purposes, mutual defense, and so on, they express their alliance by telling a tale of kinship. 'You and I are brothers; your village and my village descend from the same ancestor.' In other words, the primary function of this kind of story is to create and sustain a sense of community identity. Most of these stories are creative inventions. The kinships are invented strictly for the purpose of community identity, not because the people involved are actually related biologically. But the story is not a 'lie' since members who tell the story know that it is an invention. They believe in the family tree they narrate because it represents their social and political lives. When social and political relationships change over time, these same people will alter the family tree. 'You and I are no longer brothers; we do not descend from the same ancestor.'

The use of 'Israel' as a term designating community identity was certainly common knowledge to ancient authors of the Bible. These writers were not embarrassed to alter their family tree as needs changed. For example, a man named Zerubbabel is the son of Shealtiel in Ezra 3.2, but he becomes the son of Pediah in 1 Chron. 3.19. Another example can be seen in the Christian New Testament, in which the family tree of Joseph, father of Jesus, is traced from David's son Solomon in one biblical passage (Mt. 1.1-17), but traced from David's son Nathan in another place (Lk. 3.23-38), with the result that many of the names differ between the two lists. This is not an error, but a sign that biblical authors conceived of genealogy as something that has little to do with biology.

Also, the various ways in which the Bible employs the term 'tribes of Israel' demonstrate that the ancient authors were aware of the fluid nature of social and political affiliation. Biblical writers often speak of 12 tribes of Israel, but the precise names of those 12 tribes change from passage to passage. Sometimes Israel includes a tribe called Levi (e.g. Deut. 27.12-13), other times Levi is not listed as a tribe. In order to maintain the number 12, the tribe of Joseph is eliminated each time that Levi is missing, and they are replaced by two other tribes, Ephraim and Manasseh, the two 'sons' of Joseph (e.g. Num. 1.5-15). It gets even more complicated, however. Sometimes there are fewer than 12 tribes and their names do not correspond to the traditional names: Judges 5 lists only 10 tribes, and includes the 'tribes' of Machir and Gilead. Missing from the list are the more famous tribes of Judah and Joseph, as well as the tribes of Manasseh, Simeon, Levi and Gad. Clearly, biblical writers recognized that the concept of 'sons' of Israel was a metaphor for a complex and ever-changing process of social and political affiliation.

'Israel', then, is primarily a social or political term, though its precise definition seems to have shifted over time. Early in the Iron Age (see the chronology chart on p. 26), Israel seems to have been a term of political affiliation among loosely related tribal groups, as in Judges 5. Later, Israel became the label for a monarchy, the Kingdom of Israel, which ruled over portions of Palestine's Cisjordan Highlands. After that kingdom was destroyed by the Neo-Assyrians in the eighth century BCE, Israel seems to have become an alternate name for another monarchy, the Kingdom of Judah in the southern Cisjordan Highlands. Finally, 'Israel' became the title of choice for the Jewish people of Persian and Hellenistic times. It is important to keep in mind, when reading the Bible and when reading modern histories of ancient Palestine, that the definition of 'Israel' is never constant.

## Where was Ancient Canaan?

Ancient Canaan comprised most of modern Syria and Palestine. Ancient writers used the term 'Canaan' in varying ways, so a definition of precise boundaries is not really possible. In modern times, this region includes these political entities: Lebanon, Syria, Israel, Jordan, and the Palestinian Authority in the West Bank and Gaza Strip. The following survey will locate Canaan in its ancient Near Eastern context, emphasizing places that will play a significant role in later chapters.

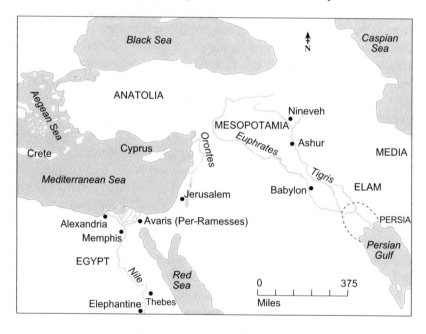

Figure 1. *The Ancient Near East.*

## The Ancient Near East

Syria-Palestine was the land 'bridge' between three great centers of ancient civilization. To the northeast lay Mesopotamia, to the north Anatolia, and to the southwest, Egypt. (Directly to the east and southeast lay vast desert wastelands that were mostly uninhabited in ancient times.)

The Greek word 'Mesopotamia' means 'between two rivers'. The two rivers are the Euphrates and the Tigris. Just to the east of the Tigris were the regions of Media (later called Parthia) in the north and Elam and Persia in the south. Important cities in Mesopotamia included Nineveh and Ashur on the Tigris, as well as Babylon on the Euphrates. Ashur was capital of an ancient empire called Assyria, the heartland of which encompassed all of northern Mesopotamia. Nineveh was an important cultural center of Assyria, and became Assyria's capital in the seventh century BCE (see the chronology chart on p. 26). Babylon was capital of Babylonia, which was southern Mesopotamia.

North of Syria-Palestine was Anatolia (modern Turkey). This was the home of a culture called Hatti. The people of Hatti were the Hittites. They had economic and political interactions with Greece, which was west of the Aegean Sea, so that some ancient Greek ideas and cultural artifacts made their way into Syria-Palestine, and vice versa.

To the southwest of Syria-Palestine lies Egypt. An ancient Greek historian named Herodotus called Egypt the 'gift of the Nile', because Egypt was all desert except the fertile land created by the Nile River's annual flooding. The region can be subdivided into Upper Egypt (the southern portion, which is higher in elevation) and Lower Egypt (the northern portion). Lower Egypt is flatter and, at that point, the Nile diverges into several branches so that, on a map, it looks like a fan. This fan-like Lower Egypt was also called the Delta. Several important locations were: a border fortress at Elephantine and a large city called Thebes in Upper Egypt; the city of Memphis at the divide between Upper and Lower Egypt; and the cities of Alexandria and Avaris (also called Per-Ramesses) in the Delta. Alexandria did not exist until the time of Alexander the Great (see the chronology chart on p. 26). The other Egyptian cities were more ancient.

Syria-Palestine is on the geographic edge of an arc-like region of fertile land called the 'Fertile Crescent'. The Fertile Crescent stretches from Babylonia north through Assyria and southwest into Syria-Palestine toward Egypt. If an army wanted to march from Babylonia to Egypt, it would have to march through this great arc, with its rivers and fertile lands. The army could not march directly westwards across the desert, for the soldiers would have died en route. That made Syria-Palestine strategically significant real estate. It was the focus of many ancient wars.

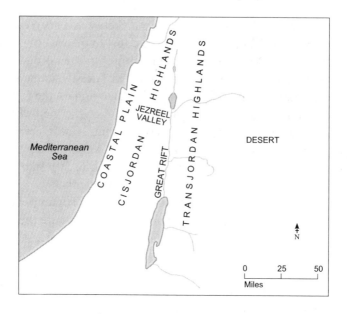

Figure 2. *Four Zones of Palestine.*

### Ancient Syria-Palestine

Syria-Palestine's terrain has been marked by a deep geological fault running north–south. This deep cut in the earth's surface extends from northern Syria (the Orontes River Valley) all the way south to the Gulf of Aqabah-Elat on the northeastern finger of the Red Sea. In fact, the geological fault created the Red Sea, and that fault continues into the African continent. Geologists call this fault the Great Rift.

Where Syria meets Palestine, the Great Rift runs between mountains called the Lebanon range and the Anti-Lebanon range, where the Orontes and Litani rivers flow. Syrian cities of note included Ugarit on the coast and Kadesh and Hamath on the Orontes. Ugarit and Kadesh were significant in the Late Bronze Age and Hamath grew in significance during the Iron Age (see the chronology chart, p. 26).

As a result of the Great Rift, Palestine's geography, south of Syria, is divided into four north–south zones:

1. The Coastal Plain, along the Mediterranean Sea.
2. The Cisjordan Highlands, between the coast and the Great Rift.
3. The Jordan River Valley, which is the Great Rift Valley.
4. The Transjordan Highlands, east of the Jordan River.

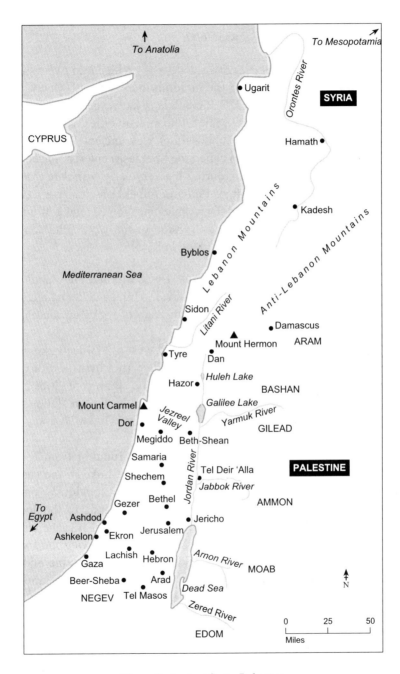

Figure 3. *Ancient Syria-Palestine.*

Each of these four zones should be studied carefully so that their distinctive features are clearly understood.

*The Coastal Plain of Palestine*. This zone was divided into two regions,
with Mount Carmel serving as the dividing line. North of Mount Carmel was ancient Phoenicia. The Phoenicians had excellent port cities
and were marine merchants. Major Phoenician cities were Byblos,
Sidon and Tyre. South of Mount Carmel was ancient Philistia. The
Philistines (and a related group called the Sheklesh) entered this coastal
region from the Aegean region during the very early Iron Age (see the
chronology chart on p. 26). Major Philistine-Sheklesh cities were Gaza,
Ashkelon, Ashdod, Ekron and Dor. Palestine got its name from the
Philistines; 'Palestine' is the Greek version of the word 'Philistia'. In
Egyptian, the Philistines were called the Peleset.

*The Cisjordan Highlands of Palestine*. The Cisjordan Highlands is a
general term for the very uneven tract of steep hills and deep valleys in
the center of Palestine. This north–south zone of rocky terrain can be
subdivided into four smaller regions:

(1) The Galilee is the highland north and west of Galilee Lake. Usu-
ally it was subdivided into the Upper Galilee (northern portion) and
Lower Galilee (southern portion). There were no significant cities in the
Galilee, but two very large cities bordered it on the Jordan Valley side.
They were Dan (also called Laish), at the foot of Mount Hermon, and
Hazor, southwest of Huleh Lake.

(2) The Jezreel is a wide and fertile valley running from Mount
Carmel in the west to the southern tip of Galilee Lake in the east. It
cuts the Cisjordan Highlands zone in two, and is not, obviously, part of
the highlands; rather, it connects the coastal lowlands to the Jordan
Valley lowlands. Near the western edge of the Jezreel was the city of
Megiddo, and at the eastern edge was Beth-Shan, bordering the Jordan
Valley. The Jezreel was the breadbasket of ancient Palestine and the
most crucial trade route connecting Egypt to Syria and Mesopotamia.

(3) The Central Hills, also known as the Samarian Hills, are the hills
and valleys wedged between the Jezreel Valley to the north and the city
of Jerusalem to the south. Several cities in this region were significant:
Samaria, Shechem and Bethel. In the Bible, this region seems to have
been the very heart of Israel. The Bible divides the Central Hills in
three: Manasseh south of the Jezreel Valley to Shechem; Ephraim south

Figure 4. *Palestine's Central Hills. The rugged terrain of Palestine's Central Hills is the primary location for many biblical narratives, from Abraham and Jacob to the battles of Israelite kings.*

of Shechem to Bethel; and Benjamin from Bethel to just north of Jerusalem.

(4) The Judaean Hills are the hills and valleys running from Jerusalem in the north to just south of the city of Hebron. The Judaean Hills are bounded by three border areas that also played a significant role in ancient Judaean experience: (a) to the west, between the Coastal Plain and the Judaean Hills, lies a fertile region of foothills called the Shephelah; (b) to the south, the Beer-Sheba Valley (extending from Beer-Sheba to Arad) marks the northern edge of a southern desert called the Negev; (c) to the east, along the western coast of the Dead Sea, is the Judaean Desert. Important cities in this region included Gezer and Lachish in the Shephelah; Jerusalem and Hebron in the Judaean Hills; Beer-Sheba, Tel Masos and Arad in the Beer-Sheba Valley. The Judaean Hills gave the Jewish people their name: 'Jew' is the Hebrew word meaning 'Judahite'—a person from Judah.

*The Jordan River Valley of Palestine.* The Jordan River originates at Mount Hermon (9000 feet above sea level), west of the city called Damascus. Its waters flow south into an ancient lake called Huleh Lake, and from there continue south into the large freshwater Galilee

Lake (also called Sea of Galilee). The Jordan continues south, rushing ever downward to the Dead Sea, the lowest spot on Earth (1300 feet below sea level). The Dead Sea got its name because it is 25 per cent salt, which means nothing can live in it. The region surrounding the Dead Sea is an arid desert. The western shores of the Dead Sea are called the Judaean Desert. Important cities in the Jordan Valley include: Dan and Hazor north of Galilee Lake, Tel Deir 'Alla near the Jabbok river, and Jericho, just north of the Dead Sea. (Qumran, where most of the Dead Sea Scrolls were found, was a very small site at the north-western tip of the Dead Sea, a few miles south of Jericho.)

*The Transjordan Highlands of Palestine.* This zone is a series of hills and valleys wedged between the Jordan Valley to the west and the great Arabian Desert to the east. At the northern tip of the Transjordan Highlands were the ancient city of Damascus and Mount Hermon. Damascus was a home of the biblical Aramaeans. Just south of Galilee Lake, the Yarmuk River divided Bashan (north of the river) from Gilead (south of the river). The River Jabbok marked the ancient region called Ammon, home of the biblical Ammonites. South of that, the Arnon River marked the territory of biblical Moab. At the southern extreme, this region became a vast desert stretching to the Gulf of Aqabah-Elat on the northeastern finger of the Red Sea. The desert south of the Zered River and north of the Red Sea was biblical Edom.

## Chronology of Ancient Palestine

The way that humans reckon the passage of time is arbitrary. Most cultures use a calendar based on Earth's orbit around the sun. This solar calendar contains 365 days per year. Since one full orbit does not end precisely with the close of day 365, it is necessary to insert an extra day into a solar calendar every fourth year. Some cultures prefer a lunar calendar, based on phases of the moon. Twelve lunar orbits around the earth coincide roughly, but not perfectly, with the earth's seasons. These constitute a year in the lunar calendar, provided an extra month is added according to some fixed schedule so that the months stay in tune with the seasons.

The arbitrary nature of time reckoning is especially apparent in our seven-day week. Why seven days? Not every culture chose to have a seven-day week. For example, prior to Caesar Augustus, the Romans observed an eight-day week. But most ancient people believed that there were seven 'planets'—that is to say, seven stars that moved in unique patterns. Each planet, which was also a god, received a day in his or her honor. Therefore, most ancient peoples observed a seven-day week, as did the Romans from the time of Augustus. Sun's day and Moon's day remain evident in our days of the week, as does Saturn's day. These names derive from the Anglo-Saxon names of the gods, as do all the names of our days: Tiw(= Mars)-day, Woden(= Mercury)-day, Thor(= Jupiter)-day, Freya(= Venus)-day. The biblical creation story in Genesis 1 is a 'de-mythologized' explanation for a seven-day week, but the seven-day week was already common centuries before Genesis 1 was written.

Our modern solar calendar is also arbitrary. It was introduced during the reign of Julius Caesar (several generations before the birth of Christ) and was modified slightly by Pope Gregory XIII in the 1500s. The numbers assigned to our years are equally arbitrary. For many centuries, a very different numbering was employed. However, as the Christian church began to dominate European culture in the medieval period, it was decided to number the years from the presumed date of the birth of Jesus Christ. A diligent medieval monk consulted the records available to him and designated a particular year during the reign of Caesar Augustus to be the year of Christ's birth. He was incorrect—off by at least four years—though he had no way to know that at the time. Nevertheless, our numbering of years remains determined by that arbitrary and incorrect decision.

Today, many people are not comfortable with the numbering of our years because it is a sectarian system, keyed to the doctrines of a religion that is by no means universal. 'AD' is short for *anno domini*, which means 'in the year of our Lord'. Therefore, a date written 'AD' is a date made as part of a religious confession of faith! But the numbering system has become so conventional that no one wants to change it. So a compromise has emerged. Increasingly, the Christian terms are being replaced but the numbers remain unchanged: 'CE' means 'Common Era' and replaces 'AD', while 'BCE' means 'Before Common Era' and replaces 'BC'. The Norman conquest of England took place in AD 1066 but now is said to have occurred in 1066 CE. Julius Caesar was assassinated in 44 BC but now we say he was murdered in 44 BCE.

Ancient cultures used a variety of calendars, and one fundamental task of the historian is to key the ancient calendar systems to our modern calendar, so that we can know when ancient events took place.

This is a complex topic that will not be surveyed here. Suffice it to say that ancient Mesopotamia has given us calendars capable of being correlated, after very careful effort, to our calendar. To a lesser degree, ancient Egypt offers some evidence for these correlations as well, although some portions of Egyptian chronology remain a little fluid. (In some cases, the dates assigned to a particular Egyptian king might vary by several decades from one history textbook to another.) To determine dates otherwise unknown, many clever methods are employed. For example, when archaeologists uncover an ancient letter written by King A to King B, we know immediately that Kings A and B were contemporaries. If King A has been correlated to our modern calendar, we now have the means to determine a date for King B as well. Moreover, if enough is known about King B's dynasty, we can calculate the dates for the kings before and after King B. When you read a history book, the dates assigned to persons and events have been determined through the painstaking process of creating these networks of correlations. Archaeologists sometimes use scientific means, such as carbon-14 dating, to determine the age of artifacts. Almost without exception, these scientifically determined dates for the artifacts are compatible with dates already determined through the 'old-fashioned' method of correlated calendar systems.

All that effort has produced a table for the reckoning of time during antiquity. This chronology chart also provides a structure for the general sequence of cultures in Syria-Palestine. It should be *memorized* as soon as possible:

| Name of Era | Dates (BCE) | One Significant Characteristic |
|---|---|---|
| Palaeolithic | Prior to c. 18000 | Hunter-Gatherer Societies |
| Mesolithic | c. 18000–8000 | Transitional Era, toward… |
| Neolithic | c. 8000–4500 | …Farmer-Herder Societies |
| Chalcolithic | c. 4500–3500 | Early Metal Working |
| Early Bronze (EB) | 3500–2000 | Invention of Writing |
| Middle Bronze (MB) | 2000–1550 | Canaanite City-States |
| Late Bronze (LB) | 1550–1200 | Egyptian Empire |
| Iron Age I (IA I) | 1200–900 | IA I Highland Villages |
| Iron Age II (IA II) | 900–586 | Regional Kingdoms |
| Babylonian Era | 586–539 | Judahite 'Exile' |
| Persian Era | 539–332 | Early Judaisms |
| Alexander the Great | 336–323 | — |
| Hellenistic Era | 332–63 | Hellenistic Judaisms |
| Roman Era | 63 BCE–324 CE | Proto-Rabbinic Judaism |

Figure 5. *A Chronology Chart.*

Several aspects of this chart should be noted. First, the dates are approximate and some resources will use slightly different dates, especially for the older periods.

Second, the 'eras' begin with labels based on technology. The three 'lithic' (stone) ages are the palaeo- (old), meso- (middle) and neo- (new). Many archaeologists prefer to call the Mesolithic the 'Epipalae-olithic', which means the period 'upon' (epi-, that is to say, 'more recently than') the palaeolithic. This book will use Mesolithic, not Epi-palaeolithic.

The technological labels continue after the lithic eras. When evidence demonstrates that humans began to smelt metal, archaeologists and historians switch to metal technologies to describe them. The Chal-colithic Age was the era of stone tools (lithic) supplemented by metal artifacts made of copper (chalco-). Later, humans realized that they could add 10 per cent tin to their copper and make an alloy called bronze, which is harder and therefore more useful than copper. Iron was known during the Bronze Age, but was harder to work and more brittle. It became widespread only as tin and copper supplies became more difficult to reach and as iron technology improved.

Towards the end of the chronology, technology is no longer the basis for the labels. The Iron Age is followed by a series of eras labeled according to political domination. This became necessary since the metal technology no longer changed dramatically. The Babylonian era and each that followed it are, from the viewpoint of technology, *still* the Iron Age. In fact, one might say that the Iron Age came to a close only a few decades ago, as computer technology began to transform our societies in the 1960s and 1970s CE.

Another important feature of this chronology chart is that most numbers get smaller as one moves towards more recent times. The year 586 BCE is older than the year 336 BCE. When time moves from Before Common Era to Common Era, numbers begin small and get larger. A year such as 70 CE is older than the year 324 CE. Except for the final chapter, this book covers dates BCE, so the numbers almost always move from large to small.

Related to this is the numbering of centuries. We just completed the twentieth century CE, and now we will live the remainder of our lives in the twenty-first century CE. But our century numerals add one digit in the hundreds column of the year dates. The twentieth century was the 1900s, and the twenty-first century will be the 2000s. This holds for ancient dates as well. The century always adds one digit in the hundreds column. The year 586 BCE was the sixth century BCE. Alexander of Macedon (336–323 BCE) was active during the fourth century BCE.

Most of this book will deal with the periods LB, IA I and IA II. Nevertheless, it is necessary to comprehend the chronological sweep prior to and after that time, and significant discussion of those other eras is included in Chapters 4 and 10.

*A Word about the Bible*

## Three Modern Bibles

| Jewish Bible | Catholic Old Testament | Protestant O.T. |
|---|---|---|
| **TORAH** | **TORAH** | **TORAH** |
| Genesis | Genesis | Genesis |
| Exodus | Exodus | Exodus |
| Leviticus | Leviticus | Leviticus |
| Numbers | Numbers | Numbers |
| Deuteronomy | Deuteronomy | Deuteronomy |
| | | |
| **FORMER PROPHETS** | **NARRATIVE BOOKS** | **NARRATIVE BOOKS** |
| Joshua | Joshua | Joshua |
| Judges | Judges | Judges |
| | Ruth | Ruth |
| 1-2 Samuel | 1-2 Samuel | 1-2 Samuel |
| 1-2 Kings | 1-2 Kings | 1-2 Kings |
| | 1-2 Chronicles | 1-2 Chronicles |
| **LATTER PROPHETS** | Ezra-Nehemiah | Ezra-Nehemiah |
| Isaiah | Tobit | |
| Jeremiah | Judith | |
| Ezekiel | Esther + additions | Esther |
| The Twelve* | 1-2 Maccabees | |
| | | |
| **WRITINGS** | **WRITINGS** | **WRITINGS** |
| Psalms | Job | Job |
| Proverbs | Psalms | Psalms |
| Job | Proverbs | Proverbs |
| Song of Songs | Ecclesiastes | Ecclesiastes |
| Ruth | Song of Songs | Song of Songs |
| Lamentations | Wisdom of Solomon | |
| Ecclesiastes | Wisdom of Ben Sira | |
| Esther | | |
| Daniel | **PROPHETIC BOOKS** | **PROPHETIC BOOKS** |
| Ezra-Nehemiah | Isaiah | Isaiah |
| 1-2 Chronicles | Jeremiah | Jeremiah |
| | Lamentations | Lamentations |
| *The Twelve: Hosea, Joel, | 1 Baruch + addition | |
| Amos, Obadiah, Jonah, | Ezekiel | Ezekiel |
| Micah, Nahum, Habakkuk, | Daniel + additions | Daniel |
| Zephaniah, Haggai, | The Twelve* | The Twelve* |
| Zechariah, Malachi | | |

Figure 6. *Three Modern Bibles.*

Ancient Palestine produced one of the most famous works of literature in the world, the Bible. Since it is a genuine artifact from the very culture to be considered in this book, the Bible will be a constant partner in our conversation.

However, discussing the Bible as though it were a single entity is rather misleading. The Bible is not a book, but an anthology of books. Prior to the Common Era, each of the books of the Bible circulated independently on its own leather scroll. During late-Roman times the codex was invented. This was the earliest version of our modern book format. With the invention of the codex, for the first time, multiple books of the Bible were bound together into one volume. In the centuries BCE no such bound volume existed. Thus, when I write about the Bible in the following pages, I am really discussing a loose anthology of literature, and a number of the documents in that anthology have very little relationship to the others.

Also, there is not one Bible, but three (or more than three, depending on how one counts). The three most widely circulating Bibles are the Jewish Bible, the Roman Catholic Bible and the Protestant Bible. The Jewish Bible is the most conservative of the three. It contains fewer books, and shorter versions of some books that appear in slightly expanded form as part of the Roman Catholic Bible. The two Christian Bibles, Roman Catholic and Protestant, call the books of the Jewish Bible the 'Old Testament', but they also rearrange the order in which some of the Jewish books appear, and the Roman Catholic Bible adds a number of books not contained in the other two. And, of course, both Christian Bibles include an appendix called the 'New Testament' that is not accepted as scripture by Jews. When I discuss a biblical book that is contained in the Christian Bibles but not the Jewish, I will clarify which Bibles are meant. In no situation, however, do I intend to suggest that I favor one Bible over the others. All three Bibles are artifacts from ancient Palestine and, therefore, all three are worthy of a historian's attention and study.

## SUGGESTED ADDITIONAL READING

*Chronology*

Bickerman, E.J., *Chronology of the Ancient World* (Ithaca, NY: Cornell University Press, 2nd edn, 1980).

*The Bible and Geography*

Frick, Frank S., *A Journey Through the Hebrew Scriptures* (Fort Worth: Harcourt Brace College Publishers, 1995).

Rogerson, John, and Philip Davies, *The Old Testament World* (Englewood Cliffs, NJ: Prentice–Hall, 1989).

*Common Bible Translations*

A Jewish Bible:

*Tanakh: A New Translation of the Holy Scriptures According to the Traditional Hebrew Text* (Philadelphia: The Jewish Publication Society, 1985).

A Roman Catholic Bible:

*The New American Bible* (London: Thomas Nelson, 1983).

A Protestant Bible:

*The Holy Bible: New International Version* (Grand Rapids: Zondervan, 1978).

An Ecumenical Bible:

*The Holy Bible: New Revised Standard Version* (Oxford: Oxford University Press, 1989).

Chapter 2

## WHAT IS 'HISTORY'?

### Introduction

Before one can discuss the ancient past, it is necessary to determine how one is able to discuss the ancient past. Historians tend to disagree on many aspects of ancient events, which is not surprising, since the events happened a very long time ago. But how does one choose between the various disagreements? How does one determine which narrative of the ancient past is most realistic? This chapter will discuss the academic discipline called 'history', emphasizing how it differs from popular, and sometimes ideological, understandings of 'history'. Also, it will describe several of the tools employed by the historian of the ancient Near East. Through this discussion, I hope that you can develop a sense of the necessity for critical judgment when engaging with any narrative that purports to be about the ancient past.

### Differing Conceptions of 'History'

History is a commonly misunderstood concept. It is confusing for several reasons. First, the word 'history' is understood in popular culture to mean 'the past'. Yet, a more formal definition of 'history' is not 'the past', but 'a narrative that presents a past'.[1] That is to say, history is not what happened; it is what a teller reports to have happened. Since history bears these two contradictory meanings in our culture, there is ample room for confusion. For example, a history can be entirely false. Fascist governments frequently publish histories that falsify the past to put the government in a positive light. This kind of history is not false history; it is true history in the sense that it conforms to a proper definition of the word 'history', a narrative that presents a past. But it is true history that tells lies. One might prefer to call it true false-history! This can be confusing for someone who uses the word 'history' when he or she really means 'the past'.

History can be confusing for a second reason. There are many varieties of history because there are many ways to narrate a past. Look at the front page of a daily newspaper. There you will find one form of history. This is an informal history about very recent events. Now look at an academic journal devoted to the study of the past. This is also history, but a much more formal variety. Each page of the academic journal contains two texts. The main text, which is always called 'the text', is a narrative about the past. The other text, which is called 'the apparatus', provides footnotes. The footnotes cite the sources used for the narration of the past that appears in the text, and they sometimes also provide supplementary information. Though often ignored by casual readers, footnotes are essential to academic history and serve a valuable purpose to the serious reader. They permit verification or refutation of the assertions made in the text. The newspaper does not use footnotes to justify assertions about the past. Therefore, the reader must accept that what the reporter has written is correct. Nevertheless, both the newspaper and the academic journal constitute 'history' because each presents a narrative about a past. Yet, they are very different kinds of history.

Finally, history can be confusing because there are a variety of reasons for narrating a past. If the reader or hearer of a history does not share the teller's assumptions about why the past is significant, misunderstanding can result. Sometimes that misunderstanding evolves into controversy. In the early 1990s, the Smithsonian Institution began plans to present a history exhibit about the bombing of Hiroshima and Nagasaki, events that took place on 6 and 9 August 1945. Those who prepared the text and images for the exhibition were academic historians, for whom the study of the past is an intellectual discipline. They presented the events of the atomic bombings in accordance with the universally accepted professional standards of academic history writing. However, a group of World War II veterans, for whom these particular past events hold great emotional meaning, were outraged by the proposed exhibit. Nowhere had the academic historians supported interpretations of the atomic bombing that were common among veterans. The veterans accused the historians of distorting history. They said the exhibit was anti-American propaganda. Needless to say, the Smithsonian's historians were shocked. They had only done their job according to academic standards. This is an example in which two groups presupposed very different reasons for wanting to narrate the past.

These three points demonstrate that history is complex. Since history is not the past but a narration of a past, a history can be false (for example, if its facts are incorrect) but can never be entirely true (even if its facts are correct). True history is a matter of degree, and the truth-value of a history lies not in its facts, but in its treatment of the facts. Consider, for example, a historical novel. The novel might narrate the facts of an event correctly, but so glamorize or pillory certain partici-pants that it renders the narrative false. Hollywood films that claim to be 'based on a true story' often distort the past in precisely this way (and frequently those films are scorned by academic historians!). Since truth is a matter of degree, not an absolute, the academic historian's goal is to present a history that *approaches* truth by avoiding false-hood. It is a history that tries to get the facts correct *and* to present those facts in a proper proportion, so that the past is not distorted by its very narration.[2]

All of this is to say that *history is always an interpretation*; it is the past as narrated, and the narration will conform to the interpretational assumptions of the narrator. There is no such thing as an objective or unbiased history since interpretation is the imposition of biases onto the topic under scrutiny. Therefore it is important to be aware of pre-cisely which kind of biases are operating in a given history. As will be discussed below, some biases are more reasonable than others; as a result, some histories are more reasonable than others. Moreover, his-tory is an interpretation that is narrated in a particular form. The form of narration conforms to the needs and assumptions of those for whom a particular history is written. Popular history can get by without the apparatus so essential to academic history. But the lack of an apparatus might entail as well a lack of disciplined judgment and a correspond-ingly less 'truthful' interpretation of past events.

With this complexity of history in mind, it is necessary to be aware of at least three genres of history that are common in contemporary Western society. Before looking at these three, a definition of genre will be helpful.

### What is a Genre?

Genre is easy to understand but difficult to define. A formal definition would be: 'Genre is any communication in which the intention of the communication is shared by the sender and the receiver'. Usually (but not always) the communication is verbal and involves conventional verbal clues that alert the hearer or reader to the intentions of the speaker or writer. For example, if I say, 'Knock, knock', you would respond, 'Who's there?' You would recognize the formal quality of a genre, in this case, the genre of the 'knock, knock' joke. You would understand instantly that the intention of this communication is to entertain with simple punning humor. Even when the joke was not funny, you would understand the *intention* of the communication.

Often, a particular genre is at home in a particular social setting. The genre of the wedding ceremony entails a very different setting than the genre of the oath of office, even though both genres involve the conventional verbal structure in which an authority figure asks questions of fidelity to another person or people. Likewise, if you are watching American television and you see Jay Leno walk on stage before an audience, you expect to hear jokes, not a political speech or a news account of recent events. Yet the subject discussed by Jay might involve politics and recent newsworthy events. How did you know what to expect? The music, stage-setting and even the words of introduction provide clues, because they differ from those associated with a news program or political convention. Professional entertainers use the term 'stand-up' as a genre label for the kind of performance associated with Jay Leno and other comics. But a history professor who 'stands up' before a room full of college students would be foolish to follow the standards of the stand-up. The college lecture is a genre in its own right, and one that differs from the stand-up by displaying its own verbal and nonverbal conventions.

Most commonly, the term 'genre' is associated with literature, not events such as stand-up comedy or public lectures, but the principle is the same: It is a communication in a recognizable setting involving familiar verbal conventions, such that the intent of the communication is shared by sender and receiver. For example, a daily newspaper carries dozens of genres in its pages. The front page contains news stories; the editorial page offers opinion pieces, letters to the editor and guest columnists. Each of these four genres has its own rhetorical style or form. In fact, almost every page of the newspaper displays a new genre, such as classified advertising, display advertising, gossip columns, comics, and so on. Each genre uses its own set of clues to convey the intention of the communication. For instance, when reading the comics, you must know the difference between

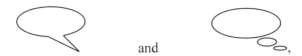

and                    ,

for otherwise, the comic will not make sense—the intention of communication has been lost. These are visual conventions of a genre. Verbal conventions (rhetorical style or form) are just as essential to the success of the communication. However, the verbal conventions associated with one genre sometimes overlap with another, which can create disorientation at times. This is obvious in a case of satire, where the similarity is employed to evoke humor. But it happens in other, more subtle ways: *The National Enquirer* pretends to be a newspaper by emulating the generic conventions of a newspaper. In a real newspaper, the news-story genre differs from the news-analysis genre, even though both genres relate very recent events, often in very similar verbal constructions, differing only in the emphases of their content. These are two genres with very subtle differences in rhetorical style or form, but very different communicative intentions; one reports, the other analyzes.

### Three Genres of History

Today, at least three distinct genres of history exist. Since each genre possesses its own understanding of the intention of a communication about the past, it is essential to distinguish among them, and not to confuse one for another. The first is called 'positivist history' and the second is 'humanist history'. The third does not have a name because it is not usually recognized as a formal genre of history. Nevertheless, it is a common genre and one that radically differs from the others as to the intention of history writing. In this study, it will be labeled 'ideological history'. It seems appropriate to look at these genres of history in turn.

Positivism is a philosophy, not a genre of history writing. However, there are historians who accept the philosophical principles of positivism, and who apply those principles to history writing. The product of their efforts is therefore called 'positivist history'. As a philosophy, positivism attempts to make a distinction between fact and opinion. Specifically, the positivist prefers to limit formal philosophical conversation to facts, eliminating all opinion. This does *not* mean that a positivist hates all opinions. It means only that the positivist prefers to limit *formal philosophical conversation* to facts.

A rule of thumb accepted by many positivist philosophers is this: 'Any statement that cannot be verified or falsified is a meaningless statement'. Consider this sentence: 'Potentially, this caterpillar will become a moth or butterfly'. This is a true, meaningful statement. Another example of a meaningful statement is: 'Frogs always become human princes when kissed'. That statement is meaningful, though false. It is meaningful since one can falsify it by experimentation (if you care to do so!). An example of a meaningless statement would be: 'The little green men on planet Vultone eat only carbohydrates'. The statement is neither true nor false since there is no way to verify or falsify it. For the positivist, this statement is also meaningless: 'In the beginning, God created the heavens and the earth'. Statements of a religious nature cannot be verified or falsified; they are meaningless, so they are excluded from positivist history writing.

When applied to history writing, positivist principles have profound implications. Since, for the positivist, an opinion is never subject to verification or falsification and is therefore meaningless, the positivist historian must find a way to deal with the subjectivity of human life and human emotion while avoiding statements of personal opinion. Consider this sentence: 'When he lived at the White House, President James Buchanan was lonely'. For the positivist historian, this statement is neither true nor false, it is meaningless. How could one ever verify or falsify claims about the emotions of a dead president? On the other hand, the following sentence would be acceptable to the positivist historian: 'In letters that he wrote while living at the White House, President Buchanan expressed loneliness'. If that sentence were followed by a footnote citation directing the reader to an archive of Buchanan's correspondence in which the president had indeed expressed loneliness, it would be a well-researched and properly articulated positivist historical assertion.

Although positivism was still popular as recently as a generation ago, only a few academic historians claim to be positivists now. Positivism suffers from difficulties that render it almost impossible to serve as an adequate genre of history. Realistically, it would be impossible to exclude all opinion from statements about the past. Indeed, *the very process of choosing to mention one fact and not another constitutes the exercise of personal opinion*. For instance, if it were a fact that

President Buchanan expressed loneliness in the White House, who is to decide whether that fact is important enough to be mentioned as part of a history? No historian is able to mention all the facts about a subject, so a selection of facts is inevitable, and therefore subjectivity is bound to be a part of even the most rigorous positivist history. Positivism reached for an impossible goal, the goal of total objectivity. It failed, but the effort was not in vain. Positivism bestowed upon the academic study of the past a method for the investigation and citation of factual data that remains a vital part of all competent history writing.

Most academic historians prefer a genre of history writing that might be termed 'humanist history'. Like positivism, humanism is a philosophy, not a genre of history. But those who accept the principles of humanism and apply those principles to history writing produce humanist history.

Humanism is difficult to define because there are many varieties of humanist philosophy. All varieties have two things in common. First, humanists promote the subjective value judgment that all human beings are dignified creatures worthy of study and respect. Second, humanism prefers to limit formal philosophical discussion to the natural world, avoiding any speculation about the supernatural, such as the possible existence of a god or gods. Like the positivist who avoids opinion but does not hate it, the humanist avoids speculation about the supernatural not because she hates such speculation, but because she prefers to avoid it during formal academic research. For example, a humanist might study the religious beliefs of a human society, but will refrain from passing judgment about the alleged truth of those religious beliefs. For the humanist, religious beliefs are just that, beliefs held by humans.

In short, the variety of humanism that undergirds humanist history writing is the humanism that created the university. Within any academic institution, a common division is used to distinguish the natural sciences, the social sciences and the humanities. The natural sciences study every aspect of the natural world. The humanities study every aspect of the human world, especially the creative accomplishments of humans, including artistic, literary, philosophical, political, social and cultural accomplishments. The social sciences straddle those two disciplines, applying the tools and methods of the natural sciences to the study of humanist disciplines. Academic historians usually perceive themselves to be part of the humanities, though a few consider themselves to be social scientists. In either case, it is the philosophical presuppositions that created the humanities as a sub-group of academic disciplines that also created history as an academic discipline.

It is easy to see that humanism is an ideal philosophical foundation for academic study of the past. Humanism's avoidance of the supernatural makes it compatible with positivism's desire to focus on meaningful statements. The formal method of gathering data and citing those data in an apparatus is as common to humanist history as it is to positivist history. Yet humanism's self-avowed subjectivity—remember that it is based on the subjective opinion that humans are dignified and worthy of study—permits the historian to be honest about subjective value judgments, such as which facts to select for history writing, and which facts to dismiss as unimportant. The humanist can admit, for example, that if a president expressed loneliness in the White House, that detail is worthy of report, perhaps only because it puts a more human and personal face on the history of a presidency. This does not mean that positivist history is factual and humanist history is opinionated. On the contrary, humanism employs all the rigor of positivism, but avoids its fallacies. It is factual history writing by historians who admit that they are fallible humans.

One might take a moment to note that the first two genres of history are very similar, and that each goes its own way only in certain respects. The intention of positivist history is to achieve an entirely objective account of the past (an impossible goal), but the intention of humanist history is to understand the human reality of the past. The positivist defines interpretation as a desire to determine precisely what happened and why it happened. A humanist defines interpretation to mean something a little more subtle: not just what happened and why, but what were these people who did these things really like? How did events mold them and how did they mold events? In short, where the positivist tends to ask 'What happened?' the humanist prefers the question 'Who were these people?' In spite of these differences, the methods used by each are quite similar. Both research all available data about a given time and place, carefully sift that evidence, and try to propose an interpretation that puts the data in a realistic light. The finished product will be a narrative of the past that has been composed for the sake of the past.

However, there are people who study the past not because they are interested in the past, but because they want to mold and influence the direction that the present is taking. Usually, these individuals are members of a group who advance a cause of some kind. The cause might be political, social, religious or even ethical. I prefer to call this kind of history 'ideological'.[3] It is a history not for the sake of the past but for the sake of the present, and perhaps the future.

Unlike the first two genres, ideological history is not founded upon a specific philosophy. However, individual examples of ideological history might well rest on a philosophy of some kind. Marxists tend to write Marxist history; capitalists promote capitalist history; Christian fundamentalists champion fundamentalist history; feminists advance feminist history. Many other examples could be listed. The common denominator in each, and that which distinguishes the ideological genre of history from either positivist or humanist history, is the *intention* for which it is written. Ideological history has been composed to advance a cause.

*It is imperative to note that ideological history is not automatically 'bad' history—though it can be.* At its worst, ideological history is merely propaganda. At its best, ideological history can make profound contributions to the academic study of the past, sometimes correcting a bias or a miscomprehension overlooked by positivists and humanists. The best way to illustrate how ideological history can be 'good' history sometimes and 'bad' history at other times is to offer a brief definition of 'ideology' and to follow that definition with an example.

The word 'ideology' has been defined in many ways. In an effort to place this word in as neutral a light as possible, I use the following definition: 'An ideology is any reasonable hypothesis designed to defend the legitimacy of an identity group'. Every word of this definition is crucial. First, an ideology must be a reasonable hypothesis. Crazed, paranoid hypotheses are not ideological, they are meaningless. For example, Holocaust denial is not a reasonable hypothesis, it is merely nonsense. Second, to be ideological, the hypothesis must exist primarily for the purpose of demonstrating the legitimacy of a particular group of people. A scientific theory is not ideological since its purpose is to comprehend the natural world and it has no bearing on the groups into which humans divide themselves.[4] Likewise, a mathematical theory is not ideological since its validity does not depend upon a group's assent. Two plus two always equals four, even if a group of people choose not to believe it. Third, an ideology attempts to legitimate a particular group who identify themselves as somehow distinct from all other groups. I, for instance, identify with the following groups:

American citizens, college professors, humanists and basketball fans. Given space, I could name many more groups with which I identify. If I develop a hypothesis to defend the legitimate existence of any one of these groups as distinct from all other groups, I have developed an ideology. For example, this statement is ideological: 'Basketball fans are uniquely valuable to society because we promote fellowship and good sportsmanship'. This is not necessarily very convincing ideology, since one could argue that many other groups do these two things as well, so there is no legitimate need for my group to exist. Ideology might or might not be convincing, but if it is a reasonable hypothesis that defends an identity group, it is ideology.

With this definition in mind, it is possible to see that some ideological history will be 'good'—that is to say, sound and reasonable—history, while other examples will be 'bad'—or unreasonable—history. The key distinction is whether the ideological historian has remained within reasonable bounds, or has permitted the ideology to veer off into indefensible (and thus meaningless) realms.

Consider this example: Joseph Stalin identified himself as a Marxist. This fact, which is indisputable, has been a problem for Marxist historians. Stalin was a ruthless man responsible for the murder of millions, and this is difficult to reconcile with the assertion made by Karl Marx, and echoed by most modern Marxists, that Marxism is a fully developed humanism, a philosophy that champions the dignity of individual humans and seeks to benefit all by creating economic equality. How does a historian who wishes to defend the legitimacy of Marxists and their philosophy deal with Stalin as a topic of historical research? Here are two possibilities. First, one might argue that Stalin was not really a Marxist—that his actions violated the basic tenets of Marxist philosophy to which he paid lip service. This hypothesis, if accepted, defends Marxism against the disastrous (pseudo-)Marxism of Stalin. Not every historian has been convinced by the argument (some have even dismissed it as a false hypothesis), but all agree that the hypothesis is reasonable, given the evidence. Another tactic that might be employed by a Marxist historian would be to argue that Stalin's crimes were not crimes, but were necessary because Stalin had the best interest of his own Russian people in mind. Although this hypothesis also tries to defend Marxism, such an approach will be rejected by all competent historians as an unreasonable interpretation, and would constitute 'bad' history writing. Thus, it is not the ideological intent of a history that determines its worth, but the degree to which that intent has either distorted or clarified the data.

One can see that ideological history, even when it is 'good' history, is a genre of history that differs from positivist and humanist history. The intention of its communication differs profoundly from these forms of history writing. In a sense, ideological history engages in what one philosopher has called 'retrospective politics'.[5] That is to say, it presents a past in order to promote an agenda in the present. The other two genres of history, by contrast, study the past because the past is interesting to study. Positivists and humanists think of the past as that which is dead, fixed, and finished, yet fascinating, and useful to the present because knowledge of the past enriches our lives in so many, often unexpected, ways.

Genre is a key concept that affects your life every day. The ability to recognize distinct genres of history enables critical evaluation of any history writing that you encounter. If you comprehend the intention of a communication about a past, you have taken the first step toward determining the worth of that communication.

## Tools for the Study of the Ancient Past

After a historian of ancient Canaan and Israel has determined the genre of history to be written, the real work begins. One must research ancient events, and ancient events are very difficult to research. Not only have all eyewitnesses passed from the scene centuries before, but the cultural assumptions of ancient people have disappeared as well. Those cultural assumptions are crucial, for they gave meaning to everything an ancient person did or said. Think of all the routine activities in your own life. Would you bother with most of them if you were suddenly transported out of your culture and into a wholly different one, with alien values and assumptions? Your deeds and words have meaning to you because they are grounded in a particular social context; out of that context, they become meaningless. It is this same subjective meaning that brings evidence from the ancient past to life. If historians examine an artifact or document from ancient times but do not know the cultural values that made the artifact or document important, how can they evaluate its significance? Both artifact and document were part of a network of interrelated activities and their associated meanings. A modern historian must develop tools for recapturing as much of that network as possible.

Two of the most significant tools available to the historian of the ancient world are archaeology and the dual field of philology and epigraphy. As I will explain in the following pages, archaeology is the systematic recovery and interpretation of the material remains of ancient societies. Philology and epigraphy are the systematic study of the documents written by ancient peoples.

*What is Archaeology?*
Archaeology is not merely digging up artifacts; rather, it is both the systematic recovery and the careful examination of artifacts. The stereotyped image of the archaeologist is a person covered in dry dust, carefully digging up an ancient Palestinian mound called a 'tel'. But sometimes archaeology is not associated with dusty tels at all. Some archaeologists recover artifacts from the ocean. Others recover objects that were not buried, only neglected. In all cases, the archaeologist does two things. First, the archaeologist recovers the artifacts in a systematic way, recording the exact find spot and the treatment of the object from the time of its finding. Second, the archaeologist examines the artifacts carefully, using methods of examination that have evolved through the combination of several academic disciplines.

Each of the two steps is essential to archaeological investigation. The first, the systematic approach to the recovery of an artifact, provides crucial documentation that becomes as valuable as the object itself. The documentation of an artifact's find spot and subsequent treatment by archaeologists is called the artifact's 'provenance'. This is important in two ways. First, every artifact that has a provenance can be compared and contrasted with all other provenanced artifacts. In this way, the archaeologist notes patterns of similarity and difference in the find spots from which the various artifacts were recovered, and then relates those patterns to the qualities of artifacts themselves. Provenance is what enables an otherwise mute object from the ancient world to tell its story about daily activity, and routine social values associated with that activity. In short, provenance gives an artifact its meaning. Second, provenance protects the artifact's value by retaining a record of its relationship to other objects from the same excavation or survey. Since archaeological research involves the destruction of the site under investigation (when an ancient village or campsite is dug up, it is destroyed), the precise recording of each find is the only record that remains. All future re-evaluations of the site will depend upon the precision with which the site was systematically documented. Provenance instills value in each object.

In contrast to properly excavated objects, many unprovenanced artifacts turn up on the antiquities market. These artifacts were not recovered by archaeologists, but were dug up by poachers who earn their living from illegal excavation. More often than not, these artifacts are utterly useless to an archaeologist precisely because they lack a provenance. Without that provenance, they remain mute curiosities, incapable of telling their stories. It is fair to say that an artifact on the antiquities market is an artifact that has been desecrated. Lack of provenance is a problem in another way as well. Fake artifacts are becoming more common. Those who earn a living from the sale of antiquities have been reading the academic journals and books published by expert archaeologists and epigraphers, in which details about the physical qualities of the artifacts are recorded. Some people who lack scruples have begun developing very sophisticated methods to trick even an expert's eye. As a result, scholars are usually very reluctant to accept historical hypotheses that rely on data derived from unprovenanced artifacts.

After the artifacts have been provenanced, the second stage of archaeological research begins. This is the systematic examination of the objects. It is impossible for one person to do this alone. The examination process involves experts from many disciplines, including geologists, chemists, cultural anthropologists (people who study the relationship of a human community to its environment and to the technology it invented for living in its environment), and even art historians and architects. The goal of examination is to reconstruct, as much as possible, the entire context of daily life in the time and place under investigation.

Every conceivable aspect of the recovered artifact is investigated. For instance, if a clay pot is recovered, it will undergo seven or more examinations. An art historian will study the shape, size and markings of the pot, comparing it to all other pottery styles known from antiquity. A scientist will perform tests such as petrography and neutron activation analysis. The former investigates the physical composition of the clay and the latter traces its geographic source. An anthropologist will study the uses to which that pot was put, comparing its function to the larger cultural matrix of which it was just one element. An economist will attempt to discern how the pot fits into the trade relationships of the community in which it was used. A botanist will examine and test the pot's content, searching, among other things, for ancient grains or traces of wine. If animal bones were found in the pot, an osteologist will examine them. If there is writing on its surface, an epigrapher will examine its letters or words to determine matters such as the identity and age of the dialect (historical linguistics) and style of formation for the individual letters (palaeography). And, of course, the content of the inscription will be of interest as well! As each artifact is studied, a body of data accumulates, so that the corporate 'personality' of an archaeological site begins to emerge.

There are several methods of field archaeology, though two are most common, horizontal and vertical. Vertical archaeology is better known. In Palestine it is usually, though not always, associated with a tel. A tel (which is the Hebrew word for 'ruin') is a mound that was an ancient city. In ancient times, it was a good idea to build the city on high ground. This offered the people of the city some protection against flood and invaders. When a city was abandoned or destroyed, its ruins were left as they had fallen. Later, when others decided to build a city, they usually built on the same spot for the same reason: the tel was high ground. After that city collapsed, another would be built on the ruins, and so forth. Over the millennia, a tel could grow through constant rebuilding to a height of fifty feet or more. Modern archaeologists will cut a trench down through the tel, removing, as it were, a 'slice of layer cake'. By so doing they are able to examine the layers of occupation that have accumulated through the ages. Each layer is called a stratum and identified by number or letter, or both.

Less glamorous but equally significant is horizontal archaeology, which is the systematic survey of land surfaces. As the centuries roll by, some of the broken pottery at a village or city site will make its way to the surface. This might happen as burrowing animals bring dirt to the surface, rains erode a hillside, or farmers plow up the ground. In fact, so many hazards befall a given section of land over the millennia that one can expect to find a reliable random sample of tiny potsherds on the surface of the site at any given time. If these potsherds are gathered in a systematic (and therefore statistically valid) way, they provide valuable data on the occupational history of a site or an entire region. Extensive regional surveys in Palestine were undertaken during the past generation or so, and many of the historical hypotheses offered in later chapters of this book derive from these data.

One very significant historical hypothesis comes from systematic surveys of this kind: estimates of population size. Frequently, in later chapters, you will read that 'X' number of people lived in a certain city or geographic region. How are these numbers determined? They are educated guesses based on the occupational history of a city or region. First, the archaeologist surveys societies of our own time whose very traditional lifestyles and daily use of objects such as pottery match those of the archaeological record. The researcher determines, on the basis of averages from many samples, the number of people who live in a given house type, village type and so forth. This provides the archaeologist with something called a 'population density coefficient' that can be applied to ancient times in which similar lifestyles were observed. The coefficient is an average number of people for a given type of occupational site. This figure varies depending on the data, but one common coefficient is the rule of thumb that, in ancient times, about 250 people lived on one hectare of land. (A hectare equals 10,000 square meters, or a little less than two and a half acres.) Naturally, estimates of this kind are not perfect—they are always guesses, but they are guesses based on rigorous research. In some cases, archaeologists disagree with one another concerning estimated numbers for a given time and place. Fortunately, even in cases of disagreement, all experts are able to agree on a maximum that a given place could have housed and fed, so that disagreements do not undermine the general understanding that we have developed about ancient populations.[6]

Pottery, especially broken pottery, is the most common category of artifact found at any archaeological excavation. The humble clay pot should be stressed, for this everyday item provides the most significant key to unlocking ancient history. All cultures used clay pots. Pottery breaks easily, so it was replaced regularly, and any given village produced thousands of potsherds. In theory, the potsherds might have been shattered into ever smaller pieces until they disintegrated to dust, but usually they remained as larger pieces. Sometimes, these potsherds were reused by the ancients in creative ways. Some of the larger pieces became stationery—writing surfaces for letters and inventory lists. Many times, large collections of potsherds were gathered and placed as floors for a room or porch. Some were employed as part of the fill

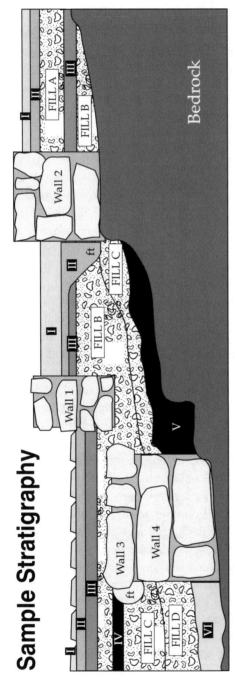

## Sample Stratigraphy

### Stratum I

Walls 1 and 2 are in use, with floors I, and cobblestone floor I. This layer was destroyed by fire, and pottery of the late 8th century BCE was found on its surface.

### Stratum II

Wall 1 is in use, and wall 2 has just been built. (Note that floor II cuts floor III, below, at wall 2. This is a foundation trench, dug to permit the insertion of the stones employed in wall 2. Called an "ft.") Pottery dates to the 8th century BCE.

### Stratum III

Wall 1 has just been built, and wall 2 does not yet exist. The floor associated with this stratum is III, and it had continued beyond the spot where wall 2 was later added. Below floor III is a layer of fill dirt, brought to the site during construction of floor III. This fill dirt (Fill B) contains 8th century BCE pottery shards.

### Stratum IV

This stratum is unclear, and appears to be damaged. Apparently wall 3 was constructed upon the previously dismantled wall 4. At the same time, floor IV was built. But floor IV seems to have been destroyed between walls 3 and 2. Perhaps this happened when floor III was built. Fill dirt (Fill C) was dumped into the area when this stratum was built. This fill contains pottery shards dating to the late 10th and early 9th centuries BCE.

### Strata V and VI (or Stratum V-VI?)

The existence of these strata (or this stratum?) is debatable. Perhaps this packed clay was the natural surface. Perhaps it is the eroded remnant of a floor associated with wall 4. Or was floor IV the floor for wall 4, which was then re-used as the floor for wall 3?

Figure 7. *Sample Stratigraphy.*

needed for the foundations of building projects. More often, however, potsherds were simply discarded. But, since they were not systematically eliminated from living spaces, a few pieces of broken pottery could be found randomly scattered in any place where humans lived. Potsherds were the roadside and curbside trash of the ancient world. Often, the strata of an archaeological dig can be dated on the basis of these potsherds. How is this possible? It is done by a method called 'pottery typology'.

Pottery typology is nothing more than the study of pottery style aimed at determining a sequence of style-change. To use a modern example, think of the way cars and trucks change design style from year to year. The person who knows enough about cars can date a car by its size and shape, the style of its bumper or headlights, its accessories and so forth. One can do the same with Coca-Cola containers. The thick, dark bottles common in the late-nineteenth century gave way to thinner, more stylized bottles in the early-twentieth century. Later, canned Coke was introduced, and eventually plastic containers. One who knows enough about Coca-Cola packaging can date a photograph by examining the Coke container held by a person in the photo. In the same manner, art historians and archaeologists have reconstructed a complex network of data on the stylistic changes in ancient pottery. The pottery, thus 'sequenced', provides a relative chronology so that pots found in an excavation can be matched to the sequence. In some cases, the sequence of pottery styles can provide an occupation date for a site to within a century or so.

Like all methods of research, archaeology has its limitations. It can do some things very well. There are many things that it is unable to do at all. Most significantly archaeology can refute a historian's hypothesis but is never able to prove a historian's hypothesis. These two points can be illustrated with three examples.

One thing that archaeology does well is to refute a historical hypothesis. All history writing involves a three-stage process. The historian examines evidence, then sets forth a hypothesis. Later, as new evidence or new ways of thinking about the evidence emerge, the hypothesis will be tested. Hypotheses that survive repeated rounds of testing tend to be elevated to the status of theory, which is the highest level of probability one can achieve in the study of the past. (A theory is a hypothesis that is highly probable and therefore tends to be accepted by most competent historians.) But many hypotheses, probably most, do not survive such testing without modification. Archaeology is one of the means by which to test and refute a hypothesis.

If new archaeological data contradict expectations derived from a particular historical hypothesis, the hypothesis is either discarded or modified. For example, some years ago a hypothesis based on the biblical books of Numbers and Joshua was common. The hypothesis suggested that the warfare described in Numbers and Joshua occurred in the thirteenth century BCE, including events such as the military destruction of Arad and perhaps Heshbon (Num. 21) as well as the destruction of Jericho, Ai and Hazor (Josh. 6, 8 and 11). The archaeologist was able to test the hypothesis by seeking in the allegedly destroyed cities a significant layer of ash (indicative of massive, citywide fire), bits of broken weaponry (such as spear heads) and so on. The results have utterly refuted the hypothesis. Several cities were not even inhabited in the thirteenth century (e.g. Arad, Heshbon, Jericho and Ai), and many that Joshua describes as either captured or destroyed betray very little evidence of military conflict at that time (Hazor is a rare exception). If Numbers and Joshua preserve memories of actual battles, the battles did not take place in the thirteenth century, as the hypothesis maintained.

While archaeology can refute a hypothesis unequivocally, it can never prove a hypothesis. This point must be stressed since some historians tend to forget this basic issue of historical method. No hypothesis, not even a theory, is ever proven. At best, archaeological data are 'compatible in every respect' with a hypothesis. In many instances archaeological data are 'compatible in most respects' with the hypothesis. To employ an example of the former, during the final decade of the eighth century BCE, a king came to the throne of the Neo-Assyrian Empire whose name was Sennacherib. In his inscriptions, he boasts that he devastated the Kingdom of Judah in Palestine and utterly destroyed the Shephelah city of Lachish. Biblical narratives also mention these events (see, e.g., 2 Kgs 18–19), although the biblical writers have romanticized the tale by inserting divine intervention into parts of it, and they have conveniently 'forgotten' to mention that Lachish was annihilated. Archaeology reveals that all of Judah suffered massive military destruction at the close of the eighth century BCE. The city of Lachish, indeed, the entire Shephelah, was devastated. In fact, the Shephelah was so badly hit that, 100 years later, it had regained only about 25 per cent of its former population. The archaeological data are compatible in every way with a hypothesis that states: 'Sennacherib devastated Judah, especially the Shephelah, in the year 701 BCE'. It should be remembered, however, that Sennacherib's signature never appears on the ruins of Judah, and the precise year-date derives from inscriptions, not potsherds. So the hypothesis is not proven, although it is reasonable to view it as an accurate theory.

Another example demonstrates that archaeological data can be, but need not be, compatible with a hypothesis. The Greek epic called *The Iliad* is a highly romanticized tale of a war at the city of Troy in the northwestern corner of Anatolia. Most experts agree that Homer's classic was composed no earlier than the eighth century BCE, yet some historians have advanced the hypothesis that the epic preserves a dimly remembered, but real, war that took place in the thirteenth or early-twelfth century BCE. Presumably, this war was of sufficient magnitude to have inspired bards to sing of it, spinning tales of heroic deeds for centuries afterwards. Archaeologically, this is problematic. Ancient Troy was a very impressive city prior to the thirteenth century and suffered massive destruction—but from earthquake, not military attack. After the earthquake, a much smaller and far less impressive city emerged on the ruin, but was attacked and destroyed by an army in the early-twelfth century. Moreover, Homer's description of Troy presumes that its inhabitants were Greeks; they seem to fight according to Greek custom and they worship Greek gods. Ancient Troy was not Greek, but Luwian, an ethno-linguistic designation for a group that was related to the ancient Hittites. The archaeological data are compatible in some respects with the hypothesis, but do they really support the hypothesis?

Each of these three examples was selected because it serves to highlight the important distinction that must be maintained between hypothesis and archaeological data. The data are essential for testing a hypothesis. They can refute a hypothesis but can never prove one. My first example was a refuted hypothesis; the second, a hypothesis compatible in every respect with the data; and the third, a very ambiguous situation in which the archaeological data are compatible in only some respects with the hypothesis.

Note as well that in each sample case the hypothesis derives from, but is not identical to, the ancient text, and that the archaeological data remain independent of both the hypothesis and the text upon which it is based. In other words, hypothesis, text and data are three distinct things that should not be confused. In one case, the text was the Bible (the books of Numbers and Joshua), in another an ancient royal inscription by King Sennacherib, and in the third, Homer's *Iliad*. In each case the data either refute or support a hypothesis—*not* the ancient text. Thus, the data suggest that King Sennacherib devastated Judah and the Shephelah—but this does not prove that Sennacherib's representation of each aspect of the event is accurate. Sennacherib's inscriptions remain political propaganda representing a past event; the inscriptions are not identical to the event, and might misrepresent it in some ways. Texts are to archaeological data as apples are to oranges. Just as each fruit offers a distinctive taste, so also archaeological data and ancient documents provide distinct information. Each certainly preserves fragments of a real past, but each does so in a way that can never be compared directly. A historian's hypothesis is what stands between text and archaeological data, drawing from each, but proving neither. As such, a historian's hypothesis is always necessary; were this not the case, text and archaeological data could never be correlated in any way.

One final and very essential point is highlighted by the three examples I have just discussed. The hypothesis advanced by a historian always stands in tension with its opposite: the possibility that the hypothesis is false. The hypothesis that Sennacherib devastated Judah and the Shephelah stands in tension with the possibility that Sennacherib did not devastate Judah and the Shephelah. Had the data not been compatible in *every* respect with the hypothesis, an opponent of the hypothesis might have been justified in challenging the historian's hypothesis, either by refuting it or modifying it. For this reason, some historians find it helpful to posit something called a 'null hypothesis'. A null hypothesis is, by definition, the simplest explanation for any given set of data. It is the historian's obligation to marshal evidence and supporting interpretations sufficient to overcome the null hypothesis. If the historian fails, the null hypothesis stands and the historian's hypothesis is refuted or modified. Thus, if the historian's data are the inscriptions of a boastful Neo-Assyrian king, the null hypothesis suggests that the boastfulness might be empty rhetoric designed to enhance the king's reputation. Only when a second set of data, the archaeological record, came into play could the null hypothesis give way to its opposite.

In sum, archaeology is a crucial tool for the historian of the ancient past. Nevertheless, its data are equivocal in many cases, and one must learn not to push its evidence beyond reasonable proportion.

Figure 8. *The Assyrian Emperor Sennacherib boasted of his brutal victory over the tiny kingdom of Judah, commissioning an elaborate stone panorama depicting the gruesome details of the sack of Lachish. Assyrian inscriptional and pictorial representations of this war—a war also described in 2 Kings 18 and 19—provide an example of the challenge facing an historian: How can we correlate ancient representations of events with the archaeological remains recovered from the soil?* (© British Museum).

## What are Epigraphy and Philology?

Simply defined, epigraphy is the study of ancient non-literary texts, such as public inscriptions, monuments, epistles (letters) and grave markers; philology is the study of ancient literature, such as Homer's *Iliad* or the Mesopotamian *Epic of Gilgamesh*. The two disciplines are, for obvious reasons, closely related. Terminology employed for this dual field of research differs from one subdiscipline to another. For example, the term 'epigraphy' is employed more loosely by scholars of ancient Palestine than by scholars of ancient Greece (whose more pre-cise terminology will not be outlined here). Moreover, there are a host of related disciplines that have a direct impact on this kind of study, including linguistics and textual criticism.

Ancient texts were written on a variety of surfaces, most of which do not survive. Papyrus, which was made from the papyrus plant that grew in marshes, was analogous to paper and used extensively in Egypt. Other impermanent surfaces included wooden tablets, wax tablets and parchment (leather) scrolls. Clay tablets were used, particularly in Mesopotamia, and were inscribed with a blunt instrument that made impressions in the soft, wet clay. These tablets are called cuneiform, which means 'wedge-shaped', because of the marks made by the blunt instrument. Because they were cheap, potsherds were employed for writing as well, and when a potsherd contains a text, it is called an 'ostracon' (plural 'ostraca'). Although potsherds are very durable, the ink on them often disappeared over time, especially if the ostracon was discarded and returned to the soil.

Thus, like our modern paper books and magazines, all these ancient texts were designed to survive for a short time, then disintegrate. If a text was intended to survive over generations, it would be etched on metal or carved on stone, and these would be displayed in a public place for all to see, or buried away in a temple or building foundation so that only the gods could read them. In some cases, a text was deemed to be permanent but any particular copy of the text was not. In those cases, fresh copies would be made as older copies disintegrated. This is how literature, such as the Homeric literature and the Bible, was transmitted over the generations. In almost every case in which ancient literature is known to the modern world, from the Bible to the Tragedies of Euripides to the Koran, it is known to us exclusively from copies that are removed from the original authors by many generations.

Each writing material lent itself to particular genres of writing. The impermanent materials were used for pragmatic purposes. Most commonly, papyri and the various types of tablets contained legal records, such as deeds of land ownership, tax receipts, contracts, property (including slave) ownership, and so on. Also, government bureaucrats kept official records on the same kinds of material. These might include tax records, daily astronomical diaries (which kept track of the changes in the stars of the heavens), chronicles of royal or religious deeds, daybooks, which were records of day-to-day activity in the court, and administrative reports from outlying regions of the kingdom. On rare occasions, literature was produced as well, but this represents a fraction of the known texts from the ancient world. The more permanent media, carved stone and etched metal, were used almost exclusively by royalty and other high-ranking leaders. Royal annals and memorials, building inscriptions, temple inscriptions, and tomb inscriptions were common. Some kings would display sample legal codes (such as the famous Code of Hammurabi, erected by a Babylonian king of the eighteenth century BCE); others would boast of their accomplishments in monuments to themselves. A few kings erected royal memorials on behalf of a predecessor.

Almost without exception, the texts that survive from the ancient world were written by professional scribes. This is because almost everyone except professional scribes was illiterate. Education was expensive, and there was no such thing as public education. Only those who could afford an education sought one. Even those who could afford to do so did not always pursue it. Generally speaking, the elite class of an ancient society had access to education and can be expected to be moderately literate. That is to say, the aristocracy, which might represent 5 per cent of the population at most, could read and write simple letters, contracts and other day-to-day texts. Many of the aristocracy did not bother to exercise their ability to read, relying on professional scribes or personal slaves to do that work for them. The lower classes were barely literate or completely illiterate, except for some merchants and slaves whose specialized work for the aristocracy resulted in the achievement of full literacy.

Complex literature was the exclusive domain of a tiny, highly educated elite group of people. Scribes, priests and a few aristocrats were the audience for literature in most cases. A text as complex as the Hebrew Bible, for example, would have been incomprehensible to the vast majority of people who lived in Jerusalem. As a matter of fact, the Bible is an excellent example of what a historian would call an artifact of privilege. It was composed by the rich, for the rich, and, for the most part, about the rich. Take, for example, the well-known Ten Commandments (Deut. 5.7-18). These commandments are not addressed to all members of society. They are addressed to those who possess male and female slaves as well as a household with fields and farm animals—in short, someone with wealth. Since the addressee also has a wife, this person would have been a wealthy male. In fact, most of the Torah stipulations presuppose an audience of wealthy landowners, men who are encouraged to treat those below them on the social and economic ladder with kindness and equity. Even passages in the prophetic books that defend the poor and the widow speak of those people in the third person. The literature of the Bible was the literature of the wealthy, which is no surprise, since only the wealthy could have read it.[7] Much later, during Hellenistic and Roman times, an effort was made to disseminate the teaching of the texts to the commoners. Even then, however, religious custom was based on, primarily, what was *heard* in a synagogue, which would have been selections from the text accompanied by a great deal of commentary. Reading was not an option for most.

The scholar who studies ancient texts faces a formidable task. In most cases, the inscriptions and manuscripts are in bad shape, worn by centuries of use, or by centuries of neglect. Parchment and papyrus rot or get eaten by worms. Ink fades, clay crumbles, stone monuments weather until they are smooth. Moreover, scribes did not always use the best penmanship, nor are ancient spelling and grammar consistent. Many ancient texts are composed in obscure dialects or wholly unknown languages. Many inscriptions lack provenance, turning up on the antiquities market. Many others were found in legitimate archaeological digs, but in 'secondary use'. (This means that in ancient times, the inscription ceased to function as an inscription, and the material on which it was written was reused for other purposes.) For example, a royal inscription on stone sometimes got buried in a newly built wall by people who no longer revered the monarch who commissioned it.

Obviously, ancient writings are beneficial to historians for the content of their texts, but that is only one of the ways that they are useful. The language in which a text is written can be studied by a linguist. This can give an indication of the social and political relationships between regions. For example, an inscription written on a plastered wall in a temple at Tel Deir 'Alla (in the early-eighth century BCE) was composed in a language that bears similarities to the Aramaic language of northeast Transjordan as well as similarities to the Phoenician-inspired languages of Cisjordan. This suggests that the people of Deir 'Alla maintained a vibrant cultural contact in both directions.

Historical linguistics can determine the age of a text on the basis of the grammar, usage of words, spelling, and syntax. Like clay pots and Coca-Cola bottles, languages evolve, their styles changing with every generation. The English of Shakespeare differs radically from the English you are reading on this page, and anyone familiar with the English language will recognize that a significant number of the differences are due to historical changes that have occurred over the past 400 years. Likewise, it is possible to create a sequential typology for ancient languages. This method has even been applied to the Bible. It has been discovered that, with the exception of two poems and a few poetic fragments, the Bible was composed in a grammar of Hebrew that dates no earlier than the Iron Age II (900–586 BCE). Except for a few biblical books and a variety of late editorial revisions to most books, nothing was composed later than the Persian period (539–332 BCE). The two oldest texts are the poetic portions of Exodus 15 and Judges 5 (but not the prose portions of those chapters), which could have been composed as early as the Iron Age I (1200–900 BCE), though this judgment is disputed by some experts. The youngest complete books of the Jewish Bible are Ecclesiastes, Esther and Daniel, which were completed no earlier than the Hellenistic period (332–63 BCE). (A few historical linguists have tried to pinpoint the compositional date for biblical texts even more precisely than this, sometimes placing a book or a portion of a book in a specific century on linguistic grounds, but their data are not compelling.)

Finally, the epigrapher and especially the philologist must become expert in textual criticism. Ancient copies of literature are like snowflakes—no two are exactly the same. For example, Homer's *Iliad* survives in a series of fragmentary manuscripts from the final centuries BCE that reflect enormous differences from the version you usually read in modern translation. The Koran, Islam's holy book, appears in early manuscripts with variant readings as well. Even biblical books appear in multiple versions among the oldest existing copies, found at Qumran near the Dead Sea. Textual criticism is the careful comparison of all the 'variant readings' in any given passage of ancient literature. Many of these variant readings are the result of errors made by scribes. Many others result from willful changes to a text by a scribe. In most cases, scribes had the authority to do that. A text could be updated, edited, altered in many ways, whenever a scribe deemed it necessary. Experts who study the textual variations among early manuscripts of Homer, the Bible and the Koran have concluded that the process of composition was fluid, continuing from generation to generation. Although a given scroll is attributed by tradition to a particular person, such as Homer, Moses, Matthew or Muhammad, in reality, many anonymous scribes contributed to the text of these books.

Archaeology, epigraphy and philology are the historian's tools. But even that is not sufficient for the writing of ancient history. A historian must have sufficient knowledge of the cultural assumptions that created ancient artifacts and texts, sustained them, and perpetuated their use through time. To investigate these matters, a historian must begin to comprehend genres of communication as practiced in the ancient world, so that he or she can know how the ancients thought and spoke about their own world. In the next chapter, I investigate one of the most significant of those ancient genres.

## SUGGESTED ADDITIONAL READING

*The Genres and Philosophy of History*

Iser, Wolfgang, *The Fictive and the Imaginary: Charting Literary Anthropology* (Baltimore: The Johns Hopkins University Press, 1993).

Stanford, Michael, *An Introduction to the Philosophy of History* (Malden: Blackwell, 1998).

Tonkin, Elizabeth, *Narrating Our Pasts: The Social Construction of Oral History* (Cambridge: Cambridge University Press, 1992).

*Archaeology*

Biers, William R., *Art, Artefacts and Chronology in Classical Archaeology* (London: Routledge, 1992).

Fritz, Volkmar, *An Introduction to Biblical Archaeology* (JSOTSup, 172; Sheffield: JSOT Press, 1996).

*Epigraphy and Philology*

Bagnall, Roger S., *Reading Papyri, Writing Ancient History* (London: Routledge, 1995).

Dalley, Stephanie, *et al.*, *The Legacy of Mesopotamia* (Oxford: Oxford University Press, 1998).

Morris, Ian, and Barry Powell (eds.), *A New Companion to Homer* (Leiden: E.J. Brill, 1997).

Ulrich, Eugene, *The Dead Sea Scrolls and the Origins of the Bible* (Studies in the Dead Sea Scrolls and Related Literature; Grand Rapids: Eerdmans, 1999).

Warraq, Ibn (ed.), *The Origins of the Koran: Classic Essays on Islam's Holy Book* (Amherst: Prometheus, 1998).

## *Sample Stratigraphy*

The sample stratigraphy diagram does not represent an actual excavation, though some of its details derive from R.E. Tappy, *The Archaeology of Israelite Samaria*. I. *Early Iron Age through the Ninth Century BCE* (Atlanta: Scholars Press, 1992).

NOTES

1.    This is the definition employed by M.Z. Brettler, *The Creation of History in Ancient Israel* (London: Routledge, 1995).

2.    Although I read and learn from postmodernists, I disagree with one aspect of that approach—a few postmodern critics of academic history writing have argued that any narration is by its very nature a distortion of the past. Therefore, all history is false. This is an extremism that can be discussed without derision in the philosophy department or after hours with colleagues but, in their study, historians usually focus on the more pressing and pragmatic task of interpreting the past.

3.    For my purposes, a definition is a working hypothesis that enhances one's ability to perceive. I suggest that the genres of history here outlined, including a genre of 'ideological' history, enable us to perceive what we are reading when we read history. That is the first step towards critical awareness.

4.    Here again I differ with the postmodern critique, at least in its common (or vulgar) form. To my mind, postmodernism is only a selection of ideas from the modernist canon. It is not post-modernism, but partial-modernism, which is why it can be insightful as a critique and yet sometimes arrives at erroneous conclusions. For a witty discussion of the problems with common postmodern rhetoric written by one who is also critical of the humanist bias I advocate, see T. Eagleton, *The Illusions of Postmodernism* (Oxford: Basil Blackwell, 1996).

5.    M. Oakeshott, 'The Activity of Being an Historian', in *Rationalism in Politics* (New York: Basic Books, 1962), pp. 137-67.

6.    For the methods of population estimation, see M. Broshi and I. Finkelstein, 'The Population of Palestine in Iron Age II', *BASOR* 287 (1992), pp. 47-60, with important bibliography (pp. 47-48, 58-60). For additional bibliography, see W.G. Dever, 'Archaeology and the "Age of Solomon": A Case-Study in Archaeology and Historiography', in L.K. Handy (ed.), *The Age of Solomon: Scholarship at the Turn of the Millennium* (Leiden: E.J. Brill, 1997), pp. 217-51 n. 8. All my population estimates derive from books or articles cited in notes or listed as part of the 'Suggested Additional Reading' sections in each chapter. In cases of disagreement among the experts, my numbers are designed to honor those disagreements while not burdening the discussion with pedantry.

7.    Some scholars have advanced the hypothesis that ancient Palestine (and specifically, Israel) was somehow exempt from the illiteracy of the ancient world, but since they evaluate the same data from which the more cautious assessment derives, their hypothesis is not very convincing. For an example of this idiosyncratic approach, see A.R. Millard, 'The Knowledge of Writing in Iron Age Palestine', in K.-D. Schunck and M. Augustin (eds.), *'Lasset uns Brücken bauen…': Collected Communications to the XVth Congress of the International Organization for the Study of the Old Testament, Cambridge 1995* (Bern: Peter Lang, 1998), pp. 33-39. (Millard seems to have misconstrued the statements by P.R. Davies [p. 36].) For a more balanced perspective, see S. Niditch, *Oral World and Written Word: Ancient Israelite Literature* (Louisville, KY: Westminster/John Knox Press, 1996); cf. J. Crenshaw, *Education in Ancient Israel: Across the Deadening Silence* (New York: Doubleday, 1998).

Chapter 3

## WHAT WAS 'HISTORY' IN THE PERCEPTION OF
## THE ANCIENTS?

### Introduction

> Hecataeus of Miletus speaks thus: I write what follows as it seems to me
> to be true; for the stories of the Greeks are varied, and, as is manifest to
> me, ludicrous.[1]

These words initiated a tradition in the ancient world. Prior to
Hecataeus of Miletus (who lived in the late-sixth and early-fifth
centuries BCE), critical history was not a recognizable genre of literature. To be sure, there were many history genres, if history is defined as
a narrative that presents a past (for the definition, see Chapter 2). For
example, ancient Near Eastern kings frequently erected stone monuments to themselves in which their deeds were narrated. Likewise, a
few ancient societies had developed a genre of chronicle, in which
events deemed to be noteworthy were listed in chronological order and
kept in an archive. Lists were a popular genre, and many king lists,
magistrate lists and other such lists were produced. Even more common
were the folk-tales and legends about the past told and retold by
peoples of every class and walk of life, many of which eventually came
to be written down and thus preserved to modern times. None of these,
however, were *critical* histories. That is to say, prior to Hecataeus, there
is no known document in which an author claims to have gathered
sources, sifted them, and made critical judgments about reliability,
dismissing the remainder as stories both 'varied' and 'ludicrous'.
Hecataeus invented history as moderns usually think of the genre.

The genre invented by Hecataeus and perfected by later Greek
authors, such as Herodotus and Thucydides, differed from all previous
history writing in the ancient world in one crucial way: the Greeks
emphasized a need for *historia*, which meant 'inquiry' or 'investigation'. Our modern word 'history' derives from the Greek term. Greek

historians insisted that before one can write competently about the past, one must investigate sources, make critical judgments, and draw reasoned conclusions about that past. When stated in this way, the Greek attitude sounds distinctly modern. The practice of *historia* was not as modern as one might think, as we shall see. Still, it was an abrupt departure from all that had preceded.

## The Practice of Ancient Historia

The modern historian gathers the evidence available related to a specific time and place, investigates that evidence carefully, then formulates hypotheses about the past. This is what ancient Greek historians claimed to have done as well, but their practice was not quite identical to their claims. Nevertheless, they did not perceive themselves to be failures who had not lived up to their boast of investigative rigor. Quite the contrary, they believed that they had accomplished fully what they had set out to do. How is it that their practice matched their preachments in their own eyes, but not in ours? The difference lies with cultural assumptions about what constitutes evidence, investigation and hypothesis. Let us look at each of these three terms.

For an ancient Greek author, evidence was something quite different from the modern definition of that word. By 'evidence' we usually mean data—artifacts and documents surviving from the past that shed light on past events and people. For the ancient Greek, artifacts and documents from the past were relatively unimportant, and were only rarely included in the category of evidence. Often, when an artifact or document was called upon as evidence, it was the unusual or atypical nature of that item that caused it to be remarked upon, another departure from the routine treatment of such items by modern historians, for whom the typical or commonplace provides a more clear comprehension of everyday reality in past times.

The ancient Greek historian defined evidence as that which seemed vividly realistic, so vividly realistic as to seem self-evident to the human mind. In other words, for the ancient historian, evidence was something that conforms to reason. For example, when confronted by the heroic tales of ancient Troy, in which mighty Achilles battles the god of the river Xanthus, Diomedes fights and even injures the god Ares, and the city ultimately falls by a ruse involving a large, hollow, wooden horse, the ancient Greek historian assumed that he was dealing with tales too ludicrous to accept. These were not evidence, for they were not reasonable. Nevertheless, within the tale are tidbits that seemed quite plausible and realistic to an ancient historian, and thus might serve as evidence. That two armies fought one another and that one ultimately destroyed the city of the other was very reasonable indeed, and therefore one will never encounter an ancient Greek writer who doubted that the Trojan War actually happened. All that was necessary was to strip the tale of its unreasonable—its non-evidential—elements, repackage what remains as a plausible, realistic narrative, and an ancient historian had produced properly critical history. Frequently, in the writings of an ancient historian, gods were eliminated from folktales, human heroes were reduced in stature, and the folk-tale was then simply repeated as fact, purged of its allegedly non-factual elements.

Investigation was not a modern concept either. A modern historian investigates as many aspects of the time and place chosen for study as is humanly possible. The ancient Greek historian was far more selective. The usual form of investigation was to review what others had previously written and published on the subject. (Publication was, of course, a process of making hand-copied volumes, and a published document in the ancient world had a far more limited circulation than publications in the modern world.) Another form of investigation was to ask living persons for the collective memories that had been passed down. Only rarely would investigation go further than this to include a study of public monuments or other easily accessible materials. The sources of investigation that are the stock in trade of a modern historian, such as archives, office records, private letters, archaeologically recovered artifacts and the like, were almost never investigated by the ancient historian, even when, on occasion, such things were known and available to him.

Each Greek historian would investigate the previously published literature about the past. Herodotus had read his predecessor Hecataeus, then Thucydides read Herodotus, and Polybius read Thucydides. Having done so, the historian would criticize past accounts, accepting in large measure the narrative received from those accounts, but adjusting it according to the criterion of evidence discussed above. Frequently, he would copy, verbatim, significant portions of a previous historical account, more often than not without explicitly indicating that this had been done. Nevertheless, he would rearrange the previous accounts into a new version, the newly 'authoritative' version, the version that seemed to him to be true (see the quotation from Hecataeus of Miletus that opens this chapter).

An excellent example of this process with which many modern students are familiar can be found in the Christian New Testament. There, a writer called Luke (who was a Greek-speaking Christian influenced by the Greek genre of *historia*) states in his opening sentence that many others have written on his topic, that he has investigated these, and that he will now produce a more authoritative version of the events. To be sure, Luke's narrative differs from many Greek histories in important ways. Luke includes miracle tales, stories about a god (specifically, the Jewish god and his relationship to the Jew Jesus) and heroic deeds that many Greek historians would have dismissed as ludicrous. But Luke's method is an excellent example of Greek *historia*: not only has he investigated previous narratives, he has copied, verbatim, large portions of one—the Gospel according to Mark—representing that narrative as his own, without even mentioning Mark's name.[2] Yet like a Greek historian who evaluates his sources according to the criterion of what seems self-evidently correct, Luke has rewritten Mark's tale as well, editing out portions of Mark's narrative that seemed unhistorical according to Luke's sense of evidence. For example, Mark's Jesus walks on water, but Luke's Jesus does not. Apparently that particular miracle was not 'reasonable' to Luke's way of thinking.

The Greek historian's investigation might have included interviews with living persons as well. If the historian was writing about very ancient times, he inquired about the traditions of local communities, then evaluated what he was told. If he was investigating the more recent past, the Greek historian would seek out eyewitnesses or others who, for some reason, might have told pertinent tales. In no case, however, would this ancient historian have evaluated the fruits of his inquiry in a manner employed by the modern historian. Where the modern historian would seek to ground such information in material artifacts and primary documents from the past, the Greek historian applied his usual sense of that which is evident to reason. The version of events that seemed most plausible was selected as the 'correct' version. If several versions seemed plausible, the Greek historian might have chosen to report each, introducing one with 'The Athenians say…' and the next with 'but the Corinthians tell it this way…', and so on.

This last point introduces a final significant difference between the modern and the ancient historian: each develops a hypothesis differently. A modern hypothesis is stated as a thesis, then defended by a survey of pertinent evidence and argumentation that demonstrates not the plausibility of the thesis but the probability of it. A modern historian desires to demonstrate that his or her hypothesis makes best sense of all available data—to convince other historians of this requires a full treatment of all that data. The ancient historian made a decision about the reality of the past, narrated that version, and put down his pen. At most, he might have attempted to refute a previously published alternate version of events, but the refutation was limited to argument derived from the historian's sense of what seemed plausible, or self-evident. Appeal to evidence (in the modern sense of that term) was rare in ancient historical debate.

The product of ancient Greek *historia* was a narrative more akin to a modern newspaper than a modern history book. Like a journalist, the ancient historian gathered information and wrote a seamless account. The reader was expected to accept that account as fact. There were few citations, no bibliography, no survey of evidence. Also, like modern journalism, ancient *historia* was a product produced both by authors of integrity and by charlatans. The ancient equivalent of *The New York Times* can be found, but the ancient equivalent of *The National Enquirer* was available as well. Bogus tales about the past were sometimes passed off with the same degree of rhetorical certainty as more reliable information. Since ancient readers knew as well as any modern reader that there were fake journalist-historians, it was imperative that the ancient Greek historian establish a rhetorical tone of authority for his narrative. It was this need for rhetorical markers of authority that led to the kind of statement one finds from Hecataeus of Miletus, quoted at the beginning of this chapter. In the next section, I will survey this 'rhetoric of authority'.

### *The Rhetoric of Authority in Ancient* Historia

One of the most difficult aspects of the history genre is distinguishing a historical narrative from a fictional narrative. A fictional narrative is *not necessarily* an untrue narrative. In fact, the best fiction is usually very true in the sense that it is true to life's experiences. Moreover, fiction can be based on real events and real people. Nevertheless, fiction differs from history in one significant way. The genre of fiction does not require its author to remain within the strict limitations imposed by the real past. For a historian, that requirement is essential. So the reader needs to be aware of the distinction between these genres and not confuse a fiction for a history.

With many modern histories, there is no difficulty recognizing a distinction from fiction. The history narrative is marked by obvious signs of nonfictional status, such as an apparatus of long, cumbersome footnote citations, chapter divisions with dry headings (such as 'Commerce in Fourth Century Anatolia: The Evidence from Potsherds') and all too frequently, a dull, sometimes stilted, writing style that could never be mistaken for great storytelling.

Now and then the line between fiction and history becomes blurred. Historical novels often take liberties with a real past that confuse an unsuspecting reader. Sometimes the genre of history dissolves into fiction completely. For example, Edmund Morris published a biography of former United States President Ronald Reagan in which Morris invented facts and even invented 'sources' for those facts.[3] Morris added to the confusion because he created an apparatus of citations in which he 'cited' his invented sources along with real sources, thus creating a fiction that conformed in every way to the normal rhetorical structure of a history. Most fiction, however, does not emulate history that deliberately.

A primary reason that history and fiction can become confused is that both are usually narrated in the past tense. At first glance, it is often difficult to distinguish the two. For example, a reader who did not know better might mistake the following for a historical account, written by a barely literate person:

> You don't know about me, without you have read a book by the name of *The Adventures of Tom Sawyer*, but that ain't no matter. That book was made by Mr. Mark Twain, and he told the truth, mainly. There was things which he stretched, but mainly he told the truth...[4]

In this passage, an authoritative voice speaks in the first person ('You don't know about *me*'), and evaluates a previously published narrative in which he was apparently mentioned. A reader who had never heard of Mark Twain, and who did not suspect that the grammar is atypical of most historical narrative, might pause for a moment before deciding that this was fiction. Consider the following quotation:

> The fog clung to the damp earth like a vaporous shroud. Leaves of the jungle underbrush collected the tropical moisture and dripped like a

thousand slowly leaking faucets. The first gray light of morning filtered
through the mist and revealed the hazy greenness of the world...[5]

This sounds very much like overwrought fiction, but it is shelved in the
nonfiction section of a library or bookstore because it is the memoir of
a soldier.

These examples demonstrate that a few rhetorical markers, such as
first-person or past-tense narration, are too ambiguous to permit 'genre'
to happen. Genre, it will be recalled, is a process of communication in
which sender and receiver share an understanding of the communication's intention (see Chapter 2). An ancient writer's desire to commu-
nicate genre to the reader was especially difficult since libraries and
bookstores did not exist, and there was no one available to shelve
the documents in sections marked 'fiction', 'nonfiction', 'biography',
'cookbooks', and so on. The ancient author was compelled to find a
way to advertise genre within his text.

With these thoughts in mind, consider the task facing an ancient
historian. Within Greek culture—or at least, within the literate portion
of Greek culture—many scrolls were circulating. There was Homer, for
example, who occasionally resorts to the first-person technique when
seeking divine inspiration for his tale, saying 'Sing to me now, you
Muses!' Hesiod, too, speaks with authority, and both Homer and Hesiod
narrate a past of sorts, one that was accepted as a true account by at
least a portion of the literate culture to whom Greek historians directed
their own writings. One reason for this credulity (which appears somewhat naive to the modern reader) is that the technical language of
literary criticism, in which words like 'genre' are common, was a language known only to a tiny educated elite in the ancient world. A philosopher such as Aristotle could analyze writings and publish a
'poetics' of literature, but few would have read it. Many people tended
to accept what was written at face value. If Homer narrates a battle
between Diomedes and the god Ares, then Diomedes must have battled
a god. To be sure, many Greeks, especially well-educated ones, learned
to be more discerning when reading such literature, but the author of a
text cannot assume that only discerning readers would see his prose.
How does the Greek historian distinguish his own literature from a
Homer or a Hesiod?

Beginning with Hecataeus of Miletus, a tradition of rhetorical techniques evolved by which the ancient Greek historians distinguished
their genre from the other literature in circulation. That tradition

included three distinct methods by which the ancient historian could tell the ancient reader that his text was a *historia*, a history. These techniques were applied in different ways by each ancient author, and each writer had his own preference. Nevertheless, all three were common.

The first distinctive rhetorical technique employed by the ancient historian was the use of an 'intrusive' third-person narrator. A narrator is the voice that narrates. A third-person narrator is one who does not take part in the tale that is told. The characters are described using third-person pronouns: '*he* did this', '*she* did that', '*they* went there'. An *intrusive* third-person narration is one in which the story is told in the standard third-person narrational voice, but a first-person narrator intrudes into that tale with sufficient regularity to remind the reader that the author is not a fictional, bodiless, and all-knowing third-person voice, but a mortal human, who speaks on the authority of his own *historia*, inquiry. I offer an example from the ancient author Herodotus:

> [T]he Carians were a people who had come to the mainland from the islands; for in old times they were islanders, called Leleges and under the rule of Minos, not (as far as I can learn from reports) paying him tribute, but manning ships for him… (Herodotus, *Histories* I.171)

The phrase 'as far as I can learn from reports' is an example of an intrusion into the third-person narrative about the Carians. This is a demonstrative example of Herodotus' use of the intrusive third-person narrative. Some ancient Greek historians made far greater use of this technique than others, but it was common to almost all.

At first glance, this technique does not seem to differ from what we find in Homer or Huck Finn, but its success was founded upon the manner in which it was inserted into the narrative. The intrusiveness of this narration was sufficiently different from that of other ancient narratives to suggest to the ancient reader that this narrative was a distinctive genre. When Homer, for example, occasionally lapses into first person, it is usually to invoke the Muse, whose authority enlightens Homer as a kind of divine inspiration. By contrast, Herodotus breaks in to remind his reader that *he*, Herodotus, has been investigating 'reports'. The Greek historians broke into first-person asides to remind the reader that the authority for these third-person narrations was *not* some ambiguous inspiration by a possibly nonexistent divinity, but the product of hard human labor and rigorous, but fallible, investigation. This is *historia*.

Nowhere was this intrusive third-person narrator more prominently displayed, or more crucial to the success of the *historia* genre, than in the prologue. The first sentence or first paragraph of an ancient scroll served as its cover and title page. It was essential to set the tone for the entire work in those opening lines. Earlier, this chapter mentioned the New Testament Gospel of Luke. The first sentence of Luke's work provides an excellent example of a typical prologue to a Greek *historia*:

> Since many have undertaken to set down an orderly account of the events that have been fulfilled among us, just as they were handed on to us by those who from the beginning were eyewitnesses and servants of the word, I too decided, after investigating everything carefully from the very first, to write an orderly account for you, most excellent Theophilus, so that you may know the truth concerning the things about which you have been instructed. (Lk. 1.1-4)

To an ancient reader, these words would mark this narrative off from other genres, and announce that the narrative to follow is the product of *historia*, careful inquiry by a historian. (It is interesting to note that Luke is the only document in the Jewish or Christian Bibles that emulates Greek *historia*. Apparently, *historia* was not the preferred genre for the literature of most literate Jews and Christians. I will discuss this issue further in a moment.)

The second and third rhetorical techniques used by the ancient historian were built on the foundation established by the intrusiveness of the narration. These two techniques were designed to *characterize* the first-person narrator who has intruded, to provide that intrusive narrator with a personality that could be trusted by the reader. On the one hand, the first-person voice is, quite often, explicitly positioned as one who is sufficiently expert to render wise judgment about each topic discussed. This could be achieved in any number of ways. Most often, passages were introduced into *historia* that would emphasize the author's high status in society, often boasting of military leadership, governmental posts, and other activities that would have placed the author in positions where worldly experience would count as a plus. On the other hand, the first-person voice is, with regularity, presented to the reader as one who is absolutely impartial in his research methods. As with the issue of expertise, the concept of impartiality could be stressed in myriad ways, such as distancing oneself from 'biased' sources of information, exerting much effort to provide two or more sides to a story, and above all, implying or explicitly stating that previous historians were not as diligent, unbiased or competent as the one who is now writing. Explicit or implicit stress on these two characteristics—expertise and impartiality—was a common feature of nearly all Greco-Roman history writing after the time of Hecataeus.

### The 'Truth' in Ancient Historia

Perhaps the one thing that most surprises a modern reader of ancient Greek *historia* is the discovery that these ancient authors did not shy from writing false statements when it suited them. As one modern historian puts it: 'No serious ancient historian was so tied to specific factual truth that he would not sometimes help general truths along by manipulating, even inventing, "facts"'.[6] Why was this the case?

The answer lies with the cultural context in which Greek *historia* was composed. Unlike his modern counterpart, the ancient historian did not operate in an academic community in which the study of the past was a profession. His readers were not other historians. Rather, they were wealthy aristocrats with time on their hands. In the ancient world, the overwhelming majority of people were illiterate. Those who could afford to buy an education were few, and the wealthy who bothered to buy an education were fewer still. Those who were educated and could read often did not bother to read lengthy documents, such as histories. Thus, the ancient historian was competing for the attention of a tiny group of discerning non-professional readers who had available many kinds of literature, from Homer to lyric poetry, philosophy to ancient science and mathematics.

Against this backdrop it is not difficult to see why the ancient historian was compelled to produce something that people would want to read. He was competing not only with other histories, but with other literature, some of which was far more exciting, erotic or aesthetically pleasing than a narrative that presents a past. As a result, *historia* was not a dry academic discipline, it was a form of literary entertainment.

It is not difficult to see why ancient history has been compared to a modern historical novel.[7] It is based on a real past, and most of the people mentioned are people who actually lived. The characters portrayed in *historia* may have done many of the things attributed to them by the narrator; in some cases, the words placed upon their lips by the ancient historian might even approximate what they actually said (though often this was not the case). But the whole account was designed to offer a satisfying reading experience. The historian developed a theme—usually a morality theme—and used the past to develop that theme. When the past did not quite match the theme, it would be 'improved'. In this respect it is similar to the modern historical novel. By 'improving' the story, the ancient historian was not telling lies, he was presenting the past in a more 'truthful' way than how it actually happened. Truth, as any great author will attest, is not always identical to real life! It exists in the mind of the one who seeks truth.

## *Is the Bible an Example of Ancient* Historia?

'Truth' is also invoked when the Bible is mentioned. In fact, I am frequently asked the question, often by total strangers: 'Is the Bible true?' I never quite know how to answer that question. After all, as Pontius Pilate asked, 'What is truth?' (Jn. 18.38). A philosopher recognizes at least three distinct kinds of truth. These are:

(A)   'Truth as Correspondence with a Real Past'. Examples: The front page of a daily newspaper attempts to offer a true account of recent events. A college history professor desires to present a true account of World War II.

(B)   'Truth as Genuine Experience of Human Nature'. Examples: A novelist invents a narrative that will capture the true emotions of a parent who experiences the death of a young child. A storyteller composes a fantastic tale about a superman with enormous strength. When exposed to a fictional natural chemical, he becomes weak. This tale of fantasy can be compelling because it reminds us how *truly* ordinary we are.

(C)   'Truth as a Logically Coherent System of Thought'. Examples: The mathematician desires to formulate a true solution to a numerical problem. The philosopher attempts to formulate a true description of the concept 'truth'.

The Bible expresses truth of each type—A, B and C. The Bible's stories and poetry reflect the life experience of those who wrote them (Type B), which is the most valuable truth any literature can offer. Many biblical passages promote logical systems of thought (Type C), such as variations on the theme that one is better off heeding the reproof of the wise than the praise of the foolish (e.g. Eccl. 7.5). As for truth of Type A, it will be demonstrated in this work that some biblical narratives even provide reliable details about real past events.

Nevertheless, given that no ancient historian was committed to writing about the past free of all invention, one should not expect *every* biblical narrative to present a truth of the 'correspondence' type—a truth of Type A. Even in cases where a biblical narrative is based on real past events, it should not surprise a modern reader if the narrative has been 'improved' in some way. If the Bible is *historia*, it is akin to a historical novel, not a modern history textbook.

This observation has not been accepted by all historians, a number of whom have tried to defend the truth of the entire Bible as a truth of Type A. More often than not, these scholars are members of a religious community for whom the historical reliability of the Bible is a matter of doctrine, and the historian's task is to defend the community's doctrinal identity. These scholars write examples of the ideological genre of history that was discussed in Chapter 2.

The religious affirmation of the Bible as historically reliable derives from the belief that the Bible is inspired by God, a belief that might be correct. (That is not for me to judge.) But, for at least some of the faithful, the affirmation contains within it an unstated assumption. The assumption is that God never writes literature in genres other than *historia*—God is a historian at all times! If God is the author of the Bible, then that assumption is false. The parables of Jesus represent a narrative genre that does not even pretend to present a real past, yet all Christians assert that these parables are divinely inspired. The psalmist speaks metaphorically, not historically, when he announces 'The LORD is my shepherd!' (Ps. 23.1), a passage affirmed as divinely inspired by Jews and Christians alike. In Judges 13–16, there are a series of tales about a superhero-figure named Samson. When his hair grows long, he is strong; when his hair is shaved off, he is weak. Nothing in the story suggests that this superman was any more real than an American comic book hero. Since there is no reason that a comic book hero's tale cannot be inspired, Samson's story is affirmed as inspired by many religious people who believe that Samson never lived.

It would seem that God is a versatile author who is comfortable composing in many genres. Thus, a divinely inspired narrative need not be a reliable account of a real past. An infallible divine being can compose infallible fiction, infallible folk-tales, infallible fables, infallible mythology. For this reason, even one who accepts religious doctrine is not able to appeal to that doctrine to demonstrate that biblical narrative was composed in a genre of history writing.

For those who prefer to determine the genre of biblical narratives without appeal to religious doctrine, comparison of the Bible to other ancient history writing has been useful. Many scholars have read carefully the writings that survive from the ancient world and compared each to the writings of the Bible. Although there is as yet no consensus on precisely how to label the biblical genre (not that there is a lack of suggestions!), the comparative studies have been fruitful. As a result of them, most scholars agree on the following two points.

First, it would be difficult to defend the hypothesis that biblical narratives are composed in the Greek genre of *historia*. Although a number of minor similarities have been noted, the differences are immense. Above all, biblical narratives lack the explicit rhetoric of authority so common to *historia*. No biblical author announces that his narrative is the truth, dismissing other tales told by the Hebrews as 'varied' and 'ludicrous'.[8] There is no biblical equivalent of Hecataeus of Miletus. With the exception of Luke, nowhere does one find in a biblical narrative an intrusive third-person narrator who is explicitly characterized as both impartial and expert (and even Luke provides only a partial parallel). In a few places, the reader of the Bible does indeed encounter a first-person narration (e.g. Neh. 1–6), but these passages appear to have been composed in a different genre, the 'personal memoir'. In any case, such first-person narratives are quite rare in the Bible, so they do not help with the question of genre as it applies to most biblical narratives.

The only biblical books that resemble *historia* are 1–2 Kings and 1–2 Chronicles. Each of these appeals to older sources of information, such as the 'Day Books' of the Kings of Israel and Judah (2 Kgs 15.6, 11, etc.)—appeals that are similar to some examples of *historia*. Also, the manner of narration is similar to that of the Greek historian Herodotus. Herodotus offers a mix of realistic (and, in some cases, accurate) narratives spiced by a series of tall tales that are easily recognized as inventions. (For example, see his narrative of 26th Dynasty kings in the latter portion of *Histories* II.) This pattern of realism mixed with obviously tall tales occurs in Kings and Chronicles as well (e.g. 1 Kgs 12–13).

Even here, however, there is an unbridgeable gulf between *historia* and biblical narrative. The delightful yarns of Herodotus pale by comparison with the wildest stories of the Bible. In the latter, straightforward reports of political history, such as the war between Kings Asa and Baasha (1 Kgs 15.16-22), mingle with utterly fantastic tales, such as Elijah's flight to the sky in a divinely provided chariot (2 Kgs 2). Elijah's fate has more in common with the Greek myth of Herakles, who was transported to Mount Olympus in the chariot of Athena, than with anything from the pen of Herodotus.

Clearly, the Greeks had a genre of *historia* but the Hebrews did not, and it is no surprise that the ancient Hebrew language contains no word equivalent to Greek *historia* or English 'history'. Most biblical scholars who find the analogy of *historia* useful for an understanding of biblical narrative genres—and many do—agree that the Bible is not directly related to, or dependent upon, the Greek tradition of history writing, even though it bears a few enlightening similarities.

A second point of agreement about biblical narrative is its relationship to Semitic history writing from ancient Mesopotamia and Syria-Palestine. These similarities are somewhat more impressive than the comparison to Greek *historia*. Semitic cultures lacked a 'critical' genre of history (which was a Greek innovation, as we have seen), but did not lack narratives that present a past. In fact, they had many narratives that can be termed 'history' in the loose sense. Biblical narratives often use plots and rhetorical structures similar to these.

An interesting example of the similarity between ancient Semitic narratives and the Bible is the way that a few biblical narratives conform to the rhetorical style of Semitic royal inscriptions. For example, the tales of conquest in the book of Joshua seem very similar to tales of conquest on the royal inscriptions of Assyrian kings.[9] Both narratives have a human hero (Joshua or the Assyrian monarch) who benefits from divine support (the biblical god or an Assyrian god); sometimes a vision of a divine warrior appears (as in Josh. 5.13-15); there is a river crossing with much fanfare (chs. 3–4); specific battles are narrated and others summarized (chs. 6–12); special emphasis is placed on the capture and humiliation of enemy kings (10.16-28); because they are terrified, a delegation from the enemy seeks peace (ch. 9); decimation of a region is followed by the settling of a new population (chs. 13–24); divine omens are not uncommon (ch. 10.12-13).

In this example, there can be little doubt that the biblical author modeled the narrative after Assyrian royal inscriptions. Like those inscriptions, the biblical narrative does not attempt to present a 'critical' history, or *historia*. Rather, common elements of folklore have been incorporated to glorify the royal hero of the tale. The Assyrian king often (though not always!) did the things narrated, albeit far less successfully than the narrative seems to imply, but the report of his activities has become a cliché, a stereotyped litany of stock events common to the genre of the Assyrian royal annal. The biblical author of Joshua has used the same stock of folklore to glorify his hero.

That which is most common to biblical and other Semitic narratives is their participation in folk tradition. Greek historians such as Herodotus participated in folklore as well. However, where the Greek historian usually attempted to extract the past *from* folklore, which was deemed 'varied' and 'ludicrous' and in need of critical evaluation, biblical narratives that present a past seem happy to steep themselves *in* folklore. Biblical authors seem to have enjoyed the challenges of working within conventional ways of narrating. Even Luke does this extensively, in spite of his Greek-like introductory statement.

Social anthropologists who have studied folklore in many cultures the world over have discovered that the past narrated in folk tradition is a past that is required for the immediate present. The details of many tales are mixed and matched to the occasion. There are many instances of this in the Bible. David kills Goliath in 1 Samuel 17, but someone named Elhanan kills Goliath in 2 Sam. 21.19. Golden calves are made by the priest Aaron and King Jeroboam I (Exod. 32.1-35; 1 Kgs 12.28-33). Psalm 34's superscription replaces Achish of Gath (from 1 Sam. 21.11-16) with someone named Abimelech, perhaps an attempted narrative fusion with the Abimelech of Gerar (Gen. 26.1-11). Some versions of the book of Joshua have Joshua build an altar on Mount Ebal (Josh. 8.30-35; this is the common English version). Other manuscripts have him build the altar at Gilgal, placing the story not in ch. 8, but in ch. 5 (this is probably the original version of the story). Some ancient manuscripts eliminate the prophet Elisha's speech to King Joash in 2 Kgs 13.14-19, and instead narrate the same speech by Elisha to King Jehu, as part of 2 Kings 10. (In this case, the common English version is more likely to be the original version.) Narrative 'switches' like these were not accidents. Ancient scribes chose to change the tales available to them. In each case, why the change was made is a matter of conjecture, but that a scribe had the *authority* to alter a story is without doubt. The ancient scribe lived in a traditional storytelling culture where such narrational alteration was commonplace, even expected.

The narration of the past within the cultural context of folklore has many effects on the stories that get told. Frequently, stock storytelling elements are introduced to a traditional tale to provide structure and familiarity for the audience. The examples above from Assyrian royal inscriptions and the book of Joshua are representative of that trend. The tale of a great warrior was expected to include those details. There are many other biblical examples. For instance, there is a pronounced tendency for people to meet near a water well (Gen. 24.10-20; 29.1-20; Exod. 2.16-22; 1 Sam. 9.11; see the New Testament tale in Jn. 4.1-26). Also common is the motif of a husband who introduces his wife to strangers as though she were his sister (Gen. 12.10-20; 20.1-18; 26.6-11). Stock miracle tales often get attributed to multiple miracle workers. Elisha feeds one hundred people with a few loaves of bread; Jesus feeds thousands with a few loaves and some fish (2 Kgs 4.42-44; in the New Testament, see Mk 6.35-44). Frequently, traditional storytellers are cognizant of, and respectful of, variant details in a single story. Have you ever asked yourself, for example, just how many pairs of each animal Noah included on his Ark? Consider the variant details in the story. Genesis 6.19-20 requires one pair of each species, but only several verses later, in Gen. 7.2-3, seven pairs of each ritually clean species are needed and one pair each of all others. The biblical author no doubt recognized these variants in the oral (or written) sources and chose to include both. Why the scribe did this will never be certain. His concern might have been nothing more mysterious than a desire to preserve variant options for the telling of an entertaining tale.

In many cases, the 'past' that is created through this dynamic process of traditional storytelling bears only remote resemblance to a past that actually took place. However, the ancient audience would not have been discomfited. Members of a traditional community often recognize that their narrative is not entirely accurate. For them, a history can be true even when not factual. The dismissive attitude of Hecataeus is not at work; rather, there is a great tolerance for 'varied' versions of a single past, no matter how 'ludicrous' those tales might seem to outsiders. On this point, too, the Bible conforms to expectations derived from social anthropology. Biblical authors seem to have taken great pride in a kind of eclectic inclusiveness. The Bible contains an amazing variety of traditional tales, poetry and song. For example, there are several versions of the creation of the world, which is a little odd if the ancient authors were trying to tell it exactly as it was after the manner of Hecataeus. In Genesis 1, humans are created after the vegetation, but in Genesis 2, they are created prior to the vegetation. Moreover, Genesis 1 seems to be a 'de-mythologized' version of an old creation story known to many ancient Semitic peoples (a version of it shows up in Babylonian writings, for instance), in which the creator deity did battle with cosmic, watery forces of chaos. A vestige of that battle with chaotic sea can be discerned in Gen. 1.1-9, but the more conservative, or 'old-fashioned', version of the creation battle is also affirmed in various biblical writings, such as Job 26.5-14 and Ps. 74.12-17.

For biblical authors and their original readers, all these traditional tales and poems were true. Some biblical stories, such as Elijah's flight into the sky (2 Kgs 2), appear naive to a modern reader only because the modern reader overlooks the degree of complexity common to a traditional culture's sense of truth. For example, it is sometimes alleged that biblical authors lacked a sense of naturalism. According to this hypothesis, biblical authors believed that miracles were possible and therefore accorded the fantastic details of their stories the same truth-value as mundane details. This hypothesis is incorrect. Biblical writers distinguished clearly between the fantastic and the mundane, as many biblical passages indicate (e.g. 2 Kgs 20.10). Social anthropologists note that the miraculous is indeed believed by the traditional teller of tales, but believed in a qualitatively different way from belief in the events of mundane stories. The fantastic is part of a moral universe, not a physical universe, and tales of the fantastic are true regardless of whether they happened. As with narratives of the past, so also with narratives of the fantastic: they can be true but not factual. Such is the nature of traditional storytelling. It is 'varied' and sublime, not 'ludicrous' at all!

## A Test Case: Establishing the Dates of the Exodus and Conquest

In sum, the Bible does not attempt to provide a reliable narrative of the past. If one were to read the Bible with the expectation that every story is true in the correspondence sense—truth of Type A—then much of its aesthetic beauty would be lost. (Perhaps much of the Bible's theological significance would be missed as well, though that is not an issue for a historian to discuss. Members of individual religious communities have the right to interpret this issue as they deem appropriate.)

Why, then, is the Bible treated as though it were a history book by some modern readers? Primarily because many modern readers are unaware of the differences between modern genres of narration and ancient genres of narration. Biblical tales that were at home in a culture that did not press them into service as reliable accounts now find themselves in a foreign environment, the modern, Western world, which seems to place a high value on narrational fidelity to the real past. In this environment, many of the Bible's narrative techniques can fool the unsuspecting reader.

Probably the thing that fools a modern reader most about the Bible is the seemingly 'historical' chronology it presents. Genesis 1 announces, 'In the beginning,' and every narrative from that point is connected to the preceding narrative by chronological links, such as 'And then', or 'In those days', or 'After these things'. Very often a precise date will be included in a biblical story. For example, genealogical lists are included that contain precise numbers of years for each generation (e.g. Gen. 5), or a leader of the community will be said to have 'judged Israel' for a specific number of years (Judg. 12.8-14). All this concern with chronology gives the modern reader the impression that the biblical authors were presenting a precise chronological history that narrates real past events.

Thus, it will come as a surprise to learn that the chronology of the Bible is almost entirely artificial. Moreover, there is every reason to believe that this chronology would have been recognized as artificial by many ancient readers, at least prior to the Hellenistic period. (During the Hellenistic period and later, readers of the Bible were influenced by Greek history writing and began to interpret the Bible as though it, too, was a *historia*. At that time, the biblical chronology began to be reinterpreted as though it was a real chronology dealing with real events.[10])

Clues to the artificiality of the biblical chronology abound. There are internal inconsistencies in the narrative itself, inconsistencies that were surely recognized by ancient scribes who nevertheless chose not to resolve them. For example, 1 Kgs 6.1 declares that 480 years passed from the time of the Israelite exodus from Egypt to the time when King Solomon began to build a temple in Jerusalem, but if one counts the chronological notices between those two events very carefully, the actual number is 481 years. Also, within those many intervening chronological notices, one encounters minor inconsistencies, such as the fact that Eli's 40-year reign as judge of Israel (1 Sam. 4.18) would have overlapped preceding reigns listed in the book of Judges. In another example, a king named Jehoram of Israel is said to have begun his reign either when King Jehoshaphat of Judah was in his eighteenth year, or when Jehoshaphat's son, also called Jehoram, was in his second year (compare 2 Kgs 3.1 with 1.17). These and other glaring inconsistencies should warn the modern reader that ancient scribes did not make chronological precision their priority.[11]

Many of these chronological markers are stereotypical clichés common to much ancient Near Eastern storytelling. For example, in the ancient Near East, when one wanted to say that a state of affairs continued for a long, but indefinite, time, one said that the situation continued for '40 years'. The number 40 was as common a cliché for the ancients as 'Once upon a time' is for us. Note that many sequences in the book of Judges last '40 years' (Judg. 3.11; 5.31; 8.28; 13.1), the Israelites wandered in the wilderness for '40 years' (Exod. 16.35; Num. 32.13; Deut. 29.4; Josh. 5.6), and both kings David and Solomon ruled for '40 years' (2 Sam. 5.4; 1 Kgs 11.42). The oddness of the '40 years' cliché did not bother the author of 2 Sam. 15.7, who states that Prince Absalom plotted against King David for 40 years, bringing his plans to completion with a visit to the city of Hebron. But the same storyteller's chronology implies that Absalom was less than 40 years old when he died (2 Sam. 3.3; 5.5; 18.15, 24-32). Apparently, some later scribes were bothered by this and changed '40' to 'four' in some copies of the Samuel scroll.

To illustrate the artificiality of the biblical chronology, let us attempt to establish the dates for the exodus of the Israelites from Egypt under the leadership of Moses and the conquest of Canaan by Joshua, two events narrated in the books of Exodus, Numbers and Joshua. For the sake of argument, let us assume that the Bible records real past events, a real exodus from Egypt and a genuine military conquest of Palestine. When did these occur?

The dates for these events cannot be determined from evidence out-side the Bible. No archaeological or inscriptional data shed light on the issue. For example, there is no evidence that Egypt suffered a massive loss of population at any time in its ancient history. The Bible would lead us to expect this massive loss of population. Ancient Egypt's popu-lation numbered about three million or so. The books of Exodus and Numbers state that some 600,000 men of military age followed Moses from Egypt. If one adds women, children and elderly men to this figure, a total of about two million is implied. It is reasonable to expect that such a massive exodus *should* be recognizable in the archaeological record of ancient Egypt. Also, there is no pattern of military conquest in Canaan in any period of its history that could be equated with the narrative of Joshua. So, if the dates of these two events are to be determined, they will derive exclusively from the Bible's chronology.

There is a biblical passage that seems to establish a very precise date for these events. As mentioned above, 1 Kgs 6.1 asserts that the fourth year of King Solomon's reign was the four hundred and eightieth year after the Israelites left Egypt. Now, if we can establish, using our modern calendar, which year was Solomon's fourth year, then we should be able to calculate the years of the exodus and conquest. Is this possible?

There is another very valuable piece of information provided by 2 Kings 24. That narrative asserts that the Neo-Babylonian King Nebuchadnezzar II attacked Jerusalem and took its king, a man named Jehoiachin, hostage to Babylon (2 Kgs 24.10-12). As luck would have it, archaeologists discovered Babylonian royal archives that also narrate this event. The Babylonian inscriptions even record daily food rations for the royal prisoner, Jehoiachin! Because the Babylonian calendar can be correlated to our modern calendar, we know that King Jehoiachin was taken captive in 597 BCE. This date is a rare, but indisputable, anchor linking the Bible's chronology to our modern calendar. Therefore, it can assist our attempt to determine the dates of the exodus and conquest.

The two books of Kings also record the precise number of years that each king reigned in Jerusalem from the time of Solomon until the time of Jehoiachin. If one adds those totals, there are 423 years from the start of Solomon's reign until the end of Jehoiachin's. Therefore, if one adds 423 years to 597 BCE, the beginning of Solomon's reign would have been 1020 BCE, and his fourth year was 1016. Now, if we add the 480 years mentioned in 1 Kgs 6.1, then the exodus from Egypt narrated in Exodus 14 took place in 1496 BCE, and the conquest after 40 years in the wilderness would have happened in 1456. These are the firm dates of the exodus and conquest according to the Bible.

It would seem that all these biblical texts add up to a precise chronology, but there is a small problem. Ancient Assyrian inscriptions mention the biblical kings of Israel and Judah by name from time to time. These inscriptions can be correlated to our modern calendar as well. When this is done, the biblical dates for the kings—as anchored by the date of King Jehoiachin's captivity—do not match the actual dates from

Assyrian inscriptions. Therefore, all modern historians have 'adjusted' the dates for the biblical kings. These adjustments vary by a few years, depending upon which modern historian is doing the calculations. According to the most common set of adjusted dates, Solomon became king around 960 BCE, not 1020, and so his fourth year would have been roughly 956. This puts the exodus in 1436 or so and the conquest in about 1396. These adjusted dates do not derive from the Bible, but from a modern reinterpretation of the biblical texts. Either pair of dates, 1496 and 1456 or 1436 and 1396, will suffice for the following observations.

The dates provided by the Bible for the exodus and conquest are impossible. These events could not have happened at that time for at least two reasons.

First, the exodus and the conquest would have occurred during the 18th Egyptian Dynasty, when the Egyptian Empire was at the height of its power. Under King Thutmoses III the Egyptian armies pushed up into Syria and the border of Egypt was established there. The whole of Palestine was an Egyptian province. In other words, Joshua's Canaan, the land flowing with milk and honey, the promised land of the Bible, was part of the Egyptian Empire! Moses led his people out of Egypt and they wandered for 40 years in a part of Egypt (the Negev and Transjordan), then Joshua brought the Israelites across the Jordan and right back into another part of Egypt! This cannot be correct, since not a single biblical author expresses any awareness that there ever had been an Egyptian Empire in Palestine.

A second difficulty is that the biblical chronology renders false a statement that the Bible made earlier in the story. Exodus 1.11 tells us that when the Israelites were slaves in Egypt, just prior to the exodus event, they were put to work in the city of Ramesses (and a city called Pithom). Historians know from Egyptian records that the city of Ramesses was built by a 19th Dynasty king, Ramesses II, in the first half of the thirteenth century. Thus, if the exodus took place 480 years prior to Solomon's time, then the Israelite slaves escaped Egypt approximately 150 to 200 years *before* those same Israelite slaves toiled in the Egyptian city of Ramesses! The Bible's own internal chronology does not work.

One could juggle the dates and details creatively in a desperate attempt to make the biblical chronology work. In fact, many biblical scholars have toiled for years doing just this, though none has ever accomplished the goal. One common 'solution' (if one can call it that) is to assume that the 480 years of 1 Kgs 6.1 is a metaphor for 12 generations. (Biblical authors usually reckon a generation to be 40 years!—this cliché was encountered earlier.) Since a genuine human generation is closer to 20 years, these scholars change 480 years to 240 years, meaning 12 *genuine* generations. That puts the exodus around 1256 (or 1196, when adjusted) BCE. In this case, the exodus took place after the city of Ramesses was built, and the kings of the time were the 19th Dynasty kings. Unfortunately, this solution also stumbles on the first objection. If anything, Egypt's rule over Palestine under the 19th Dynasty (including its twilight years) was more direct, not less so, than it had been under the 18th. The dates of exodus and conquest remain impossible.

Even if someone were to achieve the impossible by harmonizing the biblical chronology with real ancient chronology, the result, while

Figure 9. *An Egyptian Statue at Karnak. Dramatic modern lighting is designed to impress upon the mind of the tourist something that every Late Bronze Age resident of Canaan knew well: The power of Egypt was as solid as the stone from which these temple statues were carved.*

creative, would be unconvincing. It would constitute little more than desperation—the desire to create historically reliable information from an ancient folk narrative that was never intended to be interpreted as though it were reliable.

The remarkable thing about the exodus and conquest tales of the Bible is that many individual details in the stories reflect, very accurately, the world of Bronze Age Palestine. Joshua 11.10 remembers accurately that Hazor had been large and powerful in the Middle Bronze Age (2000–1550 BCE). Judges 18.29 recalls correctly that the city of Dan had been called Laish in earlier times. Also, there are personal names recorded in the book of Joshua that were common Semitic names during the era of the Egyptian Empire (the names in Josh. 10.3, for instance). Even the name of Moses sounds authentic. It is, as a matter of fact, part of a real Egyptian name—'Moses' means 'to be born' in the Egyptian language. King Thutmoses III had a 'theophoric' name. A theophoric is a sentence with a divine subject-noun. Thus the name Thut-moses means '[the god] Thut is born'. Moses is an Egyptian name in which the theophoric element has been lost.

Unfortunately, these authentic details tell us nothing about the accuracy of the exodus and conquest stories. Folklore often carries authentic fragments from the past, but in hopelessly scattered form. One researcher has likened them to the scattered remains of a supernova.[12] For example, Homer's *Iliad* contains many personal names that were authentic to the era in which the Trojan War is supposed to have taken place. It recalls as well that a place called Pylos had been an important Bronze Age kingdom. Also, some of the ancient customs and clothing are preserved accurately in Homer's epic. Historians of ancient Greece do not conclude from these details that Homer's tale is true in a correspondence sense (truth of Type A). Rather, they believe that the *Iliad* is the product of a long period of epic storytelling, during which accurate elements of the past were preserved in an almost random way. Names, particularly, tend to be preserved quite well over centuries. But the tale to which the names are attached often undergoes extreme modification over time.

Does this mean that the exodus and conquest are not 'true'? Not at all. They are true tales of human experience, in this case, the human desire for liberation from oppression and divine guidance through hardship. Just as Mark Twain created a 'true' description of the antebellum South for his fictional novel about a boy named Huck, so the

Bible has placed its main characters, Moses and Joshua, into (almost) believable narrative settings. There is no evidence in the Bible to suggest that the biblical authors desired to make of Moses and Joshua anything more—or indeed, anything less!—than two fascinating central characters for their rich and deeply spiritual tale of exodus and redemption. That is certainly an authenticity worthy of respect.

Is the Bible true? Yes indeed! But it is not history.

## SUGGESTED ADDITIONAL READING

*General*
Vansina, Jan, *Oral Tradition as History* (Madison: University of Wisconsin Press, 1985).

*Greek and Roman Literature*
Grant, Michael, *Greek and Roman Historians: Information and Misinformation* (London: Routledge, 1995).
Harris, William V., *Ancient Literacy* (Cambridge, MA: Harvard University Press, 1989).
Marincola, John, *Authority and Tradition in Ancient Historiography* (Cambridge: Cambridge University Press, 1997).
Momigliano, Arnaldo, *The Classical Foundations of Modern Historiography* (with a foreword by R.D. Donato; Berkeley: University of California Press, 1990).
Veyne, Paul, *Did the Greeks Believe in their Myths? An Essay on the Constitutive Imagination* (trans. P. Wissing; Chicago: University of Chicago Press, 1988).

*Biblical Literature*
Brettler, Marc Zvi, *The Creation of History in Ancient Israel* (London: Routledge, 1995).
Kirkpatrick, Patricia G., *The Old Testament and Folklore Studies* (JSOTSup, 62; Sheffield: JSOT Press, 1988).
Niditch, Susan, *Oral World and Written Word: Ancient Israelite Literature* (Louisville, KY: Westminster/John Knox Press, 1996).
—*Folklore and the Hebrew Bible* (Minneapolis: Fortress Press, 1993).
Parker, Simon B., *Stories in Scripture and Inscriptions: Comparative Studies on Narratives in Northwest Semitic Inscriptions and the Hebrew Bible* (Oxford: Oxford University Press, 1997).
Van Seters, John, *In Search of History: Historiography in the Ancient World and the Origins of Biblical History* (New Haven: Yale University Press, 1983).

## NOTES

1.    This translation is quoted from J. Marincola, *Authority and Tradition in Ancient Historiography* (Cambridge: Cambridge University Press, 1997), p. 5.

2.    For Luke's dependence upon Mark's Gospel, see H. Koester, *Introduction to the New Testament. II. History and Literature of Early Christianity* (Philadelphia: Fortress Press, 1982), pp. 43-49. See also, Koester's *Ancient Christian Gospels: Their History and Development* (London: SCM Press, 1990).

3.  E. Morris, *Dutch: A Memoir of Ronald Reagan* (New York: Random House, 1999). One scholar commented on the book by Morris this way: 'Morris has in fact reverted—knowingly or not—to the practice of ancient historians, aligning himself with the likes of Herodotus, Thucydides, Sallust, Livy and Tacitus in his methodological approach, in which speeches, motives, psychology, even history itself were fabricated with a great deal of freedom' (S.H. Rutledge, letter to the editor, *The Washington Post Book World* [Sunday, 19 December, 1999], p. 13).

4.  M. Twain, *The Adventures of Huckleberry Finn* (repr.; London: Octopus Books, 1983 [1884]), p. 1.

5.  D. Donovan, *Once a Warrior King: Memoirs of an Officer in Vietnam* (New York: Ballantine Books, 1985), p. 1.

6.  J.L. Moles, 'Truth and Untruth in Herodotus and Thucydides', in C. Gill and T.P. Wiseman (eds.), *Lies and Fiction in the Ancient World* (Austin: University of Texas Press, 1993), pp. 88-121 (120).

7.  M.J. Wheeldon, 'True Stories: The Reception of Historiography in Antiquity', in A. Cameron (ed.), *History as Text: The Writing of Ancient History* (Chapel Hill: University of North Carolina Press, 1989), pp. 33-63 (59-62).

8.  On this point, I disagree with N. Na'aman, 'The "Conquest of Canaan" in the Book of Joshua and in History', in I. Finkelstein and N. Na'aman (eds.), *From Nomadism to Monarchy: Archaeological and Historical Aspects of Early Israel* (Jerusalem: Israel Exploration Society, 1994), pp. 218-81, whose examples in section 7 (pp. 227-30) are more amenable to the interpretation offered here. I disagree as well with the thesis advanced by B. Halpern, *The First Historians: The Hebrew Bible and History* (University Park: Penn State University Press, 1996), which strikes me as anachronistic. For sound critical responses to Halpern, see reviews of *First Historians* by J. VanderKam, *Int* 44 (1990), pp. 293-95; M.Z. Brettler, *JR* 70 (1990), pp. 83-84; P.M. Arnold, *CBQ* 52 (1990), pp. 713-14; S.J.D. Cohen, *American Historical Review* 95 (1990), pp. 1500-501.

9.  J. Van Seters, 'Joshua's Campaign of Canaan and Near Eastern Historiography', *SJOT* 2 (1990), pp. 1-12.

10.  K.L. Noll, 'Is There a Text in This Tradition? Readers' Response and the Taming of Samuel's God', *JSOT* 83 (1999), pp. 31-51.

11.  For some aspects of this chronological complexity, see M. Noth, *The Deuteronomistic History* (JSOTSup, 15; Sheffield: JSOT Press, 1981), pp. 18-25.

12.  E. Ardener, 'The Construction of History: "Vestiges of Creation"', in E. Tonkin *et al.* (eds.), *History and Ethnicity* (London: Routledge, 1989), pp. 22-33 (29).

Chapter 4

*Introduction*

Because Charles Darwin knew nothing of DNA, he was not able to test his ideas about biological evolution. As a result, Darwin's thinking, though brilliant, was inconsistent. He would experiment first with one idea, then another. The common element in his thought was 'natural selection'. It is important to be aware that natural selection—not biological evolution—is the theoretical portion of Darwin's theory. With the scientific discovery of the chemical DNA, the *fact* of biological change over time became indisputable. This change can and does create new species. Darwin's theory merely tries to describe how change happens. His theory is that the natural environment randomly selects some species and not others. Scientists call it a 'theory' because it is a hypothesis that has been subjected to severe and repetitious testing and has, so far, survived those tests. Although a minority continues to challenge Darwin's theory, the ineffectiveness of the challenge encourages most scientists to place great trust in the theory.

Biological change occurs when random mutations emerge during the process of DNA replication. Most mutations are either benign or harmful to the creature born with them. On occasion, DNA mutation results in a creature who is better equipped to survive in its environment than the other members of its species. In more cases than not, one who is better equipped to survive will survive, and reproduce creatures bearing its DNA. Less well equipped individuals tend not to survive long enough to reproduce, so their DNA disappears with them. If, for some reason, the new variant of a species becomes geographically isolated from the earlier group, a new species will emerge gradually as thousands of generations continue to produce significant DNA mutations. Over millions of years, many mutations have resulted in many species. During that same period of time, many species have been crushed by ever-changing natural environments. This is 'natural selection', and it is why the fossil record contains so many extinct species. There are far more dead species than living species.

Three popular notions about biological evolution are false. First, a common but false objection to Darwinism is that there are no transitional forms in the fossil record, and therefore one species does not evolve into another. That notion derives from the erroneous belief that a species has an essence, a core set of invariable attributes. In reality, a species is nothing more than the label we give to an interbreeding population who share a DNA pool. No single attribute is essential to a species. Within the population, every individual is absolutely unique, yet the whole group is one species. Gradual changes occur as reproduction takes place, but a new species occurs only when creatures that were related stop interbreeding with their 'parent' population, often (but not always) due to geographic isolation. The 'parent' species never evolves into another species. The 'offspring' species has made an immediate, not gradual, mutation to a slightly different DNA structure. Each population then evolves in its own random way so that, after thousands of generations, sexual union between members of the two populations would be fruitless.

A second common misconception is that biological evolution always moves from a less complex to a more complex form of life. In other words, the popular idea is that evolution is always an advancement. This is false. Evolution is merely biological change over time. As noted above, DNA mutation is benign or harmful in many instances. Nevertheless, *if* a mutation permits its recipient to survive and reproduce itself, the mutation becomes a new pattern of DNA represented by a population of organisms who are reproducing it. The laws of probability ensure that almost any mutation that better equips a creature to survive in its natural environment will be selected by that environment. The process is random, not linear, yet its cumulative effect is continual change.

The third common misconception is that Darwin's theory is the enemy of religious faith. If this were the case, there would be no Jewish or Christian Darwinists. As a matter of fact, however, many educated Jews and Christians accept Darwin's theory. Why? Because Darwin's theory is a 'materialist' theory. That is to say, Darwin has explained material changes over time. Darwin has not explained, nor even tried to explain, the spiritual question of *why* matter changes over time. At its best, biological science can answer the 'how' questions about life, but never attempts to address the 'why' question. The 'why' question is an issue for the philosopher or the theologian. In other words, Darwin gives people of religious faith plenty of interesting things to consider and discuss! This volume will not discuss religious 'why' questions. Instead, 'when' questions will be the focus of attention.

### In the Beginning...

It is estimated that our planet is four and a half billion years old. The human story begins only a few moments ago, about 35 million years ago. At that time, a species that biologists have labeled *propliopithecus* appeared on the scene. This tiny animal was the first creature to resemble the apes. Apes were a latecomer to the planet; the dinosaurs had lived many millions of years and had died off long before *propliopithecus* emerged. After many more millions of years, a certain kind of ape, called *australopithecus*, emerged. This creature was very similar to an archaic chimpanzee. Three and a half million years ago—just a blink of an eye—some of these creatures developed 'bad' knees. That is to say, from the perspective of a chimpanzee their knees were bad, but from a modern human's perspective, their knees were good. They enabled the *australopithecenes* to walk upright. That was a new challenge, since these creatures were compelled to seek out living spaces in which their distinctive knees would not be a hindrance.

About two and a half million years ago, the Earth began to undergo a series of Ice Ages. These climatic changes made life difficult for apes because food was more difficult to obtain. Some apes with bad knees began to cope with the situation by using stones to dig and scrape the ground in search of food, and to break animal bones so that the soft bone marrow could be eaten. Creatures with a proclivity to learn this behavior had a survival advantage and therefore lived long enough to reproduce ever more creatures with a proclivity to learn.

The first humans were those apes for whom stone tools were no longer a convenience, but had become an absolute necessity for survival. At that moment, the genus *homo* had emerged. Of course, no one knows exactly when that moment arrived, but it was about two million years ago. Human speech, which is perhaps the most distinctive feature of *homo*, was an accidental by-product of two unrelated biological developments: a particular formation of tongue and laryngeal muscle combined with the abstract thinking that was required to learn the art of tool making. Speech emerged after stone tools were invented.

The most successful member of the *homo* genus has not been *Homo Sapiens*; rather, it was *Homo Erectus*, who emerged more than one and a half million years ago and disappeared only yesterday—about 300,000 years ago. So far as is known, these people were the first to move out of the African continent, and they mastered the use of fire. They gave birth to our 'parents', an archaic form of *Homo Sapiens*, near the end of their existence. However, they did not become extinct the moment Archaic *Homo Sapiens* arrived on the scene. They survived, probably in geographic isolation, for many centuries while Archaic *Homo Sapiens* multiplied and spread around the globe. Some anthropologists have discovered evidence—still considered controversial—to indicate that *Homo Erectus* might have survived to about 50,000 years ago. In any case, whether they became extinct 300,000 or 50,000 years ago, *Homo Erectus* survived for more than a million years and our immediate branch of the family has been around for only a fraction of this time. It remains to be seen whether we will enjoy the longevity of *Homo Erectus*.

In Palestine, the first evidence of Modern *Homo Sapiens*—people whose biology and ability to reason were just like ours—can be dated geologically to at least 45,000 years ago. To try to put this time frame into perspective, consider the average human generation, which is about 20 years. If, for the sake of argument, we assume that the 20-year average has been a constant, the first modern humans appeared in Palestine at least 2250 generations ago. By contrast, the invention of farming (the start of the Neolithic era) occurred about 500 generations ago. One of the Bible's presumed authors, Moses, would have been active about 170 generations ago. Jesus of Nazareth was born about 100 generations ago. Gutenberg produced the first printed Bible about 27 or 28 generations ago. In other words, the Palaeolithic Age was by far the longest era in the experience of Modern *Homo Sapiens*.

Prior to the Mesolithic era, humans lived an itinerant lifestyle. They would gather plant foods and hunt animals with sharp stone-tipped wooden weapons, cook their meals over a fire, then break camp when necessary to follow the herds. During the Mesolithic period, however, a new idea began to spread among humans: permanent residence. That innovation changed human lives forever.

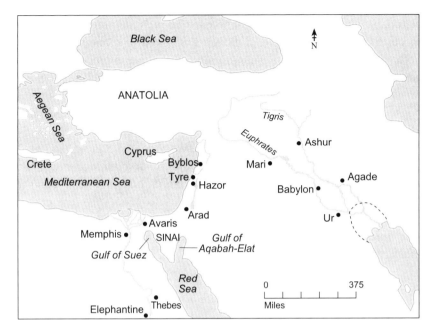

Figure 10. *The Ancient Near East Prior to the Late Bronze Age.*

## Palestine in the Mesolithic Era (18000–8000 BCE)

Twenty thousand years ago, Palestine looked different from how it does today. The climate was much warmer and wetter then. There were a few lakes in what is now the Negev desert. The sea level was lower, so the Palestinian Coastal Plain was about twice as wide as it is now. The two gulfs of Suez and Aqaba-Elat did not yet exist, so the land mass that Christians would later name 'Sinai' was not yet a peninsula. Also, the Jordan River did not exist. Rather, there was a huge salt water lake in that region, called by geologists Lake Lisan. It covered the Great Rift from north of what is now Lake Galilee to south of the modern Dead Sea. One of the interesting aspects of the Mesolithic era is the way human occupation tended to follow the receding waters of this gradually diminishing lake down the hills and, ultimately, into the Jordan Valley as it slowly emerged. That process was completed about 10,000 years ago.

Scholars call the people who lived along the receding coast of Lake Lisan, and in many other places in Palestine, the Natufian culture. The

Natufians were a very creative people. They built permanent settlements of about 100 people or fewer, and lived in stone-walled huts,
occasionally painted with a hand-crafted red-ochre pigment. So far as
can be discerned, Natufian villages display no signs of military activity
or violence. Several burials indicate that they had pets: domesticated
dogs. They hunted gazelles, hares and birds. Micro-traces of wild grain
affixed to their expertly crafted stone blades indicate that wild wheat
the primary part of their diet. They did not plant the grain, but built
their villages near sources of both wheat and fresh water. Some scholars
have suggested that it was the late Natufian culture that first began to
plant wheat, but this suggestion remains controversial. By the end of
the Mesolithic period, as Natufian culture was giving way to the early
Neolithic, Palestine's climate had become just a little cooler than it is
today, but still much wetter.

### *The Neolithic Era (8000–4500 BCE)*

This period of about 175 human generations is the most revolutionary
moment in our collective past. During the Neolithic era, farming was
invented. The invention did not occur all at once. In fact, it evolved
gradually during these 3500 years. In the present study I can only trace
some highlights in that step-by-step process. But the Neolithic era was
revolutionary in the natural realm as well as the human sphere. The
Black Sea was formed about 5600 BCE, when the sea waters from the
Aegean broke through what is now the Bosporus Straits, and flooded
the valley below. The climate of Palestine still did not match Palestine's
modern aridity. Neolithic people could expect rain to fall in the summer as well as winter, whereas rain normally falls only in the winter
today.

The first stage of the Neolithic Revolution was the domestication
of wheat. Early in the Neolithic period, traces of 'domestic' wheat
strains—strains that could not reproduce themselves without the assistance of farmers threshing seed from chaff—are found in the archaeological record. Farming had begun.

Many of these new farming villages were larger than Natufian villages had been. The Neolithic village of Ain Ghazal, at the northeastern
end of the Dead Sea, might have been home to as many as 2000 people
in any given generation. Jericho was almost as large. They were
builders, too. A wall and tower were built at Jericho in about 8000 BCE,

the first such structure known. Judging from the size of the homes, Neolithic people usually lived in nuclear families. A nuclear family consists of only two generations, parents and children. Many cultures prefer an extended family, three or more generations as part of a single family unit, including siblings, uncles, aunts and cousins. Obviously, an extended family requires a larger living space, which is why archaeologists believe many Neolithic families were nuclear.

Once farming had become the way of life, food supplies became more stable and humans could turn their attention to other creative ideas. Several new technologies developed in the early generations of the Neolithic era. Beer was invented, as were a variety of small objects that give every appearance of having been game boards. Farming permitted time for leisure! Also, Neolithic people began to make thread from various plant fibers. They braided ropes, baskets and rugs, which were used in many creative ways. For example, some baskets were used for cooking! They would line the basket with pitch, pour soup into it, then drop rocks that had been heated in fire into the soup. Linen clothing and sheets, made from the fiber of the flax plant, were created as well. Some of these fragile items have survived the centuries in the very dry climate near the Dead Sea, and were discovered by archaeologists. Other ancient textiles have left their 'mark' so to speak. Several of the Neolithic village homes have plaster floors permanently marked by the heavy coil rugs that lay on them for years.

Plaster floors under coil rugs were just one manifestation of the most important invention to emerge in the early Neolithic era: the manufacture of plaster from limestone. After it hardens, this plaster is almost as hard as the rock from which it is made, so it was a durable substance susceptible to human manipulation. Neolithic people used it for many tasks. They plastered and painted the walls and floors of their homes, built plaster hearths for cooking, and even made so-called 'white ware' bowls and cooking pots. Plaster seems to have played a role in Neolithic religion as well. At several Neolithic sites large and exquisitely crafted statues of human-like figures were found. These statues have qualities that remind an art historian of god statues from later eras, so one popular interpretation of them is that they represented the gods of Neolithic communities.

One of the most remarkable aspects of the Neolithic societies that used plaster is their burial custom. Many people were buried under the plaster floors of homes. Later, when sufficient time had elapsed to transform these bodies to bones, the plaster was broken, the grave was opened and the skull removed (without disturbing the remainder of the grave). The skulls were then plastered and molded to give the likeness of human skin. Sometimes, sea shells were employed as eyes. Eventually, sets of several plastered skulls would be reburied in a different location. This activity, which seems so odd to those who did not live in that society, did not extend to all the dead. Only some people were buried under house floors and later decapitated. Some villages favored males for this 'honor', while others preferred females.

Figure 11. *Neolithic Plastered Skull. In ancient times, the grave of this Neolithic resident of Jericho was disturbed, apparently by his own family members, so that the skull could be removed, plastered and decorated, perhaps as part of a solemn religious ceremony* (© Ashmolean Museum, Oxford).

These distinctive burial rites may have been part of ancestor worship. Worship of selected dead family members was a common phenomenon in later times, so this interpretation of decapitated burials seems reasonable. Ancestor worship served several functions. The ancestor who has become divine after death can be assumed to be biased in favor of his or her descendants, and will bestow blessings on the family. Also, an organized religion of ancestors usually signifies property ownership. 'My worship of my ancestors at this grave is evidence that I am rightful owner of this plot of land.'

Neolithic people lived in a very complex human society. Not only did some villages become very large, but most Neolithic communities were integrated into a long-distance network of trade. Villages in Palestine, for example, possessed obsidian (volcanic glass) from central Anatolia. Inland villages frequently made use of sea shells, often brought from many miles away. Moreover, most of these communities display a very similar pattern of material objects, which implies that the communities were not isolated from one another, but traded with or emulated each other.

If the early Neolithic era was known for farming and plaster, the later Neolithic saw the invention of animal herding and ceramic pottery. On the basis of these changes in technology, the Neolithic era is usually divided into the 'Pre-Pottery Neolithic' (PPN) followed by the 'Pottery Neolithic' (PN). Pre-Pottery communities relied heavily on plaster; pottery communities found that clay was an excellent substitute for many of their smaller, more portable plaster objects. The year 5500 BCE is the conventional dividing line, although the process was too gradual to pin the new PN era to a single year or even a single generation.

Pottery Neolithic communities domesticated goats and sheep first, cattle and pigs a short time later. Archaeologists discern the emergence of domesticated animals in several ways. In some cases, building structures might indicate stables or pastures. In other cases, archaeologists might note the presence of a mature animal with bone features that would have made the animal easy prey if it had been born in the wild. One important clue is a village trash dump with a disproportionately high number of butchered young male animals. A few males would be kept for stud and the females for milk, leaving an abundance of males for meat. These clues, as well as others, indicate that the animals were no longer hunted, but raised.

Not long after the domestication of animals, a new type emerged in human society: the 'pastoralist', or shepherd. Pastoralists usually move as small family or clan units from place to place, seeking grazing land for the flock. Often in winter, they settle in one place. They do some farming, but rely on herding for their livelihood. Pastoralists always live on the fringes of farming communities so they can trade with the farmers for the goods they do not raise themselves. The farmers benefit from the relationship as well, obtaining wool, milk, manure, meat, leather, bone and horns from the flocks.

Pottery was an important invention for the modern archaeologist as well as the ancient farmer. When the 'domestication' of clay begins to appear in the archaeological record, archaeologists can use pottery typology to determine the chronology of the societies they study (a technique discussed in Chapter 2). For ancient people, pottery became the most essential tool of daily life. Its most important use was for cooking and eating, as well as storage of grain, fruits and liquids. Some clay pots were tiny and used as drinking or eating vessels, while others were huge, designed to store goods over long periods of time. But pottery was useful for other purposes as well. Terra cotta figurines could be molded as children's toys or as ritual objects. They can be distinguished from each other usually in the way that the objects show signs of use, or by their find location. Also, clay tokens were made to assist in accounting and inventory.

The clay tokens used for counting highlight one important invention that did not occur to Neolithic people: writing. The development of writing would not take place until 1000 years after the end of the Neolithic Age. Before the emergence of writing there came one more extremely significant advance in technology: metalworking.

### *The Chalcolithic Era (4500–3500 BCE)*

The Chalcolithic era was relatively brief when compared to earlier eras, consisting of about 50 human generations. This period is defined as an age in which metalworking had been invented but writing had not. The exploited metal was copper. Because it was relatively soft, it was more useful for ritual and ceremonial objects than for everyday tools, although many farm implements and weapons were manufactured from it as well. It should be stressed, however, that while copper was *known* in the Chalcolithic era, it was *not* common. Many people continued to live without the new metalworking technology.

The primary effect of copper on human society was the stimulation of long-distance trade networks and, with them, more complex societies. It has already been mentioned that long-distance trade was a part of Neolithic society as well. However, the items that were traded in Neolithic times were common to many places (e.g. sea shells) and were made of substances that, while unique, could be replaced by more local substitutes (e.g. obsidian). Now, however, a commodity was in demand that was utterly distinctive—there was nothing else quite like metal. Copper mines were rare and usually a considerable distance from major sites of human habitation. That made demand high and availability low. Copper was a prestige item, and ownership of it was restricted to the newly emerging elite classes. A sophisticated network of trade routes evolved that were governed by a professional class of warriors who could protect the trade routes as well as benefit from them. Thus, copper was at least partially responsible for the emergence of a more highly stratified society, with 'haves' and 'have nots'.

This more stratified society is observable in the archaeological record, the 'material culture' of Chalcolithic Palestine. When plotted on a map, the sites where Chalcolithic-era pottery has been found reveal a distinct pattern. In any given local area, one large, centrally located village is surrounded by a cluster of smaller villages. When archaeologists compare this pattern, and other aspects of Chalcolithic material culture, with the lifestyles of living traditional societies, they recognize that the people of Chalcolithic Palestine lived in chiefdoms.

A chiefdom is a loosely structured hierarchy governed by a leader who enjoys special authority for several reasons. Primarily, he is a warrior who is able to muster and lead able-bodied males when the occasion requires military action. Usually, his status of leadership is reinforced by a religious structure that sanctions his office as divinely revealed or authorized. His place of residence becomes the center of the community, a fledgling 'capital city'. His authority is transmitted to his offspring in dynastic succession. In short, a chief is a little like a king, but rules over a far less complex society. Unlike a kingdom, a chiefdom has a small population, no bureaucracy, no standing army, no written records or law codes and, apart from the specially trained warrior class surrounding the chief, no significant social hierarchy.

Chalcolithic Palestine's chiefdoms dotted the landscape, but clustered to a greater degree in the valleys and coastal regions, since they were better agricultural lands than the highlands. The average person in this society followed a lifestyle that was identical to the Neolithic farming village, a lifestyle that would continue through most of Palestine's experience until very recently. Bread made from wheat and barley was the staple of the diet. That was supplemented by beans and vegetables, a few fruits, and a very small amount of meat. Animals were not killed for everyday meals since they were precious commodities. Later, in the

Bronze and Iron Ages, meat was eaten more often than not during agricultural festivals or on special occasions. Presumably that was the case in these earlier times as well. Sheep and goats remained the most common source of meat. Cattle were eaten sometimes. Pigs were never very popular in Palestine. In Chalcolithic archaeology, pig bones represent about 15 per cent of the butchered remains. After the Chalcolithic era, the percentage of pig consumption fell steadily until it became negligible.

The chiefdoms of Palestine collapsed and disappeared during the final generations of the Chalcolithic era. Historians are uncertain why this happened. It may have been due to changes in the climate that began about that time. The level of aridity and the weather patterns known to Palestine today began to emerge during the gradual transition from the Chalcolithic to the Early Bronze Age. Perhaps Chalcolithic communities were unable or unwilling to adjust to the changes, and migrated. Another reason for the collapse of Chalcolithic chiefdoms might have been warfare between neighboring communities. There is no sign of widespread military destruction, but sporadic warfare may have contributed to the breakdown of society, which again encouraged migration, or perhaps contributed to starvation. Whatever the cause, archaeologists discern a clear break between the close of the Chalcolithic and the first stages of the Bronze Age.

### Syria-Palestine's Neighbors During the Early and Middle Bronze Ages (3500–2000 and 2000–1550 BCE)

The Bronze Age gets its name from the art of adding a little tin to copper to make a harder metal called bronze. But this clever innovation was not this era's most valuable invention. The two most significant human inventions have been, first, the establishment of farming (in the early Neolithic), and second, the development of writing (just before 3200 BCE). At best, metalworking is a distant third.

Writing emerged in two places at roughly the same time, Mesopotamia and Egypt, in the early centuries of the Bronze Age. In both cases, the reason for its invention was quite mundane. Both regions were dry and hostile environments. If humans wished to build a society and live in these regions, they needed to work together, form a large, integrated society and pool their physical manpower to build irrigation canals and other aids for the raising of food. Large-scale cooperative effort required a small cadre of overseers to coordinate that effort. In other words, there needed to be a social hierarchy, with leaders and bureaucrats who would organize the workers. Writing was invented by these early bureaucrats to keep records. For centuries, this was the primary purpose for writing. Only much later did people develop literature.

Mesopotamian and Egyptian writings were similar in some ways, but took two different outward forms. In Egypt, the scribes wrote with pictures, which we call hieroglyphs. In Mesopotamia, they developed a system of wedge-shaped symbols, called cuneiform, to express words in syllables. Thus, neither of the original writing systems was similar to the alphabetic system you are reading now. Our alphabet consists of 26 individual signs, each representing a short sound, not a full syllable or word. (The invention of the first alphabet occurred in Syria-Palestine during the late Middle Bronze period, and will be discussed later in this chapter.)

The two massive societies that emerged in Mesopotamia and Egypt were divided from one another by the less-densely populated strip of land called Syria-Palestine. The people who lived on this land bridge found that their lives were profoundly affected by their neighbors on either side. As a matter of fact, one might say that *geography was destiny* for Syria-Palestine. Beginning with the Bronze Age, the ancient experience of this region has been frequent dominance by and response to Mesopotamia and Egypt. A very brief survey of those ancient neighbors is essential to a writing of Syro-Palestinian history.

*Mesopotamia in the Early and Middle Bronze Ages*
The land between the rivers Tigris and Euphrates has been home to a long sequence of cultures and empires. Earliest among the Bronze Age cultures were the Sumerians, who were followed by Akkadians (including Assyrians and Babylonians), among others.

The Sumerians lived in city-states along the river banks of southern Mesopotamia, from well before the Bronze Age until about 2400 or so BCE. A city-state is a little like a chiefdom in structure (see the discussion of chiefdoms above), but much more populous. The difference in population created differences in the way the two systems operated. The dynastic king of an ancient Mesopotamian city-state, like a dynastic chief, enjoyed special status reinforced by religious beliefs, and functioned as the head of the military and the religion. But, unlike a chief, the king governed a community divided into a more rigid social structure, and his administration consisted of full-time bureaucrats, a standing professional army, and a written code of law, characteristics never encountered in a chiefdom.

By about 2500 BCE, 80 per cent of Mesopotamia's population lived within city-state societies. Because these city-states were so populous (some of them numbered in the tens of thousands), society was divided into classes and labor was highly specialized. In addition to the elite class, the aristocracy who surrounded the king, there were slaves and free peasants. Labor among the peasantry was specialized; that is to say, each individual pursued one activity. The variety of specializations included farmers, pastoralists, and a host of skilled crafts, such as potters, basket makers, metalworkers, bakers, tanners, weavers, and so on. Women were a class in their own right, but not a class that possessed a recognized authority. Women were property of men in most ancient Near Eastern societies. For example, biblical authors always presupposed a cultural norm in which a young woman belonged to her father until a man paid the bride-price to purchase her. Then she became the property of her husband. As such, she was always a piece of property, not an autonomous individual like her father or husband. The only women who did not belong to a man were widows, orphans and prostitutes, and special provisions were made in biblical literature for each of those 'outsider' roles. The image of women presented by the Bible is, unfortunately, quite representative of the ancient Near East generally.

The king presided over the city-state's commerce as head of a 'redistributive economy'. A redistributive economy is one in which most goods are gathered into the central government's stores, then redistributed to the people. This type of economy had advantages for an ancient peasant as well as the king and his aristocracy. The elite classes benefited by being able to control the economic foundation of society; with this power came wealth and prestige. Peasants benefited by living in a society that was protected by a warrior class whose only real job was to train for war. Also, the peasants were usually protected in times of famine or drought, provided these calamities were not so severe or long-term that they depleted all the king's central stores. (In the Bible, the famous folk-tale of Joseph in the land of Egypt uses the motif of a redistributive economy as a crucial element in the plot's structure. See Gen. 41.)

Not only did the king control the economy, he was the head of religion as well. As a matter of fact, the king was the link between the gods and humanity. He was the chosen one of the gods or, in many cases, the chosen one of a patron god. In some cases, a king was even considered to be a god. For example, King Naram-Sin (2213–2176 BCE) was called 'god of the city of Agade'. This link between politics and religion is one that must be kept in mind when studying the ancient world. There was no division, in any ancient culture, between government and religion. The notion of a separation between 'church' and 'state' was invented by the European and American Enlightenment philosophers of the seventeenth and eighteenth centuries CE, by such thinkers as Baruch de Spinoza, John Locke and Thomas Jefferson. In the ancient world, the god (or the gods) played a vital role in each political and economic system. A temple was, among other things, the royal bank. A king was, among other things, chief priest of the kingdom's religion. At the level of the peasantry, there could be, and usually was, extreme diversity of religious belief. But at the level of the state, there was a single, official royal religion, and that religion justified the king's power and activities.

The city-state's temple was a central element in Mesopotamian society, and its importance even for commoners cannot be exaggerated. It was a vital part of seasonal agricultural festivals, since festivals always had a religious dimension. The temple was also huge, which means that no city resident could ignore it. Mesopotamia's flat landscape was transformed by the creation of an artificial mountain at the center of the city-state. This mud-brick mountain, called a ziggurat, was an elaborate platform upon which stood the primary holy place of the city, where king and priests met the city's patron god. The people of a city-state spoke of their ziggurat as the 'navel' that connects the realm of humans on earth to the realm of the gods in the sky. (Incidentally, ancient Semitic languages have no word equivalent to modern English 'heaven'. In ancient writings such as the Bible, the divine realm is the 'sky', that blue dome above us. 'Heaven' is an artificial English translation. Some ancient people believed that the dome was made of metal—see Gen. 1.6-8, for example.) The ziggurat remained a feature of Mesopotamian cities through most of the period covered in this book. Biblical writers poked fun at Mesopotamian ziggurats by telling a tall tale (pun intended) in which Mesopotamian people try to build a gigantic tower to the sky, but are thwarted by a powerful god who lives in the sky (Gen. 11.1-9).

Northern Mesopotamia was dominated by speakers of the Akkadian language. Sumerian culture and language gave way to this social and linguistic element as the two mixed freely. Much that had been Sumerian, including the ziggurats, became Akkadian. Gradually, Akkadian language and customs grew dominant, and the Sumerian language died as a spoken language, being preserved only by educated scribes who copied old Sumerian literature.

By the twenty-fourth century BCE, King Sargon of a city called Agade had accrued sufficient power and wealth to begin conquering neighboring city-states. The result was Mesopotamia's first empire. It was not an empire in the sense that Rome under Caesar Augustus was an empire, with a complex imperial bureaucracy and a percentage of the population viewing themselves as Roman citizens. Rather, it was a cluster of Mesopotamian city-states that paid taxes to a single king, Sargon of Agade. For a peasant in one of the city-states, very little changed. He was not a 'citizen' of an empire, but a peasant who paid taxes to a 'lord', his king.

The Akkadian empire (sometimes called the Sargonic empire) survived for several centuries, but gradually weakened. By the twenty-first century BCE, it gave way to a rival empire ruled from the old Sumerian city of Ur, south of Babylon. In history books, this empire is called the Third Dynasty of Ur, or Ur III. These kings attempted, with partial success, to revive the older Sumerian culture and language, but the empire survived for only about one hundred years. Its collapse around 2000 BCE marks the close of the Early Bronze Age.

Mesopotamia during the Middle Bronze Age (2000–1550 BCE) was, once again, a cluster of rival city-states. It was during this period that the cities of Babylon and Ashur became major political forces, competing with one another for control over the land between the rivers. The most famous king of Ashur (the capital of Assyria) during these centuries was a man named Shamshi-Adad I (1813–1781 BCE). Babylon boasted King Hammurabi (1792–1750 BCE), who published a law code that is often compared to aspects of the biblical legal tradition. Another significant Mesopotamian city, though less powerful than Ashur and Babylon, was Mari. Archaeologists have discovered a collection of palace archives from the Middle Bronze stratum of Mari's ruins. These archives have shed much light on the daily life of ancient Mesopotamia.

In sum, Mesopotamia enjoyed a long period of cultural vitality during the Early and Middle Bronze Ages. This brief discussion does no justice to that society's complexity. Mesopotamia's impact on

Bronze Age Syria (and, to a lesser extent, Palestine) was extensive, and will be discussed below. Bronze Age Canaan was influenced more directly by Egypt during these centuries, and that culture is the next topic of discussion.

*Egypt in the Early and Middle Bronze Ages*
Ancient Egypt was a culture whose life depended upon the Nile River. Every summer (until a dam was built in modern times), the Nile flooded its banks when it swelled with the waters of the monsoons and melting snow from Ethiopia and Sudan, where the Nile originates from two rivers called the Blue and White Niles. A complex system of irrigation made use of the annual flood to raise crops and feed the masses of people who lived along the more than 500 miles of riverbanks meandering from Elephantine (modern Aswan) down to the Mediterranean Sea. A few oases in the desert near the Nile were also inhabited, but the bulk of Egypt's ancient population lived close to the river.

To harness and fully exploit the Nile, political unification came early in the Bronze Age. The precise time and circumstances of unification are not entirely certain because they are shrouded in the pre-literate era and further confused by conflicting later traditions. When Greek *historia* began to influence Egyptian elite classes during the early Hellenistic era (after 323 BCE; see Chapter 3), an Egyptian priest named Manetho attempted to compile a complete list of all Egypt's kings. His effort produced an imperfect, but somewhat useful, list of royal dynasties, each assigned a number in what Manetho had thought was the correct chronological succession. We now know that some of these dynasties ruled portions of Egypt concurrently, not sequentially; others were not really dynasties at all, just local governorships at best. Nevertheless, the use of Manetho's dynastic numbers has become the conventional way of discussing ancient Egypt's history.

Most history books divide ancient Egypt into a series of time periods corresponding to the relative strength or weakness of the ruling dynasts of the period. Four of these groupings—the Pre-Dynastic era, the Early Dynastic Era (Dynasties 1 and 2), the Old Kingdom (Dynasties 3-6) and the First Intermediate (Dynasties 7-11)—correspond roughly to the Early Bronze Age (3500–2000 BCE). Two periods—the Middle Kingdom (late-Dynasty 11 and Dynasty 12) as well as the Second Intermediate (Dynasties 13-17)—represent the Middle Bronze Age (2000–1550 BCE). As one might guess, each of the periods labeled 'intermediate' was a time in which central authority had become weakened and several political entities (dynasties) competed with one another.

During most of the Early and Middle Bronze Ages, unified Egypt was ruled from a city that is situated between Upper Egypt to the south and Lower Egypt (called the Delta) to the north. This centrally positioned city was Memphis (modern Cairo). At times, the capital moved from Memphis to some other city, but this was rare and for only a short time. During the Middle Kingdom, there were, in effect, two capitals for a single dynasty (Dynasty 12), one capital at Thebes in Upper Egypt, the other just south of Memphis in a newly built administrative city. Lower Egypt's Delta region became a center of political influence only toward the end of the Middle Bronze (2000–1550 BCE) Age, under Dynasty 15, the so-called Hyksos Dynasty (to be discussed momentarily).

Thus, whereas Bronze Age Mesopotamia's political world had consisted of a series of city-states only occasionally unified into an empire, Egypt's civilization was a single political entity only occasionally dividing itself into regional competitors. But very much like Mesopotamia, most people did not perceive themselves to be 'citizens' of Egypt. It is reasonable to assume that they thought of themselves as peasants who owed allegiance to their god and king.

As in Mesopotamia, the Egyptian king was the link between the gods and humanity, but the nature of the link was more direct, more concrete. If Mesopotamian kings were usually the chosen favorites of the gods, Egypt's kings were gods in their own right. Each king or 'pharaoh'—a term that came to designate the kings of Egypt beginning with the Late Bronze Age (1550–1200 BCE)—of Egypt was an incarnation of Horus, the falcon god, son of the god Osiris, and associated at times with the sun god Re. The divine king bestowed *ma'at* on his land. This word is difficult to translate into English as there is no precise equivalent. The term *ma'at* meant 'order', 'truth' and 'justice', a combination of blessings that, if in correct balance, benefited all the people of Egypt. At death, the king of Egypt did not cease to be divine; his divinity was transformed into another state of being. He was associated with Osiris, the god of the underworld. During the Old Kingdom, each king was buried in a pyramid, the most famous of which are the three Giza pyramids just outside Memphis (Dynasty 4). After the Old Kingdom, royal tombs were less elaborate. From the tomb, an Egyptian king continued to live in splendor and his life-force (*ka*) bestowed influential power.

In spite of his divinity (or perhaps, at times, because of it), Egyptian storytellers did not shy from making light of the king in a variety of tales that survive from ancient times. One can understand, as well, why the biblical authors chose the king of Egypt as the villain for their exquisite story of Moses and the exodus. The reputation of the god-king of Egypt is one that was well known throughout the ancient world right down to Roman times. Hebrew storytellers and their audiences would have been very familiar with that concept. When Israel's god, Yahweh (commonly rendered in English as 'the LORD'), plays cat-and-mouse with Pharaoh by inflicting 10 plagues in succession, he is toying with a would-be god (Exod. 7–11). By telling the story in such a way that Yahweh hardens the heart of Pharaoh so that Pharaoh cannot control his own destiny, the Hebrew storyteller obeyed the first commandment of the Bible while simultaneously delighting his audience with humor and wit (see Exod. 7.3; 20.2-3).

Even before unification under Dynasty 1, Egypt had begun to exert influence on Palestine. During the Chalcolithic era, there is evidence for trade relations between the two regions. There was a similar link, much more formalized, under the first two Dynasties. At times, Egyptian kings campaigned in parts of Syria-Palestine. At other times, Egypt sent envoys to the courts of Syro-Palestinian city-states. Pottery finds suggest that the Palestinian city of Arad was, at that time, a trade center linked with Egypt. The level of Egyptian involvement waxed and waned with the phases of its own political history.

Egypt's Old Kingdom (Dynasties 3-6) had been an insulated society. The vast desert wastelands that surround the Nile valley served as a very effective buffer against military invasion. Therefore, Egypt lived in peace. Egyptians were confidently self-satisfied, attributing their good fortune to the superiority of their own culture. Outsiders, people who lived in any land other than Egypt, were regarded as inferiors. All other lands were called, collectively, the 'Nine Bows'—regions where barbarian culture suffered for lack of Egyptian civilization.

The Middle Kingdom began to expand beyond the limits of Egypt. The 12th Dynasty discovered that Nubia (modern Sudan), to the south, was rich in copper and gold, cattle and sub-Saharan trade items, and also men who could be enslaved if defeated in battle. The first attempts at Egyptian conquest and empire began at this time, though they were not altogether successful; Nubian resistance was strong. Egyptian kings also campaigned from time to time in Syria, where the massive cedar trees of Lebanon, as well as incense, oil and wine were valuable commodities. Not all contact with the outside world was hostile. The kings of the 12th Dynasty, like many kings of previous dynasties, sent envoys to establish diplomatic and trade relations with a number of Syrian city-states, especially Byblos on the Syrian coast.

A second period of intermediate dynasties closed the Middle Bronze Age (Dynasties 13-17), a period that would have a significant impact on Canaan. It was during the years spanned by these Dynasties that Semites began migrating and settling in the Delta. Eventually these Semites developed into a potent military force that conquered Lower Egypt to a point just south of Memphis. Egyptians called these new kings *heqaw khasut*, 'foreign rulers'. That word became, in the Greek language, Hyksos, and the 15th Dynasty remains the Hyksos Dynasty for modern historians.

The Hyksos were ambitious commercial entrepreneurs who engaged in trade with Canaan, Cyprus and Greece. They appear to have had direct cultural contacts with the Minoan society of Crete, in the Aegean Sea. There is even evidence to suggest that the Hyksos dominated southern Canaan, perhaps ruling over that region directly. They ruled for about 100 years, from roughly 1650 to 1550 BCE. Their territory encompassed only Lower Egypt and Memphis, and did not include Upper Egypt. The Hyksos capital was established in the Delta at Avaris. Eventually, the Hyksos were defeated in battle by a 17th Dynasty king of Thebes. The first king of the 18th Dynasty, also from Thebes, drove the Hyksos out of Egypt entirely, and reunified Upper and Lower Egypt.

The Hyksos phenomenon—which was marked by Semites ruling Egypt, then being driven out—has reminded not a few people of the biblical story of Joseph, Moses and the exodus. Even the ancient Jewish historian, Josephus, who was active in the second half of the first century CE, tried to equate the Hyksos with the Hebrew Israelites. While there are countless difficulties with such a hypothesis, this romantic idea remains popular in some circles even today. At best, the biblical story could be no more than a metaphorical impression of the Hyksos era, not a reliable account of it, since the details of the two are so radically different. It is more likely that the Hyksos memory does not stand behind the biblical tale at all.

## Syria-Palestine During the Early and Middle Bronze Ages
### (3500–2000 and 2000–1550 BCE)

Syria and Palestine were separate and unrelated cultures during the Early and Middle Bronze Ages. Palestine had been unoccupied for a number of generations after the collapse of the Chalcolithic chiefdoms, and the population that emerged there during the Early Bronze seems to have migrated from the north. Having arrived, however, these new-comers went their own way, culturally. Increasingly, Syria emerged as a vibrant cultural community, which was influenced primarily by Meso-potamia and had some economic contacts with Egypt. Palestine remained a cultural backwater, sparsely populated, and engaged in mostly local trade. Its limited contact with the outside world was with Egypt.

### Syria

By 2500 BCE many of the urban centers of Syria had grown into models of Mesopotamian city-states. One of the most important among them was Byblos on the coast. Byblos supplied Egypt with massive cedar logs, a precious commodity for Egypt, since it had very little wood of its own. Also, Byblos traded with the Mesopotamian powers, providing metals and other goods obtained from various regions around the Mediterranean, and supplying those commodities to the far-off lands between the rivers Tigris and Euphrates. As one might expect, the fortunes of Syria waxed and waned with the fluctuations taking place in Mesopotamia throughout the Early and Middle Bronze Ages.

As was mentioned earlier in this chapter, the alphabet was invented in Middle Bronze Age Syria, the economic link between Mesopotamia and Egypt. The bureaucrats of cities such as Byblos kept records of exchanges with all their trading partners. For centuries they kept these records in the languages of the lands with which they were trading. Thus, the scribes of Syria were compelled to learn Egyptian hiero-glyphs and Mesopotamian cuneiform, two highly complex systems of communication. Eventually, it became apparent that a much simpler process would be to borrow some of the most common signs and create a single system for articulating the various one-syllable sounds made by any language. The alphabet was the product of an effort to simplify communication between groups who did not speak or read the same languages. It is one of humanity's greatest cultural achievements, and it was invented in Syria around or just before 1600 BCE.

*Palestine*

Palestine in the Early Bronze Age (3500–2000 BCE) was a 'prehistoric' region. That is to say, very few writings derive from this era, and Palestine's population was, in many ways, an echo of the Chalcolithic period. During the entire Early Bronze Age, a period of some 70 or more human generations, Palestine consisted of about 20 or so small city-states, though the locations of the cities shifted over the centuries. Unlike the massive city-states of Mesopotamia and Syria, Palestine's cities were quite small, with only a few numbering more than 2000 people. Their social structures appear to have been far less complex than the cities to the north and east. Among the largest and most significant of these Palestinian cities were Megiddo, Laish (which was later called Dan), and Ai (quite close to Bethel).

The success of city life in Early Bronze Palestine could well have been directly dependent on trade relations with Egypt. When the Egyptian Old Kingdom collapsed in the twenty-third century BCE, Palestine's city-states went into rapid decline, eventually being abandoned almost completely. For the final centuries of the Early Bronze Age, Palestine's meager population consisted of not much more than a few villages and some pastoralists. The Palestinian commodities that Egypt sought from Palestine's Early Bronze cities were their most lucrative crops: olive oil and wine. The oil was the more expensive and was used for a variety of purposes. It could be made into a soap, burned in lamps, used as a liniment and, of course, served as a dressing for food. Wine was, in the ancient world, the most common drink, and there were various grades of quality.

During the Middle Bronze Age (2000–1550 BCE), Canaan was home once more to a series of urban centers, each of which ruled over its immediate rural surroundings. One archaeologist has described this era as a period of social and political complexity never before seen in the land of Canaan.[1] This may have been due to the influence of Egypt's Middle Kingdom (Dynasty 12) and intermediate Hyksos Kingdom (Dynasty 15). It was also the result of the influence of the Phoenician cities on the Syrian coast, just north of Palestine, whose material culture had a pronounced impact on northern Canaan.

A significant proportion of the population in each of these small-scale city-states lived in the primary city, but the majority lived in agricultural villages round about. The people of these city-states were ruled by an aristocratic elite class, with a king in ultimate control. The highly stratified society included an educated and wealthy elite who numbered fewer than five per cent of the population, a wholly illiterate peasantry of about 85 to 90 per cent, and others, such as merchants and slaves, most of whom were also illiterate.

Each small city-state was relatively self-sufficient, growing its own food and producing its own crafts and tools. But each of them also engaged in trade with near neighbors or, if the city-state could manage, with distant trade partners in Egypt and Syria. Predictably, most trade was local. Local commodities included food, textiles and everyday tools, such as common household pottery. Long-distance trade was the exclusive domain of the aristocratic elite class (and the merchants and slaves who served them). Trade at this level specialized in luxury goods, such as finely crafted garments and pottery, as well as metal. Metals (copper, tin, silver and gold) could be traded in worked or raw form.

Money was not in common circulation, so trade made little use of it. Peasants never had money, and all local trade was bartered. At the elite level, much of the exchange was 'gift exchange'. One nobleman would send another valuable gifts, expecting gifts in return. The process forged social alliances—and in that society, social alliances were political alliances. Elite exchange that was not governed by the social etiquette of gift exchange was paid for by weighing out silver or gold. Money as you and I know it—silver and gold coins stamped with a design—was invented relatively late, in about the sixth century BCE in the Aegean region. It did not become common until the third century BCE.

During the peak of the Middle Bronze (2000–1550 BCE), Canaan was home to about 140,000 people. Most lived in the lowlands, the coastal plain, the Jezreel and the upper half of the Jordan valley (the lower half becomes increasingly arid as it descends toward Jericho). The Central Hills were populated, but sparsely so, except in those areas where they merge into the lowlands, such as at Hazor in the Galilee.

The city of Hazor was the dominant city in Middle Bronze Canaan. It was small compared to the cities of Egypt or Mesopotamia, but absolutely colossal compared to other cities of Palestine. Possibly, as many as 20,000 people lived in Hazor during these centuries. A city of 2000 is unusually large for Palestine in any period prior to the Hellenistic era (that is, prior to the late-fourth century BCE). According to archaeological evidence and ancient Mesopotamian records, Hazor dominated trade in the northern half of Canaan. Given Hazor's location, in the fertile regions near Huleh Lake, and on the trading crossroads of the ancient world, this is not surprising. Canaan's southern half was economically controlled by the Delta region of Egypt, where the Hyksos capital at Avaris served as a commercial hub. It remains uncertain whether the Hyksos ruled southern Palestine or simply dominated economically, but their presence is evident in the large number of Hyksos royal scarabs found in southern Canaan. Thus, the cultural and economic influence in northern Palestine came from the Syrian coastal plain as well as from Mesopotamia, and the cultural and economic influence in southern Palestine came from Egypt.

Middle Bronze Palestine's society was volatile. The elite classes were trained warriors, and peasantry could be conscripted for the army in times of crisis. New war technologies were invented during these centuries, including the composite bow, the military chariot (but not cavalry, which was invented during the Iron Age II), and several kinds of siege engine (including the battering ram and the siege tower). To counter these siege engines, the primary city of a city-state evolved into a heavily fortified citadel atop a high hill. The city wall was doubly protected by a long, massive earthen rampart, often plastered, to protect against frontal attack. As a result, most of these fortified cities survived unmolested for the first 400 years of the Middle Bronze period. Invading armies would not hesitate, however, to ravage the countryside during time of war. Peasants would escape behind city walls when invading armies were in the vicinity.

Middle Bronze Palestine came to a tragic end. With a few exceptions, each of the major city-states was destroyed by military assault during a period of just over 100 years, from about 1650 to 1550 BCE. In earlier historical scholarship, a single culprit was sought for this wave of destruction. Most scholars attributed the damage to invading Egyptian armies. (A few fundamentalist Christians sought the handiwork of biblical Joshua in these ashes, in spite of the obvious chronological problems.) It is now generally recognized that the process of destruction was gradual and is not to be attributed to any single cause. Southern Canaan suffered destruction at the hands of the early 18th Dynasty Egyptians, but other portions of the land were devastated by a variety of armies, including Hurrian kings from northern Syria (to be discussed in the next chapter) and Palestine's own city-states in competition with each other.

## SUGGESTED ADDITIONAL READING

*Darwin's Theory: Scientific Aspects and Philosophical Consequences*

Deacon, Terrence W., *The Symbolic Species: The Co-Evolution of Language and the Brain* (New York: Norton, 1997).

Dennett, Daniel C., *Darwin's Dangerous Idea: Evolution and the Meanings of Life* (New York: Simon & Schuster, 1995).

Haught, John F., *God After Darwin: A Theology of Evolution* (Boulder, Colorado: Westview, 2000).

*Prehistory of the Human Species*

Banning, E.B., 'The Neolithic Period: Triumphs of Architecture, Agriculture and Art', *Near Eastern Archaeology* 61.4 (1998), pp. 188-237.

Levy, Thomas E. (ed.), *The Archaeology of Society in the Holy Land* (with a new introduction by Kent Flannery; Leicester: Leicester University Press, 1998).

Rollefson, Gary O., 'Prehistoric Time', in Gösta W. Ahlström, *The History of Ancient Palestine from the Palaeolithic Period to Alexander's Conquest* (ed. D.V. Edelman; JSOTSup, 146; Sheffield: JSOT Press, 1993), pp. 72-111.

*The Early and Middle Bronze Ages*

Ahlström, Gösta W., *The History of Ancient Palestine from the Palaeolithic Period to Alexander's Conquest* (ed. D.V. Edelman; JSOTSup, 146; Sheffield: JSOT Press, 1993).

Kuhrt, Amélie, *The Ancient Near East, c. 3000–330 BC*, I (London: Routledge, 1995).

## NOTES

1.    D. Ilan, 'The Dawn of Internationalism—The Middle Bronze Age', in T.E. Levy (ed.), *The Archaeology of Society in the Holy Land* (Leicester: Leicester University Press, 1998), pp. 297-319 (305).

Chapter 5

## The Late Bronze Age

### Introduction

The middle of the sixteenth century BCE was a turning point for
Canaan. On three sides, Syria-Palestine's neighbors were emerging as
powerful kingdoms. To the north, Anatolia had become known as the
land of Hatti. In northern Mesopotamia, a coalition of Hurrian kingdoms was called Mitanni. And in Egypt, the 18th and 19th Dynasties
were about to become the two most powerful royal dynasties ancient
Egypt would ever know.

All three of these powers had one thing in common: they coveted
Syria-Palestine. Not only did this region offer natural resources of
value, such as Syria's massive cedar trees, Palestine's oil and wine, and
the Negev's copper mines, but Syria-Palestine was also the land bridge
that stood between the three powers. Each rival king desired control of
that passageway, strategic both defensively and offensively, and each
was willing to fight for it. Syria-Palestine became the battleground for
the superpowers of the age.

Imperial policies imposed from outside affected the lives of Syro-
Palestinian people in many ways. Taxation skimmed natural resources
from the region, impressment into the armies of these foreigners took
place from time to time, and enslavement, even deportation, was not
uncommon. Thus the three foreign powers were much the same from a
local person's perspective—foreign domination was domination, no
matter which king claimed divine right to engage in it.

### Setting the Scene: Three Competing Powers

#### Egypt's 18th and 19th Dynasties

As was mentioned, the Hyksos city of Avaris in the eastern Delta
dominated trade with southern Canaan during the final century of the

Middle Bronze era. But the Hyksos (15th Dynasty) were perceived to be foreigners by the Egyptian 17th Dynasty that ruled in Thebes to the south. Rivalry between these two centers of power eventually errupted into warfare. The Theban army attacked the Delta, and the attack was continued by the founder of the 18th Dynasty, who was also from Thebes. The Egyptians drove the Hyksos out of Egypt and into southern Canaan, where the war continued until the Hyksos were destroyed.

The Hyksos war accounts for a portion of Palestine's military destruction at the close of the Middle Bronze Age, as discussed in the previous chapter. For Palestine, the end of the Hyksos marks the beginning of the Late Bronze Age (1550–1200 BCE). For Egypt, their expulsion marks the close of the Second Intermediate period (13th to 17th Dynasties; approximately 1750–1550 BCE) and the start of the New Kingdom (18th to 20th Dynasties; 1550–1070 BCE). Note that, chronologically, the New Kingdom overlaps the Late Bronze Age (1550–1200 BCE) and the early Iron Age I (1200–900 BCE). During the New Kingdom, Egyptian kings became known by the title 'Pharaoh', which meant 'the Great House'.

Although the family comprising the 18th Dynasty was from Thebes, it moved its capital to Memphis, from where the dynasty ruled from about 1550 to roughly 1300 or so. (Precise dates for this period of Egypt's history are not yet possible, so the dates given in any history book are subject to a few years' margin of error.) The 18th Dynasty came to an end not because Egypt weakened, but because male heirs died out, leaving power in the hands of leading generals and paving the way for transition to a new royal family, the 19th Dynasty, which ruled for just over a century. At that time a new city, Per-Ramesses, was built near the ruins of Avaris in the Delta, which remained the prominent northern center of New Kingdom power to the end of the 20th Dynasty.

From a Canaanite's perspective, the 18th, 19th and early-20th Dynasties represent a single period of uninterrupted Egyptian imperial presence and dominance in Syria-Palestine. Although some historians claim that the 19th Dynasty's hold on Palestine weakened as the dynasty went into decline, evidence suggests otherwise. Palestine remained in the firm grasp of Egyptian authority as the 19th Dynasty made its transition to the early-20th Dynasty at the start of the Iron Age I (1200 BCE). Thus, Canaan was an Egyptian province from the start of the Late Bronze Age (1550 BCE), until the first several generations of the Iron Age I (1135 BCE), give or take a decade.

It is not necessary to go into every aspect of Egyptian politics during this period, but the names of a few New Kingdom rulers should be committed to memory, since these monarchs played a crucial rule in Palestine's experiences, and their reigns provide chronological structure to the Late Bronze Age. The 18th Dynasty went through four phases:

| *Nubian Wars* | *Hurrian Wars* | *Peace of Egypt* | *Transitional Kings* |
|---|---|---|---|
| Late-sixteenth and early-fifteenth Centuries | Early to mid-fifteenth Century | Late-fifteenth to mid-fourteenth Century | Late-fourteenth Century |
| Four Kings, then Queen Hatshepsut (Regent for Thutmoses III) | Thutmoses III Amenophis II | Thutmoses IV Amenophis III Akhenaten | Tutankhamun Ay Horemheb Ramesses I |

Figure 12. *Four Phases of the 18th Dynasty.*

This was followed by over a century under the 19th (and early-20th) Dynasty, whose primary kings and events included:

| *Hittite Wars* | *Peace with Hatti* | *Libyan Wars* | *Sea People War* |
|---|---|---|---|
| Early-thirteenth Century | Mid-thirteenth Century | Late-thirteenth Century | Early-twelfth Century |
| Seti I Ramesses II | Ramesses II | Merneptah | Ramesses III (20th Dynasty) |

Figure 13. *The 19th (and early 20th) Dynasty.*

(Note that the name of Ramesses II appears in two columns. This king ruled for two-thirds of a century. Ramesses III of the 20th Dynasty is mentioned because of his significance, though full discussion of his deeds will appear in the next chapter.)

### Kadesh, Mitanni and the Hurrians

The Hurrians were located in northern Mesopotamia and gradually spread westward into northern Syria. They are identified by their language, which is not related to the Semitic languages common to the region. Culturally, however, they seem to have differed little from the other Semitic peoples of Mesopotamia and Canaan. By the close of the Middle Bronze Age (2000–1550 BCE), they had established political entities in Syria and had begun to dominate northern Palestine as well. Without doubt, they are responsible for some of the military destruction that marks the close of Palestine's Middle Bronze Age. Two of the most significant Hurrian centers were Kadesh on the middle Orontes River and the larger, more powerful Mitanni in northern Mesopotamia. (Archaeologists have not yet located the capital city of Mitanni.) When Thutmoses III entered the Palestinian theater of war, his first enemies were the King of Kadesh and some of his allies. After knocking out that resistance, he engaged Mitanni directly. These wars took place in the fifteenth century BCE. Within a few generations, however, the Hittites became involved as well.

### Hatti and the Hittites

Anatolia (modern Turkey) was known as Hatti-land during the Late Bronze Age (1550–1200 BCE). The Hittites are identified by their distinct language and several cultural differences from the peoples to their south. They achieved power during the later Middle Bronze era, and remained a major political force in the ancient Near East until about 1200 BCE. During the Late Bronze Age, Hatti's power gradually increased. By the mid-fourteenth century, a Hittite king was able to attack and dismantle much of Mitanni. From that time, Hatti became Egypt's primary rival in Syria.

Thus it was that three major powers shared a single goal, the domination of Syria-Palestine: Egyptians, Hurrians and Hittites. A closer look at the events of this period will put into perspective the fate of Canaan during the Late Bronze era.

### The Wars of Empire (Sixteenth–Thirteenth Centuries BCE)

#### Nubian Wars (Late-Sixteenth–Early-Fifteenth Centuries BCE)

The late-sixteenth century saw a great deal of Egyptian military activity in Nubia (modern Sudan). As mentioned in the previous chapter, Nubia had much to offer an ambitious Egyptian monarch, and the early 18th Dynasty kings were eager to seize the region. Not only did Nubia possess cattle and humans that the Egyptians wanted to exploit, but also its land was rich in copper and gold. In addition, Nubia was the land bridge to trade with sub-Saharan Africa, which offered exotic animals and animal skins, ivory and other luxury goods. Each of the early-18th Dynasty kings campaigned in Nubia. By the time that Queen Hatshepsut ruled as regent for the child Thutmoses III, Egypt was gaining control over most of it.

Figure 14. *Tomb of Hatshepsut. Carved into the cliffs not far from Egypt's Nile river, this grand monument commemmorates Queen Hatshepsut, of the 18th Dynasty. The splendid proportions and superb craftsmanship are lasting testimonies to the New Kingdom's imperial might.*

Canaan was not ignored by the early-18th Dynasty. A few of these monarchs made expeditions there as well. As a matter of fact, Thutmoses I, father of Hatshepsut, had pushed his army all the way to the banks of the Euphrates River. These were, however, military raids, not conquests. Egyptian interest in the region as a possession evolved only after significant portions of Nubia had been 'pacified' (to use the rhetoric of the Egyptian kings). The adult Thutmoses III, who became sole ruler very early in the fifteenth century after the death of Queen Hatshepsut, began the conquest of Canaan in earnest. His opponents were the Hurrians who were dominating Syria and northern Palestine at that time.

*Hurrian Wars (Early- to Mid-Fifteenth Century BCE)*
Thutmoses III sought to push Egypt's border beyond the Euphrates River. It is possible that he was motivated by a desire for vengeance against the Semitic Hyksos who had been driven out almost a century earlier, and who had been, from a proud Egyptian's perspective, foreigners unworthy of the success they had achieved in the Egyptian

Delta. A more significant (and likely) motivation was the growing presence and power of Hurrians on the border of Egypt, which no doubt raised the spectre of an eventual invasion of the Delta. To prevent that possibility, Thutmoses III struck first.

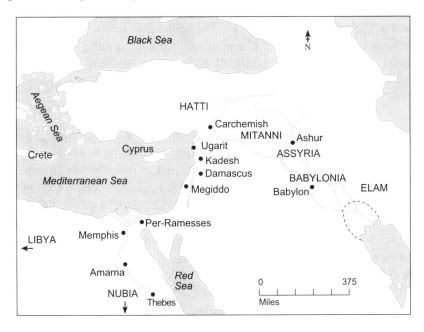

Figure 15. *The Ancient Near East during the Late Bronze Age.*

In all, Thutmoses III campaigned 17 times in this region, and he reappeared regularly to collect taxes. A crucial battle was the seven-month siege and conquest of Megiddo in the Jezreel Valley. The conquest of that strategically located city brought under Egyptian control the primary traveler's route through Canaan (northward up the coast, across the Mount Carmel foothills, through the Jezreel, and on toward either Damascus or Kadesh). This rendered the politically fragmented region of Canaan unable to resist Egypt, and drove the Hurrians northward, back toward their center of power in Syria. Thutmoses III pressed on, taking the coastal regions and then moving on the city of Kadesh, which he captured. He soon found himself facing the larger and more formidable Mitanni in northern Mesopotamia.

Thutmoses III was never able to defeat Mitanni fully, but he pushed well into Mitannian territory, reaching the banks of the Euphrates River near Carchemish. Unlike his grandfather, Thutmoses III intended to make Egyptian dominance over northern Syria permanent. Mitanni thought otherwise, and the war continued into the reign of Amenophis II. Gradually, a stalemate began to emerge, and both sides were happy to begin negotiating a peace. The marriage of a princess from Mitanni to the Egyptian heir Thutmoses IV sealed the treaty of friendship between these two powers. The border between Egypt and Mitanni was drawn roughly from a city called Ugarit on the northern Syrian coast, southeast toward the city of Damascus. Northeast of this line was Hurrian domain, southwest of it was Egyptian.

*The Peace of Egypt (Late-Fifteenth to Mid-Fourteenth Century BCE)*
The next hundred or so years are sometimes called the Peace of Egypt. From Egypt's point of view, it was just that, a peaceful era in which Canaan was a rich source of tax revenue. From the perspective of a Canaanite, however, the period was not very peaceful at all. For one thing, any hint of revolt in Canaan was crushed ruthlessly. Also, Egypt required slaves and several kings deported a significant percentage of the Palestinian population for that purpose. By the time of Amenophis III and Akhenaten (early to mid-fourteenth century BCE), Canaan had been transformed radically by Egyptian imperial rule.

In light of Egyptian imperial policies, it is not surprising that archaeologists have noted a marked population decrease in Palestine during this era. The Central Hills were all but abandoned, and most lowland communities were much smaller than they had been prior to this time. In some cases, the Egyptians seem to have relocated communities to serve Egyptian strategic interests.[1] In other cases, entire communities simply disappeared. Middle Bronze Palestine had once been home to some 140,000 people, but that number decreased to fewer than 70,000 by the middle of the Late Bronze Age.

Canaanites were not the only ones who found the Peace of Egypt less than peaceful; this was not a time of peace for Mitanni either. Thutmoses III's military success was only part of the reason why Mitanni had made peace with Egypt. The other reason was Hatti. Mitanni had been fighting two wars, against Hatti as well as Egypt. As any military strategist knows, a two-front war is a formula for failure. Mitanni chose to make peace and cede land to the more distant enemy, Egypt, in the hope of concentrating all its effort to defeat the near neighbor, Hatti. The hope was not realized. By the mid-fourteenth century BCE, a Hittite king invaded and dismantled Mitanni, leaving it a shell of its former self.

*Hittite Wars (Early-Thirteenth Century BCE)*

By the mid-fourteenth century, there were but two major powers, one holding Syria-Palestine as a series of Egyptian provinces, the other coveting that land from the vantage of its northern border. Through a series of complex diplomatic and military maneuvers, Hatti succeeded in bringing significant portions of northern Syria under its power. As Egyptian provinces in this region entered treaty alliances with Hatti, Egypt reacted. A treaty of this kind required the province in question to renounce its fealty to Egypt and pledge allegiance to Hatti instead. For the Egyptian kings of the late-18th Dynasty, that meant war. The war outlasted the dynasty, however. There came a point when male heirs were no longer available, and the surviving queen considered several options, including a peace treaty with Hatti that might have placed a Hittite on Egypt's throne. This did not materialize; instead a series of generals served as interim kings of Egypt, and a transition was made to the 19th Dynasty.

The kings of the early-19th Dynasty opposed Hatti vigorously, and this era marks the peak of the Hittite wars. This did not mean that military campaigns were conducted year on year. In fact, there were sporadic and sometimes extensive periods of quiet. But Egypt never accepted the loss of northern Syria and continued to attack Hittite vassal states in that area.

A particularly significant battle took place when King Ramesses II attempted to capture Kadesh, which was by then a Hittite enclave. His army was lured into a trap and severely beaten by a clever Hittite king. Modern historians sometimes represent this battle as a stalemate in which neither side won or lost. However, the battle was a disaster for Ramesses II, who can certainly be described as the loser. The Egyptian king never reached the walls of Kadesh, lost half his army, and faced, as a result of this defeat, sporadic rebellion throughout southern Syria and Palestine. Returning to Egypt, Ramesses II created monuments to himself in which he presented his loss as though it were a great victory. Then he quickly and ruthlessly quelled the unrest in Canaan. Also, during this period Ramesses II built near the ruin of a previously robust city in the Egyptian Delta, Avaris, and named it Per-Ramesses, 'the City of Ramesses'. This gave the kings of Egypt a nearby center from which to oversee their holdings in Canaan.

*Peace with Hatti and the Libyan Wars (Mid- to Late-Thirteenth Century BCE)*

Although Hatti had the military advantage after the Battle of Kadesh, internal strife weakened the regime. Moreover, Hatti was now facing a two-front war. The Assyrians had begun to fill the vacuum left by the demise of Mitanni, and were threatening Hatti from northern Mesopotamia. For these reasons, a Hittite king offered to make peace with Ramesses II, who accepted due to other military pressures. In Egypt, the western border was beginning to experience pressure from Libyans. The Libyan problem and the unrest in Canaan were sufficient challenges, so Ramesses II wanted to avoid more warfare with Hatti. The two kingdoms buried their differences, entered into a deep bond of friendship and became trade partners. Most of southern Syria and all of Palestine remained, by this agreement, part of imperial Egypt.

Pressure from the Libyans only increased as the long reign of Ramesses II came to an end. For his successor, Merneptah, the Libyan war became the most pressing issue. Merneptah was able to stem the tide of incoming Libyans during his lifetime (late-thirteenth century BCE). But over the next several centuries, that influx would continue to such an extent that Libyans even became pharaohs by the tenth century BCE (the 22nd and 23rd Dynasties).

During Merneptah's reign other foreign groups made their way into Egypt and served as mercenary soldiers in both the Libyan and Egyptian armies. Modern historians call them 'Sea Peoples', but this was not the name they gave themselves. They were a mix of groups with names like Sheklesh and Sherden. They came from various places, mostly from the the Aegean area (Greece, western Anatolia, Crete, Cyprus). Within a generation or two of Merneptah these groups would include a people called Peleset. In Hebrew, that group was called Philistine. They were to become a central player in the sweeping changes that mark the opening years of the Iron Age I (1200–900 BCE), to be discussed in the next chapter.

Syria-Palestine saw almost continual warfare during the Late Bronze Age. The three major foreign powers met and fought one another there. Egyptian troops marched through and despoiled the region regularly, putting down rebellion and collecting taxes. And much of Palestine was depopulated, the people carried away to serve as slaves in various Egyptian cities. Seen through the eyes of a Canaanite in this period, the world was harsh and often unkind.

*Daily Life in the Late Bronze Age (1550–1200 BCE)*

The two primary sources for a historical narrative during this period—archaeological and epigraphic—both give us wonderful insights into daily life in Palestine and Egypt. An archaeologist surveying settlement patterns in Palestine is struck by the impact that Egypt had on the region. Generally, this was a period of impoverishment, no doubt due to Egyptian taxation. The small amount of wealth clustered into the larger urban centers, where Egypt's local governors and their troops resided. The governors lived well, since the appearance of splendor was an essential ingredient in the regime's control of the Canaanite population. Conspicuous wealth creates prestige and sets the local leadership apart from the commoners. Depending upon the period, there were about 15 to 20 major Syro-Palestinian cities under Egyptian control during these centuries. Each ruled its immediate environs on behalf of Egypt.

Epigraphers are fortunate to have discovered a second source for writing history in this period, an Egyptian royal archive. The 18th Dynasty King Akhenaten was a religious maverick who built a new capital city with a name that sounds quite similar to the king's name, Akhetaten. His city survived only as long as he did. After his death, Akhetaten was abandoned by Akhenaten's successors. The royal archive was abandoned as well, and remained, untouched, in the desert sands until modern times, when it was discovered. As a result, we can read Akhenaten's mail. He received diplomatic and administrative epistles from Canaan, Hatti, Mitanni, Assyria and Babylon. These writings shed a great deal of light on daily life in this era. Usually, they are called the Amarna Archives, since Amarna is the modern name of the ancient city Akhetaten.

Pharaoh Akhenaten has been the focus of attention for many people because of his religious innovations. To some extent, however, this attention has distorted the significance attached to this king's ideas. Nevertheless, he was a remarkable man. He began life as Amenophis IV, but chose to abandon the god Amun, after whom he had been named. Instead, he worshiped the sun-disk, called the Aten. That is why he changed his name to Akhenaten, which means 'the one who is effective on behalf of the Aten'. This is another example of a theophoric name, a name that includes a divine being, as discussed in Chapter 3.

The Aten was the only god that Akhenaten acknowledged. All other Egyptian gods were shunted aside. This manifestation of monotheism has led some historians (and a great many nonhistorians) to the erroneous conclusion that Israelite monotheism was influenced by Akhenaten. Although there is some evidence to suggest that Egyptian piety had a minimal impact on the Bible (especially in Ps. 104 and Prov. 22–24), there is no justification for making a direct link between Akhenaten's religion and biblical religion. Akhenaten and his religion died centuries before the first words of the Bible were written. At best, the religion of Akhenaten continued to influence the cultural milieu that later gave rise to the Bible. The Bible manifests a religious sensibility that it shares with Akhenaten and many others (an issue that will be discussed in Chapter 9).

For Akhenaten the sun-disk was the exclusive source of all light and goodness. Although this idea can be considered monotheistic, it was not an entirely pure monotheism. Akhenaten was himself the incarnation of the Aten's light and goodness, the one who was effective on behalf of the Aten. Deity was not as singular as it seems at first glance, since it was shared with the human king. In this sense, the seemingly unconventional religious belief of Akhenaten was not very new at all. As in traditional Egyptian religion, the king of Egypt remained a god, the source of *ma'at* for his people. The outward form of the religion was new, but the inner logic of it had not changed.

Some historians believe that most Egyptians hated the new religion, despised Akhenaten, and were eager to repudiate and bury his religion the moment he died. This is possible. However, another historical hypothesis is just as likely. It would seem, from the evidence, that no one protested against the religious innovations of this king. The construction of his new city, which was huge, required a massive cooperative effort, and that effort seems to have gone smoothly. The temples of Egypt did not close, they simply directed their activities toward a new manifestation of the divine. However, there is evidence to suggest that plague struck the ancient world at this time. Akhenaten's own family seems to have suffered high death rates, and plague may have killed the king himself. After the king's death, therefore, it is possible that the coincidence of plague was interpreted to be divine displeasure at the religious changes. For that reason, Egypt's subsequent kings reverted to the more traditional version of the Nile's religious culture.[2] Whatever the reason for the abandonment of the short-lived religion, the simultaneous abandonment of the new capital city has resulted in a perfect time capsule just waiting for the modern archaeologist's spade.

While the sun-disk Aten shone over Amarna, Pharaoh's subjects in Canaan bowed 'seven times and seven times' before their god, their sun, the king of Egypt. That courtly language was typical not only when the Aten was the god of Egypt, but before and after Akhenaten's reign as well. Canaan was very much a part of the Egyptian domain, and Pharaoh was Palestine's ultimate god and king. On a more local level, there was a much more mundane governmental bureaucracy, a very human one.

Each Canaanite city-state was governed by a Canaanite mayor who had been selected by Pharaoh.[3] Usually, this man had been raised and educated at Pharaoh's court in Egypt, so that he was thoroughly Egyptianized and loyal to his lord. In turn, the mayor sent his sons to Egypt for their education, and the sons' residency with Pharaoh also served to keep the mayor in line, lest anything 'unpleasant' befall his children.

The mayor ruled with his own local militia, and sought royal Egyptian troops as need arose. The local militia was a kind of feudal aristocracy, possessing estates associated with the city-state, and supplying military duty in return. The population of Palestine was not large, as we have seen, so the warriors were not many. Since they were well-trained, it was not difficult to keep the peasantry in line. When a mayor requested additional troops from Pharaoh, he usually desired 100 men or fewer.

Most of these city-states were in the lowlands of Canaan, along the coast and in the Jezreel and Jordan Valleys. The Cisjordan Highlands were only very sparsely populated, and few lived in Transjordan. This is not surprising since the population of Palestine was meager, and the best agricultural land was in the valleys and foothills. What little population had been living in the highlands during the Middle Bronze Age had disappeared, probably absorbed into the valleys as Middle Bronze society collapsed. The Egyptian government maintained two city-states in the Central Hills, at Shechem and Jerusalem. These seats of Egyptian presence governed the very small number of people who lived in the tiny highland villages, but primarily they were there so that the hills would not be overrun with bandits or other undesirables. Likewise, Hazor maintained control over the Galilean Hills (until it was destroyed, apparently by Ramesses II, for rebellion).

A Canaanite mayor was expected to serve Pharaoh in three ways:

with troops, taxes and hospitality. His troops were at the command of the Egyptian army and could be called up for royal service if need arose. A considerable part of his city-state's surplus produce, such as grain, oil, and wine, was sent to Egypt as tax payments. The mayor also paid taxes in other goods. For example, Palestine was a land bridge for merchants, and many of the imported goods were sent directly to Egypt. These might include glass, silver, gemstones, copper, timber and incense. The Canaanite mayor was expected, above all, to provide hospitality to any Egyptian dignitaries or troops sent by Pharaoh. This was a crucial aspect of the mayor's role, and he was scrupulous in his observance of it. Pharaoh often sent dignitaries. Some were tax collectors, others military police sent on general or specific missions. All needed to be fed and sheltered, and that was the mayor's duty.

Generally speaking, the mayors of the city-states did not like each other. As a matter of fact, they competed with each other, often to the point of military action. One mayor would try to annex the land of another, invade his city, or even kill him. The Amarna archive is full of letters sent by a mayor complaining, often bitterly, about the mistreatment he has suffered at the hand of a neighbor. In some cases, the competition seems to have decayed into temporary chaos and murder. Pharaoh rarely got excited by such conflicts—so long as taxes were paid and Egypt's peace maintained, the lives of a few Canaanites were not much concern to him. The constant squabbling among these mayors was, from Pharaoh's perspective, quite a good thing—while the mayors were at each other's throats, they were not likely to organize into an anti-Egyptian coalition. When matters got out of hand, Pharaoh would send troops and restore order. Often, however, he permitted the locals to fight it out and settle the matter for themselves.

The Canaanite mayors walked a tightrope between two constituencies. On the one hand, if they seemed too subservient to the Egyptian Pharaoh, they risked losing the confidence of the people they governed. Taxes were high and the Egyptians unpopular. The local mayor needed to distance himself from the source of that resentment. On the other hand, the mayor could not afford to cross the Egyptian administration. His life depended upon subservience to Pharaoh. This give and take was part of a mayor's everyday reality. Some might play the game successfully, others might die at the hands of a violent mob, or get dragged off to face charges of disloyalty in Egypt.

This policy of indirect rule maintained by the 18th Dynasty changed somewhat under the 19th Dynasty. As Hatti strengthened its hold over northern Syria, the Egyptians, in self-defense, decided to become more directly involved in their imperial domains. Egyptian garrisons were enlarged and new ones created. More direct governance of the population resulted. Taxes increased as well. On occasion, a Pharaoh was required to put down the predictable uprisings that this policy fostered—he exercised his duty brutally. The land and people of Canaan were, from his perspective, a resource to be exploited and a military buffer against Hatti, nothing more.

This description has concentrated on the aristocracy of Canaan—but aristocrats comprised perhaps only five or 10 per cent of the population. Unfortunately, it is only the upper class that we are able to know intimately through the writings that have survived, since only the upper class were engaged with writing. Nevertheless, we also get a few glimpses of commoners in the texts and in the material culture recovered archaeologically.

Below the aristocracy, there were two classes of Canaanite peasantry, artisans and peasants. The artisans were skilled laborers who created all manner of crafts, including pottery, textiles and metal objects. They seem to have been employed directly by the aristocrats in a redistributive economy (see p. 96 for that term). Below them were the farmers, who were by far the largest element of the population. They did not own their land during the Late Bronze Age, but were, in essence, serfs who were required to work the land on behalf of the upper classes, keeping some of the produce as payment. In other words, the entire economic structure of the provincial city-states was in the hands of the elite class.

Just beyond the edge of 'polite' society were two other groups, the *shasu* and the *'apiru*. The *shasu*, a term meaning 'foot wanderers', were pastoralists. As always, pastoralists lived in close relation to the farmers, providing and receiving goods as part of an economic relationship (see the discussion on pp. 91-92). In the Egyptian texts of the New Kingdom era, these *shasu* can turn up in any number of locations, from Syria to the Negev. Sometimes they were hostile and required Egyptian 'pacification'. In time (unless it is only an accident of documentation), the *shasu* seem to have become associated primarily with the southern fringe of Palestine, particularly the area the Bible would later call Edom, southeast of the Dead Sea. The later New Kingdom documents usually place the *shasu* exclusively in that region.

One group of *shasu* has intrigued historians particularly. During the fifteenth century BCE, a place in Edom was called Yahu in the land of *shasu*. Yahu is a shortened form of the divine name Yahweh, a kind of nickname. It was not uncommon for places to be named after the god worshiped in the area. Apparently, there were some Yahweh worshipers living on the southern edges of Canaan in the Late Bronze Age.

The Bible calls its god Yahweh and places the wandering Israelites in southern Edom as part of the Exodus story, so the presence of Yahweh-worshiping *shasu* in that very place has given rise to much speculation. Perhaps the Bible has preserved the memory of an actual group of Israelites wandering on the edges of the Promised Land. This is indeed possible, though the image of these people should not be romanticized. For one thing, the *shasu* did not originate in Egypt, so they could not have been escaping slaves, as in the biblical story. Moreover, the Bible tells of 600,000 able-bodied men, not to mention women and children, marching through the desert (see Exod. 12.37-38 and Num. 1), but there were fewer than 70,000 people living in all of Palestine at this time, and the *shasu* were but a few pastoralists living on the fringe of that society. Therefore, if the Bible has preserved an accurate memory of the earliest known Israelites, it has also 'improved' the narrative about them by placing these people into the ancient equivalent of a modern action-adventure story.

Another reason for caution is that not all ancient worshipers of Yahweh were Israelites. There is no necessary connection between the people called Israel and a god whose personal name is Yahweh. Even the Bible preserves a tradition in which the people of Israel had not always worshiped their god by that name. Exodus 6.3 states that the god of Abraham, Isaac and Jacob had been El Shaddai (often translated 'God Almighty' in English versions), but that, beginning with Moses, this same god was revealed to have the name Yahweh (usually rendered 'the LORD' in English versions). A story of this kind is common among religious groups that have combined two or more gods into a single entity. The names of each original god become the multiple names of the one god. In this case, Exod. 6.3 demonstrates that biblical writers were aware of a combination of gods in their community's past, and that the Yahweh element in this deity was a latecomer to the Israelite religion.

The word 'Israel' is a theophoric name, *yisra-'el*, and as such, it demonstrates that early Israelites did not worship Yahweh. Scholars disagree on the original meaning of this archaic sentence, which could be rendered 'El strives' or 'El is a just one'.[4] In any case, the divine element in Israel is El, not Yahu or Yahweh. If the name had been Yahwistic rather than Elistic, it would have been written *yisra-yahu*, and in English, Israiah. So the biblical memory that Israel's god was originally El Shaddai (literally 'El of the mountain' or perhaps 'El of the fields') is very accurate. He was El Shaddai before he became Yahweh or Yahu. But this reality compels us to conclude that the *shasu* of the land of Yahu might or might not have been related to early Israel, who, as a people, may or may not have been worshiping a god called Yahweh or Yahu during the Late Bronze Age.

Nevertheless, most historians believe there might be a connection, however slight, between the *shasu* of Yahu and the biblical Yahweh. The Bible preserves a tradition that Yahweh used to 'live' in the south, in the land of Edom, sometimes called Seir or Teman. Apparently, in a tradition much older than the Exodus story, the mountain of god, which was called Mount Sinai (or sometimes Mount Paran, but not yet Horeb), would have been in Edom or further south, in what is now Saudi Arabia. Certain passages of poetry, one of which has been described by historical linguists as among the oldest writings to survive in the Hebrew Bible (see pp. 54-55), describe Yahweh marching from this southern home into Canaan. Thus, Judg. 5.4-5 reads:

> O Yahweh, when you came forth from Seir,
> When you marched from the fields of Edom,
> The land trembled,
> Indeed, the sky poured down;
> Yes, the clouds poured out their water;
> The mountains melted before Yahweh,
> The One of Sinai;
> From before Yahweh, the god of Israel.

Other examples of this tradition can be seen in Hab. 3.3 and Deut. 33.2. With these passages in mind, many historians believe that the Yahwistic portion of the Israelite religious tradition had its origins in Edom. Opinions are divided as to how that tradition made its way north into the Jerusalemite Bible. This issue will be discussed in greater detail in later chapters.

In addition to *shasu*, there were *'apiru* in Late Bronze Canaan. (The word is sometimes written in English letters *habiru*. This is because certain ancient letters have no precise equivalent in English letters, so they can be rendered in several ways, each of which is accurate.) The *'apiru* were, in a sense, an outlaw group. Or perhaps it would be more accurate to say that anyone deemed to be outside the law was labeled an *'apiru*. Being called an *'apiru* was not a compliment. The word literally means 'dust-maker' and seems to have designated a person who would 'make tracks' at a moment's notice, if necessary. Often, *'apiru* meant 'bandits'. In many other cases, *'apiru* were unskilled laborers who had come to a given place as refugees and had been put to work at jobs no one else wanted to do. Frequently, a governor of one of the city-states would accuse the governor of another city-state of rebelling against Pharaoh and of entering into conspiracy with the *'apiru*. In this situation, the term seems to have been nothing more than slander, not a designation of a specific social group.

Like the *shasu* of Yahu, the word *'apiru* has intrigued many historians because of a possible connection to the Bible. Linguistically, it is possible to connect this Bronze Age word with the later Iron Age Hebrew word *'ibri*, meaning 'Hebrew'. Thus, for a time, some scholars had thought that the Late Bronze Age *'apiru* were none other than the early biblical Hebrews, or Israelites. If there is a connection, however, it is indirect at best. It is now known that *'apiru* was a common derogatory term that had no ethnic connotations at all. If the early Israelites were called *'apiru* by others, they were not the only ones called that, nor would they have called themselves *'apiru*. Thus, if the biblical documents mentioning *'ibri* are connected in some way to Bronze Age *'apiru*, it would represent an instance in which an originally non-ethnic slang term has been assimilated at a later date by a group who have come to see in it an ethnic self-designation. (Such situations are known from anthropological research.)

If these possible connections to an ancient people called Israel are disappointing, there remains one other document from the Late Bronze Age that gives us a glimpse, however fleeting, of the earliest known Israelites. That is the famous Merneptah Stela.

### 'Israel' on the Merneptah Stela

In a temple dedicated to Pharaoh Merneptah at Thebes, a huge stone monument was discovered that recounts the glorious deeds of this Egyptian king. The Merneptah Stela deals primarily with the king's war against the Libyans toward the end of the thirteenth century BCE.

However, an appendix to the main narrative recounts a military campaign that Merneptah conducted in Canaan. That brief passage has become justly famous, for it is *the only ancient Egyptian text that mentions Israel*. Merneptah's boast reads:

> The princes are prostrate, saying: 'Mercy!'
> Not one raises his head among the Nine Bows.
>
> Desolation is for Tehenu; Hatti is pacified;
> Plundered is the Canaan with every evil;
>
> Carried off is Ashkelon; seized upon is Gezer;
> Yanoam is made as that which does not exist;
> Israel is laid waste, his seed is not;
>
> Hurru is become a widow for Egypt!
> All lands together, they are pacified;
> Everyone who was restless, he has been bound...[5]

The rhetoric of this inscription is the usual boastfulness that one expects from a proud king of mighty Egypt. In fact, it is the language of cliché. Nine Bows is Egyptian slang for 'all the enemies everywhere'. Tehenu was the ancient name of modern Libya. Hatti is, of course, ancient Anatolia (modern Turkey). Canaan is mentioned twice since Hurru is an alternate name for the same territory, Palestine. So Merneptah is claiming to have subdued all the enemies to the west and the northeast of Egypt's Delta region: Libya, Anatolia, Palestine. In other words, the poem consists of sweeping generalizations quite typical of pharaonic bluster, the kind of text that makes it all but impossible to determine what events gave rise to the hyperbole.

As part of this boast, Merneptah singles out four enemies whom he has subdued. In these three lines we seem to be on the level of more concrete events. The 19th Dynasty pursued a policy of direct intervention in Canaanite affairs. All four of Merneptah's enemies in this passage were in Canaan. First is the city of Ashkelon on the southern coast. A generation or two after Merneptah, Ashkelon would become a Philistine city, but during his lifetime (the final decades of the Late Bronze Age), it was simply a Canaanite city. Gezer is near Ashkelon, on the edge of the Shephelah. Yanoam is a city whose precise location is disputed, but was near the Galilee Lake. All three of these places have been written by the ancient Egyptian scribe with a particle (a part of Egyptian hieroglyphic grammar) that identifies them as 'cities'.

The fourth enemy in this list is not designated a city, but carries the particle designating a 'people' or 'ethnic group'. The group is called

Israel. This people, apparently, lived in the vicinity of Ashkelon, Gezer and Yanoam, thus, perhaps the Cisjordan Highlands or the Jezreel Valley. The latter is more likely since, from archaeological surveys, it would seem that very few people were living in the hills of Canaan. It is not impossible that Merneptah did battle with the few people who were living in the hills at that time. It would have been a short and one-sided battle! I suspect, however, that Israel was part of the lowland population. (I will discuss the location of Merneptah's Israel in much greater detail in the next chapter.)

Two additional points are raised by this enigmatic mention of a people called Israel. First, Merneptah claims to have utterly annihilated these people. Their seed is no more, a common ancient cliché. Did he really wipe out Israel? In the ancient world, a king often claimed to have annihilated an enemy, yet the enemy in question curiously appears again in later inscriptions! It was a boast, but not necessarily a reality. In this instance, if Merneptah really did annihilate his enemy, this Israel could have had nothing to do with biblical Israel, since biblical Israel appears only after the time of Merneptah. On the other hand, since the boast of annihilation is probably just a boast and nothing more, there is every reason to believe that the Israel mentioned by Merneptah is related in some way to the biblical Israel. Merneptah defeated them in battle, perhaps killing a great many, but Israel survived.

This thought leads to a second interesting point: biblical writers never mention Merneptah or a battle with an Egyptian king. As a matter of fact, biblical writers appear to have been utterly ignorant of the fact that an Egyptian empire ever existed in Palestine. There is no hint of such an empire in any of the stories that, according to biblical chronology, would have taken place during the Late Bronze Age (e.g. the books of Exodus and Joshua). Judges 5 remembers a battle in the Jezreel Valley, and most scholars believe that its archaic language indicates that the poem is very ancient. Moreover, the battle that is narrated was already an ancient battle when the poem was composed, since Judg. 5.6 places the event in the days of hoary antiquity, when an obscure figure with a Bronze Age military title, 'son of [the warrior-goddess] Anat', was supposed to have been alive (compare Judg. 3.31; the Bible knows nothing else about this legendary figure with the poly-theistic title). But the battle that is narrated in Judges 5 involves local Canaanite opponents; Judges 4, which is a much later prose revision of the poem's tale, also associates the battle with Canaanites, not Egyptians.[6] Indeed, there is no biblical memory of a military conflict with Egypt that could correspond to this event.

Several conclusions can be drawn from these observations. First, even the oldest portions of the Bible were composed after the Late Bronze era. The Bible was composed long enough after that time for scribes of Israel to have forgotten that Egypt once ruled their land. In Chapter 2, it was noted that historians arrived at the same conclusion on linguistic grounds: with few exceptions, the entire Bible was composed during the Iron Age II, the Babylonian, and the Persian periods (from about 900 to 323 BCE). The linguistic observations are compatible with the Bible's content. The Bible is younger than the Bronze Age.

A second conclusion follows logically from the first: the people of Israel had existed in Palestine for centuries before they constructed the religious traditions, poetry and narratives that the Bible contains. Although the Bible implies that a god called Yahweh chose Abraham hundreds of years before the Iron Age (Gen. 12), the reality is that a folk-tale about a man named Abraham was committed to writing for the first time only during the Iron Age II (or later), centuries after the people of Israel had come into existence as an identifiable ethnic group and were living in the land of Canaan. In this respect, the biblical authors were representative of their era. A few ancient people belonged to a highly literate stratum of society that enabled an individual to trace his or her ancestry through many generations. Even in this situation, the genealogy could be altered from time to time to accommodate changes in current status (this was discussed in Chapter 1). The overwhelming majority of ancient people did not live among the elite class, and even those who did rarely bothered to trace their family's past beyond a few generations. Almost all, therefore, lived in a community where the only tales of the past were folk-tales—stories like those about Abraham in Genesis 12–25.

These observations further clarify the Bible's genre, a topic discussed in Chapter 3. As we have seen, the writers of the Bible were aware that many of their sources were folk-tales, and they created an artificial chronology with which to link those folk traditions sequentially. Although it is unlikely that these ancient scribes would have composed something like ancient Greek *historia* even if they had been aware of the genre, we can now see why it was not possible for them to write an accurate form of *historia* even if they had desired to do so. The Bible was assembled by scribes who had no access to sources for the earliest history of their own people. They certainly did not have access to sources about a battle with Merneptah. In all probability, they were fully aware that they had little hope of ever gaining access to those sources, and they did not care.

It need not surprise us that Israel's biblical authors lacked accurate memories of, or concern about, their own people's past. Social anthropologists have noted that events of the past, even major events, tend to be forgotten unless they serve a useful social function in the community's storytelling process. For example, it is probable that you know next to nothing about the lives of your great-grandparents. Since life expectancy in our time is much longer than in ancient times, it is possible that you met members of that generation. Also, since modern Westerners take a greater interest in the past than did the majority of ancient people, you might have access to a store of information about your great-grandparents' lives that is unusually comprehensive. Yet, if you are typical of our culture, what little you do know of that generation represents isolated fragments, some very accurate, a few confused or even wholly spurious. The sum of those fragments will not provide the necessary ingredients for an accurate *historia*. Compound this problem when thinking of an ancient, predominantly illiterate, culture, which had no previous tradition of history writing, and the nature of the Bible's genre becomes clear.

A war with King Merneptah may have been a traumatic and devastating event. But, after four or five generations of oral transmission, the memory of that event would have slipped silently away from the collective consciousness of those who descended from its survivors. Such is the nature of oral traditions about a past. It is the best explanation for the otherwise inexplicable failure of the Bible to reflect Merneptah's version of Israel's past.

Merneptah and his Israelite opponents lived at the close of the Late Bronze Age (1550–1200 BCE). The Egyptian empire in Canaan survived into the early years of the Iron Age I (1200–900 BCE). Nevertheless, the demographics of Palestine changed radically after the death of Merneptah, and Egypt's role in those changes gradually diminished. Canaan in the Iron Age I is a different world from Canaan during the Late Bronze Age, and that world is to be explored in the next chapter. First, however, Late Bronze Mesopotamia deserves a brief overview.

### *Mesopotamia in the Late Bronze Age (1550–1200 BCE)*

Except for northern Mesopotamia's Hurrian population, Syria-Palestine had very little interaction with this region during the Late Bronze Age. For the most part, the political events between the two rivers played themselves out in isolation from the center of this book's focus. But that does not mean that Mesopotamia was irrelevant to the story told here. On the contrary, Late Bronze Mesopotamia molded a cultural world that would later have a direct impact on Palestine and especially on Israel. At this point, the discussion can only set the stage for that influence.

As has been mentioned, Middle Bronze Mesopotamia was the scene for a variety of competing city-states. From time to time, one city-state was able to conquer and control neighboring cities, thus carving out an empire. Two of those city-states became particularly powerful, Ashur and Babylon. Throughout the Bronze and Iron Ages, these were never the only two centers of power in Mesopotamia. Groups such as the Elamites played a role in Mesopotamian politics as well. Nevertheless, Ashur and Babylon were among the most significant political centers, so they merit special attention.

During the Late Bronze Age, Ashur (= Assyria) and Babylon again rose to prominence. With the demise of Mitanni around 1350 BCE, Assyrian power expanded considerably. In some periods after that time, Assyria even captured and controlled Babylon to the south. But Babylon's fortunes also grew during the Late Bronze Age. From the early-sixteenth century BCE, a group of kings often called 'Kassites' ruled Babylon, and presided over a period of cultural sophistication the like of which the region had never before seen. Scholars emerged in Babylon who began to gather the literature of many previous generations back to Sumerian times, giving birth to a kind of 'renaissance' enjoyed by the elite classes of Kassite society. Some of the best known Mesopotamian literature was preserved and codified in this era, such as the most common version of the heroic epic *Gilgamesh*. Many historians attribute the early versions of Babylon's famous story of divine creation, called *Enuma Elish*, to the Kassite period (though the epic was revised in later times). The increasing power of Babylon and Assyria had other, more subtle effects as well.

As Ashur and Babylon dominated their respective portions of Mesopotamia, they also began to effect a very gradual cultural change.

Northern cities and regions dominated by Ashur emerged as a territorial state, the Kingdom of Assyria. Likewise, Babylon's regional holdings in southern Mesopotamia came to be the Kingdom of Babylonia.

This was a subtle shift, largely ideological in nature, and not entirely intentional. For the average peasant, it did not result in a national consciousness of the kind we moderns take for granted. No one thought of him- or herself as a 'citizen' of the Assyrian 'nation' or a 'citizen' of the Babylonian 'nation'. Neither citizenship nor nationhood existed. Political allegiance remained a matter of a subject (or 'vassal') pledging fealty to a lord (or 'suzerain'). Nevertheless, the greater political unification—which was not constant, but increasingly prevalent—homogenized religious and cultural traditions in such a way that many people might have perceived themselves to be part of a region rather than just one city-state. In other words, a person's sense of self-identity would not have been quite so localized as it had been in previous generations. 'Just as my king rules over many cities, so also I am a part of that larger community, the people of the king's lands.' This new sense of self-identity, to the extent that it might have emerged, resulted from a shift away from the city-state and towards a larger, territorial state.

An example of this greater sense of regional connectedness can be seen in Babylonia, where there was a reorganization of an ancient New Year's festival resulting in a change of religious emphasis. The festival had been celebrated locally for ages (in the spring, at the start of the new agricultural season), but by the early Iron Age (and perhaps earlier, during the Late Bronze), Babylonia's version celebrated the kingship of Babylon's god, Marduk, over all the gods of the region. During the celebration of the new year, the gods of neighboring cities 'visited' Babylon to pay homage to Marduk, which means that their statues were transported to Babylon for the event, then returned to their original cities.[7] Marduk was viewed as the highest of all the gods, the god of gods.

This great religious festival enhanced Babylon's prestige as a regional power and its god Marduk as a powerful god; similar state-sponsored religious activites promoted the city and the god Ashur in Assyria. Because religion was an essential element in people's lives, it may have resulted in a new, more regionally focused, worldview for the commoners as well. Not coincidentally, this religious celebration also enhanced the king's prestige as the one who has been chosen by an increasingly 'henotheistic' god. The term 'henotheism' is significant. A 'theism' is a belief in one or more gods. *Heno*-theism was a kind of theism common to many parts of the ancient world, a topic to which I now turn.

### Henotheism, Monotheism and Polytheism: Varieties of Royal Theology in the Ancient World

The discussion of Marduk in the previous section gave an example of a royal theology. This was a religion promoted by the state, a religion that served, among other things, to legitimize the rule of the king. In the ancient world, royal theologies were common. Today, one witnesses a similar phenomenon every time a politician invokes the god of the state's most common religion to secure the votes of people who worship that god. In America, for example, politicians frequently invoke the Christian god during their speeches. It is easy to become cynical about this kind of religious expression since it is so easily exploited for political gain. Nevertheless, in the ancient world, many kings who espoused a royal theology actually believed in it as well. From a practical viewpoint, they need not have believed in it so long as their subjects accepted it, and probably a significant number of ancient kings were as impious as are many Bible-thumping politicians in our own day. By the same token, many commoners may have focused on their own family and community gods, taking little note of the royal theology except when it was pressed on their consciousness through state-sponsored events, such as festivals. Nevertheless, royal theologies were common, were frequently accepted by many, and are worthy of serious attention by anyone who seeks to know the people of the ancient world.

In ancient times and even today, any religion in which there are many gods but one all-powerful god who reigns over them is henotheistic religion.[8] Henotheism differs from monotheism and polytheism; yet there is similarity with each. Monotheism is the belief that one, and only one, god exists. Polytheism is any theism in which multiple gods exist, and each displays a degree of power. Since it stands between these extremes, the concept of henotheism can seem confusing, so its relationship to polytheism and monotheism requires some additional comment.

Henotheism is identical to polytheism in one way: both presume the existence of multiple gods. The similarities go beyond that basic observation. Most polytheisms assume that the gods are not of equal power, and that one or a few tend to be more powerful than all others. Likewise, a henotheistic religion assumes that the lesser gods possess a degree of power while at the same time being subservient to the highest of the gods. Thus polytheism and henotheism can seem quite similar indeed, but there is a subtle difference. In henotheism, the highest of the gods is far more powerful than others, and the primary (though not exclusive) focus of the religion is on this one high god. For example, when an ancient Neo-Assyrian king took office, the pageantry surrounding his coronation stressed the supremacy of Ashur, who was king of the gods, and whose decree it was that had permitted the human king to take office. Yet, within this celebration, the other gods were named and their selection of the human king stressed as well. The distinction can seem even more complicated when one examines the way these theisms were practiced in the ancient Near East. In a single society, one person might have experienced a religion polytheistically while another perceived the *same* religion henotheistically. Thus, a king promoted the divine power of Marduk, god of Babylon, over all other gods, but one of the king's subjects could easily have prayed to a 'lesser' god as though that god's power and importance matched or surpassed Marduk's majesty. Henotheism never existed (and never exists) in 'pure' form.

One might think that monotheism is clearly distinct from henotheism, yet this too can be complicated. Ancient henotheists often acclaimed the power of the highest god in such lofty language that they *seem* to deny the very existence of any lesser gods. In some cases, a god might seem to 'absorb' the attributes and names of lesser gods, so that the divine pantheon turns out to be 'manifestations' of the one god. In that case, the modern reader might mistake the passage as the words of an ancient monotheist. In reality, this was only the flattery of a henotheist who was trying to impress his or her god. Rhetorical appearance differs from theological reality. Likewise, a monotheist, modern or ancient, might invoke belief in some lesser supernatural beings (angels or the like), a form of rhetoric that begins to sound very much like henotheism. Just as henotheism never exists in 'pure' form, monotheism rarely exists in 'pure' form.

In spite of all these ambiguities, the distinctions between poly-, heno- and mono- theisms are helpful for recognizing subtle but significant distinctions in the way religion was practiced in ancient times. The henotheist was a polytheist who believed that one god is supremely powerful, and all other gods are subservient to that one high god. As such, ancient henotheism was a religion that stood between poly- and mono- theisms.

Henotheism served a very practical political function: the most powerful among the gods usually had a counterpart on earth, the most powerful among the people. For ancient Babylonia, Marduk's chosen city and its chosen king stood at the center of earthly power. For Assyrian kings, the god Ashur served this function. Ashur was proclaimed to be the true king, and the human king was the god's regent. In other words, in the ancient world, henotheism was a convenient method for imposing a king's rule over subject peoples: one all-powerful god means one all-powerful king as well.

Henotheism was not the exclusive religious means by which ancient kings imposed their power. Any religion could be exploited for that purpose. The so-called 'monotheism' of Akhenaten in Egypt is a good example. It made Akhenaten the 'effective one' on behalf of the only god, the Aten, the only source of power. More traditional Egyptian religion, in which the pharaoh was identified with several of the most powerful manifestations of the Egyptian divine realm (Horus, Re, Osiris), also placed the human king in a supreme position, but did so within a polytheistic religion.

Nevertheless, for an ambitious ancient king, henotheism had certain logical advantages over other religious strategies. Unlike monotheism, henotheism saved room for lesser gods and lesser powers. This permitted the gods of popular piety a place in the divine realm, which could be very satisfying for the king's subjects. At the same time, of course, all these popular gods were subject to the supreme god, just as the humans who worshiped them were subject to their king. In other words, henotheism was a religious 'umbrella' under which many little gods, and many little people who worshiped those gods, could be included.

Henotheism had certain advantages over polytheism as well. Unlike polytheism, in which various gods displayed levels of power, henotheism did not risk the sharing of power with some other contender. With a polytheistic religion there was always the possibility that some new god would come along who was more powerful than previously worshiped gods, and the human who promoted that new god might try to usurp power in the earthly realm. Henotheism gave the king the ability to protect himself, at the level of ideas if not in reality, against this type of ideological challenge. Though there were many lesser gods, there was but one all-powerful god and, therefore, there could be but one all-powerful human king, the chosen one of the supreme god. 'Ashur is king, and I—the human king—am his regent!'

Other aspects of ancient religions, including royal theologies and more localized 'popular' religions, will be discussed in later chapters.

## SUGGESTED ADDITIONAL READING

*Aspects of the New Kingdom*

Assmann, Jan, *Egyptian Solar Religion in the New Kingdom: Re, Amun and the Crisis of Polytheism* (trans. A. Alcock; London: Routledge & Kegan Paul, 1995).

Hasel, Michael G., 'Israel in the Merneptah Stela', *BASOR* 296 (1994), pp. 45-61.

Moran, William L., *The Amarna Letters* (Baltimore: The Johns Hopkins University Press, 1992).

O'Connor, David, and Eric H. Cline (eds.), *Amenhotep III: Perspectives on his Reign* (Ann Arbor: University of Michigan Press, 1998).

Redford, Donald B., *Egypt, Canaan, and Israel in Ancient Times* (Princeton: Princeton University Press, 1992).

*Studies of Early Israel*

Ahlström, Gösta W., *Who Were the Israelites?* (Winona Lake, IN: Eisenbrauns, 1986).

Frerichs, Ernest S., and Leonard H. Lesko (eds.), *Exodus: The Egyptian Evidence* (Winona Lake, IN: Eisenbrauns, 1997).

Lemche, Niels Peter, *Prelude to Israel's Past: Background and Beginnings of Israelite History and Identity* (Peabody, MA: Hendrickson, 1998).

*Bronze and Iron Age Mesopotamian Religion and Literature*

Foster, Benjamin R., *Before the Muses: An Anthology of Akkadian Literature* (2 vols.; Bethesda: CDL Press, 1993).

Hallo, William W., and K. Lawson Younger, Jr, *The Context of Scripture* (2 vols.; Leiden: E.J. Brill, 1997–2000).

Porter, Barbara Nevling (ed.), *One God or Many? Concepts of Divinity in the Ancient World* (Transactions of the Casco Bay Assyriological Institute, 1; Bethesda: CDL Press, 2000).

Pritchard, James B. (ed.), *Ancient Near Eastern Texts Relating to the Old Testament* (Princeton: Princeton University Press, 1950).

## NOTES

1.  A. Kuhrt, *The Ancient Near East c. 3000–330 BC* (London: Routledge, 1995), I, p. 196.

2.  Kuhrt, *The Ancient Near East*, p. 202.

3.  For this discussion of life in Late Bronze Age Canaan, see D.B. Redford, *Egypt, Canaan, and Israel in Ancient Times* (Princeton: Princeton University Press, 1992), pp. 192-213; Kuhrt, *The Ancient Near East*, pp. 317-29.

4.  Much depends on vocalization, and especially on the nature of the sibilant, which is uncertain. See E.A. Knauf, 'War "Biblisch-Hebräisch" eine Sprache?', *ZAH* 3 (1990), pp. 11-23 (17-18).

5.  Translation by J.A. Wilson in *ANET*, pp. 376-78.

6.  On the relationship of Judg. 4 to 5, see W.J. Houston, 'Murder or Midrash? The Prose Appropriation of Poetic Material in the Hebrew Bible', *ZAW* 109 (1997), pp. 342-55, 534-48.

7.  See A. Kuhrt, 'Usurpation, Conquest and Ceremonial: From Babylon to Persia', in D. Cannadine and S. Price (eds.), *Rituals of Royalty: Power and Ceremonial in Traditional Societies* (Cambridge: Cambridge University Press, 1987), pp. 20-55 (31).

8.  Terminology is difficult since individual scholars employ the terms in a variety of ways. My discussion is designed to be useful, but not necessarily representative of all academic viewpoints. 'Henotheism' can be understood to mean belief in 'my' god while at the same time not excluding the possibility that 'your' god exists as well. In an ancient context, this was expressed frequently as belief that 'my' god is highest of the gods: god of gods and lord of lords (cf. Deut. 10.17; Ps. 29.1-2, etc.). For a cautious, succinct discussion of Late Bronze and Iron Age Mesopotamian henotheisms, see T. Jacobsen, *The Treasures of Darkness: A History of Mesopotamian Religion* (New Haven: Yale University Press, 1976), pp. 234-36; see also the interesting summary of an unpublished paper by P. Riemann, succinctly described by P.D. Miller, *The Religion of Ancient Israel* (Louisville, KY: Westminster/John Knox Press, 2000), pp. 25-26, with the citation on pp. 227-28. A recent debate over the nature of Mesopotamian religion between S. Parpola, who advocates Assyrian monothesim, and B.N. Porter, who dissents from that thesis, can be found in B.N. Porter (ed.), *One God or Many? Concepts of Divinity in the Ancient World* (Transactions of the Casco Bay Assyriological Institute, 1; Bethesda: CDL Press, 2000). For practical applications to biblical study, the now classic article by M. Smith remains unsurpassed: 'The Common Theology of the Ancient Near East', *JBL* 71 (1952), pp. 135-47.

Chapter 6

## THE IRON AGE I

### Introduction

The Iron Age I was a time of transition. During the first decades of this era, Egypt remained in control of its Canaanite empire. But Egypt's 19th Dynasty came to an end and the 20th Dynasty emerged shortly after 1200 BCE. The 20th Dynasty began as a very strong imperial power, but quickly weakened and, by about the 1130s BCE, no longer maintained a presence in Canaan. (Egypt's control of Nubia slipped away gradually as well, so that Nubia was independent by about 1100 BCE.) Meanwhile, Hatti collapsed around 1200 BCE, liberating northern Syria from Hittite imperial rule. As a result, there were no large political powers governing Canaan during the Iron Age I.

Why did this radical political transformation occur just after 1200 BCE? No one factor is responsible. Rather, massive changes resulted from a combination of factors. The Iron Age I witnessed a series of ecological, economic and social upheavals which, together, resulted in changed political circumstances.

Ecologically, the ancient world from Asia to Africa experienced one of its regularly recurring shifts in weather patterns between 1200 and 900 BCE. Toward the beginning of this era, higher aridity resulted in a series of famines throughout Greece, Anatolia and Canaan. Even Egypt experienced lower levels of Nile flooding and increased hunger. These problems are documented in texts found throughout the ancient Near East, from Mesopotamia to Egypt.

A famine of a few years was not uncommon to these regions in any era, but greater aridity with resulting hunger over a period of several human generations is something that strikes the Near East only once every few millennia. This period of aridity must have seemed relentless to those living through it, and it motivated many groups (who could not have known how geographically widespread the effects of the climatic changes were) to uproot and migrate in search of better land. Social and economic consequences were bound to follow these migrations.

Apparently, some of the groups who migrated in search of a better life were hostile toward those they encountered along the way. Archaeologists from Greece to Palestine have found evidence for military destruction of many major cities during the final decades of the Late Bronze and early decades of the Iron Age I. Ugaritic texts mention hostile groups of people in ships who were attacking its coast. Egyptian texts also speak of wars with groups attempting to enter the Delta. It is possible that the folk memory of these times gave rise to some of the world's greatest literature, stories composed during the Iron Age II (900–586 BCE) and later eras, such as Homer's *Iliad* and *Odyssey* (twin tales of military action and migration) and the Bible's books of Exodus and Joshua (in which these two themes appear in reverse order). As we have seen, these stories were not designed to be read as *historia*, but the inspiration for telling tales of great warriors might have come from the fuzzy memory of actual warfare.

Sporadic warfare began to alter the political map while cultural exchange altered the social context. When groups immigrate in small numbers, they tend to be absorbed into the new environment without leaving much of a mark on it. But when larger groups migrate, they have an impact, much like a very small meteorite on a land's surface. The host culture is not entirely transformed, but dramatic changes occur. In this case, a large number (no one knows how many) of people from the regions now called Greece and Turkey made their way both west and south, leaving their mark on the places where they settled. Those moving west landed in places such as Sardinia and Sicily. In fact, those islands got their name from the Aegean immigrants, the people called Sherden (Sardinians) and Sheklesh (Sicilians).

Aegeans moving south landed on the island of Cyprus as well as on the coast of southern Syria and Palestine. A few even entered Egypt, and historians usually call them the 'Sea Peoples'. Apparently, wherever these Sea Peoples landed, they did not constitute the majority of the population, but they were numerous enough to have a visible impact on the material culture and lifestyle of those who had been living in the area before the immigrants arrived. The most famous group of Sea People was the 'Peleset'—the Bible calls them 'Philistines'. Other biblical ethnic groups were also part of this early Iron Age I immigration. For example, Gen. 15.19-21 mentions several groups in Canaan. This list includes the Girgashites, whose name can be traced to western Anatolia, and the Hittites, who were migrants to Palestine from Hatti as it collapsed around 1200 BCE. In a few cases, biblical authors were aware, vaguely, of migrations that had occurred generations before. See, for example, Amos 9.7, which mentions the non-Palestinian origin of the Philistines. But the biblical authors lived at a time when all memory of origins had been forgotten for some of these groups. The Hittites and the Girgashites of Gen. 15.19-21 are mentioned as though they had been in Canaan all along, grouped together with people who were either nonexistent (the legendary race of giants called Rephaim) or by definition autochthonous (which means 'native to the land'), such as the Canaanites.

With a significant minority of the population on the move in early Iron Age I, and with an economy already strained by poor crops and widespread famine, other aspects of the economy suffered as well. International trade of luxury goods decreased conspicuously since trade routes were increasingly vulnerable to attack. Also, the resulting scarcity of copper and tin motivated a new interest in iron ore, which was frequently locally available, but very difficult to work. Not surprisingly, decreased international trade was matched by decreased diplomatic relations between major states. The resulting decrease in 'cash flow' had a negative impact on the relative strength of centralized governments with their equally centralized economies. Peasant loyalty to their kings or lords was bound to decrease as well, since these governments could not be counted upon to protect hunger-stricken areas through redistribution of grain collected as taxes from more well-off portions of the kingdom. In other words, redistributive economies were undermined. These internally weakened kingdoms were therefore vulnerable to attack by aggressive migrant groups, a situation that makes the widespread destruction of cities noted by archaeologists very understandable.

After the decline of Hatti and the 20th Egyptian Dynasty, there was no centralized political structure in Syria-Palestine. As a result, the local city-states, which had been under the imperial thumb of either Hatti or Egypt, became independent, much as they had been during the Middle Bronze Age, centuries earlier. From 1200 BCE to well beyond 900 BCE, most regions of Syria-Palestine were home to small political entities, each competing with its neighbors politically and economically.

Four clusters of independent city-states emerged gradually during the Iron Age I. First, northern Syria, which had been under vassalage to the Hittites, fragmented into a series of small kingdoms. One of the most prominent of these was the city of Carchemish. Second, Phoenicia became once again a series of autonomous city-states, the most significant of which were Byblos, Sidon and Tyre. Although these cities had been a part of the region's trade economy for centuries, it was during the Iron Age I that they began to dominate Mediterranean trade, an international status they would maintain for many more centuries. Third, in southern Syria and the northern portion of Palestine, small Aramaean kingdoms emerged, two of which were Hamath and Damascus. Fourth, along the southern coast, a series of newly independent city-states, Canaanite and Philistine, such as Gezer, Gaza and Ekron, became prominent.

This chapter will focus on the decline of the Egyptian Empire, the rise of several new groups, and the resulting changes in the land of Canaan. In the history textbooks published prior to the late-1990s (and even a few more recent ones), the Iron Age I is usually labeled the 'period of the Judges'. That label derives from the biblical book of the same name, but it is a misnomer since the biblical judges were the heroes of folk legends, not the leaders of actual political units in this era. Even if a few of the biblical stories about the judges are based loosely on real persons and events, it would be useless to speculate about them in the absence of helpful evidence. Moreover, to concentrate on these tales to the exclusion of the larger context in which such tales played only a minor role would only distort one's comprehension of this era. Nevertheless, the concept of Israelite judges, derived as it is from Israelite folk memory, raises an important historical question.

Where was Israel during the Iron Age I? Pharaoh Merneptah was kind enough to let us know that a group called Israel was living somewhere in Palestine during the final decades of the Late Bronze Age. Presumably, they were still there in the following generations, since ancient documents also speak of an 'Israel' in the later Iron Age II. Is it possible to find these people in the material culture of Iron Age I Palestine and to write their history? Not surprisingly, attempts to locate Israel have been going on for generations of modern scholarship. To date, however, little has been achieved. To understand why, issues of historical method will be addressed, following which some applications of those methods will be pursued.

### *What is an Ancient Ethnic Group and How is It to be Found?*

With few exceptions, historians agree that a people calling themselves Israel lived somewhere in Canaan during the Iron Age I. Unfortunately, the Israelites are invisible. They are invisible for two reasons. First, Iron Age I Canaan was an illiterate society. There is very little evidence for writing during this period. The few individuals who were writing appear to have been living in areas where there were no Israelites, so far as anyone can tell. Second, the Israelites are invisible because the objects they made, the houses in which they lived, and the tools they used appear to have been identical to the objects, houses and tools used by all other Canaanites in this period. This problem of Israelite invisibility raises a serious question concerning historical method.

How does one find an ethnic group in these material remains when there is nothing very distinctive about the artifacts that are buried in Palestine's soil? The first step toward answering that question is to try to define, as carefully as possible, what is meant by the term 'ethnic group'. We cannot find an ethnic group if we do not know what it is that we seek.

An ethnic group is any large or small cluster of people who identify with one another and engage in a continuous, and usually informal, public conversation about who they are. That is to say, an ethnic group is a group who negotiate with one another about what it means to be one group of people rather than many unrelated individuals. On most occasions, the two topics of discussion are (1) shared stories about the past and (2) shared values in the present. Not all members will agree on the details of these shared stories and values. Indeed, on most occasions, there will be strong dissent in some factions of the group. One subgroup might, for example, protest that another subgroup has violated the moral code of the ethnic community. Or one subgroup might disagree with another on the significance of a famous event or person of the past. Nevertheless (and this is a key point), the fact that these subgroups care enough about one another to bother arguing is evidence that they are part of a single ethnic group. If they did not identify with one another at some fundamental level, they would not engage in this kind of conversation. An ethnic group is any community of people who identify with one another to such a degree that they implicitly recognize one another as members of something they call 'us'—the ambiguous and often ill-defined 'essence' that is presumed to stand at the center of the group's identity.

From this definition it can be seen that ethnic groups come in many shapes and sizes. Essentially, any clustering of people who take an interest in one another and perceive themselves to be a people are an ethnic group. The group's self-definition might reside in a religion, such as Judaism, Christianity, Islam, and so on. It might reside in the perception of biological descent, such as African Americans, European Americans, Japanese Americans, and so forth. The affiliation might be relatively weak, based on nothing more than the perception of a shared community past (a shared 'history') or shared language and geography. Or the affiliation could be a strong one that traces a demonstrable continuity over many centuries and many continents. In all cases, the key element is the group's interest in its own members and the dialogue that takes place among them.

As an example of an ethnic group's public negotiation of their own corporate identity, consider a recent Hollywood film by the African American filmmaker Spike Lee, *Get On the Bus*. This movie tells a fictional story based on a real event. The event was a rally in Washington, DC, in which thousands of African American men participated. In the film, a group of men rent a bus to drive across the United States so they can take part in the rally. Along the way, these men begin to talk with one another. As they do so, they discover the many differences between them, differences of cultural background and of worldviews. Long philosophical discussions take place, arguments break out, tempers flare, and, at times, the situation degenerates into fistfights. Nevertheless, their journey to Washington gives each man ample opportunity to explore what it means to try to live with dignity as an African American in a society where a significant portion of the power remains in the hands of European Americans.

In this film, all the men agree on one issue, and they agree on this issue without discussing it: they agree that they are 'one people'. The agreement is based on perceptions of biological descent. Each man on the bus was born to parents whose ancestors came from the continent of Africa. However, they discover, sometimes to their dismay, that they do not share identical visions about the *significance* of that blunt fact. One man tends to use the derogatory 'N' word frequently—so frequently, in fact, that the other men kick him off the bus. Another man is scornful of homosexuals, then discovers that two gay men are on the bus. Many other examples could be mentioned, but these illustrate the recurring topics of conversation within an ethnic group. On the one hand, the community discusses the significance of the past, such as the way insulting slang terms from that past continue to be directed against African Americans. On the other hand, they negotiate issues of morality, such as sexual orientation. The entire process is more or less unconscious. That is to say, the men on the bus are very aware of their differences and very eager to promote their individual solutions to those differences. But they remain unconscious of their shared presupposition. The shared presupposition is that they are indeed one group, one people, and therefore these conversations, arguments and fights are absolutely necessary—indeed, radically significant to their own sense of self-identity. Spike Lee's film presents in microcosm what every ethnic group is and does in all places around the world, in all times, past and present.

*Get On the Bus* illustrates four aspects of ethnicity that must be kept in mind if a historian hopes to identify an ethnic group, such as Israel, in the material record of the ancient past. First, a sense of ethnicity usually has much to do with perceived biological descent, though in reality it has nothing to do with *actual* biological descent. In most cases, ethnicity *appears* to be an issue of biology—some would call it 'race'—precisely because most people unconsciously identify with the group into which they were born. However, there are many instances in which a person born in one culture moves to another and adopts it so completely that she or he rejects any former sense of identity. These individuals demonstrate that 'race' is not the substance of ethnic identity. As a matter of fact, the concept of 'race' has no genuine content.[1] Biologically, all humans are one race, descendants of a particular evolutionary branch in the genus *homo*. In the film, all the men on the bus are biological descendants of one couple, but that couple lived so many thousands of years ago that no one on the bus can hope to recover their names or when they lived, nor do they even discuss that possibility. Ethnic identity, therefore, must be negotiated through public conversations of the type that take place on the bus. 'If we are one people, then what is it that makes us *us*? Are gay men in or out of the group called *us*? Is it acceptable to hurl ugly slang terms at members of *us*?' In the film, the questions go on and on. In real life, each generation of a group's members will renegotiate the answers to such questions.

Since there is no stable biological element in ethnic identity, a second aspect of ethnicity is stressed by many of the anthropologists who work with ethnic identities: ethnicity is never static and unchanging.[2] As a matter of fact, ethnic identity is subject to constant revision over the generations. This process of change is inevitable, and it is as valuable as it is necessary for the ethnic community's health. It gives each generation a stake in the process of maintaining the ethnic group's sense of corporate identity. For example, over the centuries Christians have renegotiated their values with respect to slavery. When Christianity was born, all Christians believed that human slavery was a divinely ordained station in life. (The Jewish scriptures that Christians adopted as their own presupposed a slave economy—see Exod. 21; Deut. 15). There is no record that Jesus challenged the institution of slavery. Even the apostle Paul, whose rhetoric implied that slavery was no more (Gal. 3.28), failed to challenge actual structures of slavery endemic to his world. Indeed, he even participated in them (Philemon; contrast Deut. 23.16-17; see also 1 Cor. 7.21-22). As recently as 150 years ago, some Christians in America fought to preserve the institution of slavery, calling their war a holy cause. Now, all that has changed and there are very few Christians who believe slavery is moral. The community renegotiated its values with respect to that issue. Some communities change more rapidly than in this example, but the process goes on in every community. If the group fails to 'update' its beliefs on a regular basis, members of the group have ceased to care enough to negotiate those updates, which is another way of saying that the ethnic group no longer exists. An ethnic group that does not engage in such debate dissolves into the larger cultural fabric of its human environment, a process that is called assimilation.

Constant change in ethnic identity requires historians to consider a third aspect of the issue: when searching for an ethnic group in the past, one cannot assume the stories and values that define that group in the present prevailed also in the past. Since groups change over time, their distinguishing characteristics change as well. For example, in the second century CE, many Christians were Gnostics. Gnosticism taught that a divine revealer (Jesus) showed the way to knowledge, and it was the knowledge that rewarded a person with eternal life, not the divine revealer. A modern Christian theologian has the luxury of looking back at the second century and declaring the Gnostics heretics, 'false' Christians. A historian cannot do that. In the second century, Gnosticism *was* Christianity for many people, and modern historians (at least, modern humanists and positivists who write history) accord these people the dignity of viewing them as they viewed themselves, as full members of the Christian community. The example illustrates the problem: if historians want to find an ancient ethnic group in the material remains of the past, they must be careful not to impose later conceptions of that group's identity onto the evidence. Therefore, analysis of the material remains is complicated by the uncertainty of what a historian *expects* to find in those remains.

A fourth and final observation about ethnic groups is equally essential: ethnicity is not identical to 'culture'. In popular usage, these two terms often become synonyms, but in academic study they are not. A person's ethnic identity might shift regularly in subtle or not so subtle ways, even though that person remains in one unchanging culture. How is that possible? It is possible because ethnic identity is ideological, but culture is not. An individual might identify with several ideologies, that is to say, with several ethnic groups. For example, a woman might perceive herself to be an American and not an Israeli in one social context, Jewish and not Gentile (non-Jewish) in another context, Reconstructionist and not modern Orthodox in a third context. Each of these groups with which she identifies expresses an ideology to distinguish itself from other groups. At the same time, the woman might be living in one location. Perhaps she is in Tel Aviv as part of an extended visit with close relatives, and her relatives are modern Orthodox Israeli citizens, who live in a neighborhood where Jews interact with Gentiles regularly. From day to day, this woman's culture does not change even as her identity shifts with every new interaction.

In contrast to ethnicity, culture is merely the sum of all routine aspects of a community. The routine values, activities and objects all around you are the culture in which you are immersed. These are 'routine' in the sense that everyone, or almost everyone, takes them for granted. Certain behaviors are deemed appropriate, yet people rarely discuss why. Certain activities are considered normal, but no one questions their normality. Certain objects are to be found in abundance, and no one is surprised to see them there. These three categories of 'routineness' are, collectively, the culture of a particular place. Within your culture, there are many ethnic groups, each of which more or less accepts the routine aspects of the prevailing culture. Almost everyone, regardless of ethnic background, routinely uses a telephone, routinely speaks politely when using it, and routinely places the phone on a tabletop, on a dashboard of a car or in a backpack when finished with the conversation. Most will never question the 'normality' of those objects and that behavior.

This does not mean that all aspects of the culture are shared by every ethnic group, only that most aspects are shared. Each ethnic group might dissent from, fail to participate in, or even protest against, one or two aspects of the prevailing culture. But unless the ethnic group utterly rejects *all* aspects of the routine, it will remain within the culture. If an ethnic group dissents radically from the culture, it isolates itself from the culture. For example, the Amish in many parts of northern America shun most modern conveniences such as telephones.

This observation can be useful to the historian who seeks ancient Israel in the material culture of Iron Age I Palestine. If an archaeologist who is familiar with the normal pattern of material culture finds some minor, but consistent, difference in that pattern at one location or one region, and if it can be shown that this difference reflects the community's shared values, it might be an indication of ethnic identity. Even this is risky, however, since historians of the modern era often assert that 'ethnicity' should be abandoned as a category for historical explanation. These historians assert, correctly, that ethnic identity changes too quickly and unpredictably, is almost never to be correlated to material culture, and rarely serves as an individual's *primary* center of self-identity. (More local sources of identity, such as the small village or the family, often weigh more heavily in an individual's life.) Therefore, these historians insist, determination of ethnic identity is either hopeless, or possible but useless.[3] Their insights on this issue are flawless, but not every historian agrees with their skeptical conclusion, which is why the search for ancient ethnic groups in the material culture of Iron Age I continues.

With these observations in mind, and given that Iron Age I Palestine has left us almost no writings and a relatively uniform material culture, the challenge of finding one ethnic group, the Israelites, is daunting. The material culture of Iron Age I Palestine is very uniform, with only minor variations from place to place. Even if one were to find artifacts that differ drastically from those in another location, some evidence and reasoning will be required to demonstrate that those artifacts are the material remains of a people who thought of themselves as Israelite. Not surprisingly, there have been many approaches to the problem, heated debates about the merits of each approach, and a general lack of consensus about the success or failure of each effort.

To illustrate some of these issues, a sample quest will serve nicely. We shall begin, therefore, with these questions: can the ancient people called Peleset be located in Iron Age I Canaan? If so, where were these Philistines?

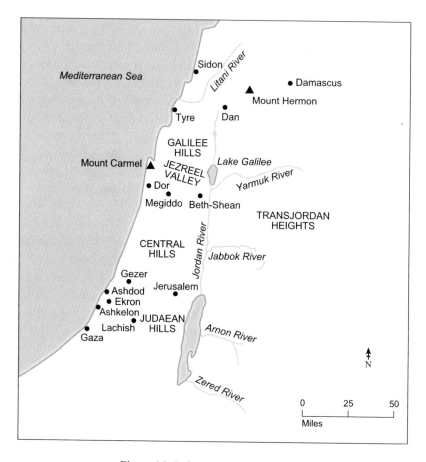

Figure 16. *Palestine in the Iron Age I.*

## Seeking the Philistines in Canaan's Material Culture

Archaeologists and historians would not bother to seek the Peleset (or Philistines) if ancient documents had not mentioned them. But this group is attested in a variety of ancient writings from Egypt and Meso-potamia, and, of course, in the Bible as well. As just discussed, it does not follow that a group mentioned in ancient texts can be found in ancient artifacts and city ruins. Only through careful research can an assemblage of artifacts be correlated with a textual reference. In the case of the Philistines, Pharaoh Ramesses III of the 20th Egyptian Dynasty (early-twelfth century BCE) offers a place to begin.

In a funeral temple dedicated to the splendor of the god Ramesses III, the king boasts of great victories over Nubia, the 'Asiatics' (people to the east of Egypt) and the invading Sea Peoples. On a variety of grounds, many historians discount much of this boast. Ramesses III did not, so far as can be determined, fight Nubians or Asiatics. His battle with the peoples of the sea is expressed in flamboyant language, the usual bluster so frequently relied upon by pharaohs eager to impress their readers—the gods of Egypt, particularly—with their deeds. For a king of ancient Egypt, the past was not what happened but what ought to have happened, given that this king is such a great warrior, a representative of the gods. Accordingly, the gods are flattered by receiving a tale of success far greater than mundane realities.

Ramesses III describes the Sea Peoples as a coalition of armies invading by both land and sea, a 'conspiracy' of chaotic forces that could only be stopped by the great Pharaoh. These mighty hordes devastated Hatti, Ugarit, Carchemish and many other cities. But Ramesses III was able to annihilate them. In his narrative of the battle, the usual cliché occurs: 'Their seed is not'. In another document, Ramesses III claims to have taken the remnant of enemy survivors and incorporated them into his own empire, settling them in various regions.

Part of this description is false and portions are certainly accurate. Carchemish, for example, did not suffer military destruction at this time. However, as observed above, many cities of Syria-Palestine did, and the empire of Hatti crumbled as well. Groups from the Aegean certainly were on the move, and some of them had even become mercenary soldiers in the employ of Egyptian kings prior to Ramesses III's reign. However, the destruction that Ramesses III attributes to one great horde is to be attributed to many more local disruptions caused by the widespread instability of the times, as discussed at the beginning of this chapter. Ramesses III preferred to depict the events as the product of one great conspiracy so that his own military accomplishment would seem astounding. (In a sense, one might call Ramesses III the first of the conspiracy theorists, whose pseudo-historical hypotheses are still common today!) In other words, stripped of the excessive aspects of its propaganda, the boasts of Ramesses III seem to fit nicely with the era in which he lived.

Historians differ on what took place during the Sea People battles with Ramesses III. Some believe that two battles occurred, one on land at the northern border of the Egyptian empire (roughly in the region of modern Lebanon) and another at sea in the Egyptian Delta. Others are convinced that the only battle was in the Delta. In any case, the war was short, and the mighty hordes were, in actuality, limited in number. All historians agree that at least one battle, however minimal it may have been, took place, and that some Sea Peoples settled in Egyptian-held lands as a result. Those lands might have been in Egypt or in Canaan. This battle (or these two battles) took place in the 1170s BCE.

If one seeks Sea People settlements in Canaan, and given that the Sea People were from the Aegean, it seems logical to search for material culture in Palestine that reflects the Aegean homeland. Probably not by coincidence, the twelfth-century strata of Palestinian coastal sites betrays widespread evidence of influence from the Aegean. A new kind of pottery is found in these strata. These pots are decorated with painted designs identical to pots found in Greece and associated with a Greek society called Mycenaean society. A few of these Mycenaean-style pots were imported, but when neutron activation analysis was performed, others were found to have been made from local Canaanite clay; in fact, the bulk of these pots were not imported through trade, but made by someone familiar with Greek culture who was living in Canaan. Also, some of the building structures (such as a particular use of hearths) reflect floorplans similar to those uncovered by archaeologists in Greece. New religious artifacts, including depictions of a goddess, are similar to Mycenaean religious artifacts. And, surprisingly, the people using these Greek pots and living in these Greek buildings ate quite a bit of pork, meat from an animal that was almost never eaten by most Canaanites. It would seem that a Mycenaean population had settled the Palestinian coast south of Mount Carmel in the twelfth century BCE.

The pattern of artifacts on Canaan's coast underwent rapid change after the generation that brought Aegean material culture. Within two or three generations at most, the pottery style had begun to change markedly. The newer pots retained elements of Mycenaean artistic style, but incorporated elements of the local Canaanite style as well. Archaeologists call the purely Mycenaean pots of the first generation

'Philistine monochrome' because they are painted with one color (black). The newer pots are called 'Philistine bichrome' because they use two colors (black and red). A third stage of the pottery style is even more like Canaanite style and less like Mycenaean, and soon after that, one no longer finds any artifacts that retain the explicit features of Mycenaean influence.

This pattern of change is precisely what an anthropologist might expect to find. It seems to follow the usual pattern for an immigrant group. At first, the new settlers retain much of their way of life from the homeland. They use tools similar to their traditional tools, speak the language of the homeland, worship the gods of the homeland, and so on. The next several generations usually begin to assimilate to the new culture. They tend to be bilingual, speaking their parents' language in the home and the local language on the street. They incorporate artistic styles and tools common to the new homeland. By the fourth and fifth generations, almost total assimilation has occurred. At best, these younger generations preserve prized aspects of the family tradition, usually carefully selected aspects that are valued as part of ethnic identity, and maybe a few words or phrases from the old language. But they will have become very 'native' in most other respects. Therefore, although they might retain an ideology of ethnic difference from other people in their new homeland, little or nothing in the material culture would reflect that ethnic difference.

The Philistines represent a model example of just what one might expect when seeking an ethnic group in ancient artifacts. Like a small meteorite, they have landed on the coast of Canaan and effected a discernible change in the terrain. But over the years, the terrain has adjusted to their presence, and they have adjusted to it.

Only a few historians dispute the evidence and conclusions discussed so far, but that does not mean that all questions about the Philistines have been resolved. As a matter of fact, two crucial questions remain: *when* did the Philistines arrive in Canaan? And *how* did they arrive in Canaan?

### When Did the Philistines Arrive in Canaan?

Everyone agrees that the Philistines arrived in the twelfth century after a battle between Sea Peoples and Ramesses III; thus they settled during or after the 1170s BCE. However, there is great disagreement as to *how soon after* Ramesses III's battle the new settlements began. Did the soldiers who battled Ramesses III settle with their families immediately, or was there a gap of a few decades before Sea Peoples began to populate the Canaanite coast? The latter is a distinct possibility. More than one wave of Aegean peoples made their way into Canaan during the course of the twelfth century BCE, and the battle with Ramesses III was only the early stage of this process. Which wave do the Philistine monochrome pots represent?

To pursue this question, a point of method should be stressed. The link between Philistine monochrome and the battle of Ramesses III is *not* a direct link. We do not know if monochrome-style pottery makers were among the soldiers who opposed the pharaoh. Rather, the earliest possible date for Philistine monochrome is determined by comparison of archaeological digs throughout Syria-Palestine and the method called pottery typology (as discussed on p. 47). For example, Philistine monochrome style must date to a time after the destruction of a Syrian city called Ugarit, because a style of pottery that is its typological 'parent' was in use at Ugarit when the city was destroyed. That was in the 1180s BCE and, at that time, the new 'offspring' style, Philistine monochrome, was not yet in use. Likewise, evidence from Tel Deir 'Alla in the Jordan Valley again places the typological 'parent' of Philistine monochrome in the 1180s, suggesting that Philistine monochrome style began no earlier than the 1170s, and possibly later. So the 1170s—the same decade as the battle of Ramesses III—is the *terminus post quem* for Philistine monochrome, which means the 'earliest possible date'. What is not yet certain is the *terminus ante quem*, the 'latest possible date' at which the first Philistine monochrome pots were made.

In the face of this uncertainty, two hypotheses have emerged for the date of the Philistines in Canaan. Both hypotheses emphasize the same important aspects of the data, but arrive at opposite conclusions. The pertinent data are these: (1) many of the cities on Palestine's coast were destroyed and the Philistine monochrome pots appear in the next stratum (e.g. Ekron, Ashkelon and Ashdod). (2) In these cities, Philistine monochrome represents a percentage of the pottery, but local Canaanite pottery styles are abundant as well. (3) Some cities in the same region at about the same time display evidence of an Egyptian military presence (e.g. Lachish and Gezer). The sites with Egyptian presence have Canaanite pottery similar to Philistine sites but do not have Philistine monochrome. Given these data, a key problem has emerged. Since pottery typology only brings us to within about 50 to

100 years, it is not certain whether the sites with Egyptian presence were *contemporary with* the Philistine monochrome or *prior to* the Philistine monochrome. (All agree that they cannot be later than the Philistine monochrome.)

The first hypothesis, which can be labelled Proposal 1, concludes from this evidence that the Philistines attacked some cities of Canaan in a first phase just after the battle with Ramesses III, in the 1170s BCE. Ramesses III lost the battle (though he claimed victory, as boastful pharaohs always do), and as a result, lost a portion of the Canaanite coast to these Sea People invaders. The Egyptians reacted by setting up Egyptian garrisons all around the new Philistine cities, thus containing the Philistines within the area of their initial conquest. But after several generations, as Egyptian power in Canaan weakened (the 1130s), the Philistines expanded, taking almost all the Palestinian coast south of Mount Carmel and much of the Shephelah near the Judaean Hills in a second phase of military activity. Thus, in Proposal 1, Philistine monochrome is equated with the first phase (1170s–1140s) and Philistine bichrome equates with the second phase (after the 1140s) of Philistine occupation. Most importantly, the Egyptian sites are *contemporary with* the Philistine monochrome sites, the first phase. During the bichrome second phase, the Egyptians were gone.[4]

An objection to Proposal 1 can be raised that leads to an alternative idea, which I call Proposal 2. In Proposal 1, the Philistine monochrome is an ethnic identifier. Philistine monochrome pottery equals ethnic Philistine occupation, and the absence of that pottery represents the Egyptian border region, pinning the Philistines down in a military containment policy. This hypothesis is not consistent with usual anthropological considerations, which hesitate to equate ethnicity with culture (see the discussion above). Pottery was a commodity, a product made of clay produced by people in the business of making and trading pottery for other goods. Without doubt, the original makers of the Aegean-style pottery were newly arrived Aegeans but, one can ask, were the *users* of Philistine monochrome *always* Philistines? The Philistine monochrome wares were highly artistic items. There is evidence that the later Philistine bichrome pots were subject to trade and distribution into Canaanite cities, and this could be the case with the earlier monochrome pots as well, depending on how the pattern of finds is interpreted. Artifacts such as pottery tend to make their way to neighboring cities even when the cities are not entirely friendly with one another, and there is every reason to believe that, if the Egyptian sites were contemporary with Philistine monochrome production, at least a few of these beautiful pots would have crossed the border into the hands of the Canaanites who also lived in the Egyptian occupied cities. Therefore, it is difficult to believe that the Egyptian sites were contemporary with the Philistine monochrome sites. If they were not, the evidence would demand that they were *prior to* the Philistine mono-chrome sites.

Therefore, Proposal 2 suggests that since the battle of Ramesses III took place in the Delta (and perhaps far to the north of Mount Carmel), it had nothing to do with the presence of Philistine monochrome in Palestine. The military destruction of sites on Palestine's pre-Philistine-monochrome coast could reflect Merneptah's wars a generation earlier. The Peleset did not enter this region in the 1170s. However, all archae-ologists agree that the Egyptian 20th Dynasty lost control of Canaan in the 1130s BCE. By that later date, evidence for Egyptian imperial pres-ence in Canaan vanishes. According to Proposal 2, this later date is when Philistine monochrome appears on the Canaanite coast. The Philistines drove the Egyptians out of the Coastal Plain during the 1130s in a battle that no pharaoh felt worthy of report on a temple wall. (What Egyptian king wants to brag about the utter and permanent loss of the Egyptian empire in Canaan?) This explains why there were no Philistine monochrome pots in the Egyptian garrison locations. Philis-tine potters did not begin making those wares until after the Egyptians were gone. Thus, in Proposal 2, the first phase with Philistine mono-chrome pottery began in the 1130s, and the second phase bichrome is dated to the next century, the eleventh century BCE.[5]

Archaeologists continue to debate these two proposals. To the unini-tiated, it may seem to be much ado about nothing, a debate over a mere half-century or so. But it demonstrates the limitations of the methods by which historians narrate a past. These limitations become all the more frustrating when seeking ethnic Israel in the material culture, as we will see momentarily. As for the Philistines, the precise date of arrival in Canaan cannot be narrowed beyond the final two-thirds of the twelfth century BCE. But another aspect of the issue further complicates any attempt to write a history of the early Philistines.

### How Did the Philistines Arrive in Canaan?
Returning to Proposal 1 above, a second objection has been raised. It has to do with how the Philistines arrived in Canaan. Proposal 1

suggests that, after the battle with Ramesses III in the Delta region, the Philistines captured part of Palestine's coast, destroyed the cities, and occupied them. Archaeological data suggest that the number of people living in all the cities where Philistine monochrome was found was about 25,000. That is an enormous number for a migrating group. Proposal 1 accounts for that mass by suggesting that boatload after boatload of Aegeans arrived and overwhelmed the Coastal Plain, an idea that has not been well received by many archaeologists. Though it is not entirely out of the question, migration in the ancient world rarely occurred on that scale. Moreover, these Sea People would have massacred a huge population of Canaanites when they set fire to the Canaanite cities, and then would have somehow managed to begin producing new Canaanite-style pottery identical to the kind produced by the people they had just annihilated (in addition to Philistine monochrome they also manufactured). Even if they found prototypes of the Canaanite-style pottery in the city ruins, what would be the motivation for emulating this style of pottery rather than just creating their own, 'native' monochrome styles exclusively? Moreover, the pattern noted above of gradual assimilation in later generations of Philistine material culture suggests that these people were not living in isolation from Canaanites, but rubbing shoulders with them every day. Not only is the date for Proposal 1 problematic, its description of events is less than convincing as well.

Thus, it is reasonable to suggest, as Proposal 3, that some Sea Peoples arrived with monochrome pottery makers among their numbers, that they did extensive military damage to the coast, killing some Canaanites, and that they settled among those they had not killed but had conquered. Well-trained warriors need not be a majority to conquer a region, since the population would be mostly peasant farmers with no military training at all. In this proposal, a Philistine city included ethnic Philistines and ethnic Canaanites as one community, the rulers and the ruled. Gradually, the ruled exerted cultural influence over the rulers, so that the process of assimilation noted by archaeologists occurred.[6]

In sum, the archaeological data, though they are clear and unambiguous, permit multiple historical narratives, each of which is compatible in many ways with the evidence. If you read the scholarship on early Philistines, you will encounter all three of the proposals discussed here, both in their pure forms, and in various combinations that include yet other proposals. This is not surprising. When one seeks an ethnic group in the material remains of the ancient world, it must be conceded that one works only with probabilities, never certainty. Some historians have evaluated the data even more critically than suggested here, thus arriving at far more skeptical conclusions. Although those who defend Proposals 1-3 may be tempted to dismiss skepticism as a kind of historical agnosticism (a few even call it nihilism), such dismissal would be as unfair as it would be dangerous. Historical narratives are interpretations of the past; they are not the past. One must learn to live with the ambiguity that reality necessitates.

### *Seeking the Israelites in Canaan's Material Culture*

If the quest for the early Philistines was difficult, the search for early Israel is more so. To begin, one starts with the textual evidence, as was the case with the Philistine example. Merneptah's Stela represents one textual source, albeit a brief and ambiguous one (see the previous chapter). The Bible represents another source, though we have seen that its memory of the Iron Age I is, at best, almost hopelessly confused. One popular interpretation of the biblical story (popular especially with a generation of historians active during the middle decades of the twentieth century CE) is that the early Iron Age I Israelites arrived in Canaan after an exodus from Egypt under Pharaoh Ramesses II (a suggestion based on Exod. 1.11). According to that hypothesis, the Israel of Merneptah had just arrived in Canaan, and one should expect to find Israelite settlement immediately after Merneptah's battle (assuming, of course, that Merneptah did not annihilate the Israel he fought, which is a safe assumption).

If one seeks Israelite settlements in Palestine, and given that the Bible's Israel had just come from a 400-year sojourn in Egypt, it seems logical to seek material culture in Canaan that reflects the Egyptian homeland. There certainly is some evidence of Egyptian material culture at that time, in the form of Egyptian imperial presence. But that is not what we seek in this situation. That evidence is part of a continuum from the Late Bronze Age, and suggests that the Egyptian empire in Palestine continued into the Iron Age I until about the 1130s BCE. What we seek is evidence that a group of people who had lived (as slaves?) in Egypt were now living (as peasants?) in Palestine. Moreover, the Egyptian presence is located primarily in the lowlands, the coast and the Jezreel and Jordan valleys. The Bible asserts that Israel was not able to live in those places because of Canaanite [sic] military strength, especially Canaanite chariots (see Judg. 1.19-34; also note v. 18 which, in the better ancient manuscripts, reads 'did not capture'). The Bible consistently places the early Israelites in the Cisjordan Hills primarily, and in the Transjordan Hills as well.

The results of a search for evidence of this massive influx of Egyptian material culture are disappointing. There is no such evidence. Unlike the evidence for Aegean infiltration on the Palestinian coast, there are no new pottery styles, no new religious artifacts, no building styles—in fact, absolutely nothing—to suggest the migration of people formerly living in Egypt. Also, the term 'Israelite' does not seem to have been associated with any land other than Canaan in any ancient written source, so we cannot trace an Israelite migration in the way that was done above for the Girgashites and Hittites. The ancient evidence refutes the hypothesis that Israel migrated in substantial numbers from Egypt. This does not rule out the possibility of a very small group of migrants who would have left no discernible trace in the data, but to posit such a group in the absence of any evidence is speculative.[7]

There is, however, a new situation in the Cisjordan and Transjordan highlands, the regions where the Bible places early Israel. The coincidence of this new situation appearing immediately after the battle of Merneptah and Israel has led many historians to far-reaching hypotheses. It is necessary, therefore, to devote discussion to the highlands of Canaan and the new situation that emerged there.

### *The Highlands of Palestine During the Iron Age I*

During the final years of the Egyptian empire, a radical increase in population appears in the archaeological record for the Cisjordan Highlands, from northern Galilee to the southern Central Hills. A far less dramatic, but equally interesting, increase of population can be discerned in a few portions of the Transjordan Highlands and the Judaean Hills. This change in the highlands is unusual given the pattern of population fluctuation for all of Canaan during these centuries. Late Bronze Age Palestine's population had dipped to fewer than 70,000 people. During the earliest stages of Iron Age I, that number continued to decline. Then, at about 1100 or so BCE, the population began to increase gradually, so that by the close of Iron Age I (during the tenth century BCE), the total population of all Palestine had risen to more than 100,000 people. When compared to these general numbers, the Iron Age I increase in the Cisjordan Highlands north of the Judaean Hills occurred more quickly and dramatically than in Palestine as a whole. At their peak, these Iron Age I settlements numbered at least 30,000 people, which is quite staggering when contrasted to any previous era in the Cisjordan Highlands. Some estimates have been higher.

The density of village settlements during these centuries fluctuated with the passing generations, and also varied considerably from subregion to subregion. Some areas, such as the Central Hills between the Jezreel Valley and Jerusalem, which was home to a handful of villages during the Late Bronze Age, were populated by about 300 small villages at various times over the centuries of the Iron Age I. Half of these were clustered into the northern half of that subregion, the portion the Bible calls Manasseh (from the Jezreel to about Shechem). The area from Bethel to Jerusalem, which the Bible calls the land of Benjamin, was unoccupied in the Late Bronze, but home to about 50 sites in the Iron Age I. Between Manasseh to the north and Benjamin to the south, the region of biblical Ephraim was almost unoccupied in the Late Bronze Age as well, and again saw a startling increase during Iron Age I to about 100 villages. The Galilee was home to about 60 Iron Age I communities, with about 40 of those clustered into Upper Galilee. The Judaean Hills became the location for more than a dozen villages during Iron Age I, though it too had been all but unoccupied during the Late Bronze Age. Likewise, Moab had almost no Late Bronze Age population, but more than 100 small villages in the Iron Age I.

Just as the number of villages differed from subregion to subregion, the population density and the relationship of each village to its surroundings differed as well. For example, in Manasseh the villages clustered along roads that connected these villagers to the economy of the cities of the Jezreel Valley and Coastal Plains. By contrast, the villages of Lower Galilee, just to the north of the Jezreel, were situated in isolation from the lowland urban centers. Population density varied considerably. While tens of thousands had moved gradually into the Central Hills, the population of Iron Age I Judah, to the south of Jerusalem, peaked at about 4500 people, or fewer. Likewise, Moab's population was thin and the rest of Transjordan even thinner.

These new highland villages were rural agricultural communities. Urban centers were nonexistent, and even those settlements called 'cities' in the scholarship were extremely small. Jerusalem in Iron Age

I probably numbered between 1000 and 2000 people. Transjordan was home to a handful of walled settlements, but these housed numbers in the hundreds.

The new village settlements of the Iron Age I are an unresolved enigma. Of course, they were not entirely unprecedented. Throughout ancient times, a few people had lived in the highlands of Canaan. In the Middle Bronze Age, a pattern of highland villages similar to the Iron Age I existed, albeit with considerably fewer people. Just before Egyptian imperial control of Canaan, as Egyptian armies, Hurrian armies, and probably Canaanite armies were bringing the Middle Bronze Age city-states to a fiery end over a period of 100 or more years, the highland villages were deserted. No one knows why they were deserted, though it is possible that the highlanders migrated into the Canaanite lowlands as better land became available. Throughout Late Bronze Egyptian dominance of Canaan, the highlands were sparsely populated. Thus, the Iron Age I marks a return to the population pattern of the Middle Bronze, but with a larger population. But who were these newly arrived highlanders?

As noted above, the Bible claims that Israel conquered the Cisjordan Highlands, but was not able to conquer most of the lowlands. As a result, biblical scholars and historians who have been seeking the early Israelites had focused on the Canaanite highlands even before archaeological surveys began to reveal a new Iron Age I village lifestyle there. Prior to those surveys, three hypotheses for the origins of Israel in Canaan had emerged and were debated among historians. Although all three models have been abandoned by the majority of scholarship in the wake of the archaeological surveys, some recent publications have continued to defend at least two of the three. It would be useful, then, to survey each hypothesis briefly.[8]

### The Conquest Model

For much of the twentieth century, this hypothesis for the emergence of early Israel in Canaan enjoyed a consensus among historians, but it has been abandoned by almost all competent historians today. Essentially, the Conquest Model was a paraphrase of the biblical story (minus the miracles, of course). The Israelites toiled in the Egyptian city of Ramesses (Exod. 1.11), then, after 40 or so years in the Negev wilderness (Exodus–Deuteronomy), they conquered Canaan (Joshua). Since the biblical tales of conquest focus on the Cisjordan Highlands, it was assumed that the Israelites conquered the highlands, but not the Coastal Plain or Jezreel Valley. If one accepts the biblical reference to the Egyptian city of Ramesses, then Joshua should have been conquering Palestine just before Merneptah fought an Israel in the Central Hills or the Jezreel Valley; that is to say, Joshua would have been active in the middle of the thirteenth century BCE. (Of course, this thirteenth century date for the exodus and conquest requires the overlooking of 1 Kgs 6.1 and other chronological snares, an adjustment in the face of chronological realities that even religious historians of the twentieth century were willing to make.[9])

Figure 17. *Iron Age Jerusalem. Every year, thousands of tourists marvel over these excavated remains of the Iron Age I city of Jerusalem. Historians debate how much influence this small city exerted over the Central and Judaean Hills prior to its growth in size and population in the Iron Age II.*

The Conquest Model has been abandoned because it is incompatible with the archaeological evidence. It has already been noted (see pp. 154-55) that there is no evidence for an influx of Egyptian material culture in Palestine. Also, if an incoming band of Egyptian slaves wrought destruction in Canaan, one would expect a series of clearly recognizable military destructions in the archaeological record. However, as noted in Chapter 2 (p. 48), there are a few sites in Palestine that suffered fire and destruction at about the right time, but almost without exception they are places not listed in the Bible. By contrast, a number of cities allegedly captured or destroyed by Joshua and the Israelites did not suffer destruction according to the archaeological record, and in some cases the places Joshua is said to have destroyed were not even inhabited in the Late Bronze and early Iron Ages. In light of the evidence, it is not possible to defend the Conquest Model.

By saying this I am not seeking to dismiss the biblical books of Numbers and Joshua as worthless to a modern historian. The distinctions between ancient texts, modern hypotheses, and archaeological data, as well as the multiple ways in which all ancient Near Eastern literatures (such as the Bible) are valuable to a historian, have been discussed in Chapters 2–3. In this instance, a few of the battle stories contained in Numbers and Joshua might reflect the dim memories of actual warfare at various times from the Late Bronze Age to Iron Age II. As such, fragments of these books might assist the historian of ancient warfare and politics. Additionally, the existence of a biblical tale narrating a single, unified conquest under the leadership of Moses and Joshua is valuable to the social historian who seeks to understand the ethos of a people who liked to tell tales of this kind. The tale of Israelite conquest is the product of a long process of storytelling over many generations. One biblical scholar suggests, plausibly, that as Iron Age Israelite construction workers encountered, from time to time, the unearthed foundationsof massive Middle Bronze Age fortifications, folk-tales of 'conquest' would arise quite naturally as a way of 'explaining' the demise of those ancient and unremembered cities.[10] The hypothesis is supported by the fact that it conforms well with the patterns of folklore throughout the world (as discussed in Chapter 3). Thus, the biblical conquest is a natural—even predictable—result of folklore; it is not an accurate depiction of Israel's entry into Canaan.

*The Gradual Infiltration Model*
As early as the first decades of the twentieth century CE, some historians had begun to recognize serious problems with the biblical narrative of conquest, and had begun to formulate a viable alternative to it. That alternative approach became the Gradual Infiltration Model. As the

name implies, the idea was that pastoralists gradually infiltrated and settled the highlands of Canaan, in regions where the Canaanite city-states had no control. There was no conquest. In fact, there was very little conflict at all. Perhaps a few battles were fought in places where the incoming pastoralists came into contact with Canaanite lowland regions, but that was all. The hypothesis was remarkably prescient, since it predicted what archaeology would later confirm: the highlands were a peripheral region mostly unconnected to the urban centers of the lowlands. In some versions of the Gradual Infiltration Model, the Egyptian texts mentioning the *shasu* are invoked, and the *shasu* are identified as early Israel.[11]

Although the Gradual Infiltration Model is still defended by some historians (in various versions of the hypothesis), it too suffers serious difficulties. For one thing, the model requires more pastoralists than can be reasonably posited. Shepherds existed on the fringes of Palestine in all periods since the late Neolithic period but they were never numerous. Usually, pastoralists numbered no more than about 15 per cent of the total population, and often were far fewer. How can an appeal to pastoralists settling down to become farmers account for the dramatic population increase in the Cisjordan Highlands during the Iron Age I?

*The Peasant Revolt Model*

A third hypothesis for the emergence of early Israel employs a more sophisticated, less literal, biblical interpretation than the others. In this approach, the Iron Age I highlands were populated by people who had formerly lived in the Palestinian city-states of the lowlands. Having become disenchanted with Canaanite culture and religion, so the hypothesis goes, these people rebelled against that lifestyle and took to the uninhabited Central Hills, where they created an all-new society, the society of Israel. This is why, these scholars suggest, the Bible encourages its reader to reject Canaanite religion and lifestyles; it was the manifesto of peasants who rejected that culture (see, e.g., Deut. 7.16-26; cf. Ezek. 16.3). In some versions of the Peasant Revolt hypothesis, a biblical exodus from Egypt is retained by claiming that a very small group of 19th Dynasty slaves escaped Egypt and brought a new god, Yahweh, to Canaan. These Yahwists became the catalyst around which the Canaanite peasants of the lowlands rallied when they took to the hills. Like the Gradual Infiltration Model, no biblical conquest is required by this hypothesis. However, the highlanders occasionally had to defend themselves in sporadic warfare with the lowlanders.[12]

An advantage of this third model is its compatibility with the material culture of the Iron Age I village settlements. The artifacts suggest that the villagers were Canaanites with cultural ties to the lowland urban centers. However, there is no evidence to suggest that these highlanders possessed a special ideology, a sense of corporate identity or ethnicity that set them apart from their neighbors. The Peasant Revolt Model seems to lack any evidence for its most crucial concept, 'revolt'. Only by reading between the lines of the biblical story can one find evidence for that concept. Thus, this model has been abandoned as well by most historians, though it still has a few defenders.

*An Alternative Approach: Symbiosis Model*
With the collapse of the three older models, a new hypothesis has emerged, but it does not yet have a label that all agree upon. A few have called their versions of the hypothesis the Symbiosis Model, and I will employ this term as a general one for all approaches that have similarity to these.[13]

In essence, the Symbiosis Model—regardless of whether one accepts the label—is a blend using sophisticated archaeological research and the best aspects of previous models. From the Peasant Revolt Model, the acknowledgement that the highland villagers were Canaanites has been retained, though the emphasis on an alleged revolt has been dropped. Likewise, from the Gradual Infiltration Model, pastoralism plays a role in this newer model, but with the acknowledgement that only some of the highlanders might be shepherds who had chosen to settle and start farming. From the social sciences, much emphasis has been placed on economic influences for human behavior.

The new model suggests that the highlanders were a blend of farmers from the lowlands and some ex-pastoralists who, together, settled into a new 'symbiotic' economic relationship in the highlands. The motivation for settling the highlands differs depending on which version of the Symbiosis Model is advanced. Since this approach is relatively new, scholars differ over many details.

In some versions of this model the highland villages were the direct or indirect result of Egyptian policy. These villages began to dot the landscape while the late-19th and early-20th Dynasties continued to dominate Palestine. Many historians believe that the Egyptians had taken a more direct role in the governance of Canaan during the 19th Dynasty. Indeed, most are convinced that Merneptah's four battles in Canaan, three with cities and one with Israel, were part of a much larger process of Egyptian consolidation of power, begun under Seti I and continued by Ramesses II.

The highland villages were a direct result of Egyptian policy if the Egyptians forced Canaanites to settle unsettled regions in order to work more land and provide a greater tax revenue for the Egyptian lords. They were an indirect result if increased Egyptian taxation of low-landers compelled two simultaneous and very spontaneous reactions. On the one hand, some lowlanders may have escaped higher taxation by moving to the peripheral highlands, and, on the other hand, pastoral-ists settled down to raise the food that was no longer available to the shepherds since the lowlanders upon whom they had previously depended for trade were now forced to pay higher taxes to Egypt. In either case, once the villages were established, they continued to thrive during the generations after the collapse of the Egyptian empire.

One aspect of the Symbiosis Model remains problematic: the ethnic identification of the highland villagers. Were these villagers Israelites? Older archaeologists, especially advocates of the Conquest Model, were eager to identify artifacts common to highland villages with Israelite ethnicity. This was an example of the common fallacy in which culture is equated with ethnicity. Although largely abandoned, one still reads from time to time in the scholarship a claim that a certain kind of pot (often one that is called a Collar-Rimmed Pot) or a certain kind of building (often, the so-called Four-Room House) is an Israelite pot or house. Most advocates of the Symbiosis Model reject these simplistic equations. They recognize, for example, that a huge pot with a rimmed collar at its top and a tapered point at the bottom was perfect for the storage of grain or liquid in a rural setting, and would be used by people with specialized storage needs, not specialized ethnic affili-ations. Nevertheless, some (though not all) advocates of the Symbiosis Model identify the Iron Age I village highlanders as early Israel. On what basis is that identification made?

The most reasonable hypothesis for equating the Iron Age I highland villages with early Israel is simple logic. Merneptah fought an Israel in the Late Bronze Age that seems to have been located either in the Jezreel Valley or the highlands. Iron Age II Assyrian inscriptions (to be discussed in Chapter 8) mention a Kingdom of Israel that was located in the highlands and the Jezreel. In between these eras, one finds the highland villages of Iron Age I. Therefore, according to some scholars, they must be the early Israelite settlements. If they were not Israelite, they were 'Proto-Israelite', a term that has caught on with a variety of historians. That means that they were the direct biological ancestors of the people who first began to identify themselves as Israelites. Of course, biology does not equal ethnic identity, but research shows that ethnicity often follows biological lines because people tend to identify with the group into which they were born. So the hypothesis is logical from a humanist historian's point of view, even if unverifiable from a positivist's perspective.

There is, however, a temptation faced by those who use this logic; they are tempted to think of *all* people living in the Cisjordan Highlands as Israelites or Proto-Israelites. That assumption is surely incorrect. Each subregion was settled in its own particular way, and those differences suggest that each community was isolated from the communities of other regions. It is doubtful, for example, that the villagers of Manasseh, who seem to have participated in the agricultural market of the Coastal Plain and Jezreel Valley, had much in common with their northern neighbors in the Lower Galilee, whose lives were lived in relative isolation from that economy.[14] Given that most travel was by foot and most peasants had little reason to travel, the individual's sense of ethnic identity—*if* she or he even had one—would have been local, not regional. It is entirely possible that local village and family identity precluded any genuine sense of larger, ethnic identity at all. (Or, to say the same thing another way, local identity *was* the individual's ethnic identity in total.) If Israel was one of the local identities, it surely was not the only one. Not all village highlanders were Israelites, though some of them certainly were.

Given that identity is likely to have been local rather than regional in the highland villages, a reconsideration of Merneptah's Israel might help us locate Israel. (See pp. 124-28 for discussion of Merneptah's Stela.) Recently, an Egyptologist has identified a second stone monument attributable to Pharaoh Merneptah.[15] This is a relief sculpture on a temple wall depicting Merneptah's battles with the enemies of Canaan: Ashkelon, Gezer and Yanoam. In addition, there is a depiction of his battle against Israel. The Israelites in this artwork are wearing the usual Canaanite clothing of the period, and they drive at least one chariot.

(By contrast, the Bible presents early Israel as having nothing to do with chariots—see Josh. 17.16-18; Judg. 1.19.)

It would seem that, at least in the eyes of Merneptah's artisans, Israel was a Canaanite group indistinguishable from all other Canaanite groups. If they were driving chariots, they probably lived in the lowlands. Since very few people lived in the highlands during Merneptah's reign (the highland villages only began to appear in his day, and did not peak until well after his time), it is likely that Merneptah's Israel was a group of Canaanites located in the Jezreel Valley. Merneptah does not associate them with a city because his battle with them took place in the plain. Possibly, then, Israel was a coalition of several Canaanite cities in the region, each of which capitulated when the coalition was defeated. Merneptah did not need to lay siege to the cities, so he emphasized the chariot battle in his poem and wall relief.

If this is the case the Israelites cannot be discovered archaeologically, though there can be no doubt that they were living in Iron Age I Palestine. Indeed, they were a part of Canaan even before the Iron Age I highland villages began to thrive. In all probability, some of those who later came to live in the highland villages were Israelites as well. Since other, non-Israelite, ethnic groups probably lived in the highlands with them, a method does not exist for distinguishing between any ethnic differences that may have existed. The Israel of this period was strong enough to resist (unsuccessfully) a pharaoh, so it should be no surprise that their descendants would be sufficiently dominant in the region to establish an Iron Age II kingdom. Only then did other ethnic groups become incorporated into an entity called Israel, and the process was politically motivated. (This point will be discussed in Chapter 8.) In between, during Iron Age I, Israelites were to be found in abundance, but would have been more easily recognized by their contemporaries among whom they lived than by us, who see only the remnant of their material culture. There is no need to call these people Proto-Israelites as long as one keeps in mind that the name of the ethnic group, Israel, remained constant even as the substance of what it meant to be an Israelite was undergoing constant revision, as is the case with any ethnic group.

### *Life in the Iron Age I Highland Villages*

Before moving to a discussion of the tenth century, a brief sketch of daily life in the highland villages of early Iron Age I is interesting.[16]

Most people living in this region did not live in urban environments. As a matter of fact, the only 'cities' were rather small villages, usually numbering a few hundred people. Even cities of that size were rare. The majority lived in villages of about 100 people or fewer. It should be stressed as well that almost all these highland villages were north of the Judaean Hills. The southern region was home to very few.

The average village consisted of 18 to 20 houses. Each house could accommodate a nuclear family: mother and father, with children. In ancient times, prior to the advent of modern medicine, the average woman would bear about six children during her lifetime, and about three or four of those children would die before the age of two. Thus the average family comprised four or five people. Often, two or three of the village houses were clustered together. These have been interpreted to be an extended family unit defined by the Bible as a *beth 'ab*, which means 'house of the father'. One of the clustered houses was home to the patriarch (eldest male) and his wife, and a son of the patriarch with wife and children lived in each of the other homes. Daughters of the family lived at home only until shortly after puberty, after which time they were married away to another extended family unit. Apparently, if there were more than two sons, the remaining sons would move to another location (in the same or another village) to begin a new extended family.

The village may or may not have contained persons who were directly related by blood to one another, but in the Bible, they are described as blood related. The term is *mishpachah*, which is usually translated into English as 'clan'. A group of *mishpachôt* (the plural form) located in the same geographic area was called a *shebet*. Unfortunately, the traditional English translation of *shebet* can mislead. The usual translation is 'tribe', which sounds like an ethnic unit. But the Hebrew *shebet* was primarily a geographic term. People who lived in the hills just south of the Jezreel were of the *shebet* Manasseh. Further south they were of the *shebet* Ephraim. If they lived in upper Galilee, they were of the *shebet* Naphtali. Since almost no one was yet living in the Judaean Hills, those who lived just north of Jerusalem, which is the southernmost portion of the Central Hills, were called the *shebet* Benjamin. In Hebrew, *ben yamîn* means 'son of the the south'. In the Iron Age II, as the Judaean Hills became populated, a *shebet* Judah emerged. But that *shebet* does not yet exist in the archaic poem of Judges 5, which may have been composed as early as the tenth century BCE (late

Iron Age I). Iron Age II (or Persian period) biblical storytellers created an elaborate (and wholly artificial) family tree out of these geographic designations (see, e.g., Gen. 29.31–30.24). At that stage, some ethnic labels, such as Dan (originally a Sea Peoples clan) and Gad (probably a Moabite clan), were incorporated into the Israelite tribal lists.[17]

To ensure the survival of the community, the risk involved in farming was spread out over several activities. If one activity failed during its season, the others could provide for the lack. Thus, each village engaged in several crop seasons each calendar year as well as animal husbandry. On average, agricultural life might include the following: the winter (rainy) months were a time for the growing of legumes (chickpeas, lentils); spring and early summer produced the most significant staples of life, the grains (barley, wheat); the later summer and early autumn was the time of the fruit harvests (grapes, olives, figs, dates). The community raised sheep and goats as well, and a few cattle. These provided milk, wool, manure and, only on special occasions, meat. The religious calendar reflects this agricultural pattern (see, e.g., Lev. 23). The biblical holidays *ro'sh ha-Shanah*, which was a new year's celebration, the Day of Atonement for sin against Yahweh (*yom kippur*), and the Feast of Booths (*sukkoth*) collectively correspond to the fruit harvests of late-summer and early-autumn. The barley harvest is known to the Bible as Unleavened Bread and First Fruits, a holiday that follows immediately after the celebration of the spring birthing of livestock, known as Passover. Early summer's wheat harvest is called the Feast of Weeks, because it falls roughly seven weeks after Unleavened Bread and First Fruits. All these holidays were given a role in the grand narrative of Moses and the exodus from Egypt, but the festivals themselves were as old as Palestinian agriculture itself (see Chapter 4).

## SUGGESTED ADDITIONAL READING

*Ethnic Identity*

Hutchinson, J., and A.D. Smith (eds.), *Ethnicity* (Oxford Readers; Oxford: Oxford University Press, 1996).

Sparks, Kenton L., *Ethnicity and Identity in Ancient Israel* (Winona Lake, IN: Eisenbrauns, 1998).

Tonkin, Elizabeth, Maryon McDonald and Malcolm Chapman (eds.), *History and Ethnicity* (London: Routledge, 1989).

Sollors, W. (ed.), *Theories of Ethnicity: A Classical Reader* (New York: New York University Press, 1996).

*History and Archaeology of the Iron Age I*

Block-Smith, Elizabeth, and Beth Alpert Nakhai, 'A Landscape Comes to Life: The Iron I Period', *Near Eastern Archaeology* 62.2 (1999), pp. 62-92, 100-27.

Finkelstein, Israel, *The Archaeology of the Israelite Settlement* (Jerusalem: Israel Exploration Society, 1988).

Finkelstein, Israel, and Nadav Na'aman (eds.), *From Nomadism to Monarchy: Archaeological and Historical Aspects of Early Israel* (Jerusalem: Israel Exploration Society, 1994).

Gitin, Seymour, Amihai Mazar and Ephraim Stern (eds.), *Mediterranean Peoples in Transition: Thirteenth to Early Tenth Centuries BCE* (Festschrift Trude Dothan; Jerusalem: Israel Exploration Society, 1998).

Gottwald, Norman K., *The Tribes of Yahweh: A Sociology of the Religion of Liberated Israel, 1250–1050 B.C.E.* (Maryknoll, NY: Orbis Books, 1979).

McNutt, Paula M., *Reconstructing the Society of Ancient Israel* (Louisville, KY: Westminster/John Knox Press, 1999).

Rogerson, John W., 'Was Early Israel a Segmentary Society?', *JSOT* 36 (1986), pp. 17-26.

Stager, Lawrence E., 'The Archaeology of the Family in Ancient Israel', *BASOR* 260 (1985), pp. 1-35.

NOTES

1.   For a discussion of the irrelevance (and nonexistence) of 'race', see R. Just, 'Triumph of the Ethnos', in E. Tonkin *et al.* (eds.), *History and Ethnicity* (London: Routledge, 1989), pp. 71-88.

2.   See, for example, R. Handler, 'Is "Identity" a Useful Cross-Cultural Concept?' in J.R. Gillis (ed.), *Commemorations: The Politics of National Identity* (Princeton: Princeton University Press, 1994), pp. 27-40.

3.   J. Vansina, *Paths in the Rainforests: Toward a History of Political Tradition in Equatorial Africa* (Madison: University of Wisconsin Press, 1990), pp. 19-20.

4.   Proposal 1 is the hypothesis advanced by L.E. Stager, 'Forging an Identity: The Emergence of Ancient Israel', in M.D. Coogan (ed.), *The Oxford History of the Biblical World* (Oxford: Oxford University Press, 1998), pp. 123-75; see also, *idem*, 'The Impact of the Sea Peoples in Canaan (1185–1050 BCE)', in T.E. Levy (ed.), *The Archaeology of Society in the Holy Land* (Leicester: Leicester University Press, 1998), pp. 332-48.

5.   Proposal 2 was advanced by I. Finkelstein, 'The Date of the Settlement of the Philistines in Canaan', *Tel Aviv* 22 (1995), pp. 213-39; see also, *idem*, 'Philistine Chronology: High, Middle or Low?', in S. Gitin, A. Mazar and E. Stern (eds.), *Mediterranean Peoples in Transition: Thirteenth to Early Tenth Centuries BCE* (Festschrift Trude Dothan; Jerusalem: Israel Exploration Society, 1998), pp. 140-47.

6.   For this suggestion, see S. Bunimovitz, 'Sea Peoples in Cyprus and Israel: A Comparative Study of Immigration Processes', in Gitin, Mazar and Stern (eds.) *Mediterranean Peoples in Transition*, pp. 103-13 (see n. 5, above). Bunimovitz accepts Stager's dates and Egyptian containment hypothesis, however.

7.   I have engaged in precisely this speculation in my article, 'An Alternative

Hypothesis for a Historical Exodus Event', *SJOT* 14 (2000), pp. 260-74. It remains to be seen whether my hypothesis is deemed credible by other historians. In the meantime, there is no need to pursue that speculation here.

8. The three major hypotheses (Conquest Model, Gradual Infiltration Model, and Peasant Revolt Model) are summarized succinctly in any number of recent publications. See R.K. Gnuse, *No Other Gods: Emergent Monotheism in Israel* (JSOTSup, 241; Sheffield: Sheffield Academic Press, 1997), pp. 23-61; F.S. Frick, *A Journey through the Hebrew Scriptures* (Fort Worth: Harcourt Brace, 1995), pp. 258-75; N.K. Gottwald, *The Hebrew Bible: A Socio-Literary Introduction* (Philadelphia: Fortress Press, 1985), pp. 261-76; Stager, 'Forging an Identity', pp. 128-41 (see n. 4, above); I. Finkelstein, *The Archaeology of the Israelite Settlement* (Jerusalem: Israel Exploration Society, 1988), pp. 295-314; W.G. Dever, *Recent Archaeological Discoveries and Biblical Research* (Seattle: University of Washington Press, 1990), pp. 37-56.

9. The three names most closely associated with the Conquest Model are the famous W.F. Albright and his two star students, G.E. Wright and J. Bright. These three, with several generations of their students, are known as the 'Albright School'. See G.E. Wright, *Biblical Archaeology* (Philadelphia: Westminster Press, abr. edn, 1960), pp. 34-52; J. Bright, *A History of Israel* (Philadelphia: Westminster Press, 1st edn, 1959), pp. 110-27. (Bright's volume went through subsequent revisions in which his thesis was modified very slightly in the direction of Mendenhall's Peasant Revolt hypothesis: see his *A History of Israel* [Philadelphia: Westminster Press, 3rd edn, 1981], pp. 120-43.)

10. B. Halpern, 'Preface to the Paperback Edition', in *idem, The First Historians: The Hebrew Bible and History* (University Park: The Pennsylvania State University Press, paperback edn, 1996), pp. xxvii-xxviii. (See Chapter 3 n. 8.)

11. The Gradual Infiltration Model was introduced by A. Alt, supported by Alt's student, M. Noth, and has been embraced in variant forms by many scholars since. This is just a selection of the publications: A. Alt, *Essays in Old Testament History and Religion* (trans. from the 1925 original by R.A. Wilson; Oxford: Oxford University Press, 1966), pp. 135-69; M. Noth, *The History of Israel* (trans. S. Godman; London: A. & C. Black, 1958), pp. 68-84; I. Finkelstein, *The Archaeology of the Israelite Settlement* (see n. 8, above); D.B. Redford, *Egypt, Canaan, and Israel in Ancient Times* (Princeton: Princeton University Press, 1992), pp. 257-80.

12. The Peasant Revolt Model was advanced by G.E. Mendenhall and refined by N.K. Gottwald. See G.E. Mendenhall, *The Tenth Generation: The Origins of the Biblical Tradition* (Baltimore: The Johns Hopkins University Press, 1973); N.K. Gottwald, *The Tribes of Yahweh: A Sociology of the Religion of Liberated Israel, 1250–1050 B.C.E.* (Maryknoll, KY: Orbis Books, 1979); see also, M.L. Chaney, 'Ancient Palestinian Peasant Movements and the Formation of Premonarchic Israel', in D.N. Freedman and D.F. Graf (eds.), *Palestine in Transition: The Emergence of Ancient Israel* (The Social World of Biblical Antiquity, 2; Sheffield: Almond Press, 1983), pp. 39-90.

13. The Symbiosis approach might be said to include at least the following, though perhaps some would reject the label: W.G. Dever, *Recent Archaeological*

*Discoveries and Biblical Research*; I. Finkelstein, 'The Emergence of Israel: A Phase in the Cyclic History of Canaan in the Third and Second Millennia BCE', in I. Finkelstein and N. Na'aman (eds.), *From Nomadism to Monarchy: Archaeological and Historical Aspects of Early Israel* (Jerusalem: Israel Exploration Society, 1994), pp. 150-78; S. Bunimovitz, 'Socio-Political Transformations in the Central Hill Country in the Late Bronze-Iron I Transition', in Finkelstein and Na'aman (eds.), *From Nomadism to Monarchy*, pp. 179-202; Niels Peter Lemche, *Early Israel: Anthropological and Historical Studies on the Israelite Society before the Monarchy* (Leiden: E.J. Brill, 1985); *idem*, 'On Doing Sociology with "Solomon"', in L.K. Handy (ed.), *The Age of Solomon: Scholarship at the Turn of the Millennium* (Leiden: E.J. Brill, 1997), pp. 312-35.

14. E. Block-Smith and B.A. Nakhai, 'A Landscape Comes to Life: The Iron I Period', *Near Eastern Archaeology* 62.2 (1999), pp. 69-92, 100-27 (71, 83).

15. F. Yurco, 'Merneptah's Canaanite Campaigns and Israel's Origins', in E.S. Frerichs and L.H. Lesko (eds.), *Exodus: The Egyptian Evidence* (Winona Lake, IN: Eisenbrauns, 1997), pp. 26-55.

16. This section depends to a significant degree on L.E. Stager, 'The Archaeology of the Family in Ancient Israel', *BASOR* 260 (1985), pp. 1-35.

17. On the Sea Peoples origin of Dan, consult the references in K.L. Noll, 'The God Who is Among the Danites', *JSOT* 80 (1998), pp. 3-23 (3 n. 2). The Moabite origin of the clan of Gad is implied by a 'plain sense' reading of the Moabite Stone. For the text of the Moabite Stone, see p. 223; see also J.A. Dearman (ed.), *Studies in the Mesha Inscription and Moab* (Atlanta: Scholars Press, 1989).

Chapter 7

THE TENTH CENTURY BCE

*Introduction*

Conventionally, the year 900 BCE has been chosen to designate the start of the Iron Age II. This places the tenth century (the 900s BCE) in the Iron Age I, as is the case in the chart on p. 26, and throughout this book. In this situation, an archaeologist would call the tenth century IA IC (which means Iron Age I, C). The 'C' represents the third and last segment of the Iron Age I period: IA IA, followed by IA IB and then IA IC.

Many archaeologists prefer to call the tenth century IA IIA (Iron Age II, A), beginning the Iron Age II with the year 1000 rather than 900 BCE. This difference in nomenclature might seem trivial since all such designations are merely labels of convenience defined by modern researchers. They were not defined or even perceived by ancient people. But it is not as trivial as it seems.

Behind this difference in terminology lurks a significant problem. According to the Bible, a man named David created a kingdom in Palestine (2 Sam. 8). Following this, his son, Solomon, presided over a huge empire, stretching from the Euphrates River to the border of Egypt (1 Kgs 5.1; in some English versions, this is 4.21). According to biblical chronology, David was active in the eleventh century BCE (c. 1060–1020 BCE). After cross-referencing the biblical data with ancient Mesopotamian records, all historians adjust the dates for David's activity down to the tenth century. Thus, David's dates are frequently listed in history books as 1000 to 960 or so BCE, and Solomon is given dates c. 960 to 920 BCE. This reflects the biblical cliché of 40-year reigns for each, which sounds suspiciously artificial. The two may have been active for less than 80 years. Nevertheless, if David and Solomon were real people, they lived in the tenth century BCE, whether it is called IA IC or IA IIA.

With some significant exceptions, those who call the tenth century IA IIA believe that the archaeological evidence is consistent with the biblical stories of David and Solomon, while those who call it IA IC are not convinced of this correlation. In other words, the difference in nomenclature determines whether the tenth century belongs with the period of political decentralization that was Iron Age I (without a large Davidic–Solomonic empire from the Euphrates to Egypt), or the period of regional kingdoms so characteristic of the Iron Age II (with a Davidic–Solomonic kingdom of significant size). The nomenclature itself is a minor issue, but these two conceptions of the tenth century are radically opposed, and a decision for one and against the other is necessary.

An issue of historical method should be stressed from the outset. Anyone who argues for a large Davidic–Solomonic monarchy must convince others that the thesis makes better sense than the null hypothesis. (For the definition of a null hypothesis, see p. 50.) In this case, the null hypothesis is that Palestine experienced a gradual transition from Iron Age I decentralized political units to the Iron Age II period, with its larger, territorial states. The null hypothesis would not expect to find a large kingdom ruling from the Euphrates to Egypt during the tenth century BCE.

The first step in dealing with the question of a Davidic–Solomonic monarchy in Palestine is to review the case in favor of such a kingdom. Next, the argument against the existence of this state will be discussed. Only then will we be in a position to continue our survey of Canaanite–Israelite history in Chapter 8.

### The Case for a United Monarchy

Those who favor the existence of a Davidic–Solomonic kingdom usually call it the United Monarchy, a term that derives from the biblical story. According to the books of Samuel, the Central and Judaean Hills were not politically unified prior to David's time. The story asserts that King Saul (1 Sam. 9–31) ruled over Israel in the Central Hills and parts of Transjordan. This king seems to have exerted nominal control over the Judaean Hills, but not full authority. The Bible describes Saul as a warrior engaged in almost constant battle against the Philistines, who controlled the Coastal Plains and the Jezreel Valley. In 1 Samuel 31, King Saul dies in a failed attempt to push the Philistines out of the Jezreel.

Intertwined with the tale of King Saul is the story of David (1 Sam. 16–2 Sam. 8). David becomes a general in Saul's army, but falls out of favor with the king. As a result, he escapes to the Judaean Hills, gathers a band of outlaws who become his personal army, and eventually joins forces with the Philistines against Saul. The story suggests, halfheartedly, that David was innocent of any treason against Saul. Saul, we are told, was demented, and David was not really loyal to the Philistines, but only used them to protect himself against Saul's paranoia. However, the storyteller planted clues to suggest the relationship between David and Saul was far more complex than that of an innocent lad and his insane lord. Artistic ironies in the plot and chronology allow for the possibility that David was not as innocent as he feigned. For the author(s) of 1–2 Samuel, there are no 'good guys', only tragically flawed people: Samuel, Saul, David, Jonathan, Michal, Absalom. As a result of this storytelling complexity, Samuel's narrative is a delightful tale to read.

The story climaxes with the elevation of David from Judaean fugitive to king of Judah, and then king of Israel and Judah (2 Sam. 1–5). When David has become king, he conquers the Canaanite city of Jerusalem (occupied by a people called Jebusites), making it his capital. In the Bible, Jerusalem is ideal for a capital because it stands between Israel to the north and Judah to the south, two distinct political entities united only by the fact that they share one king, David.

Thus, the Bible presents David's kingdom as a United Monarchy, which was inherited by his son Solomon. The process of inheritance is another opportunity for the Bible's storyteller to display his subtle craft (2 Sam. 9–1 Kgs 2). Several sons of David, the reader is told, might have become king: Amnon, Absalom, Adonijah. Instead, these men died one at a time and a younger son who played little active role in the story becomes king, a surprising outcome. After this, the tone of the story shifts to an ironic glorification of King Solomon in 1 Kings 1–10. Solomon is supposed to have presided over a massive international trade network, and to have built a temple in Jerusalem for Yahweh, god of Israel, yet he acts in ways that violate Deuteronomy's stipulations for royal conduct (Deut. 17.14-20). Finally, the story of the United Monarchy comes to a close in 1 Kings 11–14, when King Solomon commits sins against Yahweh, then dies. As punishment, Yahweh divides the United Monarchy in two, the Kingdom of Israel to the north and the

Kingdom of Judah to the south, and an Egyptian raider named Shishak steals Solomon's wealth.

Most historians agree that at least portions of Samuel and Kings are based on real events of the tenth century BCE. Saul, David and Solomon probably were real people who lived in that century. However, most historians also agree that these story-world characters have been manipulated by the creativity of the storytelling process, and do not correspond with the historical people whose names they bear. In a sense, the Bible's King David and the 'real' David are similar to the legendary King Arthur and the 'real' Arthur. Behind the Arthur tradition was the memory of Celtic resistance to the invading Anglo-Saxons in the early-sixth century CE. The Arthur legend, however, took on a life of its own. So it was with David.

Thus, like Genesis to Judges, the books of Samuel and Kings are products of folklore, yet contain genuine fragments of the past. Historians disagree on the number of genuine fragments that can be recovered from these biblical books, and their significance. Other portions of the Bible also mention David and Solomon. For example, the book of Psalms is supposed to have been composed, in part, by David, and Proverbs, in part, by Solomon. Except for Samuel and Kings, however, only the books of Chronicles have the potential to offer a historian reliable information. The majority of scholars believe that the writer of Chronicles copied much of his narrative directly from Samuel and Kings. Where Chronicles departs from that source, it is unreliable in most instances. Therefore, Samuel and Kings are the major biblical sources for the tenth century in spite of their folklore qualities.

Those who believe that a large United Monarchy existed in the tenth century base their hypothesis on two arguments. First, they believe Samuel and Kings contain passages that derive from the tenth century BCE, and that implies there was a tradition of Hebrew writing in the period when Israelite monarchy is supposed to have begun, with a reliable transmission of details about that kingdom in subsequent generations. Second, they argue that archaeological data are consistent with the existence of a centralized, region-wide monarchy in tenth-century Palestine. All agree that the second of these arguments is the more weighty of the two, but both provide valuable insight to the complexities of the issue.

*The Antiquity of Selected Biblical Texts*

Since the Bible is the product of an ancient culture in which narrative reliability was never a priority, the belief in the accuracy of biblical tales requires supporting argument. Also, given the unstable nature of oral tradition, most scholars agree that one cannot offer a hypothesis that reliable information about David and Solomon survived orally and was written down only in later centuries. The best way to defend the belief in reliable biblical literature is to show two things. First, one must demonstrate that there was writing activity among speakers of Hebrew in the tenth century BCE. Second, one must show that portions of the biblical text were composed during the tenth century, or (and this is almost as good) were copied from documents composed during the tenth century.

There is slight, but useful, evidence that writing activity began among speakers of Hebrew during the tenth century. Prior to that century, the Iron Age I offers no evidence for Hebrew writing at all.[1] The only significant tenth-century epigraph discovered so far dates to around 910–900 BCE (although even this text might date to the early-ninth century). It is a small poem about the agricultural seasons that was composed in the city of Gezer. Although the Gezer Calendar, as it is called, was not composed in standard biblical Hebrew, it bears minor resemblance to archaic portions of the Bible. As noted on p. 55, archaic linguistic features are clustered in two biblical poems. Archaisms also appear haphazardly in many other biblical texts. With the possible exception of the two poems, none of these archaic features demonstrates that the biblical passages in which they are found were composed as early as the Gezer Calendar. Rather, they demonstrate that writers of later times knew the archaic forms. These later writers used the archaisms artistically to give their writings a traditional atmosphere, much as a modern Christian employs Elizabethan English to give a prayer or hymn that effect. How did the writers of the later period know these archaic forms? It is reasonable to assume that there were some ancient texts still available, and that these texts would have been composed prior to the Iron Age II (defined as 900–586 BCE). It is not credible to speculate on Hebrew writing in the early Iron Age I, but by the transitional tenth century (IA IC or IA IIA), some archaic Hebrew texts had been composed. Unfortunately, the Gezer Calendar is the only one of these that survives.[2]

A second argument has been advanced for Hebrew writing in the tenth century BCE. Except for the Gezer Calendar, the earliest surviving non-Biblical Hebrew epigraphs date from the eighth century. The writers of these later epigraphs used a system for writing numbers in hieratic, a type of Egyptian. This particular method was no longer used by Egyptians in the Iron Age II, so one must ask where these Hebrews learned the system. The hieratic system was used by people in southern Canaan during the Late Bronze Age's Egyptian empire. Presumably, it was preserved in a few isolated locations, probably the urban centers that survived through the centuries of Iron Age I. One of those centers was the small highland city of Jerusalem. It is possible, then, that writers of Hebrew, who would have learned their craft in Jerusalem after David conquered the city (2 Sam. 5.5-8), inherited the hieratic forms from the Jebusite scribes they conquered. This second argument is weaker than the first. The point of contact with the hieratic system could have been a tenth-century city as just stated, but need not have been. Speakers of Hebrew might have learned to write the hieratic forms in later times from whomever preserved that system of notation (and that 'whomever' remains, to date, unknown).[3]

If these two arguments for writing activity among speakers of Hebrew in the tenth century are accepted, the second step is to isolate biblical passages that plausibly derive from tenth-century originals. Although many biblical scholars treat extensive texts as verbatim copies of actual tenth-century documents, this is misleading. Even if some biblical passages ultimately go back to that time, they exist now in a form of Hebrew that is much younger. Therefore, it is necessary to be cautious when assigning very early dates to selected biblical passages.

The best means for isolation of early documents in the Bible is to analyze the genres of individual biblical passages. (For a discussion of genre, see pp. 33-35.) Archaic poems such as the Gezer Calendar would not have been the most common genre of the tenth century. At that time, writing was new to speakers of the Hebrew language. In societies where writing is an innovation, 'literature' such as poetry is a minor product of writing activities. More commonly, writing is used for practical purposes, such as administrative documentation. As a matter of fact, in the ancient world, early and short examples of literature, like the Gezer Calendar, were usually training exercises for apprentice scribes who would become bureaucrats. If the Gezer Calendar was written in the tenth century, it is likely that administrative texts were also produced, and in greater quantity than the poetry.

Common genres among ancient administrators included lists of government officials, tax records, inventories, letters, liturgical or ritual texts, daybooks of mundane royal activity, sometimes also compilations of highly significant royal activity in the form of a chronicle, and, on occasion, political propaganda, such as a narrative designed to justify a king's right to rule. This last category was usually a short narrative for public display, to be read by either the gods or literate members of society, depending on where it was displayed. A few other genres for this kind of public display included dedicatory inscriptions for a building, votive offering inscriptions in a temple and royal stelae (sometimes based on information from daybooks or chronicles).

Biblical scholars have tried to isolate portions of the books of Samuel and Kings that seem to conform to these genres. Many suggestions have been made that are not very convincing and even those that are plausible are not necessarily correct. However, among the more persuasive of these efforts, one might include the following portions of 1–2 Samuel:

1. The poem of 2 Sam. 1.19-27, which claims in v. 18 to come from an older document called 'Yashar' ('Upright/Just' or 'Valiant'), could have been an old literary text similar to the Gezer Calendar. (See also the references to the document of Yashar in Josh. 10.12-13 and in some manuscript versions of 1 Kgs 8.12-13.) The poems in 1 Sam. 2.1-10 (originally attributed to a king, not the wife of a commoner) and 2 Sam. 23.1-7 could be additional examples. Such texts were used as sample writings when scribes were trained. It must be stressed that poetry is not an ideal genre for historical research. Even if a poem is based on real events (perhaps Judg. 5?), it is not in the nature of the genre to tell what happened. Could a historian, several thousand years from now, reconstruct specific events from 'The Star-Spangled Banner'? It is not very likely.

2. A few lists of royal administrators, such as 2 Sam. 8.16-18 and 20.23-25, could have been part of the royal archive or another scribal training text. (It would be more difficult to argue that 2 Sam. 23.8-39 was an old administrative list, though this folkloristic material might have been inspired by an old list.)

3. The battle narratives of 2 Sam. 8.1-14, and perhaps portions of 5.6-9, 17-25, as well as 10.6-19 and 12.26-31, could have had their origin on a public stone inscription or in an archived scroll

such as a daybook or chronicle. Perhaps 1 Sam. 14.47-48 and 2 Sam. 2.8-9 derive from a similar record of King Saul, but this is very uncertain. In each case, these texts have been rewritten by the author(s) of Samuel. It might also be noted that biblical authors seem to be aware of a few public monuments, mentioned but not quoted (1 Sam. 15.12; 2 Sam. 8.3, 13; 18.18), and these monuments might have been sources for some of the battle narratives.[4] (It would be more difficult to suggest that narratives such as 2 Sam. 21.15-22 derive from older sources. In Mesopotamia, invented narratives that emulated royal stelae were composed, and that could be the case with this and similar biblical passages.)

4.  Portions of the narrative in 1–2 Samuel are similar in some ways to ancient royal propaganda. In this narrative, King David's reputation is defended against accusations that he took part in the killing of King Saul, the murder of Saul's son Ishbaal (also known as Ishboshet) and a variety of other unsavory events. Since the story consistently exonerates David of wrongdoing in these matters, several historians have suggested that the story (or, more likely, the underlying document from which the story was created) was an old propaganda narrative. As such, its details would be a reliable witness to actual crimes of treason and murder committed by David, crimes that the propaganda was trying to deny. As one scholar asserts, this narrative can be trusted because it is 'nothing but lies'.[5]

A number of passages from 1–2 Kings may also be included:

5.  Portions of the story about Solomon could have derived from tenth-century lists or a royal chronicle, possibly the same document(s) mentioned under '1.' and '2.', above. If so, these passages have been rewritten by the author(s) of Kings, so it is difficult to be certain which aspects of the texts go back to the tenth century. Also, some biblical scholars have been eager to inflate the list of passages that could have been a part of such a document. Realistically, the passages that might have been copied from archived sources are:

     a.  1 Kings 4.2-19, a list of royal officials and districts. If this text is old, it has been modified by later scribes and is difficult to assess.

b. 1 Kings 9.17-19, a list of royal fortifications. Some scholars include v. 15 as well, but that is unlikely in light of v. 16, a point that will be discussed below.

c. 1 Kings 3.1, 7.8, and 9.16, 24, a marriage between Solomon and an Egyptian princess. In the tenth century a marriage between a minor king in Canaan and the daughter of an (equally minor) Egyptian king of the 21st or 22nd Dynasty is not out of the question. An alternate manuscript tradition of Kings (which is rarely translated in the various English Bibles) claims that Jeroboam I was also married to an Egyptian princess, which is also within the realm of possibility. (The text appears in Greek manuscripts as 3 Kgdms 12.24e, which would have appeared in English Bibles between the verses of 1 Kgs 12.24-25.)

d. 1 Kings 9.10-14, a narrative in which Solomon sells land to a king of Tyre. The author of Kings has tried to present this in folkloristic fashion as an example of the wily Solomon bettering the foolish king of Tyre. If it is from an old source, the original recorded, soberly, a sale of land in return for prestige items (gold and lumber).

e. 1 Kings 5.27-30 (in some English versions, 1 Kgs 5.13-16), a narrative about Solomon's forced labor policy. A passage in 1 Kgs 9.22 flatly contradicts 5.27-30, which suggests that the author of Kings, or a later editor, was embarrassed by the forced labor policy. The numbers in 5.27-30, like so many numbers in ancient documents, biblical and non-biblical, are grossly inflated and wholly unrealistic.

f. 1 Kings 9.26-28 with 10.11-12, a narrative about Solomon's trade venture in partnership with Tyre. This depicts a shipping port on the Gulf of Aqaba-Elat, south of Edom. (The folk-tale about the Queen of Sheba [1 Kgs 10.1-10, 13] was added to this narrative at a later time.)

6. 1 Kings 8.12-13 preserves the mutilated fragment of a temple inscription, the text of which is more complete in some biblical manuscripts than others. It is possible that this fragment was copied from a building inscription or from an anthology of poetry called Yashar, as discussed in '1.' above. (1 Kgs 6–7 describe, in great detail, the building activities of Solomon. However, the suggestion that this material derives from a building

inscription lacks support from ancient Near Eastern parallels. In reality, after the demolition of these buildings by foreign armies, someone who wanted to preserve the memory of them wrote 1 Kgs 6–7. Thus, these chapters were composed hundreds of years after the time of King Solomon and the descriptions evoke the structures as they existed just before they were destroyed.)

7. 1 Kings 14.25-28 preserves the mention of Pharaoh Shishak's military raid during the 920s BCE. This raid is known as well from an Egyptian stone monument at Thebes, in which Sheshonq I (Shishak), founder of the 22nd Dynasty, boasts of his accomplishments. The biblical version is not, unfortunately, a quotation of the source text, which might have been a Jerusalem temple inscription by a king who 'restored' that which was lost to Shishak.

This list includes only those biblical passages for which a plausible argument can be made that the information in them goes back to tenth-century sources. However, two cautions must be emphasized. First, although it might be plausible that these passages derive from the tenth century, one cannot be certain in most cases that they do go back that far. Only the final example '7.' can be demonstrated to match information from a known tenth-century source. Second, if some of these biblical texts are accepted as reliable sources for the tenth century, they require interpretation before they can yield to us their significance. In large measure, the significance of texts depends on how well they fit into the picture painted by the archaeological data for that century. In other words, the biblical data are secondary in importance to the primary artifacts recovered from excavation. So it is to the excavated evidence that we must now turn.

*The Archaeology of Tenth-Century Palestine*

Several archaeologists believe there was a centralized, region-wide monarchy in tenth-century Palestine. At first glance, this hypothesis seems unlikely. The tenth century stands between two eras. On one side, Iron Age I was a period of decentralized political units, most of which were in the lowlands. With the collapse of the Egyptian empire, Canaan saw a gradual process of rebuilding, in which the population recovered slowly after Egyptian deportations, warfare and famine. Small city-states emerged in Phoenicia and Syria. Philistine city-states appeared on the Palestinian coast. Canaanite cities continued in the Jezreel

Valley. The highlands, as we saw in the last chapter, were populated with small, unfortified villages and possessed no apparent political hierarchy. On the other side of the tenth century, Palestine's highlands became home to small, localized Iron Age II states: Israel, Judah, Ammon, Moab, and eventually Edom. Any archaeologist faced with these data from the dirt would not, in the absence of texts such as the Bible, go looking for a region-wide political unification during the transitional decades of the tenth century. If the evidence suggested an absence of such a state, no one would be surprised. Therefore, a hypothesis advancing this state's presence is a surprise.

The archaeological hypothesis for political unification in tenth-century Canaan rests on three pillars. First, Palestine displays a marked shift from predominantly rural villages to larger urban settings in the tenth century, and, as one archaeologist correctly observes, urbanization is a prerequisite to state formation in more cases than not.[6] Second, there is evidence for increased international trade during the Iron Age II (900–586 BCE), and a number of scholars have argued that this trade traveled through Canaan in the tenth century. Third, monumental building complexes, including formidable fortifications with elaborate city gateways, appear at about this time in a number of places. These fortifications are interpreted to be the product of a centralized state. Each of these arguments merits careful consideration.

The first of these pillars calls attention to an unambiguous pattern of change in Palestine's material culture. Almost all of the Iron Age I highland villages were abandoned gradually, and all but a handful were gone by the mid-tenth century. In their place about two dozen larger towns, or cities, emerged, along with numerous smaller villages. Many of the cities were already urban centers in the Iron Age I, contemporary with the highland villages, others were new, but collectively they produced a more urban society than had been the case previously. More than a dozen of these cities were home to more than 1000 people each. Gezer, one of the larger cities, numbered more than 3000, and Dan, the largest, had about 5000 people. Although the highland villages of Iron Age I were gone, the highlands were not abandoned. The population of these regions had increased. Highland cities such as Shechem and Jerusalem thrived, indicating that the highlands were beginning to be integrated into the urban culture of the lowlands. Palestine's entire population was growing, and the tenth century marks a noticeable upsurge in that process, with a total population of at least 100,000, and probably more. Of these people, nearly one in four lived in a city, which indicates a radical departure from the previous two centuries.

Closely associated with increased population and urbanization is an economy that is able to feed these people. The cities were not urban in the modern sense in which people in them were isolated from agricultural activities. On the contrary, most people, even in urban centers, walked to the fields each day to earn their living. Nevertheless, larger, centralized populations imply a workforce able to be put to work on building projects rather than farming. If these cities were under the control of a central authority, a king, there would have to be an army to protect the king's interests and a bureaucracy to serve the army. Who would feed these people? Presumably, the king controlled the economy, taxing the agricultural income. That would not, however, be sufficient income for a king to control all of Canaan single-handedly, which requires an enormous investment in manpower. This king would have to tax a revenue source from outside his own domain. In other words, there would have to have been an international network of trade in the tenth century and a Palestinian king intimately involved in that trade.

During the Iron Age II (900–586 BCE), there is evidence that Canaan was the hub for a brisk trade in goods from the south, which moved through Palestine to Egypt, Phoenicia, Anatolia and Mesopotamia.[7] Copper was transported from the Negev; spices, such as myrrh, and incense, such as frankincense, came from the lands that the Bible calls Sheba (western Yemen) and Ophir (the lands bordering the Red Sea on the western shore); rare goods, such as gemstones, gold, ivory, ebony, and exotic animals, moved from Africa and the Arabian Sea into the land of Sheba, and northward to Palestine. Without doubt, this profitable trade is one of the reasons that Neo-Assyrian kings (who will be discussed in the next chapter) took an interest in Canaan during the ninth through seventh centuries BCE.

Some archaeologists believe that this trade network came into existence in the tenth century, and that King Solomon was at its center. Following the biblical narratives (see note '5f.' above), these scholars suggest that Solomon and a king of Tyre worked together to create a trade network, and if there was a historical Queen of Sheba, she visited Solomon as part of this activity. One archaeologist suggests that a thriving city of 400 people called Tel Masos, which was located between Beer-Sheba and Arad, was the nerve center for Solomon's trade.[8] Solomon's role in the trade would have been, primarily, to provide military escort and protection to the trade routes. In return, he would tax the goods moving through his land.

A vital role in an international trade network requires a strong bureaucratic and military infrastructure, and this can be seen, suggest some archaeologists, in the fortifications that emerge during this period. Those who view Tel Masos and nearby sites as the nerve center for the Arabian goods moving through the Palestinian kingdom point to evidence for fortification and horse stables at some of these sites. Others argue that a series of fortifications to the south of the Beer-Sheba Valley was established in the tenth century.

The most debated of the fortifications attributed to King Solomon are the three examples found at the cities of Hazor, Megiddo and Gezer. Many archaeologists believe that a city wall and matching city gate were built at each of these places according to a single architectural plan. The gates are very impressive. With six large guardroom chambers, each protected its city and provided a public space where city elders could meet to settle legal disputes and conduct business. Perhaps not by coincidence, 1 Kgs 9.15 states that King Solomon conscripted forced labor to build city walls at Jerusalem, Hazor, Megiddo and Gezer.

Together, these three arguments establish a valid hypothesis that a centralized state had emerged in Palestine during the tenth century BCE. Advocates of this hypothesis conclude that since there was a state at that time, and since the Bible narrates a story of a state at that time, it follows that the state observed in the material culture is none other than the United Monarchy of the Bible. David and Solomon have been found!

### The Case against a United Monarchy

The case for a United Monarchy is very strong, and it is entirely reasonable to conclude that David created, and Solomon presided over, a unified political state in Canaan. Of course, advocates of the United Monarchy are divided over how large it was. Some historians follow the lead of 1 Kgs 5.1 (4.21 in some English translations), believing that Solomon ruled directly over Palestine, and ruled Syria through vassal kings. In that case, the United Monarchy controlled all land from the Euphrates to Egypt. Others recognize that much of the biblical story about David and Solomon is unhistorical, and conclude that Solomon's empire did not extend from the Euphrates River to the border of Egypt. Biblical writers exaggerate because that makes a better story. Nevertheless, all these scholars agree on several essential issues.

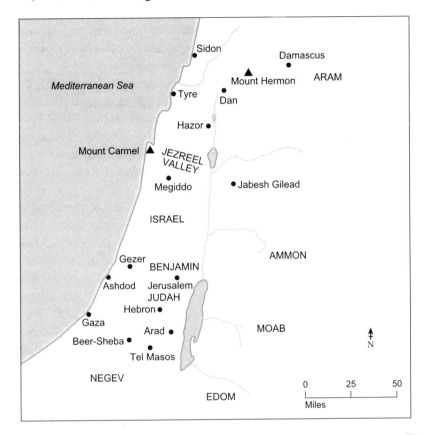

Figure 18. *Palestine in the Tenth Century BCE. The area of the United Monarchy.*

Advocates of the United Monarchy hypothesis agree that David conquered the land from Dan to Beer-Sheba and from just east of the Philistine coast to Transjordan. The Phoenicians and Philistines remained independent of David, but the former was allied with him and the latter confined by his military prowess. Most other Syro-Palestinian peoples were brought under the direct rule of the Davidic–Solomonic regime. At the death of Solomon, some 40 to 80 years after David established this kingdom, it collapsed, as narrated in 1 Kings 11–14. Shortly after that breakup, Pharaoh Sheshonq I raided Canaan (c. 920s BCE), stealing as much as he could seize, and with him went most traces of Solomon's wealth. As a result, the history of the Iron Age II (900–586 BCE) can be, and usually is, written with little or no reference to the United Monarchy. Advocates of the hypothesis affirm that the United Monarchy was only a brief and rather artificial interlude in the long sweep of Palestinian history. After the interlude, the separate kingdoms of Israel and Judah were tiny and usually powerless pawns in the larger arena that was ancient Near Eastern politics.

In my view, and in the view of a growing number of historians, this case for a large United Monarchy is not quite strong enough. There are factors that call into question each of the arguments advanced in favor of the hypothesis. As a result, many of us have decided to maintain the null hypothesis in which a 40- to 80-year United Monarchy is not a part of the historical narrative. (No mention of a United Monarchy will appear in the next chapter, for example.)

This does not mean that there was no King David. He certainly existed during the tenth century BCE, and there is direct evidence for his existence in an ancient epigraph. An Iron Age II inscriptional fragment found in excavation at Dan mentions a 'House of David' as a political entity somewhere south of Dan during the ninth century BCE, about 100 years or so after the historical David would have lived.[9] Given that the Bible calls the Jerusalem dynasty the House of David, it is reasonable to assume that the inscription from Dan refers to the royal house at Jerusalem, founded by the historical David. But David's kingdom was not the biblical United Monarchy.

It is time to look at the case against a United Monarchy. Clearly, the hypothesis in favor of it rests on the archaeological data. The Bible provided only two things: the names of the kings who ruled the United Monarchy, and sufficient textual fragments to show that records from that era survived (see the discussion above). The content of tenth-century biblical texts is not as important to the United Monarchy hypothesis as is the mere existence of tenth-century biblical documents. Their existence demonstrates that the scribal bureaucracy necessary to a kingdom was in place by that time. After archaeology establishes the existence of the United Monarchy, scholars have legitimate reason to investigate the biblical fragments and interpret their content in various ways. I stress this point because some opponents of the United Monarchy hypothesis have alleged that the entire hypothesis derives from the Bible. In reality, that is not the case; the Bible was essential to the hypothesis, but plays only a minor role in it. As a matter of fact, several leading advocates of a United Monarchy insist that, in the absence of the Bible, an archaeologist will *still* conclude that an unnamed monarchy ruled Syria-Palestine in the tenth century. Is this really the case? I think not, for at least seven reasons.

## The inscription found at Tel Dan in 1993-94

The only reference to 'David' that survives from the pre-Hellenistic world appears in this fragment of a monument. The text is far too damaged to be certain of its meaning. Some translations are more 'complete' than this one, because many epigraphers are willing to speculate about the damaged portions of the stone.

| Line | Text |
|---|---|
| 1 | ... and cut ... |
| 2 | ... my father went up ... to make war in ... |
| 3 | ... My father died. [Subject Noun] went to ... My king entered ... |
| 4 | ... [Is]rael advanced against my father's land. ... Hadad had enthroned ... |
| 5 | ... even I. And Hadad marched before me [toward] Apheq, from the seven[th] ... |
| 6 | ... my king. And I killed kin[gs] .. captives of ... |
| 7 | ... [char]iots and thousands of horsemen ... ... [ ? ]ram, son of ... |
| 8 | ... King of Israel. And ... [ ? ]yahu, son of ... |
| 9 | ... the House of David, and ... |
| 10 | ... their land ... |
| 11 | ... another ... |
| 12 | ... [rul]ed over Is[rael] ... |
| 13 | ... siege upon ... |

Figure 19. *The Inscription found at Tel Dan.*

*Seven Weaknesses in the Archaeological Argument*

There are seven aspects of the archaeological record that render a United Monarchy impossible. The first of these is the collective archaeological and epigraphic record of Egypt, Anatolia and Mesopotamia. As
was seen, the period from about 1200 to 900 BCE experienced a climatic change that devastated the kingdoms of the Late Bronze Age and
ushered in several centuries of political weakness and decentralization.
Egypt's 20th Dynasty held on for a few generations, then declined into
weakness. The Second Intermediate period had begun by about 1070
BCE, at the latest, and Egypt's weakness would continue well into the
Iron Age II. Anatolia and Mesopotamia likewise declined during these
centuries, so that little by way of international political intercourse was
taking place. In view of this 'worldwide' (from the perspective of the
ancient Near Easterners, it *was* worldwide!) political, social and economic decline, one should not expect a large region-wide state to
emerge on the periphery that was Palestine. The null hypothesis should
be maintained unless the archaeological data overwhelmingly indicate
otherwise. Although the case in favor of a United Monarchy is strong,
it is not overwhelming. Forty to 80 years is sufficient time to have left
far greater evidence (even if just fragments and refuse) than United
Monarchy advocates have presented.

Second, if, for the sake of argument, we accept the evidence for a
region-wide kingdom, there is no reason to believe that kingdom had
its capital at Jerusalem. As a matter of fact, logically, one would conclude that the kingdom's center was to the north or west of that city,
where the bulk of the Palestinian population lived. This point about
Jerusalem is difficult to press, because research is difficult in a city still
occupied in our own day. Moreover, the Muslim holy site, with its
famous Dome of the Rock mosque, covers the most significant real
estate in Jerusalem (where Solomon's palace and temple would have
been), and that land is permanently off limits to the archaeologist.
Nevertheless, extensive work has been done in some locations of Jerusalem, and *optimistic* estimates suggest that the tenth-century city was
home to as many as 2500 people. That was a large city for Palestine,
but not the largest in tenth-century Palestine. Also, nothing in the material culture of Jerusalem suggests that it was a political or cultural hub
for the region.

Of course, my last statement will inspire an advocate for the United
Monarchy to respond with a common proverb: 'Absence of evidence is

not evidence of absence'. While this proverb is true, it is also trivial. Absence of evidence is indeed absence of evidence. There is no compelling reason to make Jerusalem the political nerve center of tenth-century Palestine. (As we shall see below, not even the Bible provides compelling reason for doing so.)

What would have been the capital of a tenth-century monarchy? Dan is an excellent candidate. It was a huge city, distinct from the other urban centers of the time. Dan and its environs could have mustered and trained a larger contingent than Jerusalem and its region. One could object that Dan is geographically isolated from the region to its south, and has more natural geographic and cultural links to the Phoenician coast and Damascus. This might justify the conclusion that Dan was an independent political entity, a city-state, in the tenth century, with no ties to the south. If Dan was not connected to the Palestinian monarchy perceived to exist to its south, there remains another ideal location for the kingdom's capital—Gezer.

Gezer would be the obvious choice for capital of the Palestinian monarchy. This is especially the case if one accepts the argument that Gezer's fortification is matched by those of Hazor and Megiddo. The latter two cities were smaller than Gezer and, from an archaeological perspective, appear to have been administrative cities. That is to say, they contain relatively few domestic facilities and could be viewed as administrative outposts for a government located in another place.[10] Gezer is therefore the most obvious choice for the political center of this network. It is the only location in the tenth century that has produced convincing evidence of writing; it housed a large administrative and civilian population; and it was located in the Shephelah, where it could oversee trade routes through the Coastal Plain and up through the passes into the Central Hills and the Jezreel Valley.

My second objection assumes, for the sake of argument, that there was a United Monarchy. If it existed, Jerusalem was not its capital. Gezer may have been. However, there are other possibilities if we assume, again for the sake of argument, that there was no United Monarchy. Before exploring this approach (which will be narrated in the next chapter), let us continue with five more reasons for rejecting the United Monarchy hypothesis.

Figure 20. *The City Gate of Dan. Nearly three thousand years later, the city gate of Dan does not look very impressive. During the tenth century* BCE, *however, these ruins were resting at the center of activity in the largest city in Palestine. Was this city an Israelite city? Or was it Aramean? Or, perhaps, Dan was an independent city-state, a commercial hub between Hamath, Tyre, Samaria and Damascus.*

A third consideration is related to the second: the population of tenth-century Judah was so tiny that it could not have provided the bureaucracy and army necessary to govern an empire from Dan to Beer-Sheba, much less an empire stretching to the Euphrates. In the Late Bronze Age, almost no one lived in the Judaean Hills south of Jerusalem. During the Iron Age I, the population increased gradually and, by the tenth century, there were about 8500 people living in the region. That is a sparse group, and it indicates that Judah remained a peripheral region, as it had been in the past. Jerusalem and Judah combined represented less than 10 per cent of Palestine's tenth-century population, and would have had difficulty mustering armies capable of permanently ruling far-reaching conquests. An army need not be as numerous as the people it conquers, but an army too small cannot conquer; at best, it can raid, plunder and flee.

In this respect, the biblical battle narratives about King David listed as '3.', above, are worth considering. One of the most articulate *advocates* of the United Monarchy hypothesis has demonstrated that these narratives depict a king who did *not* impose his will on the Philistines but only defended the highlands from them; a king who did *not* conquer—or even set foot in—Syria, but defended himself against a Syrian army that had invaded Transjordan (in spite of some English translations, the Hebrew text of 2 Sam. 8.3 does not identify the 'River' as the Euphrates); and a king who did *not* reduce Damascus to a vassal, but raided some of its outlying territory. The Judaean warrior of these battle reports *did* conquer only those regions that archaeology reveals to have been even more sparsely populated than Judah: Ammon, Moab, Edom. But he was no match for larger powers unless he was defending his own territory against their invasions.[11] It is interesting that biblical David does not possess Gezer (2 Sam. 5.25; cf. 1 Kgs 9.16). There is very little likelihood that David ever set foot in the city of Dan, much less conquered it.

In light of Judah's small population in the tenth century, other aspects of the biblical material become revealing. Although some historians claim that David conquered the Jezreel Valley and Coastal Plain around Dor, there is no evidence to suggest that these areas had any relationship to Jerusalem or Judah in the tenth century. Moreover, the Bible does not narrate Davidic activity in these regions. The only biblical suggestion to the contrary appears suddenly in the Solomon story. Even here, it does not appear in the portions that likely go back to tenth-century sources. Looking at '5.' in the above list, Dor and the Jezreel Valley are mentioned in the Solomonic lists of 1 Kings 4 (see '5a.'), but most scholars agree that these lists have gone through a complicated process of editorial revision over time, and it is difficult to be sure what was original to the tenth-century text.[12] Other than 1 Kings 4, only the material about Solomon's fortresses in '5b.' hints at Solomon's control in the north. The biblical passage that is sometimes claimed to be from a tenth-century source is 1 Kgs 9.15-19, but this passage is revealing when studied carefully:

1.  Verse 15: Solomon used forced labor to build at Jerusalem, Hazor, Megiddo and Gezer.
2.  Verse 16: Gezer had been destroyed by an Egyptian king, who gave the city (presumably rebuilt with Egyptian funds) to his daughter as a dowry. The daughter married Solomon.
3.  Verses 17-18: Solomon fortified Gezer and three locations in three regions: one each in Judah and Benjamin, and one in the

desert wasteland south of the Dead Sea. (The latter would require fortification to protect southern Judah from raids by tiny but hostile groups in Moab-Edom.)

4. Verse 19: A concluding statement mentions additional fortifications at unspecified locations, which include Jerusalem and 'Lebanon'. (Many scholars agree that 'Lebanon' is an error in the biblical text. Some ancient manuscripts do not have this word, indicating either that the word was added by a later editor or that ancient scribes already realized the reference could not be correct. It is probably a misspelling of the very similar word 'Libnah', which was a city southwest of Jerusalem.)

Careful evaluation of this passage is suggestive. Gezer is mentioned three times, implying two radically different political situations. First, the city is part of a regional fortification system, then it becomes part of a local fortification system. Recalling that Gezer does not belong to David in the Samuel narratives, the tale in the middle about the king of Egypt is possible. But if v. 16 is accurate, then 9.17-18 betrays the geographic limits of Solomon's rule: he has fortified towns that guard his realm, in the Shephelah at Gezer, and in Judah, Benjamin and the southern desert. Verse 15 is odd since it lists cities far from the tightly packed network of fortresses in vv. 17-18 (and v. 19). Moreover, if Solomon inherited from David a kingdom that included Megiddo and Hazor, why did he have to wait for a king of Egypt to give him Gezer? In reality, he never ruled at Megiddo or Hazor. Those two were thriving and strategic cities during many of the centuries in which biblical texts were composed and transmitted. A scribe who wishes to transform memories of Celtic warfare into the legendary King Arthur does so in part by increasing the land under the legendary King Arthur's rule. In this case, the scribe who transformed Solomon from a local king to an emperor (see 1 Kgs 5.1 [4.21]) adds Hazor and Megiddo to the list of Solomon's forts. Fortunately, that scribe did not bother to erase the more realistic list of 9.17-18.

In other words, the Bible is consistent with archaeological estimates of Judah's population, both sources suggesting that the rulers of this southern periphery could not, and did not, establish dominion over regions to the north and west. These Judaean kings, David and Solomon, were able to carve out for themselves a portion of the Central Hills (Benjamin), and they could raid Ammon, Moab and Edom at will. But their 'empire' was no larger than the null hypothesis would expect to see in the tenth century. Their power would have been no more extensive than the limited power exerted by the biblical King Saul. The difference between Saul and David was only that Saul's base of power was Benjamin and David's power base was Judah. Neither drove Philistines from the Jezreel Valley; Saul died trying to do just that and David never tried.

A fourth argument against the United Monarchy hypothesis follows up on the discussion of Solomonic forts. Archaeologists have identified fortifications in Palestine that they assign to the building activities of Solomon. However, in many cases, these 'forts' were not *Judahite* forts, or they were not forts at all. First, the cluster of sites often labeled 'forts' in the Negev to the south of the Beer-Sheba Valley are disputed by many archaeologists. Some hold that they were not forts and others insist that they did not exist in the tenth century. Second, the fortifications in the Beer-Sheba Valley are also disputed, since pottery typology is not sufficiently precise to determine which strata date to the time of David and Solomon. For example, one archaeologist focuses on a style of pot with red-slip and hand-burnishing as its decoration. He dates these pots to Solomon's reign (mid-tenth century), and therefore associates strata at many sites with Solomon. Other archaeologists disagree, insisting that this style of pottery was in use for several generations at least, so it cannot be equated with the reign of one king. Depending upon which way one sides on the pottery issue, sites such as Tel Masos in the Beer-Sheba Valley can be assigned a date prior to David, not during the reign of Solomon.[13]

The most disputed issue, in this respect, is the question about Hazor, Megiddo and Gezer. In my discussion above, I granted advocates of the United Monarchy their interpretation of these three archaeological excavations. If their interpretation is correct, then Gezer is the best candidate for the capital of the monarchy they perceive. However, some archaeologists dispute the claim that these three cities display fortifications so similar that they must be attributed to one central authority. As a matter of fact, similar fortifications have been uncovered at other locations, cities not mentioned in the Bible's story of Solomonic fortification. Interestingly, the fortifications at Philistine Ashdod are more similar to Megiddo and Hazor than any of the three are to Gezer.[14] In other words, if a central authority built these forts, then Ashdod, Megiddo and Hazor were built by the central authority and Gezer was built by someone else. This scenario fits the biblical evidence perfectly: a coalition of Philistine powers encroached into the still-Canaanite Jezreel Valley, where Megiddo is located, and spread north to Hazor in Galilee. Meanwhile, Gezer represented the western-most border of the small kingdom (or chiefdom) of the southern high-lands, with its capital at Jerusalem. The biblical suggestion that Gezer was an Egyptian gift makes sense as well. Judah's alliance with Egypt would have forced Philistia into a hands-off policy in the Central and Judaean Hills.

Fifth, if the fortifications are not able to support the United Mon-archy hypothesis, the economic aspect of the hypothesis is in doubt as well. Clearly Palestine had become more urban in the tenth century, and with that change came a change in economic structure. Increased urbanism is a prerequisite to a unified state in many situations, but a unified state is not the inevitable result of urbanization. For example, the Iron Age II (900–586 BCE) was an urban society involving small, local political units competing with one another. Therefore, a changed economy in conjunction with increased urbanization is not sufficient to posit a unified government regionally. Not surprisingly, the United Monarchy hypothesis adds an additional aspect of economics to this urbanization argument.

Among advocates of the United Monarchy hypothesis, much is made of the trade routes from Arabia. These trade routes were active in sev-eral periods of ancient history. During the early part of the Iron Age I (1200–900 BCE) the camel was domesticated, and with this innovation the routes from the desert south became more lucrative. By the Iron Age II this industry was moving through Canaan, and Jerusalem was a part of it. However, there is as yet no evidence that Palestine was part of this trade as early as the tenth century. In this instance, archaeolo-gists operate by a reasonable inference. Since Assyrian documentation and archaeological artifacts combine to suggest that the southern trade routes were in full swing during the ninth century, it is reasonable to conclude that they were achieving that status in the tenth.

In short, the international trade of Palestine's tenth century is a hypothesis supported by reasonable conjecture but no data. In the absence of evidence, any hypothesis is possible. For example, a few scholars even push Israelite participation in this trade back to the early Iron Age I by interpreting the poetry of Judges 5 as a reference to a Canaanite attempt to cut Israel out of the lucrative industry (see, e.g., Judg. 5.6.) According to the hypothesis, the poem describes Israel's military response to that threat. Such hypotheses press the poetic genre rather too far, and also seem to forget that the poet claims to be telling a tale of hoary antiquity (see again Judg. 5.6). The poet, I suspect, had in mind a period long before the early Iron Age I. Once again, we return to the proverb: whether or not it is evidence of absence, absence of evidence is indeed absence of evidence. There is no need to posit a united political structure in tenth-century Canaan in order to have that kingdom preside over an international trade industry that was, at best, only beginning to trickle through the region.

Though the process of urbanization is not under dispute, the inter-pretation of urbanization's significance for the tenth century represents a sixth objection to the United Monarchy hypothesis. It is not sufficient to say that tenth-century Palestine was more urban than eleventh-cen-tury Palestine. From where did this process enter Palestine? After the collapse of the Late Bronze Age Egyptian empire, the Phoenician and Philistine city-states evolved independently, as did some Canaanite city-states in the lowlands, such as the Jezreel Valley. Meanwhile, small Hittite and Aramaean city-states emerged in Syria. The regions that did not emerge as centrally structured political units were the peripheral regions: the Cisjordan and Transjordan Highlands. These regions evolved more gradually. As a matter of fact, if one plots on a map the changes to Syria-Palestine over the centuries of the Iron Ages I and II, a clear pattern emerges. Urbanization and political hierarchies spread from the north and west to the south and east. First, the Phoeni-cian and Philistine coasts emerged, then the northern Syrian city-states, followed by the emergence of Samaria-Israel in the Central Hills in the ninth century. Finally, Judah, Ammon and Moab began to develop. Edom was only emerging in the final generations of the Iron Age.

Even the strongest advocates of the United Monarchy hypothesis have noted this pattern, but have not incorporated it into their thinking. Archaeologists frequently comment on the pronounced Phoenician influence in Palestine's material culture. Artistically, economically, culturally, the Phoenicians were the dominant community in Iron Age Palestine. Their architecture, alphabet, ivory carvings, pottery styles, metalworking and many other aspects of human craftsmanship were the assimilated foundation upon which the other ethnic groups built their worlds.[15]

Given this strong northwest-to-southeast pattern in the data, is it reasonable to assume that Jerusalem and Judah evolved a highly structured political unit roughly 100 years 'too soon'? Is it reasonable to make this assumption when even the biblical evidence conforms to the archaeological pattern? Since the oldest layers of the Bible place David in the periphery, and since archaeological evidence suggests that Judah was a periphery, there is little reason to believe that Judah established a kingdom with borders all the way to Syria, or beyond.[16] (This observation will be critical in the next chapter.)

There is a seventh reason for dissenting from the United Monarchy hypothesis, one that differs qualitatively from the previous six. In recent publications, one reputable archaeologist from Tel Aviv has been advocating a new chronology for Iron Age Palestine. In a previous publication, I supported this new perspective because I believe that it makes better sense of the Iron Age II.[17] However, its implications for Iron Age IC or IIA are profound. The new chronology, if correct, would bring the fortifications at Hazor, Megiddo and Gezer down to the ninth century and crush the discussion of 1 Kgs 9.15 with a resounding thud. The consequences of this chronological restructuring are far more wide-ranging than that, however. For example, the new, lower dating may bring Tel Masos back into the picture for King Solomon, though that is not certain. If it were the case, one might believe that Judah did indeed play a minor role in the Arabian trade routes during the tenth century (and give new credence to the Queen of Sheba folklore!), though, to be sure, Judah remained a peripheral player. Of course, that depends on how one evaluates the material culture at Masos and its contemporary neighbors, issues well beyond the scope of this book. All this, however, is only speculation.

The implications of the new chronology, if it were to be accepted, are far more devastating for those who advocate a United Monarchy than for those who do not. As a matter of fact, the case against the United Monarchy is almost equally strong with either chronology. Moreover, the overall portrait of Palestine's Iron Age shifts in detail but not in general with the newer chronology, and the level of discussion in this book is sufficiently general to escape the need for in-depth treatment. Given these considerations, and given that the controversy over the new chronology continues with no sign of resolution on the horizon, I have not incorporated the lower dates into the historical narratives of this book.

This chapter is more complex than most others in this book, but that was necessary, since the question of a United Monarchy remains a hot topic of debate within academe. In the next chapter, some additional comments will be made about the possible accuracy and implications of the Bible's story about Saul, David and Solomon. As always, however, the most interesting aspect of the ancient past is not the kings and the professional warriors, but the people whose everyday lives continued on their normal course no matter who received their taxes and fought their wars.

## SUGGESTED ADDITIONAL READING

Ahlström, Gösta W., *The History of Ancient Palestine from the Palaeolithic Period to Alexander's Conquest* (ed. D.V. Edelman; JSOTSup, 146; Sheffield: JSOT Press, 1993).

Ash, Paul S., *David, Solomon and Egypt: A Reassessment* (JSOTSup, 297; Sheffield: Sheffield Academic Press, 1999).

Bright, John, *A History of Israel* (Philadelphia: Westminster Press, 3rd edn, 1981).

Davies, Philip R., *In Search of 'Ancient Israel'* (JSOTSup, 148; Sheffield: Sheffield Academic Press, 1992).

Finkelstein, Israel, 'The Emergence of the Monarchy in Israel: The Environmental and Socioeconomic Aspects', *JSOT* 44 (1989), pp. 43-74.

Frick, Frank S., *The Formation of the State in Ancient Israel* (The Social World of Biblical Antiquity, 4; Sheffield: Almond Press, 1985).

Fritz, Volkmar, and Philip R. Davies (eds.), *The Origins of the Ancient Israelite States* (JSOTSup, 228; Sheffield: Sheffield Academic Press, 1996).

Halpern, Baruch, *David's Secret Demons: Messiah, Murderer, Traitor, King* (Grand Rapids: Eerdmans, 2001)

Handy, Lowell K. (ed.), *The Age of Solomon: Scholarship at the Time of the Millennium* (Leiden: E.J. Brill, 1997).

Knauf, Ernst Axel, 'King Solomon's Copper Supply', in E. Lipiński (ed.), *Phoenicia and the Bible* (Studia Phoenicia, 11; Leuven: Peeters, 1991), pp. 167-86.

McKenzie, Steven L., *King David: A Biography* (Oxford: Oxford University Press, 2000).

Miller, J. Maxwell, and John H. Hayes, *A History of Ancient Israel and Judah* (Philadelphia: Westminster Press, 1986).

Noll, K.L., *The Faces of David* (JSOTSup, 242; Sheffield: Sheffield Academic Press, 1997).

Noth, Martin, *The History of Israel* (New York: Harper & Row, rev. edn, 1960).

Soggin, J. Alberto, *An Introduction to the History of Israel and Judah* (Valley Forge, PA: Trinity Press International, 2nd rev. edn, 1993).

Thompson, Thomas L., *Early History of the Israelite People from the Written and Archaeological Sources* (Leiden: E.J. Brill, 1992).

## NOTES

1.    Several archaeologists have muddied the waters on this issue by attributing to the tenth century texts that are not relevant. For example, see the chart on p. 373

in J.S. Holladay, 'The Kingdoms of Israel and Judah: Political and Economic Centralization in the Iron IIA-B (c. 1000-750 BCE)', in T.E. Levy (ed.), *The Archaeology of Society in the Holy Land* (Leicester: Leicester University Press, 1998), pp. 368-98. Apart from the Gezer Calendar, the tenth century does not provide useful epigraphic evidence.

2. This is the most that one can conclude from linguistic analysis. Unfortunately, conclusions drawn from historical linguistics have been pushed beyond reason by a number of the method's advocates. Statistical approaches are singularly unconvincing even when the mathematics are valid, since the interpretations are usually strained beyond credulity. Traditional philology, while more persuasive in many cases, frequently assumes too much. To cite one of the finest practitioners by way of example: B. Halpern suggests that the hypothetical Yahwist (J) is an older document than the Priestly document (P) because the Yahwist employs more archaic phonology. See B. Halpern, 'Text and Artifact: Two Monologues?', in N.A. Silberman and D.B. Small (eds.), *The Archaeology of Israel: Constructing the Past, Interpreting the Present* (JSOTSup, 237; Sheffield: Sheffield Academic Press, 1997), pp. 311-41 (312 with n. 3). Also, in his discussion of Judges 5.11, Halpern asserts that תנה 'anticipates by several centuries the Imperial Aramaic rendition of *ṯ*'. See *idem*, 'Dialect Distribution in Canaan and the Deir Alla Inscriptions', in D.M. Golomb (ed.), *Working with No Data* (Festschrift T.O. Lambdin; Winona Lake, IN: Eisenbrauns, 1987), pp. 119-39 (124). In both cases, Halpern has arrived at false conclusions. In the first case, if Halpern is correct about the phonology, it demonstrates only that the Yahwist had access to a short document with archaic phonology, but says nothing about the date of the Yahwist. Moreover, Halpern's two examples are puzzling. Neither גשור nor יקשן occurs in texts universally attributed to the J source. Moreover, although there is a connection between יקשן and יקטן (Gen. 25.2-3; cf. 10.25-29), the two are not phonological variants. In the second case, if one agrees with Halpern's phonological assessment (which is debatable), then one should say that Judg. 5.11 was composed or edited no earlier than the period in which Imperial Aramaic was influencing Biblical Hebrew (i.e. the early Iron Age II).

3. N. Na'aman, 'Sources and Composition in the History of David', in V. Fritz and P.R. Davies (eds.), *The Origins of the Ancient Israelite States* (JSOTSup, 228; Sheffield: Sheffield Academic Press, 1996), pp. 170-86 (172). See also P.S. Ash, *David, Solomon and Egypt: A Reassessment* (JSOTSup, 297; Sheffield: Sheffield Academic Press, 1999), pp. 93-94 n. 179.

4. However, the date of such hypothetical monuments, even if they existed, would remain uncertain. Using compelling comparative data, N. Na'aman is convinced that no public monuments were erected by Israelite or Judahite kings until after the second quarter of the ninth century BCE. See Na'aman's 'Three Notes on the Aramaic Inscription from Tel Dan', *IEJ* 50 (2000), pp. 94-104.

5. Halpern, 'Text and Artifact: Two Monologues?', p. 330 (see n. 2, above).

6. W.G. Dever, 'Archaeology and the "Age of Solomon": A Case Study in Archaeology and Historiography', in L.K. Handy (ed.), *The Age of Solomon: Scholarship at the Turn of the Millennium* (Leiden: E.J. Brill, 1997), pp. 217-51 (249-

50). The intensity of Dever's polemics against those with whom he disagrees mars an otherwise interesting and informative essay. Perhaps it is time for a return to civility in academic discourse.

7.     I. Finkelstein, 'The Archaeology of the Days of Manasseh', in M.D. Coogan, J.C. Exum and L.E. Stager (eds.), *Scripture and Other Artifacts: Essays on the Bible and Archaeology in Honor of Philip J. King* (Louisville, KY: Westminster/John Knox Press, 1994), pp. 169-87 (179); see also K.A. Kitchen, 'Sheba and Arabia', in L.K. Handy (ed.), *The Age of Solomon: Scholarship at the Turn of the Millennium* (Leiden: E.J. Brill, 1997), pp. 126-53 (134-35).

8.     Holladay, 'The Kingdoms of Israel and Judah,' pp. 383-86 (see n. 1, above). It should be noted that most other archaeologists date Tel Masos much earlier than the time of Solomon. More significantly, the site does not provide material evidence for trade on the scale that Holladay seems to envision.

9.     For discussion, see K.L. Noll, 'The God Who is Among the Danites', *JSOT* 80 (1998), pp. 3-23.

10.    Dever, 'Archaeology and the "Age of Solomon" ', p. 227 (see n. 6, above). Dever's description fits Megiddo better than Hazor. Hazor's structures are puzzling in any historical hypothesis.

11.    B. Halpern, 'The Construction of the Davidic State: An Exercise in Historiography', in Fritz and Davies (eds.), *The Origins of the Ancient Israelite States*, pp. 44-75.

12.    P.S. Ash argued that 1 Kgs 4 does not go back to the tenth century, in 'Solomon's? District? List', *JSOT* 67 (1995), pp. 67-86. One need not accept that conclusion to heed the persuasive power of the issues Ash raises, and to proceed with great caution as a result. (It might be noted as well that folkloristic passages such as 2 Sam. 24.5-9 affirm the historian's hunch that biblical writers possessed no genuinely old traditions of Davidic–Solomonic activity in the far north.)

13.    J.S. Holladay, 'Red Slip, Burnish and the Solomonic Gateway at Gezer', *BASOR* 277/278 (1990), pp. 23-70. It should be noted that Holladay's hypothesis does *not* rest on 1 Kgs 9.15 (as is alleged by some of his critics), but on Sheshonq I's raid. Unfortunately, that does not make his hypothesis any more secure. For useful criticism, see A. Mazar, 'On the Appearance of Red Slip in the Iron Age I Period in Israel', in S. Gitin *et al.* (eds.), *Mediterranean Peoples in Transition: Thirteenth to Early Tenth Centuries BCE* (Festschrift Trude Dothan; Jerusalem: Israel Exploration Society, 1998), pp. 368-78.

14.    E.A. Knauf, 'Le roi est mort, vive le roi! A Biblical Argument for the Historicity of Solomon', in Handy (ed.), *The Age of Solomon*, pp. 81-95 (91 n. 40).

15.    Holladay, 'The Kingdoms of Israel and Judah', pp. 381-82 (see n. 1, above); cf. Dever, 'Archaeology and the "Age of Solomon" ', p. 224 (see n. 6, above).

16.    See the excellent essay by E.A. Knauf, 'King Solomon's Copper Supply', in E. Lipiński (ed.), *Phoenicia and the Bible* (Studia Phoenicia, 11; Leuven: Peeters, 1991), pp. 167-86.

17.    The new hypothesis advanced by I. Finkelstein has generated a flurry of publications. For a recent discussion with bibliography, see N. Na'aman, 'The Contribution of the Trojan Grey Ware from Lachish and Tel Miqne-Ekron to the

Chronology of the Philistine Monochrome Pottery', *BASOR* 317 (2000), pp. 1-7. For my support of Finkelstein's chronology, see 'The God Who is Among the Danites', p. 6 (see n. 9 above).

Chapter 8

## THE IRON AGE II

*Introduction*

Population increased gradually but relentlessly during the Iron Age I. It was noted in the last chapter that, by the tenth century, more than 100,000 people lived in Palestine. This steady increase would continue in the Iron Age II to the final decades of the eighth century BCE, when ancient Palestine's population reached its highest pre-Hellenistic level—about 400,000 people. At that point, wars and Assyrian imperial policies of deportation halted the natural growth in population. Nevertheless, Palestine in the Iron Age II was home to more people per generation than in any previous period.

The Phoenician and Philistine city-states of the Coastal Plain that dominated the final centuries of the Iron Age I continued to exert their influence in Iron Age II. Aramaean and Neo-Hittite city-states in Syria competed with one another and with the coastal powers during this period. Eventually, their numbers would be joined by small states in the peripheral regions, such as Israel, Judah, Ammon and Moab.

The most significant political power in Syria-Palestine during Iron Age II was Assyria. By the ninth century, this territorial state had secured its hold over northern Mesopotamia, often dominated Babylonia to the south, and had begun to expand westward into Syria. Motivated by a desire to secure the income from the international trade on the Mediterranean and the land routes from Egypt and Arabia, the Neo-Assyrian empire's unrelenting goal was to bring all of Syria-Palestine under its rule. Local Syro-Palestinian powers learned to bury their differences and cooperate in military coalitions against the common enemy from Mesopotamia. The struggle continued for two centuries before Assyria was victorious, then Palestine's final century of the Iron Age II saw a period often termed the Peace of Assyria (seventh century BCE).

Meanwhile, in the Central Hills of Canaan, an ethnic group called Israel, which had been in the region for centuries, was coalescing into a political power. By the early-ninth century (the 800s BCE), a royal family at the city of Samaria called by the Assyrians *Bit Humri* had begun to dominate the Central Hills and Jezreel Valley. These kings, also attested in the Bible, were the Omrides: King Omri, his son Ahab, and Ahab's sons Ahaziah and Jehoram. To the south, a dynasty of chiefs was consolidating power at Jerusalem as well, and would follow Samaria, becoming a complex state a few generations after the Omride rise. They were known in the Bible and in an ancient inscription as the *Bet Dawîd*, the House of David.

By what process did these ruling dynasties appear at this particular moment? The process was not a planned effort by the leaders of Israel and Judah any more than the emergence of any other political state had been. Rather, it was the net result of an organic development in the region.

The conditions permitting the rise of the Hebrew-speaking kingdoms in the Cisjordan Highlands were four regional transformations during the tenth and ninth centuries. First, the Central Hills approached a point of 'full exploitation'. That is to say, given ancient farming techniques, the Central Hills contained a population by Iron Age II that was taking advantage of all arable areas. This is due in large part to the increased population by Iron Age II. Some estimates put the number of people between the Jezreel Valley and Jerusalem above 100,000 during the peak generations of the eighth century BCE. By the late-tenth and early-ninth centuries, the region finally supported a population sufficiently large to organize into a small state.

Second, for the first time, a significant sedentary population appeared in the Judaean Hills. As we have seen, very few people had ever lived in the harsher and more arid hills south of Jerusalem prior to the tenth century BCE. That is why in early Israelite literature, such as Judges 5, a 'tribe' of Judah does not yet exist, and the southernmost existing 'tribe', Benjamin, was called by a name that meant 'the Son of the South'. (See pp. 165-66 for a definition of 'tribe'.) Why did this peripheral region's population grow? As the Central Hills reached capacity, a spillover to the south appears to have taken place, and, perhaps, some pastoralists settled down as well. Judah was never as populous as the northern Central Hills. In fact, at their peak level of human density, there were about three people in the Kingdom of Israel to the north for every one in the Kingdom of Judah in the south.[1] Nevertheless, by the eighth century BCE, Judah had become a fully settled territory.

A third radical change for the Cisjordan Highlands was the introduction of major urban centers. This region always had a few cities, but they had never been very large. With the exception of Middle Bronze Hazor (which was on the edge of the fertile Jordan Valley and on a major trade route crossroad), cities of the Cisjordan Highlands were really only large, fortified villages. During the Iron Age II, a series of cities in the Cisjordan Highlands increased their populations steadily, including Dan, Hazor, Gezer and Lachish. Most significantly, two cities dominated the highlands in Iron Age II: first Samaria in the Central Hills (ninth and early-eighth centuries, becoming an Assyrian province after that) and later Jerusalem in Judah (eighth and seventh centuries). At its peak in the middle of the eighth century, Samaria numbered 15,000 people, and in the generation or two after that, Jerusalem grew even larger. These are absolutely staggering numbers for Palestinian cities prior to Hellenistic times.

The fourth radical innovation to the Central Hills in the Iron Age II was the introduction of literacy. Archaeologists have recovered hundreds of documents, from small stamp seals to ostraca, to tomb inscriptions, and even a few fragments of royal inscriptions (such as the fragmentary remains of an Israelite epigraph that had been hauled away to Assyria as part of war spoils, then recovered by modern archaeologists at an excavation in Assyria). Collectively, these writings attest to the rise of a literate class within the previously illiterate Central Hills population. To be sure, only a few people in any generation could read and write. Given the crude nature of many of these texts, one archaeologist suggests that persons who were fully literate, that is to say, persons who could read and understand a complex piece of literature such as a biblical narrative or prophetic text, constituted only the tiny, aristocratic elite. If one surveys literacy throughout the ancient world for comparison, it is reasonable to suggest that only a small percentage of the Iron Age II Central Hills population were fully literate. Still, this would suggest that well over 1000 people could read and write in any generation of the Iron Age II period.[2]

Given these four radical changes in the Cisjordan Highlands, it is no surprise to find that region playing a role in the larger political arena of the ancient Near East during the ninth to seventh centuries. But if those four conditions set the stage for the rise of the Hebrew-speaking kingdoms, what made them a reality? The seed that gave birth to a politically unified territorial state of Israel was a specific development in the political economy of Palestine.

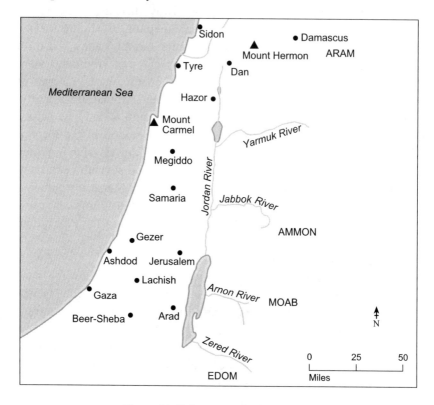

Figure 21. *Palestine in the Iron Age II.*

## The Political Economy of Palestine in the Iron Age II

We have seen that, after the collapse of the Late Bronze Hittite and Egyptian empires in Syria and Palestine, smaller independent city-states had emerged as the political players in Iron Age I. Dominant among them had been the Phoenician cities of the Syrian coast, such as Byblos, Sidon and Tyre. Palestine was a quiet backwater during those centuries. Apart from the Philistine-Canaanite coast, it was a subsistence-level region.

As mentioned in Chapter 7, the dominance of Phoenicia can be felt in the material culture of Palestine throughout the Iron Age I and II. Phoenician style in pottery, the carving of ivory, the manufacture of metal products, the design of horse-drawn chariots, the use of cedar lumber and dressed stones for buildings, to name a few, demonstrate Phoenicia's leadership role. Even the writing of Palestine owes its existence to Phoenicia: the style of alphabet adopted by Aramaic-speaking people, Hebrew speakers, Ammonites, Moabites and Edomites derives from the Phoenician script.

The pattern of archaeological evidence, in fact, suggests a core–periphery political economy. A core–periphery relationship is one in which a politically and culturally dominant core area exerts extreme influence over a less-developed peripheral region. Examples of such a relationship abound in modern times, where the influence of the Modern West results in fledgling capitalist-democracies in other parts of the world. The capitalist trinity, McDonald's, Coca-Cola and free elections, are the gospel delivered from a politically and culturally dominant core into many peripheries. Sweatshop labor and the exploitation of natural resources in those peripheries benefit the West. In ancient times, core–periphery relationships were common. We have already studied several such relationships in Palestine during the Early, Middle and Late Bronze periods, at which time the core area was primarily Egypt, while Palestine was the periphery.

In Chapter 7, it was also noted that Palestine developed from the northwest to the southeast. From the archaeological surveys and digs, it can be observed that the richest and most technologically dynamic region was the Coastal Plain, especially Phoenicia. As one moves south and east, this level of material culture gradually diminishes. At the southeast corner (Edom), one finds the least populous and least advanced— in fact, a very underdeveloped—region. Likewise, as one moves southeast, the date at which a region emerges into the advanced stages of Iron Age II culture grows ever later. The Central Hills developed prior to the Judaean Hills. In Transjordan, the region of Ammon was advanced prior to Moab, and Moab prior to Edom. It is as though a 'wave' of cultural ascent swept over Syria-Palestine, beginning with Phoenicia and moving toward the south and east.

In an imperialistic core–periphery economy, the core dominates the periphery politically as well as culturally, as was the case in Palestine's Late Bronze Age. At that time, the Egyptians invested capital in order to create a prestigious elite class of rulers in Canaan, so that Egypt could extract raw resources (oil, wine, lumber, slaves, copper, etc.) in the form of taxes and tribute. It is no surprise that the archaeological pattern of the Late Bronze period is one in which small centers of wealth existed in large regions of relative poverty. Those small centers were the government leadership sponsored by the 18th and 19th Dynasties.

A similar pattern on a less grand scale appears in Iron Age II, and suggests economic investment rather than direct imperial control. In particular, the Iron Age II city of Samaria, which according to 1 Kgs 16.23-27 was the capital of the Kingdom of Israel during the ninth and eighth centuries, has revealed to excavators remnants of a luxuriant life-style enjoyed by a wealthy ruling class. Among the many Phoenician-inspired artifacts are exquisitely designed ivory carvings. The author of Amos 6.1-8 knew well of what he wrote when he described the royalty of Samaria lying on their 'beds of ivory'. Samaria was not unique in this sense; Phoenician wealth was imported to many Palestinian cities.

It would seem, therefore, that the emergence of monarchy in the Central Hills was a product of Phoenician influence. The Phoenician centers, such as Tyre and Sidon, invested in an elite ruling class at Samaria, in return obtaining through tax or trade, or both, raw resources, such as oil and wine, as well as access to the overland trade routes running south into Arabia. It is no surprise that the Bible narrates a treaty relationship between Phoenicia and Samaria, including the marriage of a Phoenician princess to a Samarian prince, in 1 Kgs 16.29-33. This passage describes a routine alliance of peace between two powers, in which the inferior power (Ahab) becomes son-in-law to the superior power (Ethbaal), and even brings the god of the superior power (Baal) into his home city.

Why was it Israel that emerged through this process and not some other ethnic group in the Cisjordan Highlands, such as Gibeonites? In any core–periphery relationship, the peripheral region has an indigenous leadership prior to the start of the core's investment policy. More often than not, a local leadership is the primary recipient of the core's attention. In the Cisjordan Highlands, the remnant of Merneptah's Israel no doubt still lived among other Canaanite groups. Probably, they were a majority of the population, though that was not necessarily the case.

If one presumes that Israel took some form of leadership role, that group would be the beneficiaries of Phoenician investment. Biblical tales probably preserve memory of that leadership role. The biblical kings listed prior to the rise of the Omride Dynasty, kings such as Saul, Ishbaal, Jeroboam I and Baasha, probably were the regional chiefs of the highlands north of Jerusalem. Likewise, David, Solomon (Absalom?), Rehoboam and Abijam were their counterparts in the less well-developed region to the south. Both chiefdoms were independent of, or only loosely affiliated with, the few city-states in the region (Shechem, Jerusalem) until David conquered Jerusalem (2 Sam. 5.6-8), an act that would prove to be a great advantage for his descendants, jump-starting the dynasty's participation in the economic boon that Samaria and Phoenicia would bring to the region. In the north, the urbanization of the chiefdom was part of the direct investment from the coast, and the city of Samaria was built on the site of a very tiny village belonging to a man or clan named Shemer (1 Kgs 16.24).

Biblical tales of the judges and early kings, such as Abimelech of Shechem, Saul of Benjamin, and David of Judah, are the anthologized remains of many diverse, local oral memories mixed with folklore from this time. The stories as preserved differ from the real persons and events in many ways, most of which cannot be discussed for lack of evidence on the realities of those times, but certainly the narratives have been made to conform to the artificial chronological framework imposed on all the gathered traditions by the scribes who created the narrative from Genesis to 2 Kings. As one scholar has noted, it was merely the haphazard fortunes of editorial design in the literature, not because of any significant differences between them, that Abimelech wound up as a judge in the Bible whereas Saul and David became kings in that grand, epic tale.[3]

The biblical stories of 1 Kings 1–11 also reflect the period under discussion here, but in a very different manner. The core–periphery relationship between Phoenicia and Israel is personified in King Solomon at Jerusalem, particularly, though not exclusively, in those passages that might be the antique core of the Solomon tradition (as discussed on pp. 177-79). Many details in this material sound exactly like actual historical conditions at Samaria (not Jerusalem!) in the early-ninth century. Solomon possesses chariots and a cavalry (1 Kgs 5.6 [4.26 in some English translations]; cf. 10.26). This is very interesting since cavalry was invented in the early-ninth century and did not yet play a military role when Solomon lived. Solomon enters a treaty relationship with a Phoenician king (1 Kgs 5.26 [5.12 in some English translations]). The Phoenician king provides lumber and artisans so that Solomon can build a palace and a temple, and he gives Solomon great quantities of gold. In return, Solomon pays with raw resources and cedes land to

Phoenicia (land that the historical Solomon could not have had author-ity to cede; 1 Kgs 5.22-25, 32 [5.8-11, 18]; 7.13-14; 9.10-14). The description is a perfect example of the routine process by which the core invests in, and thus elevates, a local, peripheral elite class, so that resources might be extracted. Also, Phoenicia joins Solomon in a long-distance trade venture, in which Phoenicia provides its expertise on the seas while Solomon's role is to make the ships and ensure the safety of the overland route from the southern Negev to northern Palestine (1 Kgs 9.26-28).

The Bible sets its tale of King Solomon at Jerusalem in the late-elev-enth century, and modern historians set it in the mid-tenth, but the reality behind the tale belongs to the early-ninth century. Archaeologi-cal evidence to substantiate this tale is lacking for Iron Age I, as was discussed in the previous chapter. But the material cultural record supports a very similar situation in Samaria during the early Iron Age II. One historian concludes from this as follows:

> Either the Phoenician-Israelite relationships at the time of Solomon were as they are depicted in the Bible—in which case they came 100 years too early, led nowhere, and left no further trace in history beyond the literary account—or the Phoenician section in the story of Solomon is a projec-tion of relationships that had existed indeed, but 100 years after Solo-mon, when they are well attested by the epigraphical and archaeological record. Methodologically, the second option recommends itself.[4]

Why would the biblical authors transfer details of King Omri's capital at Samaria in the early-ninth century back in time to the story of King Solomon's capital at Jerusalem? The answer to this question can be inferred from two observations. First, social anthropologists who study the way in which stories about famous men of the past are told in traditional cultures have noted that there is a common tendency to these tales. The tendency is to permit details from a less famous person's story to 'migrate' toward a more famous person. In this case, the Bible was written by people who lived in Jerusalem sometime during or after the Iron Age II. These authors did not live in Samaria, and their interest in a Jerusalem king of earlier times would be much greater than any interest in a king of Samaria in earlier times. Second, it should be noted that Solomon is a hero for the authors of the Bible, albeit an ironic one (see p. 172), but Omri was a king whom the biblical storytellers appear to have disliked intensely (compare 1 Kgs 3.4-15 with 16.25-26). The natural tendency in such circumstances would be to permit favored portions of the story to 'walk' from Omri to Solomon.

To summarize this discussion, the Kingdom of Israel at Samaria appears to have emerged as a direct response to Phoenician investment in the Central Hills of Palestine. Once that kingdom was established, it became very gradually a new core area, exerting influence to the south and east. Thus Jerusalem emerged as a major city in the mid- to late-ninth and early-eighth centuries. Ammon and Moab began to develop in the mid- to late-ninth century, and Edom emerged last of all, in the eighth and seventh centuries BCE. (As discussed in the previous chapter, Jerusalem might have received some help from Egypt in the tenth century, a tantalizing possibility that remains uncertain; but if that was the case, it did not change this picture substantially.)

This situation in the Iron Age II Cisjordan Highlands raises a significant question. Biblical tradition attributes to kings David and Solomon a substantial monarchy in Palestine, especially in passages such as 1 Kgs 5.1 (4.21). Clearly such a monarchy did not exist. But then why do the stories of David and Solomon exist? What purpose did they serve? The short answer to that question is 'entertainment'. Most ethnic groups enjoy telling tales about their origins as a people, and it is not uncommon to include in those stories a series of tales about a golden age of wealth and power. David and Solomon fill that role within the biblical storytelling tradition, just as Moses served a holier purpose, presenting to Israel its code of divinely ordained conduct. That is the short answer to the question, but not the best answer. In addition to preserving, as mentioned above, the fuzzy memory of real chiefs from Canaan's late Iron Age I and early Iron Age II, these stories also seem to 'play'—in the philosophical or theological sense of the term—with the social values of Palestine's Iron Age II culture. The tales of David and Solomon, as well as the tales of their alleged predecessors, Saul and Samuel and the many judges in the book by that name, preserve, present and even probe the cultural assumptions and ethics of a patron–client style of social structure. It is to that topic that we now turn.

### *Patron–Client Relationships in Iron Age I and Iron Age II*

Although colorful biblical figures such as Deborah, Gideon, Abimelech, Saul and David are, at best, only loosely based on real persons who lived in ancient times, many details in their tales fit the period of the

Iron Age so well that they surely derive from real circumstances of the late Iron Age I and early Iron Age II. Just as a novelist today draws on his society's collective memory of the past to construct convincing and often exhilarating prose fiction, so also biblical writers tapped into genuine memories collected in their own time with which to create some of the most memorable personalities and events in the history of Western literature.

Much of what these stories describe derives from the political relationships in Palestine prior to Phoenician-sponsored monarchy at Samaria, relationships that continued in only a slightly modified form after this time. That political relationship can be called a patrimonial state, a tribal kingdom, a city-state or a chiefdom. Any of these terms (and several others) can be found in the scholarship, and this volume has used several in previous chapters. Each designated a slightly different form of social and political organization. Generally, all of them are intended to describe a (usually) small-scale political structure founded upon the concept of a patron–client relationship.

Briefly, a patron–client relationship worked this way: in a predominantly rural ancient society, the overwhelming majority of the people lived off the land as farmers and pastoralists. This lifestyle was labor intensive and provided only a small amount of leisure time. Therefore, the people were vulnerable in two ways. First, should a group of soldiers or thugs attack the village, the farmers did not possess the training or experience to defend themselves adequately. Likewise, should famine or drought attack the village, the farmers did not have the means to barter for, or even to travel and seek, food and other resources. In that situation, a person who gathers to himself a group of strong men—'mighty warriors', as they say in the folklore—and who presents himself to the community as a divinely chosen savior who will protect and provide for the community can achieve a high status. This individual becomes the patron of the community, and the village or villages under his protection are his clients. Just as he promises to guide and protect his clients, he claims also to possess the guidance and protection of a god who has chosen him for this task. Thus the human patron is also a client of a divine patron, the guardian deity. It is a hierarchy with three levels, one of them divine. The hierarchy is frequently expressed in the language of kinship—patrons are fathers or brothers, clients are sons or brothers—society is a family unit.

Throughout the ancient Near East, the institution of kingship is a manifestation of a patron–client relationship, although the patronage structure tends to give way to more formal institutions of power as the society becomes more populous and its government more complex. Purely patronage systems tend to be small-scale political units, but their principles, and especially their characteristic rhetoric, can be discerned in many ancient Near Eastern societies. Rarely does one encounter an ancient royal inscription in which it is not implied or stated that the king has been chosen by a god or the gods to bestow righteousness upon the land by protecting its people and providing for their lives. In a densely populated and economically complex society, such as Egypt or Mesopotamia, the patron–client relationship evolved into a highly complex social structure with a king, a large royal bureaucracy, a professional army, written legal records and laws, a complex religious structure and an equally complex social hierarchy of aristocrats, priests, artisans, merchants, peasants and slaves.

In contrast to Egypt and Mesopotamia, the peripheral zone of Iron Age Palestine, even at its eighth-century peak, had a small population and little sign of the rich material culture known to Egypt and Mesopotamia; here, the patron–client relationship existed at a far less complex level. Society remained rooted to its family-oriented ideology, in which affiliated villages spoke of themselves as tribes, persons who, in theory, descended from a common ancestor. Many aspects of the economy remained under the control of the elders of local villages and small cities. In this situation, the patron's standing army need not have been large, and it was always a group of men who were, for one reason or another, dispossessed from the normal kinship structures. In short, it was a mercenary army, men who were loyal to the patron personally and derived their pay (usually in kind, not cash) directly from him. In other situations, the patron might not command a professional army, but instead might rely on a militia of volunteers who were mustered to arms only in times of crisis.

This is precisely the social world implied by the tales of Judges, 1–2 Samuel and by many other parts of the Bible. The biblical authors describe a tribal society lorded over by a divine patron, Yahweh, in which the human patrons command personal armies (1 Sam. 22.1-2, 6-8), or, alternatively, the patrons display charismatic leadership which emerges only during times of crisis (Judg. 2.11-19). These charismatic leaders, either judges or kings (sometimes prophets), receive divine aid in the form of the *ruach yhwh*, which means 'Wind of Yahweh'—a metaphor of divine power. For example, 1 Samuel 11 tells the tale of an invading Ammonite army that lays siege to a small Israelite city in Gilead, called Jabesh of Gilead. When news of the crisis reaches the divinely chosen Saul, the *ruach yhwh* descends mightily upon him (11.6), he musters an army and marches to war against the Ammonites. In some of these texts, the divine patron, Yahweh, speaks of himself as Israel's king and prefers that the human patron avoid that label (1 Sam. 8.7). In other passages, Yahweh, the divine patron-king, chooses a human patron-king to save his people from crisis (1 Sam. 16.1-13; Ps. 2). In either case, the ideology is identical—similar in fact, to the Assyrian kings who were 'regents' for the divine king, Ashur, yet very much 'kings' in the eyes of their clients (see p. 132). Compare the words of a king of Hamath in Syria, whose name was King Zakkur (left column),[5] to the words of the psalmist in the Bible (Ps. 89.20-23 [89.19-22 in some English versions]):

| | |
|---|---|
| I lifted my hands to Baal of the Sky | At that time, you spoke in a vision |
| Baal of the Sky answered me | To your faithful ones, you said, |
| Baal of the Sky spoke to me | 'I have conferred power on a warrior |
|    through prophets and heralds | I have exalted one chosen from the people |
| Baal of the Sky said, | I found David, my servant |
| 'Fear not! I am he who | I anointed him with my holy oil |
|    made you king | The one with whom my hand remains |
| I stand with you | Yes, my arm strengthens him |
| I deliver you from all these kings | No enemy can rise against him |
|    who lay siege against you' | No wicked man can oppress him' |

The biblical psalm, like the Syrian inscription, depicts the human client of the divine patron who is the warrior protecting society from foreign enemies. In the psalm, as in the tales of 1–2 Samuel, and as it was experienced in Iron Age Israelite society, the human patron-king was anointed with oil as a sign of divine selection (1 Sam. 10.1; 16.13). The term for this status was *moshiach*, which is conventionally translated 'anointed one'. The Hebrew word is sometimes transliterated into English as 'Messiah', and in Greek, the anointed one is written *christos* or 'Christ'. A Messiah or Christ, in other words, was a divinely chosen human patron in a routine patron–client relationship, part of the everyday culture of the ancient Near East. There were many messiahs in the world of Iron Age Canaan.

In a patron–client relationship both partners had moral obligations, and 'morality' was defined, of necessity, in very public terms. (We moderns often think of morality as a matter of the inner heart or con-science; that idea was well known to the ancients, but not as strongly emphasized because public morality had more practical implications for society—the ancients were very pragmatic people.) Morality mani-fested itself differently for patron than for client, but both were obli-gated by the same moral code. For their part, the clients pledged fealty for the patron; they were required to, in a word, 'love' (Heb. *'ahab*) their patron, and they were expected to display 'steadfast loyalty' (Heb. *hesed*) to him alone. When the patron required services, the clients clamored for the opportunity to serve their lord. Also, the clients had an obligation to pay taxes or tribute to the patron. This was a pragmatic issue. The patron and his soldiers (if he possessed a standing army) needed to eat. Since they were professional killers, they spent most of their time training for warfare. Thus, they did not have the time to grow their own food. Taxes and tribute were the price the peasantry paid to receive the protection of the king.

The patron's moral obligations were no less essential to the relation-ship. A patron was one who benevolently 'loved' his people and showed them 'steadfast loyalty' as well, but in a different manner from the love and loyalty of the client. He performed his duty by protecting the clients from external military threat, by keeping the peace through the administration of justice, and by providing food and resources to supplement the economy (an especially significant obligation during times of want). All these obligations can be seen in the Bible's tales, such as those of 1–2 Samuel. The prophet Samuel, for instance, is rec-ognized as a divinely chosen patron because he is able to deliver the people from the Philistines (1 Sam. 7.5-17), but the patronage of his sons is rejected because they pervert domestic issues of justice (1 Sam. 8.1-5). When the patron David obtains spoils from a military conflict in a faraway place (Amalek, in the Negev), he divides his earnings with his client villages in Judah, those villages where, the narrator tells us, 'David and his men had roamed' (1 Sam. 30.26-31).

Above all, the patron deity reigns supreme in a patron–client culture. For the Israelite society described in the Bible, that divine patron was Yahweh, but Yahweh's role as patron is representative of every divine patron in Canaan, indeed, every divine patron in the ancient Near East. For Moab, the divine patron was Chemosh; for Damascus it was Hadad, who was also called Baal ('lord'); in Tyre it was lord Melqart; Sidon had lord Eshmun; in Samaria and Jerusalem it was Yahweh. Like all such divine patrons, Yahweh performed basic duties and made equally basic demands. Yahweh chose Israel (Deut. 10.15; Hos. 11.1), entered into a 'covenant' (Heb. *berîth*) relationship with Israel (Exod. 24.8), demanded 'love' and 'steadfast loyalty' from Israel (Deut. 6.4-9; Mic. 6.8) and promised the same in return (Deut. 7.9-10; Jer. 9.23). Yahweh showed steadfast loyalty to those who remained loyal to him and obeyed his teachings concerning public governance of society (Deut. 5.11-18; 7.12-15, etc.). Those who were disloyal angered Yahweh, and he vented his anger upon all the land, spitting out of that land the loyal and disloyal alike (Ezek. 21.8; Deut. 30.15-20).

The Hebrew *torah* ('instruction') was a manifestation of that world-view, a very sensible guideline for survival in a peripheral land of hardships, where life itself demanded total corporate cooperation, total obedience to the patron and total fellowship with his other clients. The biblical Torah, also called the 'Books of Moses' (Genesis, Exodus, Leviticus, Numbers and Deuteronomy), is the final product of a long process of *torah* writing and editing, and the specific moral and ritual rules contained in those five books are but a digest of the type of material common to all ancient Near Eastern patron–client societies, with their patron-god religions. Other societies did not call their rules '*torah*', for that was the distinctive Hebrew label. But every society that had a patron god had divine instruction of some kind, a public code of conduct for the clients of the patron god. It was the human patron's obligation to uphold that divine law. For example, King Hammurabi of Middle Bronze Age Babylon had himself depicted at the top of a stone monument receiving divine instruction from his patron god. The inscription below that artwork is a digest of legal material, divine law.

The Hebrew *torah* was not just good advice for the pious, it was the code of conduct for society. It was not about inner spirituality unless that inner conscience manifested itself publicly; piety was practical, it was allegiance to the social fabric. In that sense, the later Christian critique of the biblical Torah, as found, for instance, in Mt. 5.17-48, is a misinterpretation of the purpose for which the Torah had been formulated. The patron–client worldview stands at the heart of Torah, Prophets and Writings: the Jewish Bible. Why do modern Bible translations often render Yahweh 'LORD'? Because 'lord' was the proper designation for a patron in a patron–client relationship. For ancient Israel, there may have been many gods, but there was only one Lord, and that was Yahweh (Deut. 10.17; cf. 5.7-10; 6.4). In all these ways, Yahweh was similar to other Iron Age patron deities.

Many aspects of the patron–client relationship are manifested in biblical storytelling, a tradition of tales that in some cases strikes readers as utterly alien to modern sensibilities. Two examples will serve to clarify the earthy reality of this social structure and how it can seem troubling to the modern religious person.

The first example is found in 1 Samuel 25, a story in which a patron, whom the storyteller does not like, is named Nabal. Instantly, the ancient reader is alerted to the disfavor in which the narrator has placed this man. The name is a fictitious storyteller's device. In Hebrew, *nabal* means 'the Fool'. This patron, Nabal, lords over a portion of Judah, a region called Carmel (not to be confused with Mount Carmel far to the northwest of Judah). Another strong man, David, who is at this stage of the story still beginning to establish himself as a patron, has moved into the region. The new, upstart patron offers a politely worded message of peace to the Fool, the established but disliked patron. That which is not narrated, but which would have been understood by any ancient reader of the story, is that David's politely worded greeting is not polite at all. Rather, it is a direct and threatening challenge to Nabal's authority. David implies by his words that he, not Nabal, is the one who protects the region. David's men even 'protected' Nabal's men! The Fool recognizes David's threat for what it is, an attempt to usurp his authority. In this sense, Nabal is no fool at all. But the foolishness of Nabal quickly becomes apparent in another way. Rather than marching out to war against David, which is what a patron should have done in this situation, Nabal throws a party and gets drunk. The storyteller implies that the new patron, David, is a more fit patron than the one whose authority he challenged. It is no surprise to the reader when David's divine patron, Yahweh, kills Nabal, and gives Nabal's wife to David.

A second example of the earthiness with which the patron–client relationship abounds can be seen in 2 Samuel 11–12. This is a well-known story in which the human king covets another man's wife. David has sexual intercourse with Bathsheba, the wife of Uriah the Hittite, one of David's mercenary soldiers. When she gets pregnant, David orders the murder of Uriah so that he can marry Bathsheba. After the deed, Yahweh sends an angry message of rebuke and punishment by the prophet Nathan. This message provides a fascinating glimpse of the religious ideology of the patron–client society. Here is a portion of what Yahweh says to David (2 Sam. 12.7b-8):

> …Thus says Yahweh, god of Israel:
> It was I who anointed you king over Israel.
> It was I who rescued you from the hand of Saul.
> I gave you your masters' house and possession of your masters' wives.
> I gave you the house of Israel and of Judah.
> If this is not enough, I would give you twice as much…

Here Yahweh tells his human client that he, Yahweh, has been a faithful patron. Yahweh emphasizes his own fidelity to the covenant so that he can stress David's infidelity to that relationship.

Note, however, the morality of the patron–client structure, or, rather, its amorality. Yahweh asserts that he has delivered into David's bed the wives of former patrons. In a sense, Yahweh has assisted in the coveting and taking of men's wives for the sake of his client, David. If this were not enough for David, Yahweh is willing to do more. In sum, Yahweh is not angry at his client for coveting and taking another man's wife. He is angry at David for coveting and taking the *wrong* man's wife. It will be recalled that in 1 Samuel 25, Yahweh himself killed Nabal, thus permitting Nabal's wife to become David's wife. Yahweh here asserts that he has done the same with respect to Saul and his wife. (Is it coincidence that one of David's wives has the same name as Saul's wife? Cf. 1 Sam. 14.50; 25.43.) Later in his speech of punishment against David, Yahweh announces that David's punishment will include the raping of David's wives (2 Sam. 12.11). In an ancient patron–client society, the patron's wives are not people with their own dignity as autonomous individuals. Rather, the wives are 'possessions' of the patron. If a patron falls from power, his possession becomes the spoil of another man, another patron. From the perspective of a patron–client worldview, the rape of David's wives is thought to be 'proper' punishment because David, not his wives, has sinned against the patron god, Yahweh. To be blunt, the ancient storyteller has depicted the god of 2 Samuel 12 as a god who sanctions the use of women as pawns of power politics and even commands the rape of women. In this sense as well, the patron god Yahweh differs not at all from other Iron Age patron gods.

Although these narratives are not descriptions of real past events, the social and political world reflected in them was the real world of the Iron Age Palestinian highlands. Yahweh, patron god of the region, selects a series of human patrons who in turn protect and provide for the people of the land.

Interestingly, biblical writers appear to both accept and challenge the prevailing norms of the world they presupposed. The books of Samuel, for example, seem at once designed to present a *typical* patron god and at the same time to *challenge* the reader into questioning the theological assumptions of a typical patron–client-based religion.[6] Like Samuel, a number of biblical books also challenged the norm, while others accepted it. The book of Job, for example, deliberately repudiates the standard model of patron–client religion. Haggai presupposes its ideology without question, as does Deuteronomy. Modern theologians, both Jewish and Christian, continue to dialogue with one another about the religious aspects of these ancient books. From a historian's vantage, regardless of the decisions that modern religious leaders make, the texts remain an invaluable window through which to glimpse the everyday life of a fascinating, but long dead, ancient culture.

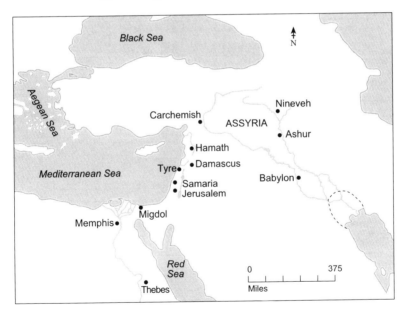

Figure 22. *The Ancient Near East in the Iron Age II.*

## *Mesopotamia in the Iron Age II*

If Israel emerged as part of Phoenician influence, it developed a life of its own within a few generations. Quickly, the Cisjordan Highlands found themselves part of the political life of Syria-Palestine. These small kingdoms were just two of many that faced the formidable challenge of Neo-Assyrian expansion during the ninth to seventh centuries BCE. The Aramaean kingdoms of Hamath and Damascus, the Phoenician city-states, the Philistine city-states, and the emerging patronage states of the highlands (Israel, Judah, Ammon, Moab), as well as a variety of other minor kingdoms in Syria-Palestine, sometimes joined forces against their common enemy and sometimes turned against one another. If one hopes to comprehend the history of Israel at Samaria, and Judah at Jerusalem, within this regional context, a brief survey of Neo-Assyrian and Neo-Babylonian history and politics is essential.

Perhaps the easiest way to comprehend the chaotic history of Iron Age Mesopotamia is to divide it into two units, Neo-Assyrian followed by Neo-Babylonian. Each of those periods can be divided into a stage of growth, followed by consolidated power, then decline. As in the case of the Late Bronze Age's Egyptian empire, students are advised to memorize the names of key Neo-Assyrian and Neo-Babylonian kings:

| Neo-Assyrian Growth | Rise of the Neo-Assyrian Empire | The Peace of Neo-Assyria | Decline of Neo-Assyria |
|---|---|---|---|
| *900–745 BCE* | *745–705 BCE* | *705–620s BCE* | *620s–609 BCE* |
| Neo-Assyrian expansion. A significant king: Shalmaneser III | Tiglath-pileser III Shalmaneser V Sargon II | Sennacherib Esarhaddon Ashurbanipal | Brief Chaos (620s) Sin-shar-ishkun Ashur-uballit II |

Figure 23. *Key Neo-Assyrian Kings.*

The Neo-Babylonian empire emerged as Neo-Assyria declined:

| Neo-Babylonian Growth | Rise of Neo-Babylonian Empire | Decline of Neo-Babylonian Empire | Rise of Persia |
|---|---|---|---|
| *620s–605 BCE* | *605–562 BCE* | *562–539 BCE* | *From 539 BCE* |
| Nabopolassar | Nebuchadnezzar II | Three Minor Kings Nabonidus | Cyrus II of Persia |

Figure 24. *Key Neo-Babylonian Kings.*

As Assyrian dominance solidified in Mesopotamia during the early Iron Age II, the kings of Ashur were tempted to increase their power and wealth by controlling the lucrative trade routes to the west. To that end, they began almost annual campaigns at times, marching through portions of Syria, collecting tribute, doing battle when necessary. The local kings usually retained their thrones by pledging fealty to their new suzerain, their lord and patron, the king of Assyria. In some cases, local kings united in opposition to the Assyrians. Of course, Syria was not the only target of Assyrian imperial lust. These kings often brought Babylonia to the south under their sway, and a variety of other small states in Mesopotamia to the east, north and south. In fact, the Assyrian empire was an intricate network of vassal kingdoms on all sides of the Assyrian heartland in northern Mesopotamia.

Local kings who were vassals of Assyria were viewed by their Neo-Assyrian lords as governors on behalf of Assyria, but they were seen as kings of their own lands by their subjects. In other words, a vassal kingdom was a kingdom that remained politically independent of the suzerain (lord), but paid taxes and tribute to that power. Also, the vassal kingdom was obligated to supply troops and resources for the suzerain's imperial army, and pursue political policies that were in the best interests of the empire.

Vassalage was common in many periods of ancient history because it was a political structure that had advantages for all parties involved. When an imperial power such as Assyria attacked and conquered a neighboring kingdom, such as Babylonia, the emperor usually preferred to permit the indigenous government to remain in power. The alternative would be to dismantle that government and transform the conquered kingdom into an imperial province. A vassal kingdom had several advantages over a province. First, the native bureaucracy was already in place, and that made for a more efficient governance than the cumbersome creation of an all-new provincial government. Second, if an outside power were to attack the region, a vassal kingdom would, in part, shed its own soldiers' blood and invest its own resources in defense, whereas a province would require imperial troops and funds for that effort. A vassal kingdom paid taxes and tribute in the same way that a province contributed to the imperial coffers, but it was far less trouble to maintain.

It should be stressed that the plight of the vassal kingdom was not entirely dreary. It is true that taxation could, at times, be very high, and that some vassal kings found themselves squeezed between the rapacious demands of the Assyrian suzerain and the unrest of commoners unable or unwilling to pay. However, more often, the burden of taxation was offset by the security that the empire promised and usually delivered. Vassal kingdoms could and did flourish under Neo-Assyrian control. Many local kings in Syria sought Assyrian suzerainty as they struggled with local neighbors. In fact, the inscriptions from a few of these kings boast proudly of their status below the powerful suzerainty of the great Assyrian king. In some cases, a vassal rose to such prominence that he could operate as a kind of miniature emperor over smaller states in his own region. Nevertheless, vassals had to be careful, lest they overstep their authority and find themselves facing the wrath of the king of Assyria.

Before narrating the history of Israel and Judah from the vantage of the vassal kings in Palestine, an overview of those events from the viewpoint of the Assyrian suzerains will place matters in perspective. This overview can be brief, since much of the political activity in Mesopotamia had no direct impact on Palestine.

The first Neo-Assyrian king who played a significant role in Palestinian affairs was Shalmaneser III (858–824 BCE). His father had subjected portions of Syria to Neo-Assyria, and Shalmaneser III was obligated to consolidate these gains, with the hope of expanding on them. His achievements were mixed. On two occasions he faced large coalitions of opposing Syro-Palestinian kingdoms. The first fought him in northern Syria early in his reign. The second, which was more significant to the present discussion, pitted Shalmaneser III against a coalition led by the king of Damascus. This coalition withstood the Assyrian king for several years, from about 853 to 841 BCE, but finally succumbed. Included in the coalition against Assyria was a king named Ahab the Israelite.

During the reign of several Assyrian kings after Shalmaneser III the empire suffered internal instability, but by 745 BCE a new king emerged who would establish the Neo-Assyrian empire firmly. Tiglath-pileser III (745–727 BCE) initiated an aggressive and largely successful policy of brutal expansion, and many of the Syro-Palestinian kingdoms collapsed before him. Israel and Judah were two of the lucky few, along with the Philistine city-states and some Syrian kingdoms, that still stood as kingdoms when Tiglath-pileser III died. However, both kingdoms had become Assyrian vassals during his reign, and both regions remained under Assyrian domination until the decline of the Neo-Assyrian empire during the chaotic years of the 620s BCE.

The kings who followed Tiglath-pileser III consolidated the empire through bitter warfare. Generally speaking, each time an Assyrian king died some of the vassal kingdoms would rebel, thinking that the next

Assyrian monarch would be too weak to do anything about it. The rebellious vassals would find that their hunch was wrong, and they would pay for their folly. Israel was one of the foolish kingdoms, and it was invaded and destroyed by Shalmaneser V (727–722 BCE) and his successor, Sargon II (722–705 BCE). After the 720s, the Central Hills were part of an Assyrian province governed by an Assyrian administrator. When Sargon II died in battle in 705, Judah made a similar mistake, rebelling against Sennacherib (705–680 BCE), who devastated Judah in 701 BCE. Luckily, Sennacherib was reluctant to transform the barren Judaean Hills into a province, so the kingdom survived, but with less territory, since portions of Judah had been depopulated and portions awarded to Philistine city-states.

After 701 BCE, Canaan enjoyed the Peace of Assyria, but other parts of the Near East experienced no peace during these decades. There was much unrest in Babylon and Elam during the seventh century (600s BCE). Moreover, Esarhaddon (680–669 BCE) and Ashurbanipal (668–620s BCE) each invaded Egypt, attacking the 25th (Nubian) Dynasty's King Taharqa. Some of the supplies for those events were provided by vassal kingdoms, including Judah. Esarhaddon conquered Memphis in 671 BCE and Ashurbanipal conquered Thebes in 663. The Assyrians established local leadership in the form of a new dynasty, the 26th, which gradually became independent of Neo-Assyria, but remained friendly with it. During the waning years of the Assyrian empire, the 26th Dynasty attempted to assist Assyria against its enemies, primarily Babylonia and Media. From about the 620s Palestine was an Egyptian province ruled by the 26th Dynasty on behalf of Assyria.

When Assyria collapsed Babylonia invaded Syria-Palestine. The 610s were a period of warfare in Syria between the 26th Dynasty and the armies of Babylon. The latter emerged victorious, and the small kingdom of Judah became a Babylonian vassal. It is now time to take a look at these events from the perspective of the Canaanite kingdoms, Israel, Judah and their neighbors.

### The Monarchy of Israel in the Iron Age II

Here is a list of the kings of Israel (names in italics need not be memorized):

| Early Kings | Bit Humri | Jehu Dynasty | Minor Kings | Anti-Assyrians |
|-------------|-----------|--------------|-------------|----------------|
| *c. 920s–880s* | *880s–840s* | *840s–740s* | *740s–730s* | *730s–720s* |
| Jeroboam I | Omri | Jehu | *Shallum* | Pekah |
| *Nadab* | Ahab | *Jehoahaz* | *Menahem* | Hoshea |
| Baasha | *Ahaziah* | *Joash* | *Pekahiah* | |
| *Elah* | Jehoram | Jeroboam II | | |
| *Zimri* | | *Zechariah* | | |

Figure 25. *The Kings of Israel.*

By the ninth century, a small Phoenician satellite state was established at Samaria in the Central Hills. Variously called Israel, Samaria or *bit humri* (House of Omri), this kingdom stood in formal alliance with Tyre (and perhaps Sidon?). One of the Omrides, Ahab, was married to a Phoenician princess, Queen Jezebel, as the Bible calls her. As part of that alliance, the capital of Samaria was home to two patron deities, the indigenous god Yahweh and the Phoenician version of a similar patron god, called by the Bible Baal. Apparently, many subjects of the Samarian crown were unhappy about the imported god, and a storytelling tradition emerged in which Ahab, Jezebel and her foreign god played the role of the villains (see, e.g., 1 Kgs 18–19 and 21). These tales are unhistorical, but the king and queen featured in them were real people. In fact, Ahab played a major role in world politics.

Shalmaneser III commemorated his 853 BCE invasion of Syria in a stone inscription called the Kurkh Stela. Although the royal stone boasts a great victory for Shalmaneser III, one is able to read between the lines to realize that the victory he claims was something more like a military stalemate. Shalmaneser III got as far as the Orontes River in Syria, but was stopped at the Battle of Qarqar near Hamath by a large coalition army, consisting of troops from a variety of Syro-Palestinian kingdoms. The coalition was led by the most powerful of the Syro-Palestinian monarchs, Hadadezer of Damascus. Prominent among his deputies is one Ahab the Israelite, who supplied the coalition army with a large number of chariots and troops. Israel during the mid-ninth century was a powerful player in the politics of the day. Interestingly enough, the Bible records nothing about this, and instead gives the reader the impression that Omri and his dynasty were minor players even within Canaan itself.

The Omride Dynasty of Samaria did not last long after the Battle of Qarqar, and it was Shalmaneser III who was responsible for its demise.

Shalmaneser III made several attempts to overcome the coalition during the decade after 853 BCE, apparently wearing down his enemy's ability to resist. The financial and physical strain of perpetual warfare seems to have led to internal unrest among some of the coalition kingdoms. By the time Shalmaneser III returned to Syria-Palestine in 841 BCE, a new king was on Samaria's throne, and Damascus had a new monarch as well. In one of his royal inscriptions, Shalmaneser III declares that Hadadezer of Damascus perished, replaced by a usurper named Hazael. The monument called the Black Obelisk depicted in relief a man named Jehu, son of Omri, doing obeisance before the Neo-Assyrian monarch and offering tribute. The Bible calls this man Jehu, son of Jehoshaphat, son of Nimshi (2 Kgs 9.2).

Figure 26. *King Jehu, 'son of Omri', kneels before the great king of Assyria, Shalmaneser III. This relief sculpture is part of a large stone monument erected by the Assyrian monarch to commemmorate his accomplishments. The capitulation of the House of Omri, albeit by a general of Samaria's army who had usurped the Omride throne, was an event that seems to have filled Shalmaneser with pride. Apparently, the Israelite kingdom was a significant, if minor, player in international politics* (© British Museum).

According to 2 Kings 9–10 Jehu was a general in the Omride Dynasty's army, was anointed (that is to say, was rendered a messiah) by a renegade band of prophets led by a man named Elisha, and committed treason against the Omrides, massacring the entire Omride family, including old Queen Jezebel. If he murdered the Omrides, why does the Assyrian monarch call him Son of Omri? Probably because, from the Assyrian perspective, the *bit humri* was *the* power of the Central Hills in Canaan. Since Jehu was pledging that power's fealty to the Assyrians, they were willing to declare Jehu the legitimate king of the monarchy called *bit humri*. Thus, by Assyrian political adoption, Jehu became a son of Omri. This is another instance in which the reliance on the patronage rhetoric of kinship plays a role in the political language of the day.

One question that plagues historians is the motivation for Jehu's bloody massacre of the Omrides. Why did it happen? The Bible's only answer is that it was divine will. The Omrides had sinned in the eyes of Yahweh their god, and so a prophet was dispatched by the deity to exterminate the dynasty (2 Kgs 10.30). Interestingly, even the Bible seems to contradict this explanation. Whereas Jehu is a chosen instrument of Yahweh in the narrative of 2 Kings (although he sinned in one respect against Yahweh, according to 2 Kgs 10.29 and 31), his bloody massacre of the Omrides, commissioned by the biblical prophet Elisha, was nevertheless condemned as sin by another biblical prophet, Hosea, in the first chapter of Hosea's short book. Even in ancient times, the motivations for, and even the merits of, Jehu's coup were debated by Israelites.

A historian's answer to the question concerning Jehu's coup appears to involve a complex set of three issues. First, Omri's Dynasty appears to have weakened considerably after the Battle of Qarqar, making it vulnerable to internal unrest. Evidence for that derives from ancient inscriptions discovered in Palestine by modern researchers. One inscription was erected sometime in the ninth century by a Moabite king named Mesha. King Mesha states that King Omri and his son dominated Moab 40 years (that is to say, for an unspecified, but long, period of time). This was because, says Mesha, Chemosh god of Moab was angry with his land (cf. the discussion of patron-god religion, above). But Mesha fought a war against the son of Omri and liberated Moab from Israelite oppression. (A folk-tale version of Mesha's war is preserved as well in the Bible at 2 Kgs 3.) Mesha appears to have been the first king to rule over a territorial state of Moab more complex than a chiefdom, and the emergence of Moab probably was stimulated by Omride investment in the region (see the discussion of the political economy, above).

# Moabite Stone

Discovered in 1868, this stone inscription from the 9th century BCE reads, in part ...

I am Mesha, son of Chemosh[yat], king of Moab, the Dibonite. My father ruled over Moab thirty years, and I ruled after my father. Now I have made this Holy Place for Chemosh in Qarhoh [DAMAGED TEXT], because he saved me from all oppressions and enabled me to gloat over my enemies.

Omri, king of Israel, oppressed Moab many days, for Chemosh was angry with his land. Then his son succeeded him, and said, 'I will oppress Moab.' In my days, he said this, but I have gloated over him and his house. So Israel perished, perishing forever.

Now Omri had seized a[ll the lan]d of Madeba. He dwelt in it in his days and half the days of his son, forty years. But Chemosh restored it in my days. I built Baal-Maon, and made the reservoir there; and I built Qiryaten.

Now the people of Gad dwelt in the land of Ataroth forever, but the king of Israel built Ataroth for himself. So I fought with the city and I took it, and I killed all the people of the city as a sacrifice for Chemosh and for Moab ...

Figure 27. *Mesha, King of Moab* (inset photo © Louvre reproduced by permission).

More evidence for Omride internal weakness is found in the north, at Dan. About the same time that Mesha erected his monument in Moab, a king, whose name is uncertain, erected a stone monument in his city of Dan.[7] The king who speaks from the Tel Dan Inscription, fragments of which were recovered in the early 1990s, states that an unnamed king of Israel encroached on the land of his father, but that he has driven the king of Israel away. Presumably, the land of the father was the city of Dan and its environs, implying that Dan was not a part of *bit humri* proper, but had for a brief period come under the suzerainty of

Samaria, probably during the 860s and 850s BCE, judging from the age of the stone fragments. At the time the stone was erected, the Israelite dominance of Dan had come to an end and the city-state was independent or under the control of Damascus.

Thus it would seem that the Omrides had carved out for themselves a miniature empire in portions of Palestine during the middle of the ninth century BCE. The Israelite empire stretched from Dan to, presumably, Judah, since the Bible implies that Judaean chiefs were vassals of Israelite kings during this era. Also included was a portion of the Transjordan Highlands, Moab (and perhaps Ammon and portions of southern Aram, though this is uncertain). By the 840s this empire was crumbling. Moab broke free, as did Dan. Then a second disaster struck.

A second complication affecting the fate of the Omride Dynasty came from Damascus. Under its king, Hadadezer, Damascus had been leader of a coalition that included Samaria. However, Shalmaneser III's inscriptional narrative relating to 841 BCE tells of a change of dynasties at Damascus. Hadadezer has been removed from the scene and replaced by one 'Hazael, son of nobody'. The Assyrian king calls Hazael 'a son of nobody' as an insult. Hazael was a usurper, not of aristocratic birth, and in open opposition to the Assyrian army. Therefore, in Shalmaneser III's eyes, he deserved no formal recognition of the kind granted to the usurper of non-noble birth, Jehu, 'son of Omri'. Shalmaneser III's rhetoric is interesting, since one former coalition member, *bit humri*, has submitted to the Assyrian king and another, Damascus, has not. This split in allegiances might be explained by a biblical tradition. According to 2 Kgs 8.28, the Omride King Jehoram and his vassal, Judah's King Ahaziah, fought together in Gilead, at a place called Ramoth of Gilead. Their common enemy was Hazael of Damascus. The usurper in Damascus apparently forfeited that city's role of coalition leader, leading to a war between former allies, Samaria and Damascus.

Thus, the second factor leading to the weakness of the Omrides was warfare with a former ally, a factor that leads directly to a third and decisive issue: the war left both Damascus and Samaria vulnerable to the return attack of the Assyrian army under Shalmaneser III in 841 BCE. Had Samaria continued to press its opposition to Assyria, it would have found itself fighting a two-front war, with one front in Transjordan against the Aramaeans and the other in the Galilee against Shalmaneser III. Jehu's coup, it can be assumed, was led by a faction of army generals wishing to avoid that two-front scenario. Jehu usurped the throne, made peace with Assyria, and concentrated on the enemy common to Assyria and Israel, Damascus, under King Hazael, 'son of nobody'.

From local inscriptions and from the Assyrian records, it would seem that King Hazael of Damascus was a very successful monarch, in spite of his two-front war with Assyria and Israel. He maintained independence from Assyria (even though Shalmaneser III claims to have defeated Hazael) and made Damascus the most powerful kingdom in Syria-Palestine. A number of the Syrian kingdoms came under his dominance, and biblical tradition claims that Samaria and Jerusalem did so as well (2 Kgs 10.32-33; 12.18-19 [12.17-18 in some English versions]). If the middle decades of the ninth century had seen success for the Omrides, the final decades of the ninth century were very much the decades of Hazael.

The early-eighth century saw the rise of another significant power in northern Syria, the city of Hamath, ruled by King Zakkur. He defeated Hazael's son in battle, and established a regional power on the Orontes. Biblical tradition also claims that a king of the Jehu Dynasty, Jeroboam II, carved out a small empire in Palestine (2 Kgs 14.23-29), but this remains unconfirmed by external evidence. Jeroboam II seems to have exerted some influence, however, since biblical traditions remember him well enough to also remember conflicting assessments of his accomplishments. On the one hand, 2 Kgs 14.25-27 presents a Yahwistic prophet named Jonah (who is also featured in a popular fable about a great fish) who promised on behalf of Yahweh to support and favor Jeroboam for the sake of his subjects, the Israelites. On the other hand, Amos 7.10-17 asserts that this same Yahweh sent the prophet Amos to condemn Jeroboam to death and to expel Jeroboam's subjects, the Israelites, from the land. From a historian's perspective, Amos was incorrect, but the jury is still out on whether Jonah was correct.

The middle decades of the eighth century BCE were a turning point for everyone in the ancient Near East. In Egypt, the first rumblings of a new and eventually very powerful dynasty, the 25th Nubian Dynasty, were being heard. During the final decades of the eighth century, the Nubian kings conquered and ruled all of Egypt. As this was happening, Tiglath-pileser III was moving into Syria-Palestine. During the early 730s, he made his way through northern Syria, conquering the region and bringing it firmly under Assyrian imperial rule.

As Tiglath-pileser III progressed, the small kingdoms of Palestine became nervous, and began planning among themselves for the inevitable assault. The result of those plans was the so-called Syro-Ephraimite

Coalition of 736 BCE. The name of this coalition is a modern one, based on the fact that one coalition leader was a Syrian, the Aramaean King of Damascus named Rezin, and the other was from the Central Hills region called Ephraim, King Pekah of Israel.

In 736 BCE the plan was similar to the one used back in 853 BCE. Together, Pekah and Rezin urged other states in the region to join against Assyria. Several did, including the son of Tubail, King Hiram of Tyre, and several kings of Philistia. In previous decades, Samaria could have expected its vassal, Judah, to follow its lead. But by the second half of the eighth century, Jerusalem had become one of the largest cities in Canaan, and was beginning to make independent decisions on matters of foreign policy. According to Assyrian inscriptions, King Jehoahaz I of Jerusalem (the Bible calls this man Ahaz) pledged fealty to Assyria, and did not join the Syro-Ephraimite Coalition.

By 734–732 BCE, Tiglath-pileser III's army had occupied Palestine. First, the Phoenician and Philistine cities were 'pacified'; then, Samaria was brought under Assyrian domination; finally, Damascus was attacked and King Rezin killed. King Pekah of Israel was killed also, but not by Tiglath-pileser III; the people of Samaria rebelled, killed him, and replaced him with a pro-Assyrian king named Hoshea. The Assyrian monarch accepted this internal revolt and confirmed Hoshea on his throne. These Assyrian records are matched by the biblical account, which describes Tiglath-pileser III as well as Pekah and Hoshea in 2 Kgs 15.29-31. (See also 2 Kgs 16.1-9, as well as the folk-lore in Isa. 7, which contains some accurate information, including the reference to the Tyrian king, the son of Tubail.) The great kingdom that Omri and Ahab had once built was now no more than a remnant. Most of Israel's land was carved into Assyrian provinces, and the vassal kingdom of Israel was reduced to a city-state consisting of Samaria and its immediate environs.

Archaeological evidence suggests that with the coming of Tiglath-pileser III and his direct control over Palestine, Jerusalem flourished, and became the economic and political center of Palestine. Jerusalem would make a terrible mistake toward the close of the eighth century (to be discussed momentarily), but except for this devastating setback, Jerusalem enjoyed direct imperial support from Assyria, and the early decades of the seventh century might well be described as the renaissance of Judah. This is also the period in which the earliest versions of biblical scrolls began to be written (though the biblical scrolls as we know them today were not edited and completed until centuries later).

Tiglath-pileser III died in 727 BCE—and when a powerful emperor dies, vassal kingdoms are tempted to rebel. King Hoshea of Samaria succumbed to just that temptation in the 720s. He is said to have appealed for assistance to a king of Egypt (2 Kgs 17.4), though the identity of this Egyptian monarch cannot be determined. At the time, Egypt was divided into local kingdoms ruled by the remnants of declining Dynasties 22, 23 and 24 in various portions of the Delta, and the rising Nubian Dynasty 25 to the south. None of these kings were in a position to assist a small Canaanite city-state even if they had desired to do so. Shalmaneser V attacked Samaria and, though he died during the war, Assyria, under King Sargon II, captured the city and deported the leading citizens of Samaria into other regions of the empire. The city of Samaria was transformed into an Assyrian province in 722 BCE. The kingdom of Israel was gone forever.

## The Monarchy of Judah in the Iron Age II

These were the kings of Judah (names in italics need not be memorized):

| Early Chiefs | Contemporary with Bit Humri | Contemporary with Jehu Dynasty | Late-eighth century Kings | Seventh and early-sixth centuries Kings |
|---|---|---|---|---|
| *940s-880s* | *880s-840s* | *840s-740s* | *740s-690s* | *690s-586* |
| David Solomon *Rehoboam* *Abijam* | *Asa* *Jehoshaphat* *Jehoram* *Ahaziah* | *Queen Athaliah* *Joash* *Amaziah* *Azariah* *Jotham* | Jehoahaz I (also called Ahaz) Hezekiah | Manasseh *Amon* Josiah *Jehoahaz II* *Jehoiakim* Jehoiachin *Zedekiah* |

Figure 28: *The Kings of Judah.*

Judah survived the dismantling of Samaria, since Jehoahaz I had not rebelled with Samaria in the 720s, but his son Hezekiah emulated Hoshea's mistake at the death of Sargon II in 705 BCE. He conspired with a Philistine king and the king of Sidon to create a new anti-Assyrian coalition. It would seem from hints in the Assyrian record that this coalition was given some support from the 25th Egyptian Dynasty. But if the Battle of Qarqar in 853 was a relative success and the Syro-

Ephraimite Coalition of 736 an almost-complete failure, the conspiracy of 705 was pure folly.

The new Assyrian king, Sennacherib, invaded Palestine in 701, defeated a nominal show of force from Egypt, wholly ravaged the entire Judahite countryside (judging from the almost-universal archaeological destructions at this time), and destroyed the city of Lachish in the Shephelah. Sennacherib was so proud of his assault that he had the fate of Lachish carved as a memorial on the walls of his throne room. These depictions present a horrifying narrative of annihilation, murder and mayhem. The archaeological destruction layer at Lachish confirms the Assyrian propaganda. The city was utterly destroyed and not rebuilt for several decades.

Sennacherib brags in his annals that he pinned up King Hezekiah of Judah like a bird in a cage at Jerusalem. Hezekiah surrendered the city, agreed to pay a heavy fine, and was, as a result of his contrition, rewarded with his life. Assyrian monarchs hated to turn vassal kingdoms into provinces, so Hezekiah remained on the throne. But it was a reduced throne, since portions of Judah's land were redistributed to Philistine vassals.

Hezekiah appears to have died shortly after this, and his son and successor, King Manasseh, remained a loyal vassal under Assyrian rule throughout his incredibly long (roughly half a century) reign. It was during this time that, judging from archaeological data, Judah enjoyed a growing renaissance supported by Assyrian domination.[8] Jerusalem seems to have regained its hinterland and benefited from continued participation in the Arabian trade, direct Assyrian support and a long period of peace. In the Bible, Manasseh is dismissed as an evil king (2 Kgs 21.1-18), but his subjects were fortunate to live in one of Jerusalem's finest moments.

All this information, derived from the Assyrian records and supplemented by archaeological data, parallels the Bible's account. The biblical version is peculiar, however, since the writer of 2 Kings 18–19 (= Isa. 36–37) wants to give his reader the impression that Yahweh, god of Israel and Judah, somehow spared Hezekiah and his people. The biblical writer fails to admit that Hezekiah's war was a disaster and that Yahweh's 'salvation' came to only three out of every four Judahites. One quarter of the population had been killed or removed. The survivors lived with the memory of military destruction and a horrifying, painful siege. The biblical story is designed for purposes other than an accurate report of what happened. Chapter 1 of Isaiah is more realistic, moaning that only 'Zion' (a term that refers to Jerusalem) is left like a booth in a vineyard (Isa. 1.8-9). The book of Kings does not mention Assyria again after this tale, giving the casual reader the false impression that Yahweh has driven the Assyrians away so that they never returned!

By the latter half of the seventh century BCE, Assyria had grown weak. The empire had become too large to maintain and the final kings of Assyria were not up to the challenge. Several vassal kingdoms in Mesopotamia went on the warpath against their suzerain. The city of Ashur was destroyed by Media in 614 BCE. Within two years, it was clear that the newly emergent power in Mesopotamia was to be shared by Media and Babylonia, the latter more dominant. In 612, the Medes were joined by the Babylonian King Nabopolassar when they attacked and destroyed the great Assyrian cultural city of Nineveh, which had also been Assyria's capital city since the days of Sennacherib. This event was also known to biblical writers. The prophet Nahum heard the news of Nineveh's demise and responded by writing three chapters of gleeful excess, heaping scorn on fallen Nineveh. Another biblical writer, who disagreed with Nahum's vindictive attitude, composed a fable about Nineveh's fate, speculating on whether it would have been possible for Yahweh to show mercy even on that 'evil' city; this fable is known to us as the book of Jonah.

The final decades of the seventh century were a confused and confusing time in Canaan. Assyrian domination was receding, but the local kingdoms could entertain no hope that they would become independent. In the 660s, with Assyria's assistance, a new and very powerful dynasty had risen in Egypt, the 26th (or Saite) Dynasty. For decades, that dynasty's King Psammetichus I ruled Egypt effectively and maintained a vibrant economic exchange with Assyria. As the latter began to weaken, Psammetichus I tried to lend support by sending troops and aid to Mesopotamia. But Egypt was unable to save Ashur and Nineveh. For a few years Egyptian forces occupied Syria-Palestine and kept Nabopolassar's Babylonian army safely on the eastern side of the Euphrates River. Then, in 605 BCE, Egypt's new King Necho II was defeated by Babylon's new King Nebuchadnezzar II at the Battle of Carchemish. Egypt's influence quickly vanished from Canaan, and Jerusalem, among others, submitted to Nebuchadnezzar II.

Babylon did not stop at Palestine. Nebuchadnezzar II hoped to conquer Egypt as well, and invaded the Delta in 601 BCE. His army was defeated and turned back, however, at the Battle of Migdol on the border between the Delta and the Sinai Peninsula. Nebuchadnezzar II was forced to return to Mesopotamia. Jerusalem rebelled, according to Babylonian records, and Nebuchadnezzar II attacked the city in 597 BCE. Judah's King Jehoiachin was captured and sent in chains to Babylon. A new Judahite king was selected to replace him on the vassal throne. But, back in Babylon, Nebuchadnezzar II faced another challenge in the form of an internal Babylonian revolt. Meanwhile news reached Palestine that Psammetichus II, the new king of the 26th Dynasty, had defeated the remnant of the 25th Dynasty in southern Egypt. This was soon followed by the Egyptian king's public relations 'victory tour' of Palestine in 593 BCE. It began to seem as though Egypt's 26th Dynasty would dominate Canaan after all.

According to the Bible (2 Kgs 25), Jerusalem rebelled a second time against Nebuchadnezzar II and, in either 587 or 586, Babylon destroyed Jerusalem. The 26th Dynasty did not come to Judah's assistance. The leaders of Jerusalem were taken in chains to Babylon, and Judah was transformed into a Babylonian province. The kingdom of Judah had ceased to exist forever.

### The Modern Theories Concerning King Josiah of Judah

2 Kings 22–23 tells a very odd tale about 'good' King Josiah. The story goes that this king renovated Solomon's temple in Jerusalem and, in the process, discovered an old scroll that had been hidden in the building. It was the book of Torah, according to 2 Kgs 22.8. In response to this scroll, Josiah is said to have undertaken sweeping religious innovations in Judah. A new covenant was made, the minor gods of the Jerusalem temple were purged, Yahwistic shrines outside Jerusalem closed. Moreover, a prophetess named Huldah predicted that the 'curses' recorded in the scroll would ultimately destroy Jerusalem, but that good King Josiah would die in peace. Later, Josiah traveled to Megiddo to encounter Pharaoh Necho II of the 26th Dynasty, who killed Josiah. (In the version of 2 Chronicles, Josiah fights a battle against Necho II and is mortally wounded, but that is not relevant to the present discussion.)

The tale of Josiah has generated no end of speculation among historians and biblical scholars. In fact, an entire historical hypothesis has been spun from this tale, a hypothesis that, in some scholarly circles, is no longer even spoken of as a 'hypothesis'. It is treated as though the hypothesis were inscribed in an ancient and trustworthy text, not merely in modern textbooks!

Although each historian differs over details, the modern hypothesis about King Josiah goes like this: an old tradition about Moses was preserved in that book of Torah discovered in the temple. In fact, the book of Torah may well have been portions of the book known to us as the book of Deuteronomy. Josiah may have planted the book so that it could be found and employed for his political agenda. Or its discovery became a convenient basis for a program that Josiah was already undertaking (since he had started cleansing the temple already). In either case, Josiah's program had as its central feature the closing of all Yahwistic temples outside Jerusalem, presumably in conformity with Deuteronomy 12, which demands that all sacrifice to Yahweh be offered in only one holy place, the one place that Yahweh will choose. A prophet named Jeremiah, whose book is somewhat similar to the theology of Deuteronomy, and who is said to have lived during the reign of Josiah, assisted this religious innovation in some versions of the hypothesis.

An unrelated aspect of biblical scholarship has become intertwined with questions about King Josiah's religious innovations. It has to do with the editorial process by which certain biblical books evolved. For centuries, readers of the Hebrew Bible have noticed that portions of the Former Prophets (that is, the books of Joshua, Judges, 1–2 Samuel and 1–2 Kings) are written in a style that is similar to the book of Deuteronomy. These portions have been called 'deuteronomistic'. During World War II, a German scholar named Martin Noth (who was in exile from his homeland because he did not side with the Nazis) wrote a book in which he advanced the hypothesis that the deuteronomistic parts of the Former Prophets were originally a single narrative history composed by a scribe who used Deuteronomy's religious beliefs as the basis for his interpretation of the past. With this hypothesis, something that scholars call the Deuteronomistic History was born.

The Deuteronomistic History has grown over the past 60 years into one of the most commonly accepted theories in biblical scholarship. Like the hypothesis about Josiah's religious innovations, the Deuteronomistic History hypothesis is no longer called a hypothesis. Most biblical scholars call it a theory, and routinely speak of 'Dtr' (the hypothetical scribe who wrote the Deuteronomistic History) as though this label of academic convenience were the name of an Iron Age man.

For many historians, Dtr lived during the reign of Josiah. For others, he lived in the century after Josiah. For some scholars, there were several Dtr scribes, a Dtr[1] and Dtr[2] or sometimes a Dtr[G], Dtr[N] and, in a few versions of the hypothesis, Dtr[P].

For those who think that Dtr lived during Josiah's reign, the assumption is that the scribe wrote on behalf of Josiah himself. He wrote a history of Jerusalem in order to further advance the agenda King Josiah was promoting. This history is none other than the books of Deuteronomy, Joshua, Judges, 1–2 Samuel and 1–2 Kings, less significant segments that scholars believe were added after the time of Dtr (such as, for obvious reasons, 2 Kgs 23.26–25.30). Moreover, according to the hypothesis, Josiah did not wish merely to reform Judah's religion. He also viewed the growing weakness of Assyria (according to biblical chronology, Josiah would have been active from the 630s to 610s BCE, when Assyria was in decline) as an opportunity to recreate the empire of King David. The death of Josiah at Megiddo (2 Kgs 23.29-30) was the unfortunate result of Josiah's unrealistic imperial ambitions, and his death clearly refuted the optimistic promise of Huldah. According to the hypothesis, the incorrectness of Huldah's prophecy demonstrates that the events of 2 Kings 22–23 are reliable and these chapters (up to 23.25) were composed prior to Josiah's death in 609 BCE.

In sum, we have two hypotheses that have become so common to biblical scholarship that most scholars speak and write about them as though they are theories. One theory is that Josiah engaged in a massive religious 'reform' driven by a political agenda. The other theory states that parts of the story in Deuteronomy through 2 Kings were written as political propaganda for Josiah's reform.

Much of what is promoted by supporters of these two hypotheses could be correct. Unfortunately, there are difficulties with each that should be kept in mind.

The theory about Josiah's religious innovation lacks any support from non-biblical evidence. Josiah is never mentioned in ancient extra-biblical documents (except for a very questionable ostracon that surfaced on the black market a few years ago and is considered to be fake by several prominent epigraphers). Although the purge of minor gods from the temple is very plausible (ancient kings had the right to make changes to their city's temple as often as they pleased), it is difficult to affirm or refute the narrative.

As for the Dtr History hypothesis, it might be that a portion of the

Bible was composed as royal propaganda for an ambitious seventh-century king—and on the other hand, maybe not. The problem is that portions of Deuteronomy and the Former Prophets seem to presuppose circumstances after the time of Josiah. Moreover, existing ancient manuscripts demonstrate that these books were still being edited centuries after the time of Josiah. Given these two realities, every biblical scholar who accepts the Dtr hypothesis differs on which portions of Deuteronomy and the Former Prophets should be attributed to the Josianic era. These differences of opinion among scholars are extreme. As a matter of fact, there does not exist one stable Dtr hypothesis in modern scholarship. Dtr hypotheses are legion. The situation has become so unstable that many scholars, in very sloppy fashion, simply refer to the entirety of Deuteronomy, Joshua, Judges, 1–2 Samuel and 1–2 Kings as though these were the Deuteronomistic History! That is utterly false and methodologically inexcusable. Yet, it is very common.

One thing is clear: The portion of the hypothesis in which Josiah is said to have closed all Yahwistic shrines outside Jerusalem and to have thus 'centralized' Yahweh worship in Jerusalem is unequivocally false. A Yahwistic temple uncovered by archaeologists at Arad in the northern Negev came into existence in the late-eighth century and remained active until it was destroyed (presumably by Nebuchadnezzar II) in the early-sixth century.[9] It was fully operative when King Josiah was active. Unfortunately, the 'centralization' portion of the modern hypothesis continues to be espoused by biblical scholars who are either unaware of, or uninterested in, archaeological data. The popularity of this portion of the hypothesis has to do with the extreme centrality of 'centralization' in the book of Deuteronomy. Let us examine this motif.

Deuteronomy 12 is devoted to, among other things, the idea that Yahweh will choose just one place from all the tribes of Israel and cause his name to dwell in that place. The place of divine choice is to be the place of the temple of Yahweh. Other portions of Deuteronomy repeat this theme, but very few other biblical books mention the motif. It does occur from time to time, and a number of passages in 1–2 Kings seem to presuppose the validity of Deuteronomy 12. In particular, each king is evaluated on the basis of whether the king did, or did not, close the shrines on the 'high places', thus rendering Jerusalem the only place with a temple (see, e.g., 2 Kgs 12.4; 14.4; 15.4, 35; 18.4). Interestingly, however, almost all of the Bible is silent on the 'centralization' motif. Exodus 20.24 (which is 20.21 in a few English versions) seems to imply that Yahweh will choose many places for his temples, and most biblical narratives take for granted—with no hint of embarrassment or censure—that there can be, and will be, temples of Yahweh all over the land where Israelites dwell.

This centralization motif *seems* to be integral to 2 Kings 23, and many scholars believe it to be at the very heart of Josiah's royal policy. It is argued that by centralizing sacrificial liturgies in the capital city, Josiah was trying to accomplish at least two goals, one political and one economic. Politically, he was issuing a religious propaganda designed to win the hearts of people living in the Assyrian province of Samaria (the Central Hills, a region that had been occupied by the Kingdom of Israel prior to 722 BCE). The propaganda promised to restore the ideal empire of Kings David and Solomon, bring the former Kingdom of Israel back to life as a Kingdom of Israel-Judah in Jerusalem, make Jerusalem the religious center for all worshipers of Yahweh and, *therefore*, make all worshipers loyal to the king in Jerusalem—the king who happened to be, not by coincidence, Josiah. Economically, the centralization program would close outlying temples, thus forcing people to bring their religious offerings (tithes), which were a form of tax, to Jerusalem. That would mean greater revenue for the crown.

As a historian, I view both these hypotheses, except for the 'centralization' portion, to be plausible. Perhaps in the future, evidence will come to light that will refute or support them. Until then, a merely plausible hypothesis does not seem sufficiently compelling to merit enthusiasm. I do not consider either hypothesis a theory, though I understand why many do. However, since these hypotheses are endemic to mainstream historical biblical scholarship and do not give any indication that they will fade away soon, it might be beneficial to look at how they can be brought into line with the compelling archaeological evidence. I do not advocate the following, I only offer it as a way to improve the Dtr and Josianic Reform hypotheses.

If one wishes to accept the hypothesis that Josiah closed a number of Yahweh and non-Yahweh temples as part of a political agenda, the 'centralization' portion of that hypothesis can be eliminated without doing much damage to the remaining details. Consider two thoughts.

First, the narrative of King Josiah's religious innovations in 2 Kings 22–23 is saturated with clichés from the book of Deuteronomy, but it need not have been based on any passage in the newly discovered book of Torah about a single place for Yahweh worship. In other words, the scroll allegedly found by Josiah's temple workers need not have contained Deut. 12.5, 11, 14, or similar passages. In the story of Kings, Josiah is engaged in the removal of royal religious traditions that no longer conform to the theology espoused in Deut. 5.7-10, 10.17, and elsewhere. In doing this, Josiah might have closed any number of religious temples that were, to his mind, so thoroughly saturated with religious objects and liturgies no longer acceptable that closure seemed more appropriate than cleansing. There is no suggestion in 2 Kings 22–23 that Josiah closed all Yahweh shrines everywhere; not even 2 Kgs 23.5, 8-9 or 19 need be so construed. (One might note that 2 Kgs 23.8-9 is inconsistent with Deut. 18.6-8.)

Second, Deuteronomy 12 is likely to have been composed at a date much later than the time of Josiah. If this chapter seeks to restrict Yahweh temple liturgy to just one location, it seems reasonable to seek a pragmatic motivation for doing so, and the motivations usually assigned to Josiah are not very pragmatic. One does not 'centralize' the collection of taxes (as in some versions of the hypothesis). That would be counter-productive because the royal administration would simply lose control of, and forfeit the payments in kind from, villagers worshiping in areas far from the capital city. Attempts to compel villagers to travel to the central shrine would be, at best, partially successful, and much revenue would slip through the king's fingers. Also, proclamation of Jerusalem as Yahweh's only legitimate holy site was as likely to offend some descendants of the former Kingdom of Israel as it was to attract some, so the policy's effectiveness would have been mixed, at best. The attempt to relate Deuteronomy 12 to 2 Kings 22–23 simply does not make much sense. As one scholar who *defends* the hypothesis put it, 'We still do not have a plausible explanation for this development. Neither purely fiscal nor purely theological hypotheses are convincing.'[10]

There is a very plausible, perhaps probable, explanation for the composition of Deuteronomy 12 that has nothing to do with King Josiah. According to Ezra 6.1-5, King Cyrus of Persia is said to have ordered the construction of a single temple for Yahweh at Jerusalem almost one hundred years after the reign of Josiah. If a small group of Jews were given permission by the reigning imperial power of their day to build but one place of worship in their homeland, it is reasonable to suppose that they would rationalize this royal decree by asserting that their god has chosen just one place, from all the tribes of Israel, to cause his name to dwell. Deuteronomy 12 and related passages (such as the evaluation of various kings mentioned above) make very good sense if they are by-products of the new political realities of the Persian-period temple restoration project at Jerusalem. At that time, Jerusalem was on its own, and its temple was a novelty disliked by at least some groups in surrounding areas. It is this moment in Judaism's past more than any other when a text such as Deuteronomy 12 might have been composed. Deuteronomy 12 has no relation to King Josiah.

## SUGGESTED ADDITIONAL READING

*Social and Political History of the Iron Age II*

Ahlström, Gösta W., *Royal Administration and National Religion in Ancient Palestine* (Leiden: E.J. Brill, 1982).

Clements, R.E. (ed.), *The World of Ancient Israel: Sociological, Anthropological and Political Perspectives* (Cambridge: Cambridge University Press, 1989).

Cross, Frank Moore, *Canaanite Myth and Hebrew Epic: Essays in the History of the Religion of Israel* (Cambridge, MA: Harvard University Press, 1973).

—*From Epic to Canon: History and Literature in Ancient Israel* (Baltimore: The Johns Hopkins University Press, 1998).

Dearman, J. Andrew (ed.), *Studies in the Mesha Inscription and Moab* (Atlanta: Scholars Press, 1989).

Finkelstein, Israel and Neil Asher Silberman, *The Bible, Unearthed: Archaeology's New Vision of Ancient Israel and the Origin of its Sacred Texts* (New York: The Free Press, 2001).

Kuhrt, Amélie, *The Ancient Near East, c. 3000–330 BC*, II (London: Routledge, 1995).

Lemche, Niels Peter, 'Kings and Clients: On Loyalty Between the Ruler and the Ruled in Ancient "Israel"', *Semeia* 66 (1994), pp. 119-32.

Smith, Morton, 'The Common Theology of the Ancient Near East', *JBL* 71 (1952), pp. 135-47.

*Deuteronomistic History Studies and Hypotheses about King Josiah*

Nelson, Richard D., *The Historical Books* (Interpreting Biblical Texts; Nashville: Abingdon Press, 1998), pp. 67-78 (Chapter 4).

Noth, Martin, *The Deuteronomistic History* (JSOTSup, 15; Sheffield: JSOT Press, 1981).

Pury, Albert de, Thomas Römer and J.D. Macchi (eds.), *Israel Constructs its History: Deuteronomistic Historiography in Recent Research* (JSOTSup, 306; Sheffield: Sheffield Academic Press, 2000).

Sweeney, Marvin A., *King Josiah of Judah: The Lost Messiah of Israel* (Oxford: Oxford University Press, 2001).

*Modern Interpretations of the Bible's Patron God, Yahweh*

Brueggemann, Walter, *Theology of the Old Testament: Testimony, Dispute, Advocacy* (Minneapolis: Fortress Press, 1997).

Clines, David J.A., *Interested Parties: The Ideology of Writers and Readers of the Hebrew Bible* (JSOTSup, 205; Sheffield: Sheffield Academic Press, 1995).

Miles, Jack, *God: A Biography* (New York: Vintage Books, 1996).

Thompson, Thomas L., *The Mythic Past: Biblical Archaeology and the Myth of Israel* (New York: Basic Books, 1999).

## NOTES

1.  Precise numbers depend on which regions are assumed to have been part of each kingdom by the eighth century. In this instance, my generalization derives from M. Broshi and I. Finkelstein, 'The Population of Palestine in Iron Age II', *BASOR* 287 (1992), pp. 47-60 (54).

2.  W.G. Dever suggests limited literacy in his essay, 'Social Structure in Palestine in the Iron II Period on the Eve of Destruction', in T.E. Levy (ed.), *The Archaeology of Society in the Holy Land* (Leicester: Leicester University Press, 1998), pp. 416-31. E. Ben Zvi offers a succinct discussion of ancient literacy, with useful bibliography, in 'The Urban Center of Jerusalem and the Development of the Literature of the Hebrew Bible', in W.G. Aufrecht *et al.* (eds.), *Urbanism in Antiquity: From Mesopotamia to Crete* (JSOTSup, 244; Sheffield: Sheffield Academic Press, 1997), pp. 194-209.

3.  E.A. Knauf, 'King Solomon's Copper Supply', in E. Lipiński, *Phoenicia and the Bible* (Studia Phoenicia, 11; Leuven: Peeters, 1991), pp. 167-86 (181 n. 55). For my views on the process by which these tales coalesced, see my *The Faces of David* (JSOTSup, 242; Sheffield: Sheffield Academic Press, 1997), pp. 40-42. See also, *idem*, 'Is There a Text in this Tradition? Readers' Response and the Taming of Samuel's God', *JSOT* 83 (1999), pp. 31-51.

4.  Knauf, 'King Solomon's Copper Supply', p. 178.

5.  For the text, see J.C.L. Gibson, *Textbook of Syrian Semitic Inscriptions*. II. *Aramaic Inscriptions* (3 vols.; Oxford: Clarendon Press, 1971–82), pp. 8, 10.

6.  Noll, *The Faces of David* (see n. 3 above).

7.  Some have argued that the unknown king who erected the Tel Dan inscription was Hazael of Damascus. In this case, Dan was not an independent city-state, but under the sovereignty of Damascus for most of the Iron Age II. For discussion with bibliography, see K.L. Noll, 'The God Who is Among the Danites', *JSOT* 80 (1998), pp. 3-23.

8.  I. Finkelstein, 'The Archaeology of the Days of Manasseh', in M.D. Coogan *et al.* (eds.), *Scripture and Other Artifacts: Essays on the Bible and Archaeology in Honor of Philip J. King* (Louisville, KY: Westminster/John Knox Press, 1994), pp. 169-87.

9.  D. Ussishkin, 'The Date of the Judaean Shrine at Arad', *IEJ* 38 (1988), pp. 142-57.

10. N. Lohfink, 'The Cult Reform of Josiah of Judah: 2 Kings 22–23 as a Source for the History of Israelite Religion', in P.D. Miller *et al.* (eds.), *Ancient Israelite Religion: Essays in Honor of Frank Moore Cross* (Philadelphia: Fortress Press, 1987), pp. 459-75 (468).

Chapter 9

THE RELIGIONS OF CANAAN: A SHORT TOUR

*Introduction*

One of the humanist historian's goals is to make ancient lives intelligible. This chapter offers a tour of ancient Canaanite religions with this goal in mind. Naturally, the religions of Israel and Judah will be treated as examples of the Canaanite religions. I will not discuss the minutiae of religious doctrines, priesthoods and sacrifices. Rather, my goal is to paint a realistic portrait of ancient religion's relationship to everyday life, and its relationship to the modern world.

What is a religion? Social anthropologists continue to debate the question, and I could write a book, not a chapter, on the topic.[1] For present purposes, there are two elements to consider. The first is theism and the second is an experience of the sacred. Belief in a god or gods is called theism; lack of that belief is called atheism. Also, a sense of mystery about life is an experience of the sacred; a lack of the sacred experience is a secular experience.

Generally speaking, a religion participates in one or both of the two categories, theism and sacredness, but to *be* a religion, it needs to participate in only one of the two. Consider this chart:

| First Ingredient | Second Ingredient |
|------------------|-------------------|
| Sacred | Theism |
| Secular | Atheism |

Figure 29: *Religious Categories.*

By merging the ingredients, one arrives at a continuum of religious experience, from sacred-theism through sacred-atheism to secular-theism and finally secular-atheism. Three of these are religious in some sense. The fourth is not. A secular-atheist does not believe in any supernatural beings and believes there is nothing mysterious about life. In many cultures, perhaps most, the secular-atheist is not commonly encountered.

Sacred-theism is the category modern Westerners usually recognize as religion. Judaism, Christianity and Islam, when they are observed in their most traditional forms, are examples. A sacred-theist is convinced by doctrines about a god and participates in sacred activity, such as worship services, prayer, divinely defined moral conduct and so on. Usually, the sacred-theist believes that she has experienced a transforming relationship with the divine through those activities.

Sacred-atheism can be philosophical, can include rituals, and always develops a set of morals, but does not need a divine being. For example, many Buddhists would answer the question, 'What is eternal?', as follows: 'Life is an eternal flame. We are but candles. Each candle burns for a moment and burns out, but the flame of life is eternal.' In this example, a sense of sacredness resides not in a deity, but in life. This is sacred-atheism.

Often, secular-theism is not recognized as a religious experience, but it is just that. Many people believe in divinity, participate in the rituals and customs of a religion, follow divinely revealed moral guidelines, but do not experience a sense of the sacred. This does not mean that these people are faking their religious experience; they are not hypocrites or 'closet' atheists. These people remain secular-theists even if they experience an occasional sense of the sacred. In the Bible, the proverb 'Is Saul too among the prophets?' expresses the human experience of one who is usually a secular person, but occasionally enters the realm of the sacred (1 Sam. 10.11-12; 19.24).

These categories offer a first point of entry into the religions of ancient Canaan. Textbooks usually assert that all people in the Bronze and Iron Ages were religious. Religion, it is said, permeated all aspects of daily life. That is certainly correct, but only half the story. One would have been hard-pressed to find a secular-atheist anywhere in the ancient world (though there were a few; the Greek historian Thucydides comes to mind). However, this does not mean that the daily experience of religion was qualitatively different from daily experience in the modern West. People in the ancient world did not walk about in a perpetual state of sacred awe. Rather, the difference between then and now is quantitative. For instance, if one gathers an anthology of great twentieth-century American writing, it will include a few passages by sacred-theists, but not many. By contrast, the Bible is an anthology of ancient Jewish literature, and a majority of its passages express sacred-theism. However, there are *secular-theistic* documents in the Bible as well. Certainly, one will seek in vain a secular-atheist among biblical authors. Just as certainly, one cannot read Qoheleth (known in English as Ecclesiastes) expecting the same expression of sacredness one reads in the Psalms. Consider these two passages from Qoh. 6.3 (on the left) and Ps. 8.4-5:

| | |
|---|---|
| If a man were to father one hundred, | When I observe your skies, |
| And the years of his life are many, | These works of your fingertips, |
| And great are the days of those years, | The moon, the stars, which you made! |
| Yet his desire is not saturated with pleasure, | What is a man, that you think of him? |
| Or there is no burial for him, | A human, that you take note of him? |
| I say: Better is a stillborn than he! | |

Here we have a clash between secular and sacred views of the world. One writer expresses a jaded attitude—not quite cynicism—in which the goal of life is to seek some pleasure for a while, then hope someone will dispose of his body honorably. There is no more to life than this, says Qoheleth, for all is 'emptiness' (Qoh. 1.2). The other biblical author cannot stifle his inner sense of reverence before the majesty of the cosmos. Observation of mundane reality, expressed by Qoheleth with the dismissive phrase 'there's nothing new under the sun' (Qoh. 1.9), is the inspiration for the psalmist's shout of unbridled joy in the divine. For the psalmist, something is new every moment!

Both writers were theists. They stood under the sovereignty of the same god, Yahweh. Neither author would deny Yahweh's reality or his power. Each responds to Yahweh differently. One is a secular-theist, the other a sacred-theist. The Bible has made room for both. That is why the Bible contains erotic poetry (Song of Songs), ribald folklore (the tales of Samson in Judg. 13–16), and stories of greed, lust, rape and mayhem (1–2 Samuel). These are not religious writings, at least not if the definition of religion is limited to a single melody, the sacred-theistic melody.[2] As an anthology, the Bible *becomes* religious as the secular-theistic texts blend their voices in harmony with sacred-theistic documents, such as Leviticus, Psalms and Isaiah.

This first step toward an understanding of the religions of Canaan emphasized the distinctive ways an individual experiences, then expresses, religion. A common ancient expression of religion was myth, and this complex topic is the next stop on our tour.

### *What is a Myth? What is Mythology?*

A myth is any story involving a god or gods that is repeated often. Sometimes a myth is part of a religious observance, called liturgy. (In scholarship, liturgy is sometimes called 'cult', which is a technical term meaning 'liturgy' and not a reference to a religious fringe group.) When it is not part of a liturgy, a myth is a form of folk entertainment.

In the ancient world, many myths were localized. Others enjoyed wider circulation. Most were not known to wide audiences. The myths of ancient Greece are better known today than they were to ancient Greeks.

Mythology is the compilation of myths as literature. For example, in ancient Greece, many stories were told about the origins of the gods. Hesiod gathered a number of these stories, strung them into a single narrative, and produced mythology, the *Theogony*. The mythology did not correspond to the myths. Hesiod's invention was an anthology linking originally separate tales of the gods, creating an artificial poetic narrative. Ancient readers of Hesiod would have recognized the mythology for what it was, a pastiche of myths.

Myths were believed or not, depending on the social circumstances in which they were told. Some hearers of myth accepted them literally. Others found metaphorical or allegorical meaning. Some dismissed myths as nonsense.

Perhaps the best way to comprehend the relationship of myth to religion in the ancient world is to learn from an ancient Roman scholar named Varro.[3] He asserted that any god or goddess can be conceptualized in three very different ways. There were, he said, the gods of the poets, gods of the philosophers and gods of the city. For example, in Homer's poetry, the Greek god Zeus was a powerful but lusty god easily swayed by the seductions of a pretty woman or goddess. By contrast, for some philosophers, Zeus was a metaphor for a highly abstract conceptualization of the divine. For city dwellers who worshiped Zeus during local festivals and holy days, Zeus was the powerful, holy and just god, who was lord of the pantheon. In the latter instance, the myths about Zeus were entertaining, but would not have played a vital role in the worship of Zeus.

Thus, myth was a complex and versatile genre of communication, which could play an important religious role in some cases, and no religious role in others. This is similar to our culture. The god of the

Bible appears frequently in storytelling that is not religious. Films, television shows, even comics, occasionally trot the all-powerful deity on stage as part of the plot. The vaudeville comedian George Burns even played god in a film entitled *Oh God!* In other cases, modern myths play a religious role. Sometimes, elaborate stories based loosely on biblical stories are told by those who teach religious doctrine. In a few cases, these newer myths became mythology, compiled into books that, for some, have even become scripture.

In ancient Palestine, the documents known to us as the Bible were the mythology compiled by the 'Hesiods' of Jerusalem. The Bible contains the Yahweh of the poets, the Yahweh of the philosophers, and the Yahweh of the city. Only one of these three Yahwehs was worshiped by those who created the biblical texts. In Gen. 11.1-9, one encounters the Yahweh of the poets. This is a very comical god with limited intellectual and physical abilities. For one thing, he must travel 'downward' to see what humans are doing. When he observes their activity, he becomes absurdly jealous of their accomplishments. The tale is delightful, but hardly religious in the sacred-theistic sense. The Yahweh of the philosophers is exemplified by the book of Job, a story about a righteous man whose god tests him with hardships. The story was based on an old myth but moves beyond it, being composed as very sophisticated literary entertainment for a well-educated audience. It is written in an idiosyncratic dialect of Hebrew involving elements of Aramaic and Phoenician, which would have taxed a poorly educated Hebrew reader. The god of Job is a god whose majesty transcends human concerns such as reward for the righteous and punishment for the evil. The god of Job does not reward or punish. This stands in contrast to the Yahweh of Deuteronomy, who is a god of righteous judgment, a god of the city who demands (and no doubt received) pious worship.

How can one Hebrew anthology contain opposing images of Yahweh? In the same way that a group of Jews, suffering in a Nazi concentration camp, put their Lord on trial for injustice, found him guilty, and then performed their usual evening prayers! During the trial, they were thinking philosophically about the divine; after that, they were moving into the realm of sacred piety. Myth played an important, yet different, role in each instance. Thus, myth can be an essential part of a living religion. Humans often find that one 'doctrine' of god is not enough, and the storytelling process inherent in myth gives ample room to seek out variant conceptualizations. The truth is called Legion, for they are many.

These first two stops on our tour of ancient Canaanite religions have revealed some strong similarities with the modern Western world. Theism and myth were, and are, secular and sacred. One topic that seems to present a radical divide between the ancient and modern worlds is the diversity of ancient theisms, which is the next stop on our tour.

### The Gods of Ancient Canaan

The religions of ancient Canaan were theistic, without exception. As we have seen, however, they were not always sacred-theistic. In fact, the diversity in ancient theisms went well beyond a simple distinction between sacred and secular. The theisms of ancient Canaan were so complex that the following description can provide only a general introduction.

Our best evidence about the gods stems from the highest ranks of society, who did all the writing and designed most of the public buildings. Even within this small segment of Canaanite society, the number and variety of the gods can seem bewildering to the uninitiated. To bring some degree of order to the data it might be helpful to consider again the concepts introduced toward the end of Chapter 5 (pp. 131-34): polytheism, henotheism and monotheism. These concepts are artificial in the sense that no ancient person used these three labels and, in many cases, a single religion might conform to more than one category. Nevertheless, the three labels will help us identify some important patterns in the theisms of Bronze and Iron Age Canaan.

#### Bronze Age Polytheism

The ancient city of Ugarit on the northern coast of Syria is the best preserved example for a study of Late Bronze Age religion in Canaan. Ugarit was one of the cities that collapsed just after 1200 BCE (as discussed in Chapter 6). It did not exist in the Iron Age.

At the highest elevation of Ugarit stood the city acropolis, a sacred precinct housing temples that towered over the people and could be seen far from shore by sailors. The two primary temples were dedicated to two male gods, Baal and Dagan. Religious structures were found in other parts of the city as well, suggesting that places of worship were a part of 'street life' and not just the separated realm of the holy precinct.

One very interesting set of artifacts from Ugarit is a collection of mythology found written on clay tablets in a house that seems to have been the home of a priest. This mythology is populated by a diverse pantheon of gods. In the poetic stories (called epics), Baal figures prominently, but Dagan does not. This and other clues suggest that the mythology was not a vital part of the worship taking place in the two primary temples.[4] If that is correct, then the mythology of Ugarit was typical of mythology in the ancient world. Even so, when these tales are compared to the liturgical and administrative documents of Ugarit, it is obvious that the mythology names gods commonly worshiped. Although the mythology does not set forth a doctrine of Ugaritic religion, the stories no doubt reflect some very general presuppositions about the relationships between the gods, and between the gods and people. The following description is based on those general relationships, while recognizing that the gods of Ugarit's poets differed from those of the city.

Ugaritic religion was polytheistic, and yet the primary gods of this city fall naturally into four levels of hierarchy. There was a pecking order in the divine realm, as there was in human society. Thus, the gods of Ugarit can be arranged into a pyramid, with two executive gods at the top, a handful of highly powerful gods in the second rank, minor gods in the third rank, and very many servant gods in the lowest rank. In other words, this was a polytheism that was moving in the direction of henotheism, yet perhaps not fully henotheistic.

The two executive gods were El and Asherah, who were married. El was creator of earth and humanity. He was an aged, wise and benevolent god, a divine shepherd who lived at a place where the sources of fresh-water rivers flow to Earth (compare Gen. 2.10-14). El's wife was Athirat (written Asherah in other ancient texts), who was mother of the gods. She was called 'great Asherah of the sea' as well, though no one is quite sure what that title meant. Her symbol was a stylized 'tree of life' (compare Gen. 2.9; see also Prov. 3.18).

In the second rank, below the two executive gods, were the cosmic gods. These were the gods of 'natural' phenomena, such as sun, moon, storm, death and even war.

Perhaps most significant among the cosmic gods was Baal, god of storm and provider of fertility. His actual name was Hadad, but Baal, which means 'lord', was used very commonly in place of the name.

Baal is said to ride the clouds through the sky, and presented as doing battle with two of his divine siblings, Mot and Yamm. Together, these three brothers symbolized three natural realms, the sky (Baal), the earth (Mot) and the sea (Yamm), but victorious Baal was the 'king' of the others (with El's approval, of course). Yamm was a god of chaos, which is no doubt what the sea seemed to ancient peoples. Mot was god of the underworld and death. The underworld was not a place of punishment like 'hell' in the modern, Christian sense. Mot and the realm of death were the final destiny of all people, whether they were good or bad. The underworld was really just a metaphor for nonexistence. No one went to heaven since there was no heaven. The sky (= heaven) was the realm of gods, the 'heavenly host' as the Bible calls them (1 Kgs 22.19; Lk. 2.13), not a place for human souls. Except for a handful of Hellenistic-era additions to the text, the Jewish Bible shares this understanding of the underworld, which calls it Sheol.

There were other very significant cosmic gods. Baal's father was Dagan, god of grain. Baal's wife, who was also his sister, was Anat, goddess of war. She was a mighty deity who saved Baal from defeat at the hands of Mot. The moon was Yerach and the sun was Shapash (written Shemesh in other ancient texts). Resheph was god of pestilence. He was worthy of worship so that he would not inflict pestilence on humanity. In ancient artwork, Resheph looks very much like Baal, and one must examine the details of each to distinguish between them. A female named Astarte seems to have been a goddess of love, similar to Greek Aphrodite, but not much is known about her.

A third level of the divine realm were gods of utility, but they are rarely mentioned by name in the Ugaritic texts. These gods ruled over practical aspects of life, such as craftsmanship. In addition to gods of utility, this rank of the divine realm included a few dead humans. At death, a king or important person became one of the *rephaim*, divinized dead humans who enjoy the company of the other gods. In the Bible, for example, the dead prophet Samuel is a 'god' (Heb. *elohim*) in 1 Sam. 28.13.

The lowest rank of deities were the servant gods, most of whom held the title of *malaak*, which means 'messenger'. These were gods who ran messages back and forth between gods, and also brought messages from a god to humans. In Greek, the word 'messenger' is written *angelos*, which became 'angel' in English. Later Jewish, Christian and Islamic teaching demoted the angels from gods to creatures of only semi-divine status, but in pre-Hellenistic times, all these gods were fully divine and part of the polytheistic pantheon. When one reads of an 'angel of the LORD' in the Bible, the ancient author of that passage had a fully divine being of low rank in mind (e.g. Num. 22.21-35). Sometimes, a *malaak* is not called *malaak*, but has a more specific title, such as the 'Prince of the Army of Yahweh' in Josh. 5.14.

In the Bible, another set of servant-level gods were the *seraphim* and the *cherubim*, whose presence symbolized royalty. For instance, Yahweh sits enthroned between two *cherubim* (1 Sam. 4.4; 1 Kgs 6.23-30, etc.), which means that Yahweh is king of the gods (see Ps. 97). We know from a variety of ancient Near Eastern artworks, from Mesopotamia to Egypt, that a *cherub* (the singular form of the word) had the body of a lion, the hooves of a bull, the wings of an eagle and the face of a man (compare the even more complex imagery of Ezek. 1). A *seraph* was a snake, or at least a snake-like being, with wings. The prophet Isaiah sees some of these gods in his temple vision in Isaiah 6, another passage in which Yahweh is depicted as a king.

Ugarit was a Bronze Age city, and its polytheism reflects a political hierarchy that differed from the political world of the Iron Age that followed Ugarit's collapse. Nevertheless, as the examples drawn from the Iron Age Bible demonstrated, there was much continuity from one era to the next—probably more continuity than discontinuity.

## Iron Age Henotheism

As the city-states of Iron Age I gradually emerged, they expanded into small territorial states, a small-scale reflection of Late Bronze Age Mesopotamia (see pp. 129-31). Although evidence for Iron Age religion is less complete than for the Bronze Age, the new political reality of the Iron Age seems to have resulted in a new religious expression.

With some exceptions, Iron Age religion seems to have developed into henotheism. One god, usually the god of the capital city, emerged as the most powerful of the gods. This movement towards henotheism probably reflects the political subordination of some cities to others as territorial states grew and developed, as had happened in Mesopotamia. The new henotheism was at home among the elite classes who wrote the ancient texts now available to us, but this theological shift might not have been the common religious perception among peasants. Perhaps at the 'popular' level, the gods of the Iron Age were much the same as they had been in the Bronze Age.

Not surprisingly, the four-rank divine hierarchy of Ugarit is more difficult to discern in the surviving Iron Age data. This might be an accident of preservation. Nevertheless, given the data, one might think of Iron Age Canaanite pantheons as having just two ranks, the high god and his wife at the top, and all other gods at the rank of servant gods, below. Sometimes a female deity was the highest of gods, but usually it was a male deity; this god could be either a bachelor or married. Chemosh was high god of Moab; in Damascus it was Hadad; Tyre's divine king of the city was Melqart; Hamath's divine patron was Ashima; in Sidon it was Eshmun. A very interesting and ambiguous case is Philistine Ekron, where two goddesses and a divine epithet are named in inscriptions, though they might well be three references to the same deity. She is (or they are) Asherah and an unpronounceable name, Ptgyh, as well as the epithet Qudshu, which means Holy One. Also mentioned is Baal, who was, *perhaps*, considered the husband of Asherah-Ptgyh at Ekron. This is entirely uncertain, but an intriguing possibility.[5]

Usually, the Iron Age high god was similar to Bronze Age Baal, but with some attributes of El. In a few instances, the opposite was the case: the high god was similar to El, but with attributes of Baal. In the Bible, Yahweh is presented as a Baal, riding through the clouds on a *cherub* with smoke pouring from his nostrils, in Ps. 18.7-20 (in some English versions, 18.6-19). Other typically Baal-type portraits are Psalms 29, 74 and 93, where Yahweh as Baal has defeated chaotic waters. Yahweh is described as El in Gen. 49.24-26, with its image of the divine shepherd, divine father, provider of blessings, including the blessings of breast and womb (probably a vestige of Asherah's role). In a very late Hellenistic text, Dan. 7.13-14, El is the 'Ancient of Days' and Baal is the 'One like a Son of Man', the latter no longer a god, but a metaphor for the Jewish people (Dan. 7.27).

The henotheistic high god sometimes absorbed the roles and titles of other gods. For example, an increasing 'solarization' of many henotheistic high gods can be discerned in the Iron Age II. Numbers 6.24-26 is an interesting case. It is a blessing of 'grace' in the name of an El-like Yahweh, yet this god 'shines' his light on the worshiper as would Shemesh (Shapash). Other lesser gods could also be absorbed, or they might remain independent gods at the high god's command. In Hab. 3.5, for example, a Baal-like Yahweh may have absorbed aspects of Resheph, unless Resheph is simply by Yahweh's side in this poem. In other cases, the high god's wife might have become a manifestation of the god himself. Evidence for this is unclear and hotly debated by scholars. For example, at Elephantine, the Persian-era Jews (whose religion was nearly identical to Iron Age II Judahite religion) worshiped Anat-Yahu, wife of Yahweh (Yahu = Yahweh). Because the name is written in a way that can be translated 'Anat of Yahu', some scholars have suggested that she was no longer just Anat, but a part of Yahu: Yahu's Anat. It is difficult to explain what this fusion of husband and wife means. A few scholars have suggested that the wife was becoming a 'hypostasis' of her husband.[6] (A hypostasis is a term borrowed from Christian doctrine, where it describes the relationship of Jesus-the-Son to God-the-Father.) If Anat-Yahu was a hypostasis of Yahweh, then other biblical terms probably were as well, including: the 'glory' of Yahweh (Ezek. 10.4, 18; 11.23, etc.) the 'name' of Yahweh (Deut. 12.5; 18.7, etc.) and the 'wisdom' of Yahweh (Prov. 8.1-36, esp. vv. 22-31; see also Wisdom of Jesus ben Sirach 24.1-34).

Figure 30. *Baal, God of Storm. One of the most common cosmic deities of the ancient Near East was the god of storm. Here, the militant posture in the Ugaritic representation of that god displays his characteristics. Baal ('Lord') Hadad is a smiting god, whose activity also brings new life, as symbolized by the sprouting staff in his hand* (© Louvre).

From many of the examples provided above, it should be clear that the best preserved example of Iron Age Canaanite henotheism is the anthology we call the Jewish Bible (Christian Old Testament). Although the Bible contains a few late additions designed to transform its religion into monotheism, the overwhelming majority of its texts are henotheistic. To be more precise, the Bible usually expresses monolatry, which is a more extreme form of henotheism. Whereas henotheism believes in many gods, but with one supremely powerful god, monolatry believes in many gods, but with only one god that is worthy of worship. Thus, the monolatrist is a henotheist who acknowledges lesser gods but refuses to worship them. Some scholars use the two terms interchangeably, which is a little misleading, but they do so because they correctly realize that henotheism and monolatry are extremely similar religious world views. Neither of them is monotheistic, however.

Monotheistic passages are rare in the Bible. For example, the famous Shema, a fundamental Jewish confession of faith found in Deut. 6.4, is grammatically ambiguous in the original Hebrew, but no matter how this grammar is interpreted or translated, the passage does not affirm monotheism. Either the text says that Yahweh is 'one god' (perhaps a polemic against the high god's absorption of lesser gods?) or it affirms that Yahweh 'alone' is Israel's god (which is monolatry, not monotheism).[7] The only portion of the Bible with a relatively high cluster of monotheistic affirmations is the second half of Isaiah (chs. 40–66), which many scholars call Deutero-Isaiah, and date to the late-sixth century BCE. The remainder of the Bible contains random monotheistic statements among monolatrous and henotheistic passages.

A very good example of monolatry in the Bible is the dual stipulation in the first two of the famous Ten Commandments, a stipulation that presumes the existence of lesser gods, but prohibits worship of them because the high god is 'jealous' of them (Deut. 5.7-10). Years after the Ten Commandments had been formulated, a scribe interpreted them to mean that Yahweh is the only god who exists, and so added Deuteronomy 4, a chapter that includes two explicitly monotheistic verses (4.35, 39). When a biblical text was updated in this way, biblical scholars call it 'redaction' (or 'editing') of the text. In this instance, Deuteronomy 4 offers 'redactional' reinterpretation of Deuteronomy 5. Sometimes the redaction is such a short addition that it is better to call it a 'gloss' on the text.

Here is an example of a monotheistic gloss in a henotheistic biblical poem found at 1 Sam. 2.2:

> Verse 2a: None are holy like Yahweh
> Verse 2b: For none exists except you
> Verse 2c: And there is no rock like our god

The first and last portions are henotheistic. The poet proclaims that Yahweh is supreme over other gods. The middle portion (v. 2b) is clearly monotheistic, affirming that there is no god except Yahweh. But this phrase does not exist in some ancient manuscripts of this passage, which suggests that it was a later addition that failed to make its way into some manuscript copies. In those manuscripts that include the phrase, there is a grammatical indication that it was not part of the original poem. Notice that v. 2a and v. 2c are written in the third person but v. 2b is in the second person. Applying the historical method called textual criticism (defined on p. 55), the middle portion is judged to be a monotheistic gloss, a later addition to an originally henotheistic poem.

These examples from Deuteronomy and 1 Samuel demonstrate that the Bible's religion is a representative example of Iron Age Canaanite religion. Those who are committed to the Jewish and Christian religions are sometimes troubled by this—but there is no reason to be troubled. All religion is a product of social circumstances. It is not possible for a religion to exist otherwise. Why? Because a religion has to be comprehensible to the people. If it is not understandable it will not survive. People will simply ignore that religion and embrace one that makes more sense to them. During the Iron Age, the religion that made sense was henotheism. Therefore, it is no surprise that those who worshiped Yahweh expressed their worship henotheistically. Monotheism began to make sense later.

Just as the modern and ancient worlds share sacred- and secular-theisms, as well as sacred and secular uses of myths and mythology, so also the two worlds share a conception of the divine: although modern people, including Christians, believe angels and devils are compatible with monotheism, they are best understood as components of henotheism.[8] Since our culture has been shaped by the finest surviving example of ancient henotheism, the Bible, modern preferences for henotheism are not as surprising as it might at first seem.

*The Rise of Yahweh as Israel's High God*

The Bible differs from other Iron Age henotheisms in only one respect: The name of the Bible's highest god is Yahweh. This was not the name of a high god in any other known henotheism. Some divine names in the ancient world were distinctive in this sense. For example, the high god Ashur was worshiped only by Assyrians. Many ancient high gods, however, migrate from place to place, showing up as lesser gods in the pantheons of neighboring religions; Marduk of Babylon, for example, was worshiped by the Assyrians. So Yahweh might have been—like Ashur, but unlike Marduk—something of a loner.

Who was Yahweh, and when and and how did he become associated with a group of El-worshipers called *yisra-'el* (Israel)? These questions do not yet have answers, but some of the evidence for addressing them will be discussed here.

Although modern people automatically equate the two, it was not inevitable that Israel and Yahweh would match up. Tiny fragments of evidence suggest that Yahweh was not quite the loner that Ashur had been. Yahweh may have been worshiped by people who are not likely to have identified themselves as ethnically Israelite. For example, a small eighth-century BCE epigraph provides the name of a man who was a priest of Canaanite Dor. His name was Zechariah, which is a theophoric, a sentence-name using Yaw (= Yahweh) as subject noun: *zekar-yaw* means 'Yahweh has remembered'. Although some historians think that Dor was an Israelite city, there is neither biblical nor archaeological support for the assumption.[9] Thus, while it is just about feasible that Zechariah considered himself ethnically Israelite, the balance of probability is that he, his parents who named him, and as many of his ancestors as he could remember, were ideologically committed to Dor, an ethnically non-Israelite city. Yet, presumably, Zechariah or his parents worshiped Yahweh.

Some of the earliest evidence of Yahweh does not mention Israel. We have seen in Chapter 5 that Yahweh was worshiped by pastoralists (Shasu) somewhere in Edom during the Late Bronze Age. By this time, the Israelites were already in the vicinity of the Jezreel Valley and Central Highlands, as implied by Pharaoh Merneptah. So it was not Israel who brought Yahweh to Canaan, nor did Yahweh bring Israel to Canaan. One of the two archaic biblical poems mentioned above (p. 55), Exod. 15.1-18, tells of a migration of some people into a new land. The people, however, are not named, except in the prose introduction that was added long after the poem was written. Therefore, it cannot be assumed that the later biblical tradition correctly associates Exod. 15.1-18 with Israel. In folk tradition, poems like this can move from group to group with ease.

It would seem that by the late Iron Age I or early Iron Age II, Yahweh and Israel have found one another, but the evidence is not as secure as one would wish. In the other of the two archaic biblical poems, Judges 5, Yahweh is god of a coalition of local chiefdoms called Israel, so the Israelites have become Yahweh worshipers. But, the early compositional date of Judges 5 has been challenged by some scholars.[10] Although I disagree with them, their challenges are not entirely without merit. Is there more secure evidence for the relationship of early Israel with early Yahweh? The Moabite Stone, an inscription mentioned in Chapter 8, dates to the latter half of the ninth century BCE, and its text suggests that Israelites were worshiping Yahweh in Moabite land occupied by Israelite forces. King Mesha of Moab claims to have attacked an Israelite city called Nebo, killed everyone in it, and dragged a ritual object devoted to Yahweh away as victory spoil. However, since the land in question was Moabite and only occupied by Israelite military forces, the ritual object could have been part of a city religion prior to Israelite occupation. To my mind, it seems reasonable to assume Yahweh was Israel's god on the Moabite Stone and in an early poem (Judg. 5), but is there more secure evidence?

Some of the kings of Israel and Judah had theophoric names using Yaw or Yahu (= Yahweh), which might suggest that Yahweh was high god in these kingdoms. For example, Jehoshaphat (1 Kgs 22.41) means 'Yahu has judged'. If one assumes that royal names use the city's high god as subject, then it is interesting that a pattern of Yaw- and Yahu-names becomes dominant at both Samaria and Jerusalem beginning with the Jehu Dynasty in 841 BCE. Prior to that time, each royal list contains only one or two such names. This suggests that Yahweh became high god after the Omride Dynasty mentioned on the Moabite Stela. However, royal names are not the best indication of the high god's identity. In Neo-Babylonia, for example, the god Nabu was as common in royal names as the high god Marduk.

By the early-eighth century BCE there is at last clear evidence that Yahweh had become high god of Israel at Samaria. A small stopping station along the southern desert trade route, called Kuntillet 'Ajrud, contained pottery with drawings and writings on them. Some of this material is Phoenician, which is no surprise (see Chapter 8). But a partially damaged inscription offers a blessing to the reader on behalf of 'Yahweh of Samaria and his Asherah'. Another epigraph offers blessing in the name of 'Yahweh of Teman and his Asherah'. (Teman was a part of the southern desert regions.) Apparently, Yahweh had risen to prominence throughout the southern half of Palestine. He was identified with El, the original god of Israel, so his wife was Asherah. Some scholars argue that, on grammatical grounds, the phrase 'his Asherah' cannot refer to the goddess per se. Rather, the blessing is given in the name of the god and the liturgical symbol of the goddess. The Bible speaks sometimes of a goddess Asherah (1 Kgs 18.19) and other times of asherah-poles, wooden objects in the temple that represented the goddess (Deut. 16.21). Biblical authors hated these objects and the goddess they represented, but their hatred obviously stems from the reality that Asherah and her symbolic objects were common to Israelite religion. Whether the Kuntillet 'Ajrud inscriptions refer to the goddess or her symbol, it is clear that Yahweh and his wife Asherah were the highest gods at Samaria and Teman by the early-eighth century. Thus, the 'when' question remains difficult. Yahweh was Israel's high god by the early-eighth century and probably before. But how long before is uncertain.

The other part of the question, then, is *how* did Yahweh become high god in Israel's henotheistic pantheon? One would expect El to hold that position, so the question 'how?' is even more difficult to answer than the question 'when?'. Yahweh's rise in status can be documented only very partially, because the literary tradition revised its texts each time its theology shifted. Most biblical passages have been 'levelled off' at a relatively late stage.

A cryptic biblical passage hinting that Yahweh began his career as a lesser god in someone else's pantheon has survived—barely survived—redactional activity by later scribes. This text, Deut. 32.8-9, appears in two versions among the best ancient manuscripts:

*The Common Hebrew Version:*

When Elyon gave peoples their inheritance,
When he divided up humanity;
When he fixed the boundaries of countries,
*According to the number of the sons of Israel;*
Then the portion for Yahweh was his people,
Jacob, the allotment of his inheritance.

*An Alternate Hebrew Version:*

When Elyon gave peoples their inheritance,
When he divided up humanity;
When he fixed the boundaries of countries,
*According to the number of the sons of god;*
Then the portion for Yahweh was his people,
Jacob, the allotment of his inheritance.

According to the alternate version of this poem, Elyon (an alternate name for El), as highest god, divided all the people of the Earth into political groups and assigned each group an inheritance (of land) and a patron god (one of his divine sons). At Bronze Age Ugarit, El had 70 divine sons, so we can assume the poet has quite a few kingdoms in mind. One of the divine sons, Yahweh, received the people Jacob, an alternate name for Israel. Thus Yahweh is a son of Elyon, a lesser god in the high god's pantheon.

The common version is a 'doctored' version of the poem. Apparently, in a later period, it was no longer acceptable to assign Yahweh a lesser status in the Canaanite pantheon. So the scribe changed one word. Hebrew *bene-elohim* ('sons of god') became *bene-yisrael* ('sons of Israel'). This one small change did away with any hint of multiple gods in the poem, and therefore permitted a reader to equate Elyon in the first line with Yahweh near the end of the segment. Now it is Yahweh-Elyon who divides the people, and retains one of those groups, Israel/Jacob, for himself. Of course, the scribe who made this small change has introduced a small problem as well. The passage in the common version makes no sense. Literally, it means that the number of political units on Earth equals the number of Israelites! Nevertheless, the scribe has accomplished what mattered most to him; he has brought Deut. 32.8-9 into line with the henotheism of other biblical passages, such as Mic. 4.5: 'As each of the peoples walk in the name of their god, so we will walk in the name of Yahweh our god, for all time'.[11]

The value of Deut. 32.8-9 to a historian is that it offers a glimpse of

Yahweh's status in Israel prior to his rise as high god. Yahweh was a part of the Israelite pantheon as a son of the high god; only later was he equated with the high god. The high god was El, sometimes called Elyon, and also called El Shaddai. Biblical authors remembered quite clearly that this was the case. For example, in Gen. 33.20, the ancestor Jacob is reported to declare 'El is the god of Israel'. The name El Shaddai in the key passage of Exod. 6.2-3 also suggests that Israelite scribes remembered, and were satisfied with, the deliberate fusion of Yahweh and El: 'God spoke to Moses, "I am Yahweh. I appeared to Abraham, Isaac and Jacob as El Shaddai. But my name, Yahweh, I did not reveal to them."'[12]

Interestingly, the book of Psalms preserves an alternate 'explanation' for Yahweh's ascent to high god, one that is far more entertaining, and may have been preserved for precisely that reason. Psalm 82 tells a delightful tale that seems to presuppose the tradition of Deut. 32.8-9:

> God stood in El's courtroom,
> Among the gods, he judged.
> 'How long will you gods judge wickedly?
> How long will you favor dishonesty?
> Bring justice to the weak and the orphan,
> Favor the oppressed and impoverished,
> Release the weak and the poor.
> From the power of the wicked, rescue!
>
> 'They do not know and they can't perceive,
> In darkness they all walk about,
> So the foundations of the Earth will stagger.
>
> 'I declare, "Gods are you!
> Sons of Elyon, all of you!
> Yet, like humans you shall die,
> As any ruler, you will fall!"'
>
> Rise, O god, judge the earth!
> You shall inherit all peoples!

This poem presents a minor deity in revolt against all his divine siblings, the sons of El. He kills them as though they were merely human, then he 'inherits' their allotments of humanity. The poet has in mind the myth we encountered in Deut. 32.8-9, in which El parcels out the peoples of the Earth, assigning a patron god to each. The allotments had been made, but the sons of El had ruled their fiefs corruptly. The one just god convicts them and overthrows them. Who was that one just god? He is called, simply, 'god'. The poem was preserved in a portion of the book of Psalms that is called the Elohim Psalter (Pss. 42–89). It is called Elohim because these psalms usually substitute the generic term *elohim* ('god') for the personal name *yhwh* ('Yahweh'). It is probable, therefore, that before it was gathered into the Elohim Psalter, the original poem identified 'god' as Yahweh. This psalm records the myth in which Yahweh ascends from a minor deity in the pantheon to only god of the cosmos. Yahweh has created monotheism by deicide!

So the Bible preserves at least two versions of Yahweh's rise to high god. In one version, Yahweh was simply equated with El Shaddai. In the other, Yahweh killed El and his sons and took over, thus becoming the sole god, not just the high god. Perhaps the creators of the biblical anthology saw these two traditions as steps in a single progression. Yahweh reveals that he is El, then El-Yahweh kills his own sons. One need not press the evidence into a single chronological sequence, however. Myths and mythology rarely functioned as 'doctrine'.

It was a short step from the monolatry of Deut. 10.12-22 to the fledgling monotheism of Psalm 82, and an even shorter step to the full monotheism of Isa. 45.5: 'I am Yahweh and there is no other; apart from me, there is no god!' The modern world seems to admire monotheism as though it were somehow morally and intellectually superior to any other theism. In reality, monotheism is simply different from the other theisms, such as polytheism and dualism. (Dualism is the belief in two gods, one evil and one good.) As a matter of fact, the polytheist and the dualist have an advantage over the monotheist and the henotheist, because evil can be ascribed to a malignant supernatural being whose power is independent of the high or only god. For example, the dualism of the New Testament routinely forgives god for evil by blaming it on an evil lesser god, the devil. This permits New Testament writers to make sweeping statements that a monotheist is not able to affirm, such as: 'God is light and in him there is no darkness at all' (1 Jn 1.5). By contrast, monotheists and henotheists must concede that god is amoral, or, as theologians might prefer to say, god transcends human conceptions of morality (see, e.g., the book of Job). So a monotheistic god certainly does have darkness 'in him'. In fact, if there is only one god, then god is the source of light and darkness: 'I am Yahweh and there is no other; the shaper of light and the creator of darkness; I make peace, and I create evil; I am Yahweh, maker of all that is' (Isa. 45.6b-7).

This final step to full monotheism seems to have occurred in the late-sixth century BCE, possibly as a highly intellectual theological response to the crisis of the Babylonian exile (see the next chapter). Some scholars have argued that it happened well before then, and a few suggest that it was much later. The timing really does not matter so much as the effect. Monotheism—genuine monotheism—is so radical, so intellectually and emotionally demanding, that few have ever embraced it. A monotheistic god too often seems, rightly or wrongly, to be a cold and uncaring god. Perhaps it is human nature to prefer a god who is the 'good guy', and that requires a theism with other powers who can be contrasted or opposed to him (or her!). For this reason, monotheism often gives way to a dualism or lax henotheism, in which less powerful supernatural beings can play a role in a person's life.

So far, we have seen that theism and myths can be secular and sacred, and that the theism of the Bible was not originally monotheism. Moreover, we can see that Yahweh's career betrays a progression from a low god to a high god. Both the Bible and the religion of Yahweh (which were never identical until the Roman era, a point to be discussed in the next chapter) became monotheism through a process of reinterpretation over the centuries. All four points help to clarify the peculiar diversity of materials that one encounters in the pages of the Bible, as well as the way that religion was experienced in the everyday life of Canaan. Nevertheless, everyday life is always more complex than the few observations that can be reduced to words. Part of that complexity has to do with the multiple levels of society always encountered by each individual. These levels also affected the religions of ancient Canaan, and they are the next stop on our tour.

## Religion at Three Levels of Society

Religion is a social phenomenon, one that is experienced by the individual within a social context. That is to say, religion is not a thing, but an event; it 'happens' as individuals experience, quite subjectively, the religion in relationship to other people (or, in the case of the religious hermit, by overt rejection of a former relationship to other people). Most religions make affirmations about a 'truth' of some kind, but the primary function of religion is not to propound eternal verities; rather, religion serves as a kind of social 'glue', binding people to each other.

Within ancient society, a person experienced religion at three social levels: the family (*beth 'ab*), the community (*mishpachah*), and the territorial state (the region ruled by a city, such as Samaria, Ashdod or Jerusalem). Each level generated a distinctive religious ethos. The boundaries between levels were fluid, but relatively distinct, and an individual's religious experience differed at each level of society. Of course, it is difficult to discuss religious practice at any of these levels since the evidence is sparse and derives, usually, from the upper classes in the form of literature and epigraphs. Nevertheless, the following very general observations seem probable, given the artifacts and texts known to us.

*Religion in the Family*

At the family level (*beth 'ab*), ancient Canaanite religion emphasized the everyday and practical necessities of life. Common themes were an inner sense of morality, personal piety, and aspects of survival, especially fertility of the land and the womb.

Inner morality mixed with piety is a family theme in biblical literature. For example, Proverbs, a book that stresses the teaching of children, offers advice for healthy and happy living—the ancient equivalent of the modern self-help manual so popular on the nonfiction best-seller lists. Proverbs 6.16-19 reads:

> Six are these that Yahweh hates,
> Nay, seven disgust his soul:
> Arrogant eyes, deceptive tongue,
> Two hands shedding innocent blood,
> Heart plotting its wicked will,
> Impatient feet running to evil,
> A false witness producing lies,
> An inciter of family fights.

As this passage suggests, household wisdom was pragmatic, sometimes artistically articulated and, from a modern perspective, not always 'politically correct'. For example, the Israelite lad was advised on erotica in highly metaphorical language: 'May your fountain be blessed, and find joy in the wife of your youth. A loving doe, graceful goat, may her two breasts satisfy you always. In her love, may you be intoxicated continually' (Prov. 5.18-19). Or practical counsel on marriage could be stated more bluntly: 'A gold ring in a pig's snout is a gorgeous woman lacking sense' (Prov. 11.22).

Emphases on family fertility and piety can be seen in the material culture of Palestine. One popular religious artifact at Israelite and Judahite sites was a small female figurine cupping her breasts. These were goddesses, and tend to turn up one to a household, or one to a grave. It is likely, therefore, that this goddess was an important household deity whose popularity was widespread. The emphasis on her breasts implies an emphasis on maternal care. The Canaanite goddess Asherah was mother of the gods, and the Bible indicates that Asherah was popular in Israel and Judah, at least at the royal level (1 Kgs 15.13; 2 Kgs 21.7; 23.4). Another popular figurine in Canaan was a monstrous little fellow with exaggerated features, who came from Egypt and was called Bes. Although it is not entirely certain what role he played, he is likely to have protected the family, especially women during childbirth.

Together with others, these household gods may have been the biblical *teraphim*. Some of these were small (Gen. 31.19, 34-35) and others quite large (1 Sam. 19.13, 16). Some biblical authors did not like the *teraphim* and condemned them as evil (Zech. 10.2). One should not be swayed by the prejudice of a few Yahweh worshipers writing against the remaining Yahweh worshipers. The data suggest that most Israelites and Judahites (including some biblical writers) accepted *teraphim* as part of their religious culture. There is no need to respect them any less because some of their contemporaries disagreed with this aspect of the culture. (From archaeological evidence, or rather, lack of evidence, rejection of household gods became widespread in the Persian period.)

In an agrarian society like that of ancient Canaan, fertility was the most important concern, and fertility lay at the center of most religious practice. Just as the household goddess figurines attest to this from the archaeological record, so also biblical texts often focus on the fertility of the crops, the flocks, herds and even the human womb. Prophets such as Hosea and Haggai stress that fertility is in the hands of the divine, and that only 'proper' worship of the divine will ensure it (see, e.g., Hos. 2.10-15; Hag. 1.2-11). Of course, each prophet had his own definition of 'proper' worship, and no doubt others in the community had their definitions as well. At the family level, it is difficult to tell what rituals were performed specifically to seek divine aid in fertility.

The religious emphasis on family and field fertility has, unfortunately, led to a serious misunderstanding in modern academic research. Based on evidence concerning religious practices in Mesopotamia and

Greece, a hypothesis emerged some years ago about Canaanite fertility religion in Palestine. The hypothesis was that men would have sexual intercourse with women at the temple as a kind of religious magic that would ensure fertility in the land. Key biblical texts were interpreted to support this idea. Deuteronomy 23.18 is the most important of these: 'There shall not be a *qedeshah* from the daughters of Israel and there shall not be a *qadesh* from the sons of Israel'. The next verse (v. 19) prohibits using prostitution money to pay a religious vow. Because these verses appear back-to-back, the key Hebrew terms have been misinterpreted to mean 'religious prostitute', both male and female. This misinterpretation has been applied to all other biblical passages in which these Hebrew words appear (Gen. 38.21-22; 1 Kgs 14.24; 15.12; 22.47; 2 Kgs 23.7; Hos. 4.14). As a result, English Bibles frequently mislead a modern reader to believe that male and female prostitutes offered sex as part of religious ceremonies in the temples of Canaan.

The words *qadesh* and *qedeshah* mean 'holy one', in masculine and feminine form. They do not mean prostitute in any known ancient Hebrew text. In Mesopotamia, these same terms appeared, also meaning 'holy one', and referring to low-level temple servants, male and female. They were people who did important, but non-priestly, work at the sanctuaries. In a society where one of the deities was Ishtar, goddess of love, a holy one was sometimes (though not always) a provider of sex, but the intercourse she or he offered was not religiously motivated. As a matter of fact, it was a simple, secular business transaction in which the temple of the goddess received the income. This was not considered respectable or honorable, but it was not immoral either, for the sex act was viewed as part of the divine structure of the world. In Mesopotamia (and in Greece), a secular brothel could even be called a house of the love goddess.

In sum, no one was having sex as part of a religious ceremony, which is what many biblical scholars usually imply. From the texts, it would seem that no ancient biblical author ever *thought* that someone was having sex as part of a religious ceremony. Biblical prophets often use sexual imagery to slander religious practices that they do not like very much (e.g. Jer. 5.7-8), but one has to read into these texts the implication of sexual rituals. Deuteronomy 23.18 simply abolishes the offices of *qadesh* and *qedeshah*, offices that had been a part of Yahweh religion at one time. Probably, the office was abolished because these temple servants were known to be sexually available in Israelite society, as they were in Mesopotamian society (see Deut. 23.19; 1 Sam. 2.22; Hos. 4.13-14).[13]

Much of the misunderstanding about the *qedeshah* derives from a misinterpretation of Genesis 38. It is usually claimed that this story equates the words 'prostitute' (*zonah*) and 'holy one' (*qedeshah*), making no distinction between them. As a result, some translations make no distinction either, which is a shame because the irony of the tale is lost. In the story, a man named Judah sees his widowed daughter-in-law in a town where she is not expected to be and wearing a disguise. He mistakes her for a prostitute (*zonah*) and propositions her. She has been trying to get pregnant, so this is her opportunity. They have sex on the agreement that he will later send payment. Judah sends the payment by a friend, who pretends that he seeks to give payment to a *qedeshah*. This is very clever. In that society, a holy one might well receive payment connected to (non-sexual) services in the local temple. This gives the villagers the false impression that the payment might be for a religious vow and not for sex. They answer that they know of no *qedeshah* in the town, so the man leaves without making the payment, and the villagers are not wise to what has been happening in their quiet little town. Judah's reputation is not smeared, which is an issue that, according to the story, is very much on his mind (38.23). It is a very clever passage, but it does not imply that a *qedeshah* performed sex as part of a religious ceremony.

I have devoted considerable space to this point for two reasons. First, the example illustrates a way in which the ancients were indeed very different from modern Westerners. Our culture holds much the same attitude towards sex: it is secular, it is fun, and people are willing to pay for it. But the ancients were willing to attribute that reality to a goddess (Ishtar, Astarte, Aphrodite). The line between secular and sacred blurred because the ancient world was so much more comfortable with secular-theism than many in our culture; the divine was a part of all aspects of life and, significantly, morality was not established in defiance of human sexual drives. The ancient view was not necessarily superior to a modern view, which usually disassociates sex from religion, but it should not be misrepresented either. Second, the point illustrates the fallibility of historical research. Hypotheses are sometimes incorrect. History sometimes changes as new data, or new ways to interpret the data, arise. The hypothesis of Canaanite 'sacred prostitution' is no longer tenable.

A final aspect of family religion might be mentioned, namely devotion to family ancestors. Archaeological evidence is abundant for the feeding and consulting of the dead as a common practice, and biblical texts mention the practice as well. For example, Deut. 26.14 prohibits giving tithed food to the dead. As noted in Chapter 4, ancestor worship was a rational practice. These minor gods would favor their descendants and veneration of them at a tomb was a visible sign of land ownership. Deuteronomy's prohibition in 26.14 should not be construed to mean that henotheism outlawed the veneration of ancestors. Tithed food was more like a state or local tax, produce offered to the priesthood, so it was not to be kept for family religion. Untithed food, of course, could be given to ancestral gods. Some biblical writers ridiculed the practices associated with the dead (Isa. 57.6-9), but they were in the minority. (Incidentally, an ancient text that ridicules the practice of another is always a little suspect. The author of the text could well have distorted the practice he describes as part of his effort to discredit it.)

*Religion in the Community*

The religious concerns of the community (*mishpachah*) differed from those of the family (*beth 'ab*), although there was overlap to a degree. Fertility remained absolutely central at both levels, though it resulted in different types of ritual at each. For the family, the goddess and Bes figurines were significant. For the community, participation in the agrarian religious rituals and holidays was central. Agrarian holidays were community events and were fundamentally religious, celebrating the Baal who provided fertility. Baal was not a name, it was a title, meaning 'Lord'. In the Bronze Age, Baal's name was Adad or Hadad. In the Iron Age, a variety of gods may have held the title. Biblical and epigraphic data suggest that Yahweh was a Baal until a rather late period, when scribes began to make a rigid distinction between Yahweh's title of Adonai (which also means 'Lord') and the newly banned title Baal.[14]

The three most important agrarian holidays were the barley harvest, wheat harvest and a combination of grape and olive harvests. The first, called by the Bible Unleavened Bread, was celebrated in the spring and was associated as well with Passover, the birthing of the flocks. Midsummer was the time for the Feast of Weeks, the wheat harvest. And Tabernacles was the late summer gathering from the orchards, in which temporary living quarters (tabernacles) were constructed near the fruit so that harvesting could be completed quickly. The Bible summarizes the major festivals in Leviticus 23 (see also Exod. 23.14-17; Num. 28–29).

These festivals were, of course, also associated with the storytelling tradition about Moses and the exodus from Egypt, so that the spring festival was claimed to have been part of the mythical exodus event, the summer festival commemorated the giving of the Torah at the exotic Mount Sinai, and the fall festival commemorated the tradition of a 40-year wandering in the wilderness. These pseudo-historical associations were late additions to festivals that had existed in Canaan from hoary antiquity. In fact, biblical references to the festivals demonstrate that even in this late period of Canaanite culture, each festival continued to undergo changes in ritual and observance over time. For example, sometimes the biblical discussion of the spring festival presupposes that the celebration took place locally, in homes within the community (Exod. 12). At other times, the Bible suggests that the spring festival had become part of a state-level system of taxation in which the event took place at a centralized temple (Deut. 16). The latter might be nothing more than a government scribe's wishful thinking, but there is no doubt that, as monarchy emerged in the Iron Age II, there would have been a taxation imposed on these agrarian events. Nevertheless, the festivals themselves probably never became severed from the local farming communities for whom they were so significant.

Participation in the agrarian festivals of the community probably went beyond the need to honor the god(s) who bestowed fertility; it was also a mark of public identity and allegiance to the social agenda. It was the community level of religious experience that was most concerned with the public behavior of individuals. In fact, social control seems to have been exerted primarily at the community level.[15]

Israelite communities were governed by elders (males who had attained sufficient status to be accorded public honor) who sat in the gate of the village or city, dispensing justice and monitoring trade. Heavy stress was placed on morality, but in a way that differed from family concerns of morality. Where parents tried to instill an inner morality, the community had a practical interest in monitoring public morality. Religious righteousness was equivalent to civil law; it covered matters such as murder, treatment of slaves, weights and measures, and observance of rituals for holy days. Leviticus 19.13-16 offers an eclectic litany of observance that runs the gamut of social-religious preoccupations:

You shall not defraud your neighbor. Do not steal. Do not withhold payment to a laborer overnight. Do not ridicule the deaf. Never set a stumbling block before the blind. You shall venerate your god, I am Yahweh. Never render unfair judgments in the law. Do not favor the poor or show deference to the rich. Always judge your neighbor fairly. Do not utter slander among your people. Do not profit by the blood of a neighbor. I am Yahweh.

These issues and others like them focus on public action. The family emphasizes the good character of the moral person, the community focuses on the practical deeds that result from good or bad character. Public teaching began with a litany of 'shall' and 'shall not' legislation, but that was only half the teaching. The 'shall/shall not' style of law quoted above was supplemented by its necessary twin, case law, usually stated in the form: 'if this, then that'. These twin forms were inseparable, and there could not have been a community in which one existed without the other. The first establishes general guidelines for conduct and the second provides for the consequences of misconduct. They are two sides of one coin.

This combination of 'shall' and 'shall not' as well as 'if this, then that' stipulations was not a law code in the formal sense, but an oral tradition that guided the elders when judging activity in the community. For example, Deut. 22.25-29 stipulates that if a man rapes a married woman, then he shall be put to death; but if he rapes an unmarried woman, then he shall pay a fine and marry the woman he has raped, without the right to divorce her. This example demonstrates *both* the community's concern to apply balanced punishment fitting the severity of a crime, *and* the ancient patriarchal society's values. Their assumptions about what is 'fitting' punishment reveal their ideas on the relative worth of humans in society. Typically women were property and the majority of men were either property (slaves, indentured servants) or free commoners. Punishments were meted out on the basis of the status of victim or perpetrator or both, which meant that the same crime might carry different punishments, depending on who was involved. In the case of Deut. 22.25-29, if a man raped a married woman, he had violated the property of her husband; if he raped an unmarried woman, he had violated the property of the father. In each case, it is a male who had been damaged, at least according to ancient opinion. Punishment in this instance is determined by the relationship of damaged property to owner. The married man cannot recoup his loss, but the father can, so punishment is more severe in the former situation. As this example demonstrates, religious morality is always a by-product of prevailing social prejudice and assumptions. Whether it conforms to social norms or reacts against them, it owes its origin to the practical necessities of people who are trying to live together as one people.

Although the examples have been drawn from the Bible's Torah (Lev. 19.13-16; Deut. 22.25-29), that Torah was not really a genuine legal code. Rather, the Torah is a digest, or compendium of sample materials. This is deduced from the fact that several such digests are embedded in the one biblical Torah, and each is relatively autonomous. One is found in Exod. 20.22–23.33, and is called the Covenant Code, because it was inserted into the biblical narrative at the point where Yahweh makes a covenant with Israel through Moses at Sinai (Exod. 19–24). Another of these codes appears in Leviticus 17–26 and is called the Holiness Code, because the authors stress divine holiness and its human response. The so-called Deuteronomic Code is found in Deuteronomy 12–26, considered by some to be the oldest material in Deuteronomy, prior to redactional activity. Several other codes and fragments of codes include the laws of sacrifice in Leviticus 1–7, laws of ritual cleanliness in Leviticus 11–15, and a miscellany of stipulations here and there in Numbers.

There are several striking features of these Torah materials: first, there is much overlap between them, second, there is a degree of inconsistency in them. These two features lead to the logical conclusion that each is independent of the others, and that their appearance together as one Torah of Moses is the product of an editorial process. A third striking feature is that none of these codes is 'complete'. That is to say, the Torah, even in final form, does not cover all the topics required to be a functional, living community guide. That is why the rabbis supplemented Torah with Mishnah and Talmud. The observation has also resulted in some recent, creative attempts by scholars to determine why the various codes were composed. Two points that seem clear are that each Torah code was intended to be a collection of sample stipulations, guidelines only, and none was designed to be read in conjunction with the others, though all of them have been read in this way for 2000 years or more.

*Religion in the Kingdom*
The state had concerns that transcended community focus, and religion at state level differed accordingly. Community religion measured an

individual's commitment to the community; state religion attempted to wed that individual to the state. In most cases, state religion did not conflict with community identity, though that might have happened from time to time since each corporate body was vying for the individual's allegiance. More often, state-level religion was symbolic, highly emotive, and sometimes jingoistic. Its purpose was to rally support for state activities, particularly warfare. It was the royal god who would lead the army to victory in times of war. King Mesha of Moab, for example, attributed his royal victories to the Moabite god, Chemosh, on his stone monument from the ninth century BCE.

In times of peace, state religion probably did not enter into the consciousness of most commoners (whose primary religious concern remained ever focused on the fertility of soil and womb) except perhaps when taxes were due. Taxes were paid in kind, since there were no coins prior to the Persian era, and would be offered to the human king as a religious offering to the divine king, the patron god. For example, a Philistine inscription on a storage jar that had contained grain or oil reads, 'For Baal and for Padi'. We know from Assyrian inscriptions that Padi was an Iron Age II Philistine king, and this storage jar was found in the ruins of a Philistine temple dedicated to the goddess who was, apparently, the Philistine Baal's wife. The biblical concept of the 'tithe', one-tenth of one's produce paid to Yahweh (Deut. 14.22-29), is probably a Persian-era descendant of an Iron Age II royal tax paid to the patron god of Samaria or Jerusalem. (Even the Bible recalls that kings would require one-tenth from their subjects; cf. 1 Sam. 8.15-17.) Also, the biblical portrait of the Levites represents a highly idealized literary construct of the Persian era, in many ways unrealistic, but probably based on an Iron Age II reality. The Levites were tax collectors, that is to say, priests attached to the king (the word 'Levite' derives from the Hebrew word meaning 'to accompany/to be attached'[16]), dispersed through the kingdom (e.g. the Levitical cities in Josh. 21), and recipients of tithed offerings (e.g. Num. 18). It needs to be stressed that, contrary to a common biblical motif, this state-sponsored Yahweh religion was not *the* religion of 'all Israel' (an impression given by biblical books such as 1–2 Chronicles), but only *one* aspect of a person's religious life, the aspect that wed an individual to the larger geographic region ruled by his human patron, the king.

In other words, individuals and communities did not participate in state religion; rather, state religion encroached from time to time into the individual's and the community's religious life. Animal sacrifice that had been, for countless generations, consumed as part of a community fertility festival became tithed as well for the benefit of the kingdom's bureaucracy. Likewise, grain, oil and wine offerings at community level were appropriated by the state. Sometimes, local sanctuaries became state shrines, such as the one mentioned in Amos 7.13. The king and his entourage of priests could justify this encroachment by pointing to the obvious benefits that the peasantry enjoyed, such as military protection, and there is no reason to believe that peasants resisted or resented state intervention in their religious lives. The state religion would have been added to the peasant's normal religious experience, but would not have replaced that more localized experience.

Using the Bible as an example, the rhetoric of ancient Canaanite state religion can be observed. Yahweh, god of Judah, was presented as the patron of the king, and it is through that king that Yahweh's blessings were bestowed. This divine patronage was similar in every respect to the patron gods of all ancient Near Eastern governments. Consider Psalm 2:

> Why do the countries conspire,
> And peoples plot emptiness?
> Earthly royalty take their stand,
> While princes take counsel against
> Yahweh, and against his Messiah!
> 'Let us break their cords,
> And toss down their ropes.'
>
> Sitting in the sky, laughing!
> My lord is mocking them.
>
> At that moment,
> he spoke to them in anger,
> terrified them in rage,
> 'But I—
> I have set my king on Zion,
> Mountain of my holiness!'
>
> Let me tell of Yahweh's decree:
> He said to me, 'My son are you!
> I have this day begotten you.
> Ask from me that I might give
> peoples as your inheritance—
> And your possession, Earth's foundations.
> You may smash them with iron mace,
> As potter's vessels, you may shatter!'

So now, O kings, be wise,
Be warned, O earthly rulers!
Serve Yahweh with fear,
Shriek with trembling,
Kiss this 'son' lest he be angry.
Then your path perishes,
when his wrath flares quickly.

Happy are those who take refuge in him.

Although tiny Judah was nothing but a peripheral state on the edge of the Neo-Assyrian empire, the rhetoric in this psalm presents the king of Jerusalem as a client of a powerful patron-god who can crush enemies at will and grant access to the very foundations of the earth. Patriotic rhetoric need not be realistic. The United States of America has never actually delivered 'justice and liberty for all', but that does not stop people from celebrating the ideal every fourth of July. So it was with state religion in the ancient world. Kings were powerful, divinely begotten, righteous, and easily provoked to anger against the forces of chaos. This was true even of petty kings in peripheral provinces!

The imagery of Psalm 2 is mythic. A god sits enthroned in the sky, chooses a human and adopts him as son of the god. This king is endowed with superhuman ability and can conquer the whole earth. Such language is typical of ancient Near Eastern royal ideologies (as was discussed on pp. 131-34). Often, the divinely chosen king was affirmed by a human prophet who spoke for the god. Prophets are best known to modern people from the pages of the Bible, but prophets were common to the entire Fertile Crescent in ancient times. These holy men and women will be the final topic on our tour of Canaanite religions.

## What was Prophecy?

### The Prophet and Divine Revelation

The religions of the ancient Near East were 'revelatory' religions. That means that people believed in gods who revealed themselves to humans. Stories of divine revelation are common from Mesopotamia to Egypt. For one who wants to understand what the believers thought was happening in a revelatory experience, the sheer variety of alleged revelations can be bewildering. How does one analyze these many ancient sources?

After comparison, three general categories of divine revelation seem to emerge. These categories are, of course, merely descriptive, designed to help a scholar or student of religion comprehend the varieties of alleged revelatory experience. In some cases, revelation occurs because the gods initiate contact with a human, and in others, it occurs because a human initiates contact with the gods. Also, the type of knowledge gained through the revelation can be verbal or experiential.

| Type of Revelation | Initiated by | Type of Knowledge |
|---|---|---|
| Prophecy | Deity | Verbal |
| Mysticism | Human or Deity | Experiential |
| Divination | Human | Verbal |

Figure 31: *Knowledge Through Revelation.*

Prophecy might be defined as revelation in which the gods begin the process of divine-human communication. The message of a prophet is called an 'oracle'. The prophet receives contact with the divine in some manner, perhaps a vision, a dream or a voice. Usually, the content of the revelation can be reduced to words, even if no words were spoken during the revelatory experience. Therefore, the knowledge that the gods impart by prophecy can be classified as verbal knowledge. Usually it is a concrete utterance, the meaning of which might be cryptic, but the structure of which is intelligible, provided a prophet is on hand to interpret it correctly (cf. the folk-tale of Dan. 5). An example of divine initiation can be seen in the ancient city of Mari on the Euphrates River. The king of Mari received a message from a woman who had been told in a dream by the god Dagan that only he, the king, could save a young woman who had been abducted. The message came as a surprise to the king and, it would seem, to the woman who had the dream.[17]

If a human initiates the revelatory experience, it is called divination. Divination can take many forms. The only common feature is that the human addresses a specific question to the gods. The manner in which the question is placed differs from example to example. In the Bible, something akin to rolling dice seems to have been called Urim and Thummim (1 Sam. 28.6; Ezra 2.63; and some ancient manuscripts of 1 Sam. 14.41). No one is exactly sure what these things were, but the idea was that a yes-or-no question was put before Yahweh and then the lots were cast (e.g. 1 Sam. 23.2). A common form of ancient divination was the interpretation of the livers from sacrificed animals. Some ancient priests even made clay models of livers, marked with information on how to interpret various parts. In most cases, the divine response to divination can be expressed in human words even when the experience was not verbal, so again the knowledge derived from the revelation would be termed verbal.

# 'The gods came to him in the night.'

### Inscription from Tel Deir 'Alla

A prophet mentioned in the Bible appears as well in an epigraph found at Tel Deir 'Alla, in the Jordan River Valley. Balaam son of Beor is a non-Israelite prophet who becomes the spokesman for Yahweh, god of Israel, in Numbers 22-24:

## 'God came to Balaam in the night.'
NUMBERS 22.20

At Tel Deir 'Alla, Balaam was a prophet of the gods of Canaan. The badly preserved inscription seems to describe a prophecy in which Balaam warns his people of disaster. In both stories, Balaam is visited by the divine during the night, perhaps in a dream. These two traditions about the same prophet suggest that Balaam might have been a prophet of the Iron Age II, whose reputation survived in the folklore of Yahwistic and non-Yahwistic peoples. Neither the Bible nor Tel Deir 'Alla provides sufficient data with which to recover the man's deeds or words, and the possibility that he was an invented figure cannot be ruled out.

Figure 32. *Balaam at Tel Deir 'Alla.*

Mysticism is a more difficult category to discuss than the other two since it is sometimes indistinguishable from either. Usually, the mystic initiates the experience through meditation, ritual, or even music and dance. However, in some situations, the gods initiate contact with an unsuspecting human. Therefore, the method of initiation is not always a reliable indication of mysticism. Nevertheless, mysticism differs from prophecy and divination in a crucial way. The prophets and most diviners emerge from the revelatory experience with a verbal content, a message to be imparted. The mystic emerges from the experience with the memory of an event that cannot be described, a mystical experience but no message. Even this distinction can be slightly problematic. Some prophets and diviners seem to have mystical experiences, trances, ecstasies and so on, and a few mystics 'preach' the mystical experience.

A biblical story illustrates how muddy the distinctions between the three categories in a revelatory experience can be. In 2 Kings 3, the commanders of an army approach a man identified as a 'prophet', by name of Elisha, and ask him whether their military mission will succeed. Already the line between divination and prophecy is blurred. Elisha commands that a musician play for him, which is often a sign of mysticism, more blurring of the lines. While listening to the music, Elisha experiences the 'hand' of Yahweh, then he utters a verbal prophecy. The 'hand' is unusual and seems to imply a sensation of presence that would be non-verbal experience. One would expect the divine 'wind' (sometimes translated 'spirit') in this passage, not the 'hand'; not surprisingly, a few ancient manuscripts of this tale replaced the 'hand' with the 'wind' of Yahweh. Thus, elements of all three categories are present in the tale. Although he is called a prophet, Elisha functions as a diviner who seeks knowledge from the god. He experiences something possibly mystical while listening to music, and then utters a traditionally formulated prophetic oracle. Prophecy, mysticism and divination are closely intertwined.

*Prophets, Miracles and Magic*

In some portions of the Bible prophets are associated with miracle-working. Why is this the case? An answer to this question gives unexpected insight into the ancient conceptualization of the kind of person who was a prophet. The ancients often thought of the prophet as a shaman or magician—as one who had access to, and was able to manipulate, supernatural powers. This conclusion requires some explanation, so let us begin by looking at the *type* of miracle a biblical prophet usually performs.

Usually, a biblical prophet's miracles were of one particular type: the 'local' miracle event. Other biblical miracle stories, stories in which a prophet is not the one who actually performs the miracle, frequently depict a miracle on a much more grand scale. With exceptions, the Bible's most famous miracles tend to be 'great events' that, if they had occurred, might have been witnessed by thousands of people or perhaps all people of the earth. For example, Noah's ark floats above a flood that has covered the whole earth (Gen. 6–8), Moses parts the waters of an entire sea before the eyes of hundreds of thousands of people (Exod. 14; cf. 12.37-38), and Joshua makes the sun stand still in the sky above Gibeon while two armies battle one another (Josh. 10). These tales do not feature a prophet. Although Moses elsewhere receives the title of 'prophet' (e.g. Deut. 34.10), his role in Exodus 14, like that of Joshua in the tale of the solar miracle at Gibeon, is very unlike that of the usual biblical prophet. Rather, it is one of great leadership over many people, a role *never* performed by the majority of biblical prophets.

With some exceptions (such as 1 Sam. 7, in which the 'prophet' is also a military leader), the prophets are presented consistently as people who engage others in small-scale settings and localized activities. They do not usually lead great hordes of people or whole armies, but operate on a personal level. Likewise, most miracles associated with biblical prophets are local events. That is to say, unlike Joshua's motionless sun, the miracles of the prophets are witnessed by a few onlookers only. Thus, for example, the prophet Elisha revives a dead child, purifies poisonous spring water at Jericho and poisonous soup at Gilgal, multiplies loaves of bread, makes a metal object float on water, and so on (2 Kgs 2.19-22; 4.32-37, 38-44; 6.1-7, etc.). Even Isaiah's miraculous reversal of the sun's shadow is depicted to be an event of much more 'local' significance than that of Joshua at Gibeon (2 Kgs 20.1-11). Since the New Testament seeks to present Jesus as a biblical prophet (Mk 6.1-6), it is no coincidence that he performs 'signs' of a similar local nature: he raises a dead child, multiplies loaves of bread, makes himself (instead of a metal object) float on water, and so on (Lk. 7.11-17; Mk 6.32-52, etc.). This tendency of the prophet to perform local miracles is the key to understanding the nature of such stories.

Anthropologists have noted that in many traditional cultures, the shaman (the person who acts as a link between humans and the gods) is able to perform ritual acts that seem to cause local benefits, such as healings, revivification of the dead, and so on. These ritual actions are 'magic' actions. Magic is a ritual performed in order to enlist a supernatural power, usually a god, for the benefit of humans. But the god has never *initiated* the process; the god has *reacted* to the manipulative action—the magic—of the shaman. Why? The reason is purely pragmatic.

As a practical matter, the shaman is not able to go about performing unsolicited miracles. The shaman is not 'sent' to save all the world, to heal and purify everyone. Nor is a shaman able to free an entire people from slavery or lead an army to miraculous victory over the enemy. Those events are at home in the realm of folklore, while the shaman is a real, flesh-and-blood human engaged in real events in a genuine traditional culture somewhere on our planet. If a god were interested in doing the great things that happen in folklore, such as rescuing 600,000 people from slavery in Egypt, the shaman would be a useless 'middleman'. It is interesting to note, in this regard, that Moses plays a very peripheral, perhaps useless, role in the events of Exodus 14; Yahweh does all the work while Moses merely waves a stick *in response to* divine command. The tale of Exodus 14 does not attempt to depict a real-life event; therefore the miracle described can be as grand as human imagination will permit, so grand that it dwarfs the role of a mere mortal like Moses. By contrast, the real human shaman responds to those who seek magical services on an individual basis. Likewise, biblical prophets are usually depicted responding to individual requests. This is why most biblical prophetic miracles are local events.

In short, the biblical portrait of the prophet is a portrait of the common shaman or magician as known from many cultures the world over. Because ancient storytellers knew the prophet as one who performed the social role of the shaman, the stories they told about prophets reflect that small-scale social setting. Only rarely did a biblical prophet's image become inflated, through repeated storytelling, far beyond the local setting. Moses, who became the rescuer of an entire people, and Samuel, who came to be patterned on the model of the military chieftain in 1 Samuel 7 (compare 2 Sam. 5.17-25) are exceptions, not the rule.

Did the local miracles described in prophetic biblical tales actually occur? Did Elisha and Jesus really feed many people with only a few loaves of bread, or revive dead children? The same questions can be asked of the tales so common in many other traditional societies, where the shaman is often said to have done these things. The answer in every case is difficult, since all cultures share a tendency toward narrational exaggeration and even invention (see Chapter 3). Most tales of this kind are designed to be wholly fantastic and, to be fair to the storytellers, should be interpreted as fantasy stories. Nevertheless, a few of the shaman-prophet stories do not seem entirely out of the realm of normal experience. When Elisha performs the elaborate ritual of 2 Kgs 4.32-37, the narrator seems to be describing actions designed to 'shock' or 'stimulate' a body toward resuscitation, just like a modern medic does. Even if one assumes that the story is not a reliable account of a real event (which is the most reasonable of assumptions), the tale might reflect the real *expectations* of ancient people who were accustomed to interacting with a shaman, a prophet. After all, if success is to come to any magician in any culture, it usually requires three elements: the magician must possess the ability to discern what is possible under the circumstances, must hope for a little good luck, and must rely on the participants' good will and willingness to believe in the power of the supernatural. On these elements, the reputation of the shaman-prophet stands or falls.

### Did Prophets Foretell the Future?

An aspect of divine revelation that is frequently miscomprehended is the issue of fortune-telling. In modern culture, the task of a prophet is popularly assumed to be the telling of future events. This idea was not unknown to the ancient world (see, e.g., Isa. 44.7-8), but there are significant nuances that are usually overlooked in the modern popular conception.

First, a prophet of the ancient Near East (including biblical prophets) did indeed attempt to announce the future, but almost without exception, it was a short-term future event. Prophets did not proclaim what was to be the case five or 10 generations later. They announced an event to take place tomorrow, next week or next year. In some cases they tried to predict circumstances a generation or so from their own time, but this is about as far into the future as any of them ever tried to gaze. It would have been impractical and unnecessary to try anything more ambitious. Prophecy, like any genre of communication, is designed to be meaningful in the present moment. For example, if I tell you what will happen 400 years from now, you will not be impressed. You will yawn, stretch and walk away. Likewise, ancient written prophecy was not composed for many later generations, but for the immediate generation. If it survived longer than one generation, it was certain to be either reinterpreted or rewritten, or both.

Belief that prophets were able to foresee long future events is a misconception that derives, in part, from a genre of literature bearing superficial resemblance to prophecy. That genre was apocalyptic. An apocalyptic document is *not* a prophecy, though it gives the impression of being prophetic. Apocalyptic is usually a narrative about a prophet with a characteristic plot: the prophet sees a vision or receives a visit from a divine revealer (usually of lower rank), and is granted a tour of the divine realm. Sometimes, the tour of things divine will include a 'tour of history' as well. That means that the divine revealer tells the prophet what will take place for many generations to come. However, the interesting feature of an apocalypse is that this genre describes past events *as though* they were future events. As a matter of fact, the modern reader is able to tell when an apocalypse ceases to describe past events and begins to attempt the future: this will be the point in the narrative when the details become inaccurate! That is why apocalyptic literature should never be confused with prophecy. It was a *vaticinia ex eventu*, which means 'prophecy after the event', a fictional narrative designed to assure the reader that *past events* have been under divine control. In the Bible, three excellent examples of apocalyptic narrative are Daniel 7–12, the New Testament book of Revelation, and Mark 13 (in which Jesus is the divine revealer of lower rank, and the disciples learn the divine view of things from him). In each case, the narrative was composed using story-world characters of a past generation to whom future events are 'revealed'; yet each of these texts was composed by an author living *after* the events described.

Second, a prophet who announced a future event was, quite frequently, incorrect. For example, a prophet at the Mesopotamian city of Mari announced, in the name of the god Dagan, that the king of Babylon had done evil and would be punished. He would be delivered into the power of the king of Mari, said the prophet. This prophecy proved incorrect. Mari's king was defeated by the Babylonian king. Likewise, biblical prophets were wrong from time to time. After Babylon's victory at Carchemish in 605 BCE, Jeremiah had the temerity to predict that his lord, Nebuchadnezzar II, would invade Egypt successfully (Jer. 46.13-24), but the invasion of 601 BCE was turned back at Migdol. Jeremiah was incorrect.

When a prophet was incorrect about a future event, it was an embarrassment, but it did not necessarily wreck the prophet's career. The prophetic reputation was not affected because *the prophet's task was not to announce the future but to shape the present*. This was the key issue, the one universal aspect of all prophecy. A prophet spoke on behalf of a god, urging his listeners to act now. If the future was already fixed, there would be no motivation for listening to a prophet's message. But most people believed the future was not fixed. Another example from ancient Mari illustrates the point. A prophet urged the king of Mari to be more diligent in the administration of justice, saying 'When a wronged man or woman cries out to you, stand and let his/her case be judged'. The very fact that the prophet believed he could influence the king's behavior implies that any warning about the future was not cast in stone. The king's decision could change his destiny. This is precisely Jeremiah's point when he also urges kings to be more diligent in the administration of justice (Jer. 22.1-5). Another example is more explicit. When Yahweh sends the prophet Jeremiah to the temple to preach, Yahweh says, 'Perhaps they will listen and repent, each from his evil, so that I may revoke the punishment I am planning...' (Jer. 26.3). That word 'perhaps' indicates a great deal. This is a god who is uncertain about the future of the afternoon's events! In the genre of prophecy, the future is not fixed and certain, so 'prediction' cannot be certain either.

Third, popular confusion about prophecy is created by the Bible itself, which gives a casual reader multiple and confusing attitudes toward prophecy. In a late era (Hellenistic and Roman times), when the activity of prophecy had given way to the more trite literary clichés of apocalyptic narrative, there seems to have been a desire to discourage men and women from acting as prophets. Passages such as Zech. 13.2-6 suggest that prophecy had become a discredited social role, and equally late texts such as Joel 3.1-2 (2.28-29 in some English versions) suggest an attempt to 'democratize' the role of prophet and thereby empty it of any significance. (If everyone is a prophet, then no one is a prophet.) By the time of Jesus and his followers, a wholesale conceptual change had taken place because the old social context of prophecy had long since died away, and no one in that generation possessed the research tools with which to recover it. That is why New Testament writers lack any understanding of the prophetic genre. They are not able to distinguish between prophetic genres and non-prophetic genres in the Jewish Bible. They treat every Jewish text in a 'flat' manner, as though it were *all* prophecy. For example, Mark 15 borrows motifs from Psalm 22, Mt. 1.23 treats the folk-tale of Isaiah 7 as though it were a prophetic oracle, Jn 1.51 transforms Genesis 28 into an allegorical narrative about the Christ. New Testament ignorance of prophecy is typical of the Roman era. Jewish writers of the Roman-era Dead Sea Scrolls were equally incapable of distinguishing prophecy from other genres.

With these late passages goes a curious text in Deut. 18.21-22, a short passage that might be the central cause of the confusion I am discussing. Here the reader is advised that the way to discern whether a prophet is truly sent by Yahweh is to wait until the prophecy has been fulfilled. At a casual reading, these two verses give the impression that prophecy was mechanical prediction of future events. Those who cannot predict are not prophets. Not only is this a false impression of ancient Near Eastern prophecy, but it is, from a pragmatic viewpoint, horrible advice. What good is it to make a decision about a prophetic utterance after it is too late to respond to the prophetic sermon? Would the advice of Deut. 18.21-22 have served the royal officials who were compelled to make a decision about Jeremiah's prophecy in Jer. 26.1-19? One presumes that, had they employed the 'wait and see' approach, they would have ensured the destruction of their city and themselves! Likewise, would the people of Nineveh have been better off to use this 'wait and see' method in the book of Jonah? The advice of 18.21-22 seems designed to ensure that no one who reads and accepts Deuteronomy will trust the words of any prophet. That is the key to understanding this strange passage.

As a historian of ancient religion, I am convinced that the reader was not supposed to read Deut. 18.21-22 out of literary context. As a matter of fact, this passage is a purely literary device, not meant to have any function in a real, social world. Allow me to explain: Deuteronomy is a highly complex and artistic religious tract. Its primary purpose is to convince its reader that (1) there is no god worthy of worship except Yahweh (e.g. 6.4-9), and (2) there has been no prophet of primary importance except Moses (e.g. 34.10-12). Yet, Deuteronomy promises the coming of a great prophet, a Prophet-like-Moses (18.15-20). Superficially, this seems to mean that, one day, there will be an equal to Moses and the book of Deuteronomy will become irrelevant, since a book is not as important as a prophet of Moses's stature. In reality, the book of Deuteronomy has no intention of ever relinquishing its religious authority to a man (or woman); rather, it is designed to be the Prophet-like-Moses for all times. The scroll purports to be the words of Moses in the past, but the final passage is written from a much later perspective, since it knows that there has never been an equal to Moses. Indeed, it is not the final passage alone that is composed from the later perspective, but the whole scroll. As a scroll, Deuteronomy is *designed to transcend time*. Moses speaks to every generation through this scroll (e.g. 5.1-5). Thus, the Prophet-like-Moses promised in 18.15-20 is perpetually fulfilled each time the scroll is read (31.10-13). No wonder 18.21-22 follows immediately, for if the Prophet-like-Moses lives perpetually in a text, he cannot appear in the flesh—ever. Verses 21-22 are designed to ensure that the reader will never follow a living prophet. Deuteronomy 13.1-6 is a passage that reinforces this anti-prophetic stance.

To summarize our discussion of prophecy, the prophet in the ancient Near East was a common figure, and the genre of prophetic communication was well known to all. The Bible preserved the most extensive collection of prophecy to have survived from ancient times, and it is informative because it is representative. These texts reflect the diversity of prophetic practice throughout the Fertile Crescent, a diversity that cannot be reduced to neat categories, but mixes divination, prophecy and mysticism with magic and short-term fortune-telling.

### The Prophet's Performance: Three Elements

One final question that bedevils modern readers of the Bible as much as it bothered ancient people is: how does one distinguish between true and false prophecy? This goes back to the discussion of truth as it relates to genres of communication. The measure of truth depends on the intent of communication (see p. 68). As a practical matter, it is not possible to make such distinctions with prophecy, since the claim of divine revelation is not really an adequate source of human knowledge. Human knowledge derives from human perception. Therefore any extra-sensory source of knowledge is as impractical as trying to carry an ice cube through the Sahara. Even if the ice cube is real, it is no match for the sun; even if divine revelation is real, its knowledge is no match for sensory-based knowledge. The genre of prophetic communication, by its very nature, cannot utter truth or falsity. It is always a subjective utterance running underneath truth's radar. A prophet was, fundamentally, a person who was steeped in a religious worldview and employed that worldview in a radically simple (but not simplistic) way. The prophet did three things every time he or she spoke or wrote: (1) the prophet interpreted the present situation (2) in light of the religion's past teachings (3) in order to persuade people about immediate future action. Prophecy was as simple *and* as complex as that.

## Conclusion

This concludes this very brief tour of ancient Canaanite religions. I have not discussed the complexities of ancient priesthoods, systems of sacrifice, or the many doctrinal subtleties. Rather, my purpose was to offer a general portrait that might highlight the rich diversity of ancient religious experiences, as well as the many ways that ancient religion was similar to, and very different from, modern religion. Above all, I hope that this discussion demonstrates the humane elements in ancient religious sensibilities. Religion was not an exotic, other-worldly phenomenon, not even for the prophet or the mystic. Religion was the medium through which the most common and mundane aspects of daily life were conceptualized, analyzed, rationalized and accepted. Religion was a vehicle for the travel through life.

### SUGGESTED ADDITIONAL READING

*Studies in Religion*

Guthrie, Stuart Elliott, *Faces in the Clouds: A New Theory of Religion* (Oxford: Oxford University Press, 1993).

Hinde, Robert A., *Why Gods Persist: A Scientific Approach to Religion* (London: Routledge, 1999).

Morris, Brian, *Anthropological Studies in Religion: An Introductory Text* (Cambridge: Cambridge University Press, 1987).

*Canaanite and Israelite Religions*

Collins, John J., *The Apocalyptic Imagination: An Introduction to Jewish Apocalyptic Literature* (Winona Lake, IN: Eisenbrauns, 1998).

Day, John, *Yahweh and the Gods and Goddesses of Canaan* (JSOTSup, 265; Sheffield: Sheffield Academic Press, 2000).

Edelman, Diana V. (ed.), *The Triumph of Elohim: From Yahwisms to Judaisms* (Grand Rapids: Eerdmans, 1996).

Fitzpatrick-McKinley, Anne, *The Transformation of Torah from Scribal Advice to Law* (JSOTSup, 287; Sheffield: Sheffield Academic Press, 1999).

Gordon, Robert P. (ed.), *The Place is Too Small for Us: The Israelite Prophets in Recent Scholarship* (Winona Lake, IN: Eisenbrauns, 1995).

Grabbe, Lester L., *Priests, Prophets, Diviners, Sages: A Socio-Historical Study of Religious Specialists in Ancient Israel* (Valley Forge, PA: Trinity Press International, 1995).

Gnuse, Robert Karl, *No Other Gods: Emergent Monotheism in Israel* (JSOTSup, 241; Sheffield: Sheffield Academic Press, 1997).

Hadley, Judith M., *The Cult of Asherah in Ancient Israel and Judah: The Evidence for a Hebrew Goddess* (Cambridge: Cambridge University Press, 2000).

Handy, Lowell K., *Among the Host of Heaven* (Winona Lake, IN: Eisenbrauns, 1994).

Keel, Othmar and Christoph Uehlinger, *Gods, Goddesses and Images of God in Ancient Israel* (Minneapolis: Fortress Press, 1998).

Nelson, Richard D., *Raising Up a Faithful Priest: Community and Priesthood in Biblical Theology* (Louisville, KY: Westminster/John Knox Press, 1993).

Overholt, Thomas W., *Cultural Anthropology and the Old Testament* (Minneapolis: Fortress Press, 1996).

Smith, Mark S., *The origins of Biblical Monotheism: Israel's Polytheistic Background and the Ugaritic Texts* (Oxford: Oxford University Press).

Smith, Mark S. *et al.*, *Ugaritic Narrative Poetry* (Atlanta: Scholars Press, 1997).

## NOTES

1.　My description of 'religion' is reductionistic, but will suffice for present purposes. My goal is not to probe all the complexities of the social phenomenon, but to offer something a little more realistic than is usually presented in academic biblical scholarship. For example, the competent, if conventional, volume recently published by P.D. Miller, *The Religion of Ancient Israel* (Louisville, KY: Westminster/John Knox Press, 2000), represents the difficulty as usually encountered. Miller's first sentence leads the reader astray: 'The center of ancient Israel's religion was the worship of a deity named Yahweh' (p. 1). Since Yahweh was not always the primary god of Israel, the statement is false. More importantly, the worship of a deity of particular name is not the 'center' of *any* religion, not even a theism. The metaphysical aspects of religious ideology are but one portion of its ideology, and the ideological aspects of a religion are but one portion of the social reality. For most participants in a religion, that level of intellectualism is of minor significance. But like the ancient author of Deuteronomy (who also dwells on the name of Yahweh), Miller has neglected the commonalties of ancient religious experience and instead focused on dogmatic minutiae. (Note, for example, his use of the misleading categories, 'orthodox, heterodox and syncretistic' Yahwisms [pp. 47-62].)

2.　I am frequently intrigued by the way modern sacred-theists attempt to bring secular biblical texts into the sacred realm by means of very creative interpretation. See, for example, the honest struggle with and against Qoheleth by my dear friend and teacher, W.S. Towner, 'The Book of Ecclesiastes: Introduction, Commentary and Reflections', in *The New Interpreter's Bible* (Nashville: Abingdon Press, 1994), V, pp. 265-360. An interesting volume dealing with these issues is P.R. Davies, *Whose Bible Is It Anyway?* (JSOTSup, 204; Sheffield: Sheffield Academic Press, 1995).

3.　Varro's ideas are preserved for us in Book VI of Saint Augustine's *City of God*.

4.　However, some scholars equate Dagan with El and conclude that the mythology did have at least an echo in the temple services. For example, see G. del Olmo Lete, *Canaanite Religion According to the Liturgical Texts of Ugarit* (trans. by W.G.E. Watson; Bethesda: CDL Press, 1999), p. 74.

5.　S. Gitin and M. Cogan, 'A New Type of Dedicatory Inscription from Ekron',

*IEJ* 49 (1999), pp. 193-202; see also S. Gitin and T. Dothan, 'A Royal Dedicatory Inscription from Ekron', *IEJ* 47 (1997), pp. 1-16.

6.   For example, P.K. McCarter, 'Aspects of the Religion of Israelite Monarchy: Biblical and Epigraphic Data', in P.D. Miller *et al.* (eds.), *Ancient Israelite Religion: Essays in Honor of Frank Moore Cross* (Philadelphia: Fortress Press, 1987), pp. 137-55. However, McCarter's presentation of this thesis is marred by a desire to disassociate 'Israelite' religion from 'Canaanite' religion. For example, his conclusion that 'Yahweh's asherah is not...the Canaanite Asherah' (p. 149) is refuted by the data he discusses.

7.   S.A. Geller rejects the translation of אחד with English 'alone' and substitutes the superlative, 'number one/supreme', which is certainly possible and, of course, similarly henotheistic, though perhaps not monolatrous. See Geller, 'The God of the Covenant', in B.N. Porter (ed.), *One God or Many? Concepts of Divinity in the Ancient World* (Transactions of the Casco Bay Assyriological Institute, 1; Bethesda: CDL Press, 2000), pp. 273-319 (290-93).

8.   For a defense of the 'Kaufmann School', in which the term 'monotheism' becomes sufficiently elastic to include almost any metaphysical speculation, see B. Halpern, '"Brisker Pipes than Poetry": The Development of Israelite Monotheism', in J. Neusner *et al.* (eds.), *Judaic Perspectives on Ancient Israel* (Philadelphia: Fortress Press, 1987), pp. 77-115.

9.   For the epigraph, see N. Avigad, 'The Priest of Dor', *IEJ* 25 (1975), pp. 101-105. On the ethnicity of Dor: Josh. 12.23 implies that Israelites conquered the city (or perhaps the region to the east), a claim that is denied by Judg. 1.27. Both passages are, of course, part of the Iron Age II (or later) conquest tradition, with no value for determining the ethnicity or political control of Late Bronze or Iron Age I cities. Joshua 17.11 calls the dwellers of Dor and its nearby villages an Israelite border region, a tradition modified in 1 Chron. 7.29. Both texts date to a period when no Israelite or Judahite political entity could have had any control over Dor. Only 1 Kgs 4.11 implies a genuine Israelite presence at Dor. If accurate, the text asserts that the region (not necessarily the city) was held politically by Israel for less than one generation in the tenth century BCE. The seal of Zechariah, the priest of Dor, dates to the late-eighth century. In his many publications, the excavator of Dor, Ephraim Stern, does not describe anything that implies an Israelite presence there, which is unsurprising in light of the Bible's testimony. Dor was never Israelite.

10.   For example, see T.L. Thompson, *Early History of the Israelite People from the Written and Archaeological Sources* (Leiden: E.J. Brill, 1992), pp. 19-20. The sober form criticism offered by J.W. Watts suggests as well that conclusions about the origins of Judg. 5 are far from settled; see his *Psalm and Story: Inset Hymns in Hebrew Narrative* (JSOTSup, 139; Sheffield: JSOT Press, 1992), pp. 206-20.

11.   For another biblical fragment that suggests Yahweh's subordination to a high god, see E.A. Knauf, 'Le roi est mort, vive le roi! A Biblical Argument for the Historicity of Solomon', in L.K. Handy (ed.), *The Age of Solomon: Scholarship at the Turn of the Century* (Leiden: E.J. Brill, 1997), pp. 81-95 (82-86).

12.   It is possible that Yahweh was an epithet for El in an early period, as frequently suggested in the scholarship. If this was the case, the epithet had become

detached from El as an independent deity well before traditions recorded in the Bible were conceived. The reuniting of El and Yahweh in the Iron Age is not surprising since Yahweh would have retained much of El's personality, making fusion natural. For the epithet hypothesis, see F.M. Cross, *Canaanite Myth and Hebrew Epic: Essays in the History of the Religion of Israel* (Cambridge, MA: Harvard University Press, 1973), pp. 60-75. That the ancient author of a text such as Exod. 3.14 did not employ the form reconstructed by Cross (pp. 68-69) suggests that the Iron Age II memory of Yahweh's origin as an epithet was vague, at best.

13. For a recent publication with nearly comprehensive bibliography on this topic, see P.A. Bird, 'The End of the Male Cult Prostitute: A Literary-Historical and Sociological Analysis of Hebrew *qades-qedesim*', in J.A. Emerton (ed.), *Congress Volume, Cambridge 1995* (Leiden: E.J. Brill, 1997), pp. 37-80.

14. The eighth-century Samaria ostraca contain a number of personal names using Baal as the theophoric element (edited by G.I. Davies *et al.* [eds.], *Ancient Hebrew Inscriptions: Corpus and Concordance* [Cambridge: Cambridge University Press, 1991], p. 316). These might represent the god Baal or Yahweh's epithet, or both, if Yahweh was Baal. In the Bible, characters who are presented as part of the story's Yahwistic community bear Baal theophorics (e.g. Ishbosheth = Ishbaal, in 2 Sam. 2.8). See also Hos. 2.18, a polemical text that indicates the use of Baal as an epithet for Yahweh. Given that Yahweh is so frequently presented as a Baal in biblical poetry (e.g. Ps. 29), there is every reason to believe that Yahweh was often conceived to be Baal in ancient Judahite and Israelite communities. This would be no surprise, since Baal was the provider of fertility and fertility was the primary religious concern in an agrarian society.

15. This is uncertain, however. For various viewpoints, see the summarizing discussion (with bibliographic citations) in P. McNutt, *Reconstructing the Society of Ancient Israel* (Louisville, KY: Westminster/John Knox Press, 1999), pp. 100-101 (citation 134, p. 237) and pp. 174-76 (citations pp. 94-95, 248-49).

16. G.W. Ahlström, *Royal Administration and National Religion in Ancient Palestine* (Leiden: E.J. Brill, 1982), pp. 44-74; also *idem*, *The History of Ancient Palestine from the Palaeolithic Period to Alexander's Conquest* (ed. D.V. Edelman; JSOTSup, 146; Sheffield: JSOT Press, 1993), pp. 478-79.

17. All the Mari examples used here are discussed by A. Malamat, 'A Forerunner of Biblical Prophecy: The Mari Documents', in Miller *et al.* (eds.), *Ancient Israelite Religion*, pp. 33-52 (see n. 5 above).

Chapter 10

AFTER THE IRON AGE II

*Introduction*

With hindsight, one can see that the destruction of Jerusalem by the Babylonian army in 586 BCE was not an end, but a beginning. After the Judahite people lost their monarchy, and with it the state-sponsored theology so typical of Iron Age Syro-Palestinian patron-god religions, they were in a position to take up the fragmented traditions of the past, reflect on them, and create something new and distinctive: the Bible. The period from the sixth century BCE to the early second century CE— a period of roughly 700 years—was the era in which the Bible gradually emerged. Although the Bible speaks, for the most part, about the period we have already studied, it breathes the air and reflects the worldview of the era we are about to study. In sum, the Bible is an anthology of literature designed to both preserve fragments of a lost past and reflect on these fragments, interpreting them for a new present—the 'now' that was experienced by the biblical authors and editors of the Babylonian, Persian, Hellenistic and Roman eras (586 BCE–324 CE).

*Babylonian Period (586–539 BCE)*

Hindsight may tell us that the fall of Jerusalem was really a beginning, but to those who experienced that fall, it was certainly an end, a bloody and excruciatingly painful end. The biblical book of Lamentations perhaps expresses that pain more eloquently than any modern historian could hope to express. Or one might turn to Psalm 137's haunting words to experience the event from the inside:

By the rivers of Babylon,
There we sat,
Sat and wept,
As we thought of Zion.

Upon the trees in her midst
We hung our harps.
For there they asked us,
Our captors, for words of song,
Our tormentors, for joyfulness.

'Sing for us a song of Zion!'

How can we sing
The song of Yahweh
Upon alien soil?

If I forget you, Jerusalem,
May my right hand be forgotten;
May my tongue cleave to my palate,
If I fail to remember you;
If I don't lift Jerusalem
above my greatest desire.

Remember, Yahweh, the Edomites!
On the day of Jerusalem
Those shouting 'Strip!
'Strip her to the foundations!'

Daughter Babylon, devastator!
Blessed be he who repays you
Your payment you paid to us!
Blessed be he who seizes, smashes
Your babies on the rock!

To one who lives comfortably, insulated from the brutality of war, the pain of loss, the alienation of captivity, the first half of this poem is lyrical, lush, lovely—and *spoiled* by the vindictiveness of the last part. But to one who has experienced this devastation, the poem hangs together as a single harmony, the soprano and the bass, a glimmer of consolation in the face of a blank, bleak future.

Judah was transformed by King Nebuchadnezzar II into a province. The leaders of Jerusalem, that is to say, the literate, wealthy, educated elite class of the city, were deported from Palestine to Babylon. The remaining population, including the majority of the illiterate, poor, uneducated peasantry, remained right where they had always been.[1] When modern historians speak or write of the so-called Babylonian

Exile (a common phrase in the scholarship), they are really only describing the event from the viewpoint of a tiny minority, not from the perspective of most Judahites. However, since that minority were the ones who possessed the intellectual capacity and the means to record their experience (as in Ps. 137), it is no surprise that both the Bible and many modern histories view the matter through their eyes.

The Bible is an artifact of privilege. It was composed by and for the elite minority who were the leaders of Judahite society. Indeed, the tone of many passages betrays the class conflict that took place after 586 BCE, as the exiles in Babylon tried to cling to their former status and sought ideological justification for viewing themselves as the 'true' people of their god vis-à-vis the 'people of the land' who had not been deported. The books of Jeremiah and Ezekiel, for example, contain passages contrasting the piety of the exiles to the allegedly perverse state of those who remained in Judah (see Jer. 24; Ezek. 8–11, etc.). Sometimes the polemical excess of such texts makes it difficult for a historian to know whether their content accurately reflects the lives of the people being described.

After the war, life from a peasant's perspective in the Judaean Hills did not worsen, and may well have improved. Though the provincial system required more effort for the authorities burdened with reconstructing a government in a devastated land, commoners might have benefited in some ways. First, when the kings of Judah reigned as vassals of foreign powers, the peasants were, in effect, double taxed, paying to feed the local nobility and the Babylonian authority. Under the provincial system, they were taxed only by the latter. Second, many of the peasants had been tenant farmers working land owned by elites who lived in Jerusalem. With the deportation of those elites, ownership of the land seems to have fallen to the tenant farmers (2 Kgs 25.12; Jer. 39.10).

Life for those in exile was not physically oppressive either. It was certainly painful emotionally and spiritually to be wrenched from one's homeland and deported to a faraway land, and no doubt the horror of the war and the loss of loved ones remained a bitter memory. But Neo-Assyrian and Neo-Babylonian policies of deportation were not designed to inflict unspeakable terror on those who were deported. Quite the contrary, the policy of deportation was a very pragmatic one. The assumptions behind that policy went like this: the imperial power (either Assyrian or Babylonian) perceived itself to have been compelled to attack and capture city X because city X rebelled against the empire. Why did city X rebel? Because the elite leadership of the city organized the peasantry into a hostile force. Therefore, the imperial power reasoned that if the city leadership were removed, the peasantry would become passive. There would be peace. Moreover, the city leadership consisted of the best and the brightest of that land. It would be tragic to destroy that talent, but it could be useful in another part of the imperial realm. In that place, these leaders would constitute a minority, would not be able to organize rebellion, and would instead devote their talents to productive activities. In short, from the Assyrian and Babylonian perspectives, deportation was a humane solution to the problem of civil warfare. (To see the policy in action from the exile's viewpoint, read Jer. 29.)

From the data in Babylon, it would seem that many of the deported groups maintained their own identities in the foreign land. One residential quarter in Babylon housed a group calling themselves Ashkelon and another Gaza.[2] Likewise from the Bible, we can see that the deported Judahites maintained a community and an identity through the years of exile. They retained the worship of Yahweh and preserved some ancient writings that would become the nucleus around which the biblical anthology grew. Because they were from Judah, they began to call themselves, and were called by others, the Judahites—identical to our modern term, the Jews.

While the families of the exiles and the peasants of the Judaean Hills rebuilt their lives, international politics continued on their chaotic pathways. Nabopolassar and Nebuchadnezzar II proved to be the only genuinely successful kings of the short-lived Neo-Babylonian empire. They were followed by the brief reigns of several unremarkable men, and then, in 539 BCE, Babylonia fell before a new emperor, Cyrus II of Persia.

### Cyrus the Great, Messiah of Yahweh

According to ancient traditions, the Persians had been subjects of the Medes, but that may not have been the case. It was the Medes who had assisted Babylon in the devastation of the Assyrian empire during the final decades of the seventh century. They were situated north and east of Babylonia. Archaeological evidence suggests that they never became the power that ancient historians such as Herodotus claim them to have been. Nevertheless, they were a significant, if minor, player in the politics of this era, and they were the first obstacle to Persian ascent. In the mid-sixth century, a Persian king named Cyrus II eliminated the Median king and established a new empire in Mesopotamia. Within a few short years, the Persians ruled all the way to Anatolia, having bypassed Babylonia in their spread northward and westward.

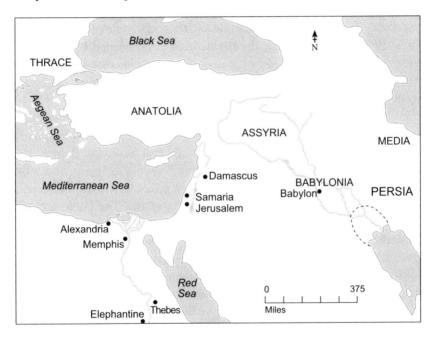

Figure 33. *The Ancient Near East after the Iron Age II.*

A nameless biblical prophet, whose writings have been incorporated into the book of Isaiah (modern scholars call him Second- or Deutero-Isaiah), praised Cyrus II with these words (Isa. 44.28–45.1a):

> The one who speaks of Cyrus, my shepherd,
> All that I desire you shall fulfill!
> You will say to Jerusalem,
> 'You shall be built!'
> And to the temple,
> 'You shall be founded!'
> Thus says Yahweh to his Messiah,
> To Cyrus, whose right hand I have grasped!

What motivated these words of praise? In 539 BCE, the Persian army defeated the Babylonian army at Opis, just northeast of Babylon, then marched, uncontested, into the city as the self-appointed 'liberators' of Babylon. Cyrus launched a vigorous public relations campaign designed to win the hearts of his new subjects. Judging from the Jewish prophet's enthusiasm, it seems to have worked. The prophet acclaims Cyrus as the Messiah of Yahweh. No doubt, Cyrus claimed the title as well. Surviving inscriptions demonstrate that Cyrus claimed many such titles. For the Babylonians, the royal rhetoric positioned Cyrus as the chosen one of Marduk, god of Babylon. In the city of Nippur, Cyrus was the favored of the moon good Sin. In short, the policy was this: you name your patron god and Cyrus is his chosen agent!

Part of the public relations policy seems to have included repatriation. Apparently, Cyrus decreed that the descendants of certain groups whose ancestors had been deported as part of standard Babylonian policy could return to their respective homelands. For many who took advantage of this policy, the 'return' was to a land they had never seen, since they were second- or third-generation exiles. The Bible records two texts that biblical authors attribute to the administration of Cyrus. Some historians doubt the authenticity of these passages (with good reasons). However, even if the texts are forgeries, they capture the spirit of a genuine and sufficiently documented Persian policy. The first, Ezra 1.2-4, permits any willing Jew to go to Jerusalem and build, on behalf of Cyrus himself, a temple for Yahweh. The second, Ezra 6.3-5, focuses more narrowly on the building project, stating that royal coffers will pay expenses and ordering the return of temple furniture taken by Nebuchadnezzar II.

The biblical books of Ezra and Nehemiah attest that at least some Babylonian Jews responded to the repatriation policy. Unfortunately, it is not clear how many responded, when, and in what manner. The biblical narratives are hopelessly confused, and do not mesh easily with the archaeological data. Before dealing with those problems, it would be helpful to establish the context by reviewing briefly major events in Persian history.

### The Persian Empire (539–331 BCE)

The kings of Persia were:

| Rise of Persia (559–522 BCE) | Early Empire (522–404 BCE) | Middle Empire (404–338 BCE) | Late Empire (338–330 BCE) |
|---|---|---|---|
| Cyrus II | Darius I | Artaxerxes II | Arses |
| Cambyses II | Xerxes | Artaxerxes III | Darius III |
| | Artaxerxes I | | |
| | Darius II | | |

Figure 34. *The Kings of Persia.*

The Persian empire at its height encompassed roughly as much real estate as the continental United States. It was the largest empire the Near Eastern world had seen to that time. Moreover, the Persian kings desired to make it bigger. Cyrus II (559–530 BCE) died fighting for ever more land. He had been a remarkable soldier whose military tactics and use of speedy marches and surprise attacks won him a reputation as a conqueror comparable to Alexander the Great. Those who benefited from his success called him Cyrus the Great, though one suspects that his victims had other choice titles in mind.

Cyrus II was succeeded by Cambyses II (530–522 BCE), who expanded Persian frontiers by conquering Egypt. In ancient Greek history writing, Cambyses II has a reputation as an oppressor and a brute. From surviving Egyptian evidence, one gets the opposite impression. Cambyses II seems to have respected the sensibilities of the people who lived along the Nile, conformed his image to the tradition of Egyptian royalty, and honored Egyptian religious rituals and piety. But Cambyses II died mysteriously in 522 and was succeeded by a usurper, Darius I (522–486 BCE). Darius I left a legacy of very heavy-handed propaganda designed to cover up his treachery in seizing the throne, but the Persian public was not fooled, and there were numerous revolts, some inspired by outrage at the coup, others inspired by the opportunity to break away from the Persian overlords during the transitional chaos. Remarkably, Darius I proved to be as shrewd as he was brutal, and kept the empire together, even expanding the borders in a few regions.

Darius I consolidated the empire by establishing a series of administrative units, each governed by a Satrap (governor), who possessed complete administrative control, but only partial military authority, the crown retaining direct influence over the military for itself. Palestine was part of a Satrapy called 'Across the River [Euphrates]'. This

Satrapy was further subdivided into provinces. At first glance, these provinces seem to have been relatively autonomous. For example, the province of Sidon (all of the Phoenician coast to, and including, Dor) was ruled by a king. But it was not a vassal state in the older sense, since a Persian provincial governor also resided in Sidon and commanded a Persian force. Nevertheless, at the provincial level, indigenous elites took the lead on many fronts. Darius's administrative excellence created a number of innovations, such as a network of royal roads, completion of a canal connecting the Nile with the Red Sea (a project that had begun under Necho II of the 26th Dynasty), and one of the earliest systems of coinage. The Daric coin became the standard in monetary transactions for almost two centuries.

If Darius I could have his wish, he would be remembered not for consolidating the empire and creating an efficient bureaucracy, but for expanding the empire into Europe. He annexed Thrace and Macedonia, just north of Greece, and attempted to conquer the Greek city of Athens. It was Darius I's troops who lost the famous Battle of Marathon in 490 BCE. The Persian king hoped to pin the Athenian army down by landing a Persian force at the opposite end of Attica, the peninsula on which Athens is located. Then, with the Athenian defenders occupied by that land invasion, Darius planned to send his navy around the peninsula for a direct attack on the city. The Athenians won a swift victory at Marathon, marched quickly across Attica, and defended themselves against the Persian navy. Darius I was forced to retreat. (This event, incidentally, also marks the beginning of the so-called Classical era in Greek history—490 to 323 BCE—the period that produced the tragedians Aeschylus, Sophocles and Euripides, and the philosophers Socrates, Plato and Aristotle.)

At his death, Darius I had been planning another invasion against Athens, and that expedition was carried out by his successor, Xerxes (486–465 BCE). Once again, the tiny but committed forces of the Greeks thwarted the massive invasion of the Persians, this time in a naval battle at Salamis in 480, just southwest of Athens. This would not have been the end, of course, since the Persians had the means to keep pressing invasion after invasion against the smaller population of Greece. But fate intervened in the form of anti-Persian revolt in Babylon, forcing Xerxes to focus attention closer to home. As a result, the pressure applied against Greece was never as intense after 480 BCE, and the Greek Delian League was able to defend the Aegean region.

Persia never conquered the Greek mainland, but the relations between Greece and Persia remained tense. Their stories are intertwined.

The middle years of the fifth century BCE saw political disturbances that may have had a direct impact on Palestine. The early reign of Xerxes in the 480s marked a period of unrest in the Central Hills, while revolt was also taking place in Egypt. Unfortunately, no documents survive to explain what happened in Palestine, but archaeologists have noted military destruction at numerous sites in the Central Hills. Throughout the Persian Empire, revolts emerged in the late-460s and early-450s, when Artaxerxes I (465–424) came to the throne. Of significance for Palestine was a revolt in Egypt, abetted by troops from Athens. With unrest in Palestine just a few years earlier, this region was sure to come under suspicion as the authorities quelled revolt to the southwest.

The late-fifth century found Persia once again interfering in the affairs of Greece, and this marked the beginning of Persia's decline, though no one realized this at the time. Sparta and Athens were fighting the Peloponnesian Wars (433–404 BCE), and Darius II (424–404 BCE) intervened several times. His agent was one of his sons, the Persian Satrap in Anatolia, Cyrus the Younger, who ultimately lent his support to Sparta, giving it the edge needed to defeat Athens. Darius II died that year (404 BCE), and Cyrus the Younger immediately employed Greek mercenary troops to help him fight the new Persian king, his own brother, Artaxerxes II (404–358 BCE). Cyrus the Younger was killed in the battle, and Artaxerxes II retained his throne.

The civil war distracted Persia and enabled Egypt to gain its independence under a succession of three short-lived dynasties, the 28th, 29th and 30th (404–342 BCE). This was not the only misfortune for the Persians, however. The reign of Artaxerxes II was one of almost perpetual revolt in one portion of the empire or another. Not surprisingly, the archaeology of Palestine again betrays military destruction, this time in the Shephelah and Negev (c. 380 or so BCE). Possibly this is connected to the invasions of the 29th Egyptian Dynasty, whose two kings, Nepherites and Achoris, briefly controlled significant portions of Palestine (390s–380s).

A brief renaissance emerged under the next Persian king, Artaxerxes III (358–338 BCE), who managed to bring Egypt back under Persian domination in 342. But it was too little too late. At the end of his reign, internal unrest developed, Artaxerxes III was assassinated, and an ineffective king named Arses reigned briefly before also falling victim to an assassin (probably the same assassin). By 336 BCE, Persia was in turmoil. An able new king, Darius III (336–330), took the throne, only to face a much more able man, the Macedonian invader, Alexander III, called by some 'the Great'.

### The History of Yehud (Persian-Era Judah)

The foregoing discussion is the background against which the story of the Persian-era Jews must be sketched. And it can be little more than a sketch, for the data are scarce. Although precise boundaries are uncertain, the province of Yehud seems to have consisted of the Judaean Hills from north of Hebron to somewhere near Bethel, and from Jericho to the eastern edge of the Shephelah. In other words, Yehud was a smaller geographic entity than the old Iron Age II Kingdom of Judah had been at its peak, and correspondingly less populated. Yehud at its most populous was home to perhaps just over 20,000 people, though some estimates are lower. Jerusalem during these 200 years housed a peak population of about 1500, and far fewer in some generations.

Since Yehud was a province of a great empire, it certainly had connections to that larger world. Indeed, without those connections, the economy of this tiny entity would have imploded. There is evidence to suggest that the province participated in the larger commercial trade of the region, producing its oil and wine and receiving other goods in return.[3] International trade with Greece and the west increased throughout this period, so much so that some portions of Palestine can be described as 'Hellenized' (*hellene* is the Greek word meaning 'Greek', and those who have adopted a Greek-like culture are said to be Hellenized).

Not everyone benefited equally from the trade economy. The elite classes who participated in the money economy were in a more secure financial position than the peasantry who continued, as in every era, to live close to subsistence level. It is no surprise to read, for example, of physical hardships, poor harvests and general poverty in the biblical books that were composed during the Persian era (e.g. Hag. 1). The elites of the region took advantage of the poor when they had opportunity to do so. The book of Nehemiah records a situation in which the poor were compelled to sell children and land, or to go into debt-slavery, in order to buy food or pay royal taxes (Neh. 5.1-19). In such situations it was the wealthy who benefited, being in a position to buy at low prices from the desperate, or to keep tenant farmers in perpetual debt. Portions of the Torah appear to have been formulated to provide relief in just these situations (e.g. Lev. 25.8-55), though there is no evidence to suggest that these aspects of Torah law were ever implemented.

Although the Bible contains several books narrating events during this period, it is difficult to rely on those documents. Most significant among these books are Ezra and Nehemiah. Ezra is said to have been a priest who was sent from Babylon to Yehud to instruct the people in the Torah of Moses. Nehemiah was sent by the Persian king to restore the walls of Jerusalem and govern Yehud. Each, the narratives imply, arrived at about the same time (Neh. 12.26). Yet their activities seem to parallel one another while simultaneously ignoring (or displaying a lack of awareness about) the other. Most historians have concluded that if the two men were real historical persons, they could not have been active at the same time. But when were they active? Evidence can be strung together to formulate a hypothesis. Nehemiah interacts with a priest named Eliashib (Neh. 13.4, 7), and Ezra interacts with a priest named Jehohanan, son of Eliashib (Ezra 10.6). Thus many historians believe that Nehemiah was active about a generation before Ezra.

If one assumes that Nehemiah and Ezra were real people, it is difficult to determine when each arrived in Jerusalem and for what purpose. Nehemiah arrived during the twentieth year of *a* King Artaxerxes, and returned to Babylon in the thirty-second year of that king (Neh. 5.14; 13.6). Which Artaxerxes? Two of the three kings of that name reigned longer than 32 years, so Nehemiah could have been active from about 445 to 433 BCE or from 384 to 372 BCE. In either case, Nehemiah's arrival might have been motivated by the Persian king's desire to pacify the region during a period of unrest. (Recall that military destruction occurred in Palestine about 480 or so and again c. 380.) Since some Jewish documents uncovered in Egypt (to be discussed below) date to the final two decades of the fifth century BCE, and those documents mention a Jerusalem priest named Jehohanan (= Ezra 10.6?), many historians place Nehemiah in Jerusalem in 445–433 BCE and bring Ezra to the city in 398 BCE (Ezra 7.7).

All this reasoning is predicated on the assumption that the books of Ezra and Nehemiah are reliable for historical reconstruction. But are they? A look at the contents of each book leads to ambivalence.

Nehemiah's book consists of at least three genres of literature. Portions are composed in the first person and appear to have been a memoir written by Nehemiah himself (roughly Neh. 1–6, 13). Other chapters are lists of various kinds (Neh. 7, 11–12) and three chapters narrate activities of Ezra (Neh. 8–10). The book of Ezra contains a long and chronologically confused narrative about events allegedly taking place prior to Ezra's arrival (Ezra 1–6) followed by a narrative about Ezra (Ezra 7–10). Many scholars have found reason to trust the details in the Nehemiah memoir, but the Ezra narratives give the impression of being a rather shallow imitation of the Nehemiah story. Ezra does not seem to hold a realistic office, possess a believable genealogy (cf. Ezra 7.1-6), or perform actions that make sense in historical context. Also, it is interesting to note that later Jewish writers of the period Before Common Era are aware of a historical Nehemiah, but no Jewish author mentions an Ezra until about the first century of the Common Era. All things considered, it is very likely that Ezra is an invented character of relatively late origin, whose story is partially modelled after that of Nehemiah.

There are other difficulties with the narratives of Ezra and Nehemiah. For instance, Ezra 2 (= Neh. 7) provides a list of those who are said to have responded to Cyrus II's decree of repatriation. The number of returnees was, according to this document, more than 42,000 people—an impossibly high figure. Some scholars have tried to accept the document's reliability by arguing that the list is cumulative: it contains the returnees over a number of generations. But even this explanation seems unconvincing in light of the demographics for Persian-era Yehud; there would not have been a sufficient number of generations for this massive horde of returnees to appear.

Another example of difficulties in these books concerns the activities of the protagonists; the new foundations are said to have been rebuilt upon the ruined temple of Yahweh twice, once by a man named Sheshbazzar (Ezra 5.16) and again by someone named Zerubbabel (Ezra 3.8). Also, if the chronology of Ezra 1–6 is accepted as narrated, the activity of Zerubbabel extended from the reigns of Cyrus II to Darius II—more than 100 years! Routinely, biblical scholars assume that the narrative contains 'flashbacks' and 'flashforwards'. This assumption is designed to solve the chronological difficulty and to compress Zerubbabel's activity into a shorter, more believable period of time. Ancient authors employed those devices from time to time, and they usually provided rhetorical indications when they did. Unfortunately, the biblical author provides no such indication in Ezra, so the modern hypothesis is probably only a clutching after straws. Suffice it to say that the narrative of Ezra 1–6, which is the only independent narrative of a Jewish return in response to the decree of Cyrus II, is hopelessly garbled, and its details are of uncertain merit.

There can be no doubt that a group of Jews responded to the Cyrus II decree and returned to Jerusalem, for the theological attitude expressed in the edited, Persian-era form of many biblical books presupposes the existence of such a group. They thought of themselves as a 'remnant' spared by Yahweh after the destruction of Jerusalem by Nebuchadnezzar II, and brought back to the Land of Promise by divine mercy (Isa. 10.20-22; 11.11-16; cf. Jer. 23.3). Interestingly, they called themselves 'Israel', a label that seems to have migrated to Jerusalem only after the old Iron Age II kingdom of Israel collapsed in the 720s BCE. Moreover, the Nehemiah memoir gives a brief glimpse of life among the children of those returnees. Nevertheless, a historical narrative of the events during this era is not possible until more sufficient evidence surfaces.

## The Varieties of Judaisms During the Persian Era

That which might seem most surprising to one unfamiliar with Jewish history is the extreme diversity of Judaisms during the Persian period. The Rabbinic Judaism of today had not yet even begun to appear; the precision of Talmudic tradition was still centuries in the future. What did appear in Persian times was a period of transition and the molding of ideas among Jews.

In fact, after the collapse of the state-sponsored patron-god religion of the Iron Age II in 586 BCE, an ongoing conversation seems to have developed among the Yahweh worshipers of the ancient world. Since Judaism as a religion was just being born, it took time for the 'normative' aspects of what we now recognize to be Judaism to evolve and become widespread. Although evidence is scarce, historians can piece together at least four differing Judaisms in this period, only one of which seems to have survived into the Hellenistic era.

The first of the four Judaisms is the one most familiar to us today, exemplified by the memoir of Nehemiah. This Jew loved that which became the pillars of later Rabbinic Judaism: a Torah of Moses (probably not quite identical to the final version of Torah just yet), the city of Jerusalem, the land of Israel. In his memoir, Nehemiah displays an intense jealousy as he guards these institutions against the allegedly slack practices of other Jews in or near Jerusalem. He refuses, for example, to permit Jewish men to marry women from the neighboring provinces of Samaria, Ashdod, Moab and Ammon, even driving from his presence a Jewish priest who had married into the Jewish(!) family of Sanballat from Samaria (Neh. 13.23-28).

The rigidity of Nehemiah repels some modern readers (even some modern Jewish readers), but it was a reasonable policy at the time, grounded in a desire to defend the Jewish community's sense of corporate identity. This sense of identity as 'Jewish'—that is to say, as descendants of the Judahites—had become central to the worldview of the Babylonian Jews who had lived amid the temptations of assimilation into Babylonian culture. Many of Judaism's most distinctive features *became* distinctively Jewish features precisely so that they could be affirmed ideologically, to reinforce the community's sense of cohesion, oneness, family. Circumcision, for example, had been relatively common among the many peoples of Palestine's Iron Age (with the exception of Philistines), but became a distinctive Jewish trait during the Persian period. Jews deliberately retained the practice while many other communities did not, even awarding it divine sanction in the form of a folk-tale explaining its origins (Gen. 17).

A second kind of Judaism can be discerned among the alleged enemies of Nehemiah's memoir, especially Sanballat of Samaria and Tobiah of Ammon (Neh. 2.10, etc.). From documents found at Elephantine in southern Egypt (discussed below), it is clear that the Sanballat family was Jewish, but Nehemiah's rhetorical broadsides give the impression that they were not. No doubt, from the perspective of Nehemiah, the Sanballats practiced a form of Judaism that could not be accepted as genuine Judaism. Likewise, Tobiah bore a Yahwistic name (*tôb-yahu* means 'Yahu is good') and had family ties to the Jerusalem priests, but he was governor in the 'foreign' province of Ammon. The Tobiad Jewish family remained a powerful presence in Ammon well into Hellenistic times. It is impossible to penetrate the murkiness of Nehemiah's polemical characterizations of these 'enemies', so it is not really possible to describe the nature of their versions of Judaism. But these were Jews descended from Judahites who had not gone into exile at the time of Nebuchadnezzar II. Thus one suspects that the Judaism they practiced was a linear descendant of the Judaism in the land prior to the arrival of the repatriated descendants of Babylonian exiles. As such, their Judaism was in all likelihood a more relaxed tradition, devoid of the rituals and symbols so essential to a Jewish community clinging to its identity in exile.

From a small community called Elephantine in southern Egypt comes evidence for a third Judaism. The evidence takes the form of letters and legal documents written in the final decades of the fifth century BCE. These documents are invaluable to historians of early Judaism because they were composed by Jews. From the documents, it seems that these Jews were descendants of Jewish soldiers hired as mercenaries by the 26th Dynasty several centuries earlier. The Elephantine Jewish community had existed from the final decades of the Iron Age II until the time of our extant documents, in the middle years of the Persian era—more than 200 years.

The Jews of Elephantine were in touch with the Jews of Persian-era Jerusalem. They also corresponded with the Sanballat family living in Samaria. But Judaism at Elephantine was rather different from Judaism as known from Persian-era Jerusalem. These Egyptian Jews worshiped Yahu along with a variety of lesser deities. They did not possess, so far as can be determined, any scripture. Apparently, they were unfamiliar with most of the liturgical holidays as described in the Bible (they received instructions about Passover from a Jew outside their community), and their temple (which, at one point, was destroyed by a mob of unruly Egyptians) violated Deuteronomy 12's insistence that there be only one temple for Yahweh, and that in the land Yahweh had given to the Israelites. Although the Elephantine papyri were composed around the time of Nehemiah's memoir at Jerusalem, the Judaism at Elephantine is radically different from, and probably more conservative than, the Judaism of Nehemiah. Elephantine's Judaism was the Judahite religion of common soldiers at the time of King Josiah, with, perhaps, a few additions picked up from Egyptian religious culture in the intervening years.

A fourth Judaism is almost impossible to reconstruct, but a tantalizing glimpse of it has been preserved from a non-Jewish, Hellenistic source. A late-fourth-century BCE Greek historian named Hecataeus of Abdera (no relation to the much earlier Hecataeus of Miletus) recorded some traditions about the Jews which he learned from some Jews of his day. These traditions were copied again by a first-century BCE historian named Diodorus of Sicily. The process of transmission no doubt permitted corruption of the tradition, and as a result, many historians dismiss this source as useless. But several features in it are intriguing. For example, the Jews who informed Hecataeus believed in a Moses who led the settlement of Israel in Canaan, including the founding of the city of Jerusalem; this sounds very much like an 'alternate' Moses tradition also preserved in a single fragment from the Bible. In 1 Sam. 12.8, Moses (with Aaron) is credited with settling the Israelites in Canaan. Since this assertion flies in the face of the narrative in the books of Numbers to Joshua (where Moses and Aaron die before Joshua brings the people into Canaan), it may represent that which the social anthropologists encounter with regularity in traditional cultures, namely, variant versions of heroic tales about the community's past. Another example from the Hecataeus tradition is the claim that Moses built a temple on the mountain of Jerusalem, which contradicts the tale about Solomon in 1 Kings 5–8, but might be compatible with a minority tradition preserved at Exod. 15.16-17, which seems to move directly from migration to a temple in the Promised Land. The evidence is slim, but significant nevertheless, and suggests that the Jewish tradition about Moses had not yet reached a singular, authoritative form by the closing decades of the Persian period.[4]

To summarize, although a narrative of Jewish history cannot be written for the Persian period, enough evidence survives to give a clear picture of daily life in Yehud as well as the evolving nature of the Jewish religion. Prior to the destruction of Jerusalem in 586 BCE, Judahite religion was a very representative example of the standard patron-god state religion common to Iron Age Canaan. With the exile in Babylon, new circumstances began to breed new religious options and ideas. Ultimately, a version of Judaism similar to that of Nehemiah emerged victorious, and served as the foundation for the Judaisms of the Hellenistic era. But the evolution of Judaism was not complete even then. For one thing, Judaism did not yet have a Bible, although many sacred books were beginning to circulate. The transformation of those sacred books into a canon (which means 'official list') of scripture is a process that unfolded after Alexander swept through the Persian empire.

*The Hellenistic Era (332–63 BCE)*

When the Persian empire suffered internal instability in the early-330s, Philip II, King of Macedon and Greece, saw an opportunity. He made plans to invade Persia, but was killed by an assassin in 336. As a result, his 20-year-old son and heir, Alexander III, was left to carry out the ambitious plan. Alexander's own generals were not convinced that the lad had the capacity to lead, but he soon surprised them. Like a tidal wave, Alexander the Great swept through the ancient Near East. He conquered all the way to the Indus River Valley and only turned back when his exhausted troops refused to go any further.

Flesh wounds and possibly malaria combined to take Alexander's life at the young age of 33. At his death in 323 BCE, the Persian Empire was but a memory, and several of Alexander's generals competed with one another to carve up the far-flung empire he had created. The final decades of the fourth century BCE witnessed political machinations and warfare. When the dust began to settle in the early-third century, the political map of the ancient Near East consisted of a series of Greek-like kingdoms; this is the era called Hellenism.

Egypt was ruled by a family of Greeks named Ptolemy. The region from northern Syria to Babylon was under the dominion of the Seleucid dynasts. (Anatolia and Greece were also ruled by Alexander's successors, but discussion of these regions takes us too far afield.) Palestine found itself, once again, on the landbridge between Syria-Mesopotamia (the Seleucids) and Egypt (the Ptolemies). Throughout the third century BCE Palestine was ruled by the latter, whose capital city was Alexandria in the northeast Delta. Early in the second century a Seleucid king fought a Ptolemy and defeated him near Dan. Palestine became a province of the Seleucids, whose capital was at Antioch in northern Syria.

Under Ptolemaic rule, the Jews thrived. Jerusalem and Alexandria became dual centers of Jewish life and learning. It would seem, from evidence to be discussed below, that the earliest formation of a Jewish Bible reached its penultimate stage in this century; at that time, the 'Bible' was 'the five books of Moses', but these five scrolls were not really a Bible in the sense that their content was not yet considered sacrosanct and unchangeable. Scribes could and did make alterations to the text as they deemed necessary. Moreover, many books that later became part of the Bible were circulating by this time, but were not yet regarded as sacred, and a few biblical books (e.g. Esther, Daniel) had not yet been composed. In a predominantly oral culture, however, the formation of a sacred text is secondary to religious tradition in any case. The Bible did not create Judaism; Judaism created the Bible. Even after the Bible was formed, the majority of Jews remained illiterate, and their knowledge of the religion was aural and participatory; texts were of secondary importance.

Life for Jews was not as pleasant under Seleucid rule, in the early decades of the second century (the 100s BCE), as it had been under the Ptolemies. The written sources exaggerate the hostilities and paint caricatures of the Seleucids and their supporters. As a result, it is difficult to determine the nature of the problems, but certainly part of the problem was Jewish resentment of the increasingly Hellenized Jewish leadership in Jerusalem. Whatever the precise cause, a Jewish revolt exploded in 167 BCE when the Seleucids attempted to Hellenize the Jewish temple in Jerusalem. Called the Maccabean Revolt (led by Judas the 'Maccabee', which means the 'Hammerer'), this war was ferocious, but succeeded in pushing the Seleucids out of Palestine. The recapture and 'cleansing' of the temple in 164 BCE is still commemorated in the Jewish calendar; it is called Hanukkah, which means 'Dedication'.

The Jewish leadership during the Maccabean Revolt evolved into a dynasty of priest-kings known by their family name, the Hasmoneans. They gradually conquered almost all of Palestine and southern Syria, creating the largest Yahwistic state in antiquity, which reached its height in the reign of the last and most famous Hasmonean, King Herod the Great, from 37 to 4 BCE. The Hasmoneans seem to have pursued a policy of forced conversion to Judaism in regions they conquered, a policy that is partially responsible for transforming Palestine into the predominantly Jewish world that it had become by the arrival of the Romans in the first century BCE. Not all subjects complied with forced conversion, however. As a matter of fact, one group of resisters were themselves Yahweh worshipers, the Samaritans.

Both the Samaritan and Jewish communities invented explanations for their differences, and each of those folk-tales pushes the animosity between Jewish and Samaritan religion back to the Iron Age (the Jewish version can be found in 2 Kings 17; the Samaritan version blames Eli of Shiloh in 1 Samuel 1–6 for causing Jews to abandon 'true' Yahwism). In reality, little distinction between Jew and Samaritan could be discerned as late as the mid-fourth century BCE. When Alexander the Great swept through Palestine in 332, the city of Samaria at first supported, then revolted against, the new Greek rulers. As a result, Alexander's troops destroyed Samaria. After that, the Samaritans established themselves at a traditional Israelite city, Shechem, southeast of Samaria. There they built a temple on Mount Gerizim, which overlooks Shechem in the valley below, claiming it to be the fulfillment of Deuteronomy 12. This placed Samaritan religion in competition with the Jewish interpretation of Deuteronomy 12, which views Jerusalem as the place of Yahweh's choice. This was the beginning of the Jewish–Samaritan rift. One of the Hasmonean kings, John Hyrcanus (135–104 BCE), persecuted the Samaritans and destroyed their temple on Mount Gerizim. In spite of the hatred on both sides, the differences between Samaritan and Jewish religion remained minuscule in this period. Gradually, as Jews increased the number of books they considered sacred, the Samaritans rejected those additions, accepting only the five books of Moses.

### *The Roman Period (From 63 BCE)*

The Hasmonean rise in power coincided with the rise of a much greater power in the west: Rome. During the course of the second century BCE, the Romans gradually spread eastward, bringing most of the Mediterranean world under their dominion. In the mid-first century, Hasmonean family members were competing with one another for power, and some Jews decided to appeal to the Roman general Pompey as an arbitrator in the dispute. The Romans responded by placing Jerusalem under siege for three months, and the day that Pompey marched into Jerusalem, in 63 BCE, the Hasmonean kingdom became a vassal of Rome. This situation was disrupted only briefly in 40 to 37 BCE, when Parthians from Mesopotamia invaded Syria-Palestine. But Rome reconquered the eastern Empire and sponsored a young man who had been in the employ of the Hasmoneans, Herod, to reconquer Jerusalem on behalf of Rome. Herod the Great married into the Hasmonean family, and so reigned as the last of the Hasmoneans and as the 'friend of Rome'.

King Herod received bad press from ancient New Testament writers, and he was certainly a ruthless king. However, he was also an extremely successful administrator and builder, who transformed Palestine, bringing it fully into the Roman world. In addition to rebuilding thoroughly the temple of Jerusalem, and completing massive building projects throughout Palestine, Herod brought trade to the region that increased its prosperity and even eradicated much poverty at the level of the peasantry. By this time, the population of Palestine, which had been increasing gradually since the Persian era, had swelled to more than two million people. The majority were Jews, but not all. Palestine was home to many ethnic groups and many religions; the Galilee had a particularly eclectic population.

During the final centuries BCE and the first century of the Common Era, the Jewish people of Palestine pursued their Jewishness in a variety of ways. Sects arose that attracted some support, but the vast majority of Jewish peasants followed a set of Jewish customs that were relatively uncomplicated. Circumcision, sabbath observance and a series of holy festivals marked the Jewishness of most. The emphasis on particular aspects of Jewish tradition differed from place to place. Several of the sects of Jews are famous from the New Testament, but New Testament writers did not attempt to present these people in a fair and unbiased way. Sadducees were a tiny sect, consisting almost exclusively of Jerusalem priests. The term 'Sadducee' is the Greek form of the Hebrew 'Zadokite', a very significant priestly group since at least the time of the Judahite monarchy. The Sadducees were deeply conservative people, and their version of Judaism conformed to older traditions (such as that of Nehemiah) more closely than perhaps any other of the period. Pharisees were, for the most part, wealthy laity. Although they got involved in politics on occasion, they desired above all to see their fellow Jews live a life of piety, and so they pursued a program of instruction centered on the institution of the synagogue. New Testament diatribes, such as Matthew 23, falsely charge the Pharisees with hypocrisy, but in reality, their teachings differed little from those attributed to Jesus by the author of Matthew's Gospel, particularly the teachings of Matthew 6 and 7. Another Jewish sect was called the Essenes. Much has been published about this group because many scholars believe they wrote the Dead Sea Scrolls. It is not clear, however, just what the Essene sect taught and did. It should be emphasized, however, that all these sects—Sadducees, Pharisees and Essenes—were tiny minorities within Palestinian Judaism. Many Jews were able to live their lives and die never having met a member of one of these sects.

At the death of Herod in 4 BCE, his kingdom was divided among three sons, Archelaus, Herod Antipas and Philip. Archelaus received the largest portion, the Central Hills. Herod Antipas received the Galilee and part of southern Transjordan, and Philip ruled the northeastern

Transjordan south of Damascus. Archelaus proved incompetent and was replaced by direct Roman provincial rule from 6 CE. The other sons ruled until the 30s CE, and their tetrarchies (they were not called kingdoms) passed to a third generation of the Herod family, Herod Agrippa I, who also received the Central Hills from the reigning Caesar in 41, and died in 44 CE. Except for that brief period in the early 40s, the Central Hills were ruled directly by Roman governors, and it was the poor public relations between those governors and the Jewish people that led to a violent uprising in 66 CE.

The reasons for the First Jewish Revolt against Rome in 66 to 73 CE are many and complex. The two central issues were, first, a deep-seated Jewish cultural clash with their Roman lords, and second, oppressive Roman taxation (it is no surprise that New Testament writers equate the office of tax collector with the general term 'sinners'). The war was bloody, and its consequences far-reaching. Jerusalem was destroyed in 70, and the last of the Jewish rebels held out on a mountaintop fortress (that had been built by Herod the Great) called Masada, in the southern Judaean desert, until committing suicide in 73 CE. Many of the sects died out or were dispersed from Palestine in the war. Others, such as the early Jesus movements, were, by their reaction to the war, catapulted on a social and intellectual trajectory that would lead them away from the Jewish religion entirely.

Thus, prior to 66 CE, the Judaisms of Palestine were many, and there existed no central authority in Jewish religion to declare one version of the religion more orthodox than another. After 73, one Jewish sect survived that could provide guidance to the Jewish people. That one sect was the Pharisee movement (or something related to it), which regrouped on the Coastal Plain at a place called Yabneh, south of Dor, where they began to gather ancient texts and comment upon them. Although they did not set out to do so, their activities eventually produced the canon known as the Jewish Bible (or Christian Old Testament).

The Jewish War of 66–73 CE was the first of three major Jewish rebellions against Rome. In 115–117 CE, Jews of the Diaspora (that is to say, Jews who did not live in Syria-Palestine) rose up against the Roman authorities in response to a complex set of slights and oppressions. In spite of Roman recognition of Judaism as a legal minority religion, most Roman citizens understood little of Judaism, and satisfied their ignorance not by learning about it, but by replacing knowledge of the Jews with rank rumors and superstitions. Thus, Jews were thought to be atheists who practiced immoral customs. The Diaspora rebellion, reacting to bigotry and hatred in many places, rose up and was cut down ruthlessly by the emperor Trajan, who annihilated the Jewish population of Alexandria.

Another Palestinian Jewish rebellion—confusingly labeled the Second Jewish Revolt—took place in the Judaean Hills from 132 to 135 CE. This rebellion was a much smaller affair than the First Jewish Revolt of 66–73, but no less bloody. It was led by a Jew named Simon Bar Kosiba (Simon, son of Kosiba). His supporters nicknamed him Bar Kokhba, 'Son of the Star', and thought of him as Messiah. This Messiah lived out his final days in a Judaean Desert cave, hiding from the Romans, his followers utterly defeated.

Rome adopted a pragmatic response to the Jewish Wars. The goal of the Roman authorities was to keep the peace in Palestine, so that the grain trade from Egypt to Rome would not be threatened by the Parthians to the east of Palestine, who otherwise might have employed Palestine's unrest as a wedge through which to pry into Roman affairs and take over the eastern Roman empire. Apparently, Jews were banned from rebuilt Jerusalem after the war, but otherwise were not unduly oppressed (except for the continued taxation suffered by Jew and non-Jew alike). As a matter of fact, Judaism was accorded a special legal status exempting Jews from participation in the Roman imperial religion (required of all others as a form of patriotism).

Under Emperor Domitian, c. 95 CE, an office of Jewish Patriarch was established by the Romans in Galilee, and this Jewish leader was recognized by Rome as the spokesperson for the Jews. As such, the office evolved into a highly authoritative and influential leader for Jews throughout the ancient world. Since these office-holders were Pharisaic in outlook, the Pharisaic—or Rabbinic as it came to be known—version of Judaism gradually became the uniform version of all Judaism. The office of Patriarch continued until about 425 CE, when the Roman empire, by that time a thoroughly Christian state, ceased to have an interest in protecting the Jews from Christian hostility.

### The Emergence of the Bible

The Jews produced one of the most remarkable and influential anthologies of literature the world has known: the Bible. This achievement was

Figure 35. *Jerusalem, the Holy City. Jerusalem came to be conceived as a 'Holy Land' in the days of King Herod, who promoted the sacredness of the city among Jews throughout the Roman Empire. In the fourth century CE, this city became a 'Holy Land' for Christians when Roman Emperor Constantine built large Christian churches here and in other parts of Palestine. After the seventh century CE, Jerusalem became a 'Holy Land' for Islam as well, and the beautiful Dome of the Rock, seen here, remains one of the world's most famous Muslim buildings.*

many centuries in the making, and was not complete until about the second century or so CE.

The earliest known biblical text was recovered by archaeologists near Jerusalem at Ketef Hinnom and dates to about 600 BCE. This consists of two small pieces of very thin silver, each rolled carefully and worn on necklaces by wealthy children. The texts contain variant versions of the so-called Priestly Blessing, a version of which is also found in the Bible at Num. 6.24-26. However, these small silver texts are not really 'biblical' texts at all. There is no evidence to suggest that an anthology of scrolls—a Bible—existed as early as 600 BCE. Without doubt, many writings later incorporated into the Bible had been composed earlier than 600. Many narratives and poems were composed during the eighth and seventh centuries. All these pre-Babylonian era writings were preserved by the elite classes who were deported to Babylon in the sixth century BCE.

It would seem that the earliest version of a Hebrew literary anthology came together in Babylon during the exile. At that time, literature was composed that presupposes the existence of such compilations. For example, an anonymous prophet, whose writings assume sixth-century circumstances as a given, attached his writings to, and even commented upon, a collection of writings deriving from the time of the Judaean monarchy in the late-eighth and early-seventh centuries BCE. The resulting combination is the earliest form of the biblical book of Isaiah (which went through later revisions as well). In the Isaiah scroll, the peculiar combination of eighth to seventh-century writings with sixth-century writings can be explained if, and only if, a scroll of eighth to seventh-century materials was known to this exiled prophet in Babylon.

Although this evidence makes it clear that the biblical anthology was emerging by the sixth century, additional consideration of the evidence renders it equally clear that the anthology did not come together earlier. Almost without exception, biblical scrolls contain ample material that dates to the Babylonian and Persian eras, thus indicating that a burst of literary activity took place in these centuries. For example, the Torah of Moses contains a wealth of material—usually labeled by modern scholars as the 'priestly' (P) stratum—which presupposes the exile and the repatriation of Jews to Jerusalem. Had the anthology of scrolls been treated as a single unit prior to this time, one would expect a pattern of uniform material presupposing an earlier period to appear in each of the scrolls. Therefore, the first stage in which an anthology of scrolls was gathered and edited was the sixth century BCE.

One can readily imagine the crisis of the Babylonian deportation serving as a catalyst that motivated Judaean scribes to begin gathering documents of an at-that-time bygone era, lest the documents be lost forever. The sources from which the documents were gathered might have been varied: elements from a royal archive, temple records, public monuments, and even small collections of writings housed in the homes of prominent priests. (By comparison, note that such private collections were found in a home of a priest at the Late Bronze city of Ugarit.) The process of gathering would, in turn, generate commentary on the texts thus gathered. The Torah's priestly stratum and the final, edited version of Isaiah are logical—almost predictable—outcomes of such a process.

The anthology of literature brought together in the sixth century was not a body of religiously authoritative literature—it was not yet a 'Bible'. At least four considerations point to this conclusion.

First, the Elephantine Jews of the fifth century BCE, who were in co-tact with Jerusalem, seem to have known nothing of an authoritative religious literature, suggesting that there was no attempt to circulate the scrolls being produced at Jerusalem in that period.

Second, the anthological format of the literature does not give the impression that the scribes were trying to create authoritative documents. For example, the Torah of Moses actually consists of several torah codes, such as the Covenant Code (Exod. 20.22–23.33), the Holiness Code (Lev. 17–26) and the Deuteronomic Code (Deut. 12–26). Since no attempt was made to harmonize the sometimes conflicting elements in these codes, it would seem that the motivation for the Torah's existence was one of preservation of variant traditions and not promotion of a single religious viewpoint.

A third, more practical, consideration also leads to the conclusion that the anthology was not at first designed to be authoritative religious literature. Literature can be read only by the literate, and since most Jews were illiterate, there would be no practical means by which a complex literature could serve as an authority, even if it had been designed for that purpose. Much later, in medieval times, the Jews as a minority group represented one of the most learned societies in Europe. When most European Christians were illiterate, a substantial number of male Jews enjoyed full literacy. But that was the product of centuries in which the reading of the Bible and the other Jewish writings had become a focal point of Jewish communal identity. This aspect of Jewish tradition did not appear until well into the Common Era. In Judaism, widespread literacy followed from the creation of scripture, it did not lead to it. Even most Jews at the time of Jesus in the first century CE could not read and write.[5] An anthology of literature cannot serve as authority for a large population of illiterate people. For example, note that the Christian Protestant movement, with its claim that the Bible is the sole authority for Christian religion, emerged as a popular idea only after Gutenberg's press (as well as the Christian Humanist movement) had made Bibles widely available and had increased the literacy rate of Europe. To be sure, the notion of *sola scriptura* had been a minor theme among a few Christians prior to the sixteenth century CE, but Protestantism's version of *sola scriptura* as a widespread religious idea simply could not have existed at any earlier moment. Likewise, on purely practical grounds, one should not call the Babylonian/Persian-era Hebrew anthology a 'Bible' in the later, religious, sense of the term.

A fourth reason to avoid thinking of the early Hebrew anthology as an authoritative body of literature for those who read and transmitted it is the very nature of the manuscripts themselves. The earliest surviving versions of scrolls that later came to be known as biblical were found in caves overlooking the Dead Sea near a settlement called Qumran. These ancient scrolls date to the final centuries BCE and first century CE—the Hellenistic and early Roman eras. Among these manuscripts are hundreds of variant readings. Many of these variations are merely the result of scribal errors, such as misspelling or accidental loss of a few words or lines from a text. But many others indicate quite clearly that the ancient scribe did not simply copy the scroll before him. He made editorial revisions of a text when and as he saw fit. As a result, in ancient times, there were alternate versions of a given scroll in circulation simultaneously. For example, historians know of two very different versions of Jeremiah, additions to the tale of Nahash the Ammonite found in 1 Samuel 11, alternate versions of the David and Goliath story in 1 Samuel 17, and so on. Some scrolls, such as Esther, may not even have existed at the time that the bulk of the Dead Sea Scrolls were copied.

With all these variations in the Hellenistic-era manuscripts, it is safe to conclude that every book of the Bible was still undergoing frequent, and sometimes extensive, editorial revision during pre-Hellenistic times. Thus, although it is possible that scribes of the Babylonian and Persian eras found something of religious value in the manuscripts they were creating and recreating, it is unlikely that they thought of these texts as religiously authoritative. In other words, the texts might have been sacred, but were not yet considered to be a divinely ordained 'rule and norm' to guide the belief and practices of all Jews. As was noted previously, Jewish belief and practice prior to the rise of the Patriarchate was dictated primarily by local custom and contemporary needs, not by texts.

The anthology began in the sixth century BCE, and was edited continually through the Persian period, but the number and titles of the scrolls in this anthology were not yet identical to the books of a modern Bible. The five books of Moses surely existed in roughly their final form by the late Persian period, and the Former Prophets (Joshua, Judges, 1–2 Samuel, 1–2 Kings) were nearing completion. Minor changes would be made, of course, for generations to come. The Latter

'Those born of truth spring from
a foundation of light,
but those born of falsehood
spring from a source of darkness.'

DEAD SEA SCROLL 'COMMUNITY RULE'

More than 800 scrolls were stored in eleven caves near Qumran overlooking the Dead Sea. Those who put the scrolls in that unlikely place were, apparently, hiding these precious writings during the First Jewish Revolt against Rome, 66-73 CE. Perhaps they planned to retrieve the scrolls after the war. Ironically, their loss has been a great gain for modern historians, who have learned much about early Judaisms from these writings.

Among the Dead Sea Scrolls are the earliest known copies of the books that later became the Jewish Bible, as well as many Jewish writings that had never been known to exist prior to this discovery in 1947. None of the scrolls survived in a perfect state, and most are severely damaged. Had it not been for the arid climate of the Judaean Desert, all the scrolls would have distintegrated centuries ago.

Figure 36. *The Dead Sea Scroll.*

Prophets (Isaiah, Jeremiah, Ezekiel, the Twelve Minor Prophets) appear to have gone through an editorial process for another few generations after the time of Alexander. For instance, Isaiah 24–27 seems to presuppose (although the point is sometimes disputed) the sacking of Samaria by Alexander's troops in 332 BCE. The Writings remained in a much more fluid state well into Roman times. At Qumran, two versions of the Psalms enjoyed equal status. Job may have been written in the late-Persian period, Qoheleth (known in English as Ecclesiastes) was first composed during Ptolemaic times, Daniel was written in response to Seleucid oppression and Maccabean revolution (160s BCE), and a few short books were parables composed at an uncertain, but very late, date: Ruth, Esther, the 'Ezra' portions of the books called Ezra and Nehemiah (Ezra 7–10; Neh. 8–10). In other words, although the anthology began to be compiled as early as the sixth century BCE, the completion of the anthology was accomplished much, much later.

The anthology expanded throughout the Hellenistic period, with a variety of books composed and added along the way. Books such as Judith, Tobit, Wisdom of Jesus Ben Sirach, Baruch, 1 and 2 Maccabees, *1 Enoch, Jubilees,* and several documents known to us only from manuscripts found among the Dead Sea Scrolls were composed during the second and first centuries BCE. Others, such as 1 and 2 Esdras, the Prayer of Manasseh, Wisdom of Solomon, *3 and 4 Maccabees,* *2 Baruch* and some late additions to Daniel and Esther, were composed in the first and second centuries CE. (The New Testament, incidentally, was also composed during the second half of the first century and the first half of the second century CE. For obvious reasons, the New Testament was never included in any version of the Jewish Bible.) More such works were produced in later centuries, too numerous to list here. Judging from some early Christian Bibles (since the early Christians often simply adopted the Jewish holy books in the region in which they lived), it would seem that no attempt had been made to create a single, uniform Bible among Jews much before the late-first or early-second century CE.[6]

No one knows why or how the Jews ultimately adopted the specific books that now make up the Jewish Bible. The decision-making seems to have reached its most important stage between the First and Second Jewish Revolts (73–132 CE), and many historians conclude, therefore, that the Bible was, in effect, a 'replacement' for the lost temple of Jerusalem. When the temple no longer served as the center of Judaism, and hence Judaism's authority, the sacred scrolls were adapted to fill that role. The Bible came to be *the* Bible in order to assist the Jewish people in their attempt to retain a distinctive corporate identity in a changing social and political environment. Even then, however, the anthological nature of the Bible rendered it difficult to apply as an authority for Jewish daily piety. The community created commentary to assist in the interpretation of this new authority. Just after 200 CE, the patriarch Judah haNasi, at Sepphoris in Galilee, gathered and edited rabbinical sayings concerning temple observance, ritual observance, legal issues, holiday observance, and so on, and produced a book known to Judaism as the Mishnah, or 'second Torah'. The Mishnah subsequently served as the nucleus for a great body of complex rabbinical commentaries called Talmud. Talmudic Judaism emerged from about the third to the twelfth centuries CE. It was the Talmud, above all, that gave the Jewish Bible its stamp of authority at the head of the Jewish religion and community. Thus the Bible was a product of well over 1000 years of faithful Jewish scholarship and transmission, from generation to generation.

## Postscript

In this book, we have explored a few aspects of a fascinating world. That world is dead, fixed and finished. Its people are lost in the dust, most of their names forgotten. The desire of the historian is to revive their memory for a moment, give them a chance to speak. Among those lost faces were good people, not-so-good people and a few monsters. They were not heroes and villains, just people. They earned their living from a harsh land that often failed to cooperate. They competed with one another, hated one another, allied with one another, loved one another. My hope is that this survey has given you a sense for their integrity, their fallacies, their ingenuity, their fears, and their hope. It is the hope that is most inspiring. Ancient people are our family members. The ancient world is a legacy, a gift for the modern world to cherish, protect and explore. The ancient past is the heritage of all, the possession of none.

## SUGGESTED ADDITIONAL READING

*The Babylonian and Persian Periods*
Carter, Charles E., *The Emergence of Yehud in the Persian Period: A Social and Demographic Study* (JSOTSup, 294; Sheffield: Sheffield Academic Press, 1999).
Grabbe, Lester L., *Judaism from Cyrus to Hadrian. I. The Persian and Greek Periods* (Minneapolis: Fortress Press, 1992).

*The Hellenistic and Roman Periods*
Jaffee, Martin S., *Early Judaism* (Eaglewood Cliffs, NJ: Prentice–Hall, 1997).
Grabbe, Lester L., *Judaism from Cyrus to Hadrian. II. The Roman Period* (Minneapolis: Fortress Press, 1992).

*Specialized Studies*
Cohen, Shaye J.D., *The Beginnings of Jewishness: Boundaries, Varieties, Uncertainties* (Berkeley: University of California Press, 1999).
Theissen, Gerd, and Annette Merz, *The Historical Jesus: A Comprehensive Guide* (Winona Lake, IN: Eisenbrauns, 1998).

*The Evolution of the Bible*

Davies, Philip R., *Scribes and Schools: The Canonization of the Hebrew Scriptures* (Library of Ancient Israel; Louisville, KY: Westminster/John Knox Press, 1998).

Stegemann, Hartmut, *The Library of Qumran: On the Essenes, Qumran, John the Baptist, and Jesus* (Leiden: E.J. Brill, 1998).

Trebolle Barrera, Julio, *The Jewish Bible and the Christian Bible: An Introduction to the History of the Bible* (Grand Rapids: Eerdmans, 1998).

Vermes, Geza, *The Dead Sea Scrolls in English* (Sheffield: JSOT Press, 3rd edn, 1987).

## NOTES

1. The Bible gives witness to a gradual solidification of prejudice by the Judahites who were deported against those Judahites who were not deported. Jeremiah 52 reports that a few thousand Judahites were deported by the Babylonians, but the similar story in 2 Kgs 24–25 inflates the numbers, implying that all of Jerusalem and many others were taken to Babylon. Later, the author of 2 Chron. 36 implies that every single survivor of the war went into exile. This gradual exclusion from the story of those who had been left in Judah reflects the attitude of the 'exile' group who wrote the texts now included in the Hebrew anthology. They wrote their less articulate opponents, 'the people of the land', out of the story.

2. D.B. Redford, *Egypt, Canaan, and Israel in Ancient Times* (Princeton: Princeton University Press, 1992), pp. 455-56.

3. E. Stern, 'Between Persia and Greece: Trade, Administration and Warfare in the Persian and Hellenistic Periods (539–63 BCE)', in T.E. Levy (ed.), *The Archaeology of Society in the Holy Land* (Leicester: Leicester University Press, 1998), pp. 432-45; see also, C.E. Carter, *The Emergence of Yehud in the Persian Period: A Social and Demographic Study* (JSOTSup, 294; Sheffield: Sheffield Academic Press, 1999), pp. 249-85.

4. P.R. Davies, 'Scenes from the Early History of Judaism', in D.V. Edelman (ed.), *The Triumph of Elohim: From Yahwisms to Judaisms* (Grand Rapids: Eerdmans, 1995). For other possible evidence of Jewish diversity in the Persian period, see L.L. Grabbe, 'Israel's Historical Reality After the Exile', in B. Becking and M.C.A. Korpel (eds.), *The Crisis of Israelite Religion: Transformation of Religious Tradition in Exilic and Post-Exilic Times* (Leiden: E.J. Brill, 1999), pp. 9-32.

5. Meir Bar-Ilan, 'Illiteracy in the Land of Israel in the First Centuries C.E.', in S. Fishbane, S. Schoenfeld and A. Goldschlager (eds.), *Essays in Social Scientific Study of Judaism and Jewish Society* (New York: Ktav, 1992), II, pp. 46-61.

6. The statement by Josephus (*Against Apion* 1.37-43) does not contradict this judgment. See n. 15 in my article 'The Kaleidoscopic Nature of Divine Personality in the Hebrew Bible', *BibInt* 9 (2001), pp. 1-24.

# INDEX

## INDEX OF REFERENCES

### BIBLE

# INDEX OF SUBJECTS

# INDEX OF AUTHORS